A Biblical Morning & Evening Prayer Manual

A Biblical Morning & Evening Prayer Manual

*A Modern Book of Hours,
Ways to Begin and End the Day*

Morning & Evening Prayer

MARK G. BOYER

RESOURCE *Publications* • Eugene, Oregon

A BIBLICAL MORNING & EVENING PRAYER MANUAL
A Modern Book of Hours, Ways to Begin and End the Day

Copyright © 2024 Mark G. Boyer. All rights reserved. Except for brief quotations in critical publications or reviews, no part of this book may be reproduced in any manner without prior written permission from the publisher. Write: Permissions, Wipf and Stock Publishers, 199 W. 8th Ave., Suite 3, Eugene, OR 97401.

Resource Publications
An Imprint of Wipf and Stock Publishers
199 W. 8th Ave., Suite 3
Eugene, OR 97401

www.wipfandstock.com

PAPERBACK ISBN: 979-8-3852-3433-2
HARDCOVER ISBN: 979-8-3852-3434-9
EBOOK ISBN: 979-8-3852-3435-6
VERSION NUMBER 12/19/24

Scripture quotations taken from *The AMPLIFIED Bible* (AMP), Copyright © 1954, 1958, 1962, 1964, 1965, 1987, 2015 by The Lockman Foundation. All rights reserved. Used by permission (www.Lockman.org).

Excerpts from the English translation of the *Catechism of the Catholic Church* for use in the United States of America Copyright © 1994, United States Catholic Conference, Inc.—Libreria Editrice Vaticana. Used with Permission.

Scripture quotations marked (CEV) are from the *Contemporary English Version* Copyright © 1991, 1992, 1995 by American Bible Society, Used by permission.

Scripture quotations marked CSB have been taken from the *Christian Standard Bible*, Copyright © 2017 by Holman Bible Publishers. Used by permission. *Christian Standard Bible* and CSB are federally registered trademarks of Holman Bible Publishers.

Scripture quotations from the ESV Bible (*The Holy Bible, English Standard Version*), copyright 2001 by Crossway, a publishing ministry of Good News Publishers. ESV Text Edition: 2016. Used by permission. All rights reserved. The ESV text may not be quoted in any publication made available to the public by a Creative Commons license. The ESV may not be translated into any other language.

Scripture texts taken from the *New American Bible* (NAB), *revised edition* © 2010, 1991, 1986, 1970 Confraternity of Christian Doctrine, Washington, D.C. are used by permission of the copyright owner. All Rights Reserved. No part of the *New American Bible* may be reproduced in any form without permission in writing from the copyright owner.

Scripture quotations taken from the (NASB) *New American Standard Bible*, Copyright © 1960, 1971, 1977, 1995, 2020 by The Lockman Foundation. Used by permission. All rights reserved. lockman.org.

Scripture quotations taken from the *New English Bible* (NEB), copyright © Cambridge University Press and Oxford University Press, 1961, 1970. All rights reserved.

Scripture quotations taken from *The Holy Bible, New International Version*, (NIV), Copyright © 1973, 1978, 1984, 2011 by Biblica, Inc. Used by permission. All rights reserved worldwide.

Scripture quotations taken from the *New Revised Standard Version Bible* (NRSV), copyright © 1989 by the Division of Christian Education of the National Council of the Churches of Christ in the U.S.A., and are used by permission. All rights reserved.

Scripture quotations taken from *The Message: Catholic/Ecumenical Edition* (TM), Copyright © 1993, 1994, 1995, 1996, 2000, 2001, 2002, 2013. Used by permission of NavPress Publishing Group.

... [P]rayer by the people of God is rightly considered to be among [their] primary duties....

—GILH, par 1

... Morning and Evening Prayer form a double hinge of ... daily [prayer] and are therefore to be considered the principal Hours and celebrated as such.

—GILH, par 37

Contents

Abbreviations | ix
Introduction | xiii

1 Morning Prayer | 1
2 Evening Prayer | 7
3 Season of Ordinary Time | 13
4 Season of Advent | 78
5 Season of Christmas | 114
6 Season of Lent | 148
7 Holy Week | 212
8 Season of Easter | 231
9 Major Special Days | 328

Bibliography | 393
Recent Books by Mark G. Boyer | 395

Abbreviations

Bibles

AMP = The Amplified Outreach Bible

CEV = The Contemporary English Version

CSB = The Holy Bible: Christian Standard Bible

ESV = The Holy Bible: English Standard Version

NAB = The New American Bible

NASB = New American Standard Bible

NEB = The New English Bible

NIV = Holy Bible: New International Version

NRSV = The Access Bible: New Revised Standard Version

TM = The Message: Catholic/Ecumenical Edition

BCE = Before the Common Era (same as BC = Before Christ)

CB (NT) = Christian Bible (New Testament)

Acts = Acts of the Apostles

Col = Letter to the Colossians

1 Cor = First Letter of Paul to the Corinthians

2 Cor = Second Letter of Paul to the Corinthians

Eph = Letter to the Ephesians

Gal = Letter of Paul to the Galatians

Heb = Letter to the Hebrews

ABBREVIATIONS

Jas = Letter of James

John = John's Gospel

1 John = First Letter of John

Luke = Luke's Gospel

Mark = Mark's Gospel

Matt = Matthew's Gospel

1 Pet = First Letter of Peter

2 Pet = Second Letter of Peter

Phil = Letter of Paul to the Philippians

Rev = Revelation

Rom = Letter of Paul to the Romans

1 Thess = First Letter of Paul to the Thessalonians

1 Tim = First Letter to Timothy

Titus = Letter to Titus

CCC = Catechism of the Catholic Church

CE = Common Era (same as AD = *Anno Domini*, in the year of the Lord)

GILH = General Instruction of the Liturgy of the Hours

HB (OT) = Hebrew Bible (Old Testament)

Amos = Amos

1 Chr = First Book of Chronicles

2 Chr = Second Book of Chronicles

Dan = Daniel

Deut = Deuteronomy

Exod = Exodus

Ezek = Ezekiel

Ezra = Ezra

Gen = Genesis

ABBREVIATIONS

Hab = Habakkuk

Hos = Hosea

Isa = Isaiah

Jer = Jeremiah

Joel = Joel

Jonah = Jonah

Josh = Joshua

Judg = Judges

1 Kgs = First Book of Kings

2 Kgs = Second Book of Kings

Lev = Leviticus

Mal = Malachi

Mic = Micah

Nah = Nahum

Num = Numbers

Prov = Proverbs

Ps(s) = Psalm(s)

Ruth = Ruth

1 Sam = First Book of Samuel

2 Sam = Second Book of Samuel

Zech = Zechariah

Zeph = Zephaniah

OT (A) = Old Testament (Apocrypha)

2 Esd = Second Book of Esdras

Jdt = Judith

Sg Three = Prayer of Azariah (Song of Three Jews)

Sir = Sirach (Ecclesiasticus)

Tob = Tobit

Wis = Wisdom (of Solomon)

ABBREVIATIONS

par(s) = paragraph(s)

Punctuation Usage

/ = indicates where one line of poetic text ends and another begins

(biblical notation) = see the specific biblical verse(s) in parentheses for more information

– = range of verses following a colon (8:3–4)

— = range of verses from a verse in one chapter to a verse in another chapter (8:3—9:4)

a, b, c = designates first (a), second (b), third (c), etc. sentence in a verse of Scripture or a line of poetic text

Introduction

Title: *A Biblical Morning & Evening Prayer Manual*

Biblical

All the entries in this book come from the Bible. A variety of English translations of the Bible have been used to create this book. A list of those translations can be found at the top of the Abbreviations page or on the Bibliography page.

Morning & Evening Prayer

According to the Acts of the Apostles (1:14, 2:42), from Christianity's very beginning, people have been praying. At first, they prayed together; then, over the course of time, they began to pray alone in the morning and in the evening. In monasteries, morning and evening prayer were enhanced with midday prayer and night prayer; then, midmorning and midafternoon prayer were added. While that was possible for communities of monks and nuns, it did not fit the daily routine of ordinary people. Even after revisions to the daily rhythm of prayer in the last century, there were still too many hours for ordinary people, not to mention the

INTRODUCTION

need to purchase four volumes to have the complete books of prayer. Morning & Evening Prayer remain the most important hours of the day, and in this book they are simplified for the ordinary person, so he or she can sanctify the day at its beginning and give thanks for it at its end.

Manual

This book is a manual, one that is meant to be held in the reader's hands. It is also a complete handbook that contains information and instructions about biblical morning and evening prayer.

Subtitles: *A Modern Book of Hours, Ways to Begin and End the Day*

A Modern Book of Hours

As a modern book of hours, presented in these pages is a process for prayer for modern people. It doesn't take an hour to pray in the morning and/or in the evening. However, daily morning and evening exercises are designed for ten to fifteen minutes before one begins his or her busy day and when finishing the same busy day. In previous books of hours, as already noted above, there were up to seven or more times for prayer during the day. And while that is laudatory, it is not practical for modern people.

Ways to Begin and End the Day

Presented here are ways to begin and to end the day. A morning exercise (prayer) can be prayed to enrich one's spiritual life with a cup of coffee at hand before going to work, taking children to school, shopping, etc. An evening exercise (prayer) can be prayed immediately before going to bed or immediately after getting into bed and falling asleep. Morning Prayer attempts to get one's focus on what lies ahead and see it as an opportunity to entertain the divine presence. Evening Prayer attempts to get one's focus on what went before and be thankful for the divine presence.

INTRODUCTION

Using This Book

This book is designed to be used by individuals for private morning and evening prayer. The goal of this book is to foster spirituality. While the basic structure of Morning Prayer & Evening Prayer with explanation for the parts is provided in chapter 1 (Morning Prayer) and chapter 2 (Evening Prayer), a basic overview is given here.

Morning Prayer consists of a beginning verse, followed by an antiphon, a few verses from a biblical psalm, the repetition of the antiphon, the reading of a passage of Scripture, an exercise designed to make the prayer personal, the praying of the Lord's Prayer, a Blessing Prayer, and a Conclusion.

Likewise, Evening Prayer consists of a beginning verse, an antiphon, a few verses of a biblical psalm, the repetition of the antiphon, the reading of a passage of Scripture, an exercise designed to make the prayer personal, the praying of the Lord's Prayer, a Blessing Prayer, and a Conclusion.

Thirty-one exercises, corresponding to thirty-one days in a month, are provided in chapter 3, Season of Ordinary Time. For those who like to mark the seasons of the liturgical year, chapter 4, the Season of Advent, contains exercises for up to twenty-eight days. The Season of Christmas, chapter 5, contains exercises for up to twenty days. While many people think of the Season of Lent as consisting of forty days, it, in fact, consists of forty-three days; those exercises are found in chapters 6 and 7.

Easter, which lasts for fifty days, is found in chapter 8 with exercises for all its days. Throughout the liturgical year, there are Major Special Days; exercises for each of those are found in chapter 9.

While using this book, readers will need four bookmarks. One should be placed at the beginning of chapter 1, Structure of Morning Prayer. Another bookmark should be placed at the beginning of chapter 2, Structure of Evening Prayer. The third bookmark should be placed in the season (Ordinary Time, Advent, Christmas, Lent, Easter) one is observing. In the reader intends to mark major special days, the fourth bookmark should be placed in chapter 9.

INTRODUCTION

Notes on the Bible

Three Parts

The Bible is divided into two parts: The Hebrew Bible (Old Testament) and the Christian Bible (New Testament). The Hebrew Bible consists of thirty-nine named books accepted by Jews and Protestants as Holy Scripture. The Old Testament also contains those thirty-nine books plus seven to fifteen more named books or parts of books called the Apocrypha or the Deuterocanonical Books; the Old Testament is accepted by Catholics and several other Christian denominations as Holy Scripture. The Christian Bible, consisting of twenty-seven named books, is also called the New Testament; it is accepted by Christians as Holy Scripture. Thus, in this work:

—**Hebrew Bible (Old Testament)**, abbreviated **HB (OT)**, indicates that a book is found both in the Hebrew Bible and the Old Testament;

—**Old Testament (Apocrypha)**, abbreviated **OT (A)**, indicates that a book is found only in the Old Testament Apocrypha and not in the Hebrew Bible;

—and **Christian Bible (New Testament)**, abbreviated **CB (NT)**, indicates that a book is found only in the Christian Bible or New Testament.

In notating biblical texts, the first number refers to the chapter in the book, and the second number (following the colon) refers to the verse within the chapter. Thus, HB (OT) Isa 7:11 means that the quotation comes from Isaiah, chapter 7, verse 11. OT (A) Sir 39:30 means that the quotation comes from Sirach, chapter 39, verse 30. CB (NT) Mark 6:2 means that the quotation comes from Mark's Gospel, chapter 6, verse 2. When more than one sentence appears in a verse, the letters a, b, c, etc. indicate the sentence being referenced in the verse. Thus, HB (OT) 2 Kgs 1:6a means that the quotation comes from the Second Book of Kings, chapter 1, verse 6, sentence 1. Also, poetry, such as the Psalms and sections of Judith, Proverbs, Isaiah, and others may be noted using the letters a, b, c, etc. to indicate the lines being used. Thus, Ps 16:4a refers to the first line of verse 4 of Psalm 16; there are two more lines of verse 4: b and c.

Because there may be a difference in the verse numbers between the *New Revised Standard Version* (NRSV) and the Vulgate (the Latin translation of the Septuagint, such as *The New American Bible Revised Edition* [NABRE]), alternative verse numbers appear in parentheses or

INTRODUCTION

brackets as necessary. This is true particularly with the Psalms, but with other books as well. Thus, NRSV Isaiah 9:2–7 is NABRE (Vulgate) Isaiah 9:1–6; NRSV Isaiah 9:2–4, 6–7 is NABRE (Vulgate) Isaiah 9:1–3, 5–6. Introductory material to Bibles usually indicates which verse-numbering is being used.

In the HB (OT) and the OT (A), the reader often sees LORD (note all capital letters). Because God's name (Yahweh or YHWH, referred to as the Tetragrammaton) is not to be pronounced, the name Adonai (meaning *Lord*) is substituted for Yahweh when a biblical text is read. When a biblical text is translated and printed, LORD (Gen 2:4) is used to alert the reader to what the text actually states: Yahweh. Furthermore, when the biblical author writes Lord Yahweh, printers present Lord GOD (note all capital letters for GOD; Gen 15:2) to avoid the printed ambiguity of LORD LORD. The Psalms in *The Message*, substitutes GOD (note all capital letters) for Yahweh. When the reference is to Jesus, the word printed is Lord (note capital L and lower-case letters; Luke 11:1). When writing about a lord (note all lower-case letters; Matt 18:25) with servants, no capital L is used.

In this book, *cf* (meaning *confer*) has not been used. Biblical notations placed in parentheses indicate where the reference can be found in the Bible. For example, the Second Book of Samuel records King David writing a song (2 Sam 22:1–51). The notation in parentheses is given to the reader, who may wish to look up the full reference in his or her Bible. In some instances, a few notations appear in parentheses; again, the reader may wish to see the references in their contexts.

Bibles

Most Bible readers are not aware that there is no such thing as the original Bible! The fact is: There are Bibles. First, there is the Jewish Bible, often called the Hebrew Bible; its books were collected and completed between 70 and 90 CE based on the Jerusalem canon (collection) in this order: Torah (Genesis, Exodus, Leviticus, Numbers, Deuteronomy), Prophets (Isaiah, Jeremiah, Ezekiel, etc.), and Writings (Job, Psalms, Proverbs, etc). It is important to note the arrangement of the collected books. Second, there is—for want of a better name—the Christian Hebrew Bible, completed in the fourth century CE, but not defined until after the Reformation. It consists of Torah, Writings, and Prophets. It is important to

INTRODUCTION

note the (re)ordering of the collected books. Christianity took the Jewish (Hebrew) Bible and rearranged the order of its books! Then, Christianity named it the Old Testament.

The Jerusalem canon, obviously, is the collection of biblical books used in Jerusalem and its environs. A large community of Jews, however, lived in Alexandria, Egypt. To the Jerusalem canon (books in Hebrew and Aramaic) they added books in Greek, the language they spoke; this collection is the Alexandrine canon. They also translated the Jerusalem canon's books from Hebrew and Aramaic into Greek. That translation, containing books and parts of books not in the Jerusalem canon, is called the Septuagint (abbreviated LXX). Later, the Septuagint was translated into Latin; it is known as the Vulgate. Every time a book of the Bible is translated, it picks up something and it loses something; that is because there is no such thing as literary equivalence.

Thus, we have (1) the Hebrew Bible—the Jewish Bible, (2) the Hebrew Bible (Old Testament)—the rearranged books of the Hebrew Bible, and (3) the Christian Bible—twenty-seven books originally written in Greek. The Protestant Bible contains only the books in the Jerusalem canon, but rearranged into the Old Testament, plus the Christian Bible books; the Catholic Bible contains the books in the Alexandrine collection plus the Christian Bible books.

The extra books or parts of books found in the Catholic Bible (and coming from the Alexandrine collection of the Jewish Bible), but not found in a Protestant Bible, are collectively referred to as the Apocrypha or Deuterocanonical Books. They include Tobit, Judith, additions to Esther, Wisdom of Solomon, Sirach (Ecclesiasticus), Baruch, Letter of Jeremiah, Prayer of Azariah (addition to Daniel), Susanna (addition to Daniel), Bel and the Dragon (addition to Daniel), 1 Maccabees, 2 Maccabees, 1 Esdras, Prayer of Manasseh, Psalm 151, 3 Maccabees, 2 Esdras, and 4 Maccabees. Not every Christian group, such as Catholics, accepts all the books in the Apocrypha as Scripture; for example, out of the four books of Maccabees, Catholics accept only 1 and 2 Maccabees. In Catholic Bibles, the additional books are placed with similar books. Thus, First and Second Maccabees are inserted with the historical books; the books of Wisdom and Sirach are found in the wisdom literature section.

Thus, there is no single or original Bible; there are many Bibles; it depends on what books a specific denomination or group (Jews, Christians) accepts as Scripture. The Bible that contains any book that any group accepts as Scripture is *The Access Bible* (updated edition): *New*

INTRODUCTION

Revised Standard Version with the Apocrypha, general editors Gail R. O'Day and David Petersen, published in New York by Oxford University Press in 1999 and updated in 2011.

Thus, a Bible reader should keep in mind the following: In a Christian Bible, The Old Testament consists of the rearranged books found in the Hebrew (Jewish) Bible. Roman Catholics and some others add some books and parts of books to that Old Testament because they were found in the Alexandrine collection. In general, Protestants do not add books to the Old Testament; they follow the Jerusalem collection of books, but rearrange them as noted above. Almost all Christians accept the twenty-seven books of the New Testament; there are a few groups that reject one or another of the books in the collection.

Thus, as you can see, this can become difficult to navigate, especially when someone says, "The Bible says . . . ." The astute Bible reader needs to ask, "Which book in which Bible says that?" There is no such thing as the original Bible. There are Bibles, various libraries of books collected over three thousand years by individuals and groups who declared their collection (canon) to be Scripture. When engaged in Bible study, it is also important to note that the Bible is a library of books written by different authors at different times in history; it is not a single book.

Presuppositions

The HB (OT) begins as stories passed on by word of mouth from one person to another. Sometime during the oral transmission stage, authors decided to collect the oral stories and write them. A change occurs immediately. One does not tell a story the same way one writes a story. Repetition and correction occur in oral story-telling. Except for future emendations by copyists, single statements by characters and plot structure dominate written stories. Furthermore, in both oral and written story-telling, types or models are employed. In the HB (OT), for example, Joshua and Elijah are types of Moses. In the CB (NT) Elizabeth becomes a type of Hannah, who is herself a type of Sarah. When orally narrating or writing a story, the teller or author consciously creates one character as a type of another in order to make the character and his or her words and actions intelligible to the hearer or reader.

In the CB (NT) the oldest gospel is Mark's account of Jesus' victory. The author of Matthew's Gospel copied and shortened about eighty percent of Mark's material into his book and then added other stories to make the work longer. The author of Luke's Gospel copied and shortened about fifty percent of Mark's material into his orderly account and then added other stories to make the work much longer. The material shared by Matthew and Luke is called Q—from the German word *Quelle*, meaning *Source*—by biblical scholars. Mark's Gospel begins as oral story-telling, lasting for about forty years in that form. An unidentified author, called Mark for the sake of convenience, collects the oral stories, sets a plot, and writes the first gospel around 70 CE. Because Jesus was expected to return soon, no one had thought about recording what he had said and done until Mark came along and realized that he was not returning as quickly as had been thought. About ten years after Mark finished his gospel, Matthew needed to adopt Mark's narrative—originally intended for a peasant Gentile readership—to a Jewish audience. And about twenty years after Mark finished his gospel, Luke needed to adapt Mark's poor Gentile-intended work for a rich, upper class, urban, Gentile readership. The author of John's Gospel did not know the existence of the other three works collectively named synoptic gospels. A point often overlooked by modern readers is the fact that they are not the intended readers of biblical texts. Every biblical book was written to a specific group of people at a specific time in history. Thus, Paul did not write to people living in the United States; he wrote in Greek to people living in Rome, Corinth, and Thessalonica. Modern readers are reading an English translation (and interpretation) with Roman-Greco cultural presuppositions underlying the text.

Furthermore, letters and gospels were not first intended to be read privately as is done today. They were meant to be heard in a group. The very low rate of literacy in the first century would have never dictated many copies of texts since most people could not read, and their standard practice was to listen to another read the letters and stories to them. Thus, what began as oral story-telling passed on by word of mouth became written story-telling preserved in gospels. A careful reading of Mark's Gospel will reveal the orality still embedded in the text, especially evident in the repetition of words and the organization of stories in three parts. In rewriting Mark, Matthew and Luke remove the last traces of oral story-telling.

The letters of Paul are older than the gospels. Biblical scholars divide the letters of Paul into the authentic letters—those written by Paul (Romans, Galatians, Philippians, etc.)—and those written by someone else in Paul's name—second generation Pauline letters (Ephesians,

INTRODUCTION

Colossians, Titus, etc.). The latter group of letters usually develop Pauline thought for a new generation of Christians. The reader of letters needs to keep in mind that the letter was not addressed to him or her; it was addressed to a specific group of believers in the mid- to late-first century CE. In addition to the Pauline body of letters, there are other letters that were gathered and placed in the CB (NT) canon (collection), such as James, 1 and 2 Peter, Jude, etc. These anonymous letters were written in the name of an apostle to give them authority in the Christian communities to which they were addressed.

1

Morning Prayer

Overview of the Parts of Morning Prayer

Beginning

The Beginning, as the name implies, is where the pray-er begins. Ten beginnings, a through j are given as choices. The pray-er needs to choose one that he or she likes, or to rotate using the ten choices.

Antiphon

After turning to a season (Ordinary Time, Advent, Christmas, Lent, Holy Week, Easter, Major Special Days), the pray-er reads the antiphon, a verse of two of a psalm meant to give focus to the exercise.

Psalm

Following the antiphon is a selection from one of the one hundred fifty psalms or one of the many canticles that appear in biblical literature. The psalm should be prayed slowly and thoughtfully. At the end of the psalm selection one may choose to add the Glory to the Father prayer; it is optional

Repeat Antiphon

After praying the psalm selection and/or the Glory to the Father prayer, the pray-er proceeds to the Reading, a passage of Scripture from the Bible. Sometimes, the passage is semi-continuous from one day to the next. Sometimes, it is a random passage that fits themes of a liturgical season. In Major Special Days, the Reading highlight the feast being celebrated.

Meditation/Journal, Reflection, Activity, Silent Prayer, Points to Ponder, Intercessions

A variety of responses to the Reading follows it. A **Meditation/Journal** response provides questions for the pray-er to answer through meditation; for those who like to journal, either with pen and paper or electronically, the questions may be used in that way.

Sometimes a **Reflection** is provided. A spiritual reflection is the author's exposition of the Scripture text which preceded it. The spiritual reflection is an exercise in spirituality, the method one chooses to nourish his or her spirit. The practices of spirituality are as varied as the people living on the earth. In this book, biblical passages with reflections are designed to nourish spirituality. This author has written about spirituality extensively in other books; the reader can find a list of those at the back of this book.

When reading the Bible, readers must place themselves in each book's author's time, rather than presume the readers' time. Presuming the standards of modern time, when reading a biblical book or a passage from a biblical book, ignores the total context of the passage and the book. Removing the context gives Bible readers the opportunity to make any text mean whatever they want it to mean; removing the context often deprives readers of the deeper meaning of a biblical text. It is also important to recognize that an English-speaking reader is reading a translation of Hebrew, Aramaic, and Greek, and words in one language do not have a literary equivalent in another language. What is very specific in one language (like breath in English) is ambiguous in another language (like breath, wind, spirit in Hebrew [*ruah*] and Greek [*pneuma*]).

A Reflection is based on the root word of spirituality: spirit. In the twentieth-first century, each person must be the keeper of his or her own flame of spirituality. The spiritual world gives reality to the ordinary world we experience. In his own time and place, Jesus of Nazareth used parables of the natural world as images for the spirituality of all things. The revelation of God takes place through our connection to all things Spirit. This author's contention is that the Divine Spirit seeks to connect to the human spirit so that we have access in one Spirit to the Father (Eph 2:18).

Throughout the Reflection, the masculine pronoun for God, LORD, LORD God, etc. is used. The author is aware that God is neither male nor female, but to avoid the repetition of proper nouns repeatedly, he employs male pronouns, as they are also used in most biblical translations.

If a Meditation/Journal question is not given, and if there is no Reflection, the author may provide an **Activity**. An activity can take many different forms, but a typical one is Lectio Divina (Divine Reading). The pray-er is encouraged to find a word or phrase in the psalm or reading and indicate what it means. After spending time thinking about it, the pray-er is asked to indicate how the word or phrase helped to make him or her aware of God's presence.

In lieu of any of the given responses to readings, a pray-er may choose to sit or stand in **Silent Prayer**. Sometimes words—spoken or recorded—get in the way of spirituality. From time to time, thinking silently may be the best form of prayer.

Points to Ponder are presented for some responses to readings. A Points to Ponder exercise presents in numbered order pieces of information about the psalm or reading that can be helpful to the pray-er. Usually, background biblical information is provided, but the author also provides information on context, specific words, and scenes.

An important part of an exercise can be **Intercession**. Intercessions are prayers for others. A general list is often given, but pray-ers are encouraged to create their own list of people for whom they pray. After finishing the response to the reading, the pray-er returns to chapter 1 to resume and conclude the exercise.

The Lord's Prayer

Following the response to the reading, a pray-er is encouraged to say the prayer Jesus taught. This book presents TM's presentation of the two versions of the Lord's Prayer found in the Bible (Matthew's Gospel and Luke's Gospel). Because TM's translations are modern and fresh, the reader may choose either the Matthean version or the Lukan version. Of course, he or she may also choose the version that most pray-ers memorize as children.

Blessing

There are two elements that conclude the exercise: Blessing and Conclusion. For the **Blessing**, a pray-er has five choices. He or she can pick the one liked the best, or the person can rotate the five choices.

Conclusion

The purpose of the **Conclusion** is to bring the exercise to an end. Six choices are given; a pray-er may choose his or her favorite, or the person can rotate the six choices.

Structure of Morning Prayer

Beginning (choose one):

(a) Unbutton my lips, dear God; / I'll let loose with your praise. (Ps 51:15, TM)
(b) I shout praises to GOD, / I raise the roof for the Rock, who saved me! (Ps 95:1, TM)
(c) What a beautiful thing, GOD, to give thanks, / to sing an anthem to you, the High God! (Ps 92:1, TM)
(d) O LORD, You preserve man [and woman] and beast. (Ps 36:6c, AMP)
(e) Be pleased, O LORD, to save me; / O LORD, make haste to help me. (Ps 40:13, AMP)
(f) O You who hear prayer, / To You all [human]kind comes. (Ps 65:2, AMP)
(g) How lovely are Your dwelling places, / O LORD of hosts! (Ps 84:1, AMP)
(h) I will hear [with expectant hope] what God the LORD will say, / For He will speak peace to His people, to His godly ones. (Ps 85:8, AMP)
(i) O give thanks to the LORD, call upon His name; / Make known His deeds among the people. (Ps 105:1, AMP)
(j) Seek and deeply long for the LORD and His strength [His power, His might]; / Seek and deeply long for His face and His presence continually. (Ps 105:4, AMP)

MORNING PRAYER

Antiphon: (see the appropriate day in Advent, Christmas, Ordinary Time, Lent, Holy Week, Easter, or Major Special Days)

Psalm: (see the appropriate day in Advent, Christmas, Ordinary Time, Lent, Holy Week, Easter, or Major Special Days)

(Optional: At the end of the Psalm there is a tradition of adding: *Glory to the Father, and to the Son, and to the Holy Spirit; as it was in the beginning, is now, and will be forever. Amen.*)

Repeat Antiphon: (see the appropriate day in Advent, Christmas, Ordinary Time, Lent, Easter, Holy Week, or Major Special Days)

Meditation/Journal, Reflection, Activity, Silent Prayer, Points to Ponder, Intercessions: (see the appropriate day in Advent, Christmas, Ordinary Time, Lent, Holy Week, Easter, or Major Special Days)

The Lord's Prayer (choose one):

(a) My Father in heaven, / Reveal who you are. / Set the world right; / Do what's best—as above, so below; / Keep me alive with three square meals. / Keep me forgiven with you and forgiving others. / Keep me safe from myself and the Devil. / You're in charge! / You can do anything you want!/ You're ablaze in beauty! / Yes. Yes. Yes. (Matt 6:9–15, TM)

(b) Father, / Reveal who you are. / Set the world right. / Keep me alive with three square meals. / Keep me forgiven with you and forgiving others. / Kee me safe from myself and the Devil. (Luke 11:2–4, TM)

Blessing: (choose one)

(a) GOD bless me and keep me, / GOD smile on me and gift me, / GOD look me full in the face and make me prosper. (Num 6:24–26, TM)

(b) Bless the LORD, you His angels, / You mighty ones who do His commandments; / Bless the LORD, all you His hosts, / You who serve Him and do his will. / Bless the LORD, all you works of His, in all places of

His dominion; / Bless and affectionately praise the LORD, O my soul. (Ps 103:20ab, 21–22, AMP)

(c) Bless and affectionately praise the LORD, O my soul! / O LORD my God, You are very great. (Ps 104: 1, AMP)

(d) May the glory of the LORD endure forever; / May the LORD rejoice and be glad in His works. (Ps 104:31, AMP)

(e) Blessed be the LORD, . . . , / From everlasting even to everlasting. / And let all the people say, "Amen." / Praise the LORD! (Hallelujah!) (Ps 106:48, AMP)

Conclusion (choose one):

(a) I love you, GOD—/ you make me strong. (Ps 18:1, TM)

(b) Be brave. Be strong. Don't give up. / Expect GOD to get here soon. (Ps 31:24, TM)

(c) Your love, GOD, is my song, and I'll sing it! / I'm forever telling everyone how faithful you are. (Ps 89:1, TM)

(d) . . . [C]ertainly God has heard [me]; / He has given heed to the voice of my prayer. (Ps 66:19, AMP)

(e) Blessed be God, / Who has not turned away my prayer / Nor His lovingkindness from me. (Ps 66:20, AMP)

(f) God be gracious and kind-hearted to [me] and bless [me], / And make His face shine [with favor] on [me]. (Ps 67:1, AMP)

2

Evening Prayer

Overview of the Parts of Evening Prayer

Beginning

The Beginning, as the name implies, is where the pray-er begins. Ten beginnings, a through j, are given as choices. The pray-er needs to choose one that he or she likes, or to rotate using the ten choices.

Antiphon

After turning to a season (Ordinary Time, Advent, Christmas, Lent, Holy Week, Easter, Major Special Days), the pray-er reads the antiphon, a verse or two of a psalm meant to give focus to the exercise.

Psalm

Following the antiphon is a selection from one of the one hundred fifty psalms or one of the many canticles that appear in biblical literature. The psalm should be prayed slowly and thoughtfully. At the end of the psalm selection one may choose to add the Glory to the Father prayer; it is optional

Repeat Antiphon

After praying the psalm selection and/or the Glory to the Father prayer, the pray-er proceeds to the Reading, a passage of Scripture from the Bible. Sometimes, the passage is semi-continuous from one day to the next. Sometimes, it is a random passage that fits themes of a liturgical season. In Major Special Days, the Reading highlights the feast being celebrated.

Meditation/Journal, Reflection, Activity, Silent Prayer, Points to Ponder, Intercessions

A variety of responses to the Reading follows it. A **Meditation/Journal** response provides questions for the pray-er to answer through meditation; for those who like to journal, either with pen and paper or electronically, the questions may be used in that way.

Sometimes a **Reflection** is provided. A spiritual reflection is the author's exposition of the Scripture text which preceded it. The spiritual reflection is an exercise in spirituality, the method one chooses to nourish his or her spirit. The practices of spirituality are as varied as the people living on the earth. In this book, biblical passages with reflections are designed to nourish spirituality. This author has written about spirituality extensively in other books; the reader can find a list of those at the back of this book.

When reading the Bible, readers must place themselves in each book's author's time, rather than presume the readers' time. Presuming the standards of modern time, when reading a biblical book or a passage from a biblical book, ignores the total context of the passage and the book. Removing the context gives Bible readers the opportunity to make any text mean whatever they want it to mean; removing the context often deprives readers of the deeper meaning of a biblical text. It is also important to recognize that an English-speaking reader is reading a translation of Hebrew, Aramaic, and Greek, and words in one language do not have a literary equivalent in another language. What is very specific in one language (like breath in English) is ambiguous in another language (like breath, wind, spirit in Hebrew [*ruah*] and Greek [*pneuma*]).

A Reflection is based on the root word of spirituality: spirit. In the twentieth-first century, each person must be the keeper of his or her own flame of spirituality. The spiritual world gives reality to the ordinary world we experience. In his own time and place, Jesus of Nazareth used parables of the natural world as images for the spirituality of all things. The revelation of God takes place through our connection to all things Spirit. This author's contention is that the Divine Spirit seeks to connect to the human spirit so that we have access in one Spirit to the Father (Eph 2:18).

Throughout the Reflection, the masculine pronoun for God, LORD, LORD God, etc. is used. The author is aware that God is neither male nor female, but to avoid the repetition of proper nouns repeatedly, he employs male pronouns, as they are also used in most biblical translations.

If a Meditation/Journal question is not given, and if there is no Reflection, the author may provide an **Activity**. An activity can take many different forms, but a typical one is *Lectio Divina* (Divine Reading). The pray-er is encouraged to find a word or phrase in the psalm or reading and indicate what it means. After spending time thinking about it, the pray-er is asked to indicate how the word or phrase helped to make him or her aware of God's presence.

In lieu of any of the given responses to readings, a pray-er may choose to sit or stand in **Silent Prayer**. Sometimes words—spoken or recorded—get in the way of spirituality. From time to time, thinking silently may be the best form of prayer.

Points to Ponder are presented for some responses to readings. A Points to Ponder exercise presents in numbered order pieces of information about the psalm or reading that can be helpful to the pray-er. Usually, background biblical information is provided, but the author also provides detailed and insightful information on context, specific words, and scenes.

An important part of an exercise can be **Intercession**. Intercessions are prayers for others. A general list is often given, but pray-ers are encouraged to create their own list of people for whom they pray. After finishing the response to the reading, the pray-er returns to chapter 2 to resume and conclude the exercise.

The Lord's Prayer

Following the response to the reading, a pray-er is encouraged to say the prayer Jesus taught. This book presents TM's presentation of the two versions of the Lord's Prayer found in the Bible (Matthew's Gospel and Luke's Gospel). Because TM's translations are modern and fresh, the reader may choose either the Matthean version or the Lukan version of the Lord's Prayer. Of course, he or she may also choose the version that most pray-ers memorize as children.

Blessing

There are two elements that conclude the exercise: Blessing and Conclusion. For the **Blessing**, a pray-er has eight choices. He or she can pick the one liked the best, or the person can rotate the eight choices.

Conclusion

The purpose of the **Conclusion** is to bring the exercise to an end. Eight choices are given; a pray-er may choose his or her favorite, or the person can rotate the eight choices.

Structure of Evening Prayer

Beginning (choose one):

(a) Blessed be the LORD God, . . . / Who alone does wonderful things. (Ps 72:18, AMP)
(b) Blessed be [the LORD God's] name forever; / And may the whole earth be filed with His glory. Amen and Amen. (Ps 72:19, AMP)
(c) I will give thanks and praise You, O Lord my God, with all my heart; / and will glorify Your name forevermore. (Ps 86:12, AMP)
(d) Sing to God, sing praises to His name; / Lift up a song for Him who rides through the desert—/ His name is the LORD—be in good spirits before Him. (Ps 68:4, AMP)
(e) Praise the LORD (Hallelujah!) / Oh give thinks to the LORD, for He is good; / For His mercy and lovingkindness endure forever! (Ps 106:1, AMP)
(f) O GOD, my heart is steadfast [with confident faith]; / I will sing, I will sing praises, even with my soul. (Ps 108:1, AMP)
(g) Praise the LORD! / For it is good to sing praises to our [gracious and majestic] God; / Praise is becoming and appropriate. (Ps 147:1, AMP)
(h) Praise the LORD! / Praise the LORD from the heavens; / Praise Him in the heights! (Ps 148:1, AMP)
(i) Praise the LORD! / Sing to the LORD a new song. (Ps 149:1ab, AMP)
(j) Praise the LORD! / Praise God in His sanctuary; / Praise Him in His mighty heavens. / Praise Him for His mighty acts; / Praise Him according to [the abundance of] His greatness. (Ps 150:1–2, AMP)

EVENING PRAYER

Antiphon: (see the appropriate day in Advent, Christmas, Ordinary Time, Lent, Holy Week, Easter, or Major Special Days)

Psalm: (see the appropriate day in Advent, Christmas, Ordinary Time, Lent, Holy Week, Easter, or Major Special Days)

(Optional: At the end of the Psalm there is a tradition of adding: *Glory to the Father, and to the Son, and to the Holy Spirit; as it was in the beginning, is now, and will be forever. Amen.*)

Repeat Antiphon: (see the appropriate day in Advent, Christmas, Ordinary Time, Lent, Holy Week, Easter, or Major Special Days)

Meditation/Journal, Reflection, Activity, Silent Prayer, Points to Ponder, Intercessions: (see the appropriate day in Advent, Christmas, Ordinary Time, Lent, Holy Week, Easter, or Major Special Days)

The Lord's Prayer (choose one):
(a) My Father in heaven, / Reveal who you are. / Set the world right; / Do what's best—as above, so below; / Keep me alive with three square meals. / Keep me forgiven with you and forgiving others. / Keep me safe from myself and the Devil. / You're in charge! / You can do anything you want!/ You're ablaze in beauty! / Yes. Yes. Yes. (Matt 6:9–15, TM)
(b) Father, / Reveal who you are. / Set the world right. / Keep me alive with three square meals. / Keep me forgiven with you and forgiving others. / Kee me safe from myself and the Devil. (Luke 11:2–4, TM)

Blessing (choose one):
(a) Rejoice in the LORD, you righteous ones [whose moral and spiritual integrity places them in right standing with God], / And praise and give thanks at the remembrance of His holy name. (Ps 97:12, AMP).
(b) Let the peoples praise You, O God; / Let all the peoples praise You. (Ps 67:3, AMP)

(c) . . . [T]hey cried out to the LORD in their trouble, / And He saved them from their distresses. / He sent His word and healed them, / And rescued them from their destruction. / Let them give thanks to the LORD for His lovingkindness, / And for His wonderful acts to the children of men [and women]! (Ps 107:19–21, AMP)
(d) Blessed be the name of the LORD / From this time forth and forever. / From the rising of the sun to its setting / The name of the LORD is to be praised [with awe-inspired reverence]. (Ps 113:2–3, AMP)
(e) The LORD has been mindful of [me]; He will bless, / He will bless . . . . / He will bless . . . . (Ps 115:12, AMP)
(f) May you be blessed of the LORD, / Who made heaven and earth. (Ps 115:15, AMP)
(g) May the LORD bless you . . . , / And may you see . . . prosperity . . . all the days of your life. (Ps 128:5, AMP)
(h) The blessing of the LORD be upon [me]; / [I] bless you in the name of the LORD. (Ps 129:8bc, AMP)

Conclusion (choose one):

(a) I love you, GOD—/ you make me strong. (Ps 18:1, TM)
(b) I called to You, O LORD, / And to the Lord I made supplication (specific request). (Ps 30:8, AMP)
(c) Be brave. Be strong. Don't give up. / Expect GOD to get here soon. (Ps 31:24, TM)
(d) Be pleased, O LORD, to save me; / O LORD, make haste to help me. (Ps 40:13, AMP)
(e) Your love, GOD, is my song, and I'll sing it! / I'm forever telling everyone how faithful you are. (Ps 89:1, TM)
(f) I love the LORD, because He hears [and continues to hear] / My voice and my supplications (my pleas, my cries, my specific needs). (Ps 116:1, AMP)
(g) In my trouble I cried to the LORD, / and He answered me. (Ps 120:1, AMP)
(h) I will exalt You, my God, O King, / And [with gratitude and submissive wonder] I will bless Your name forever and ever; / Every day I will bless You and lovingly praise You; / Yes, [with awe-inspired reverence] I will praise Your name forever and ever. (Ps 145:1–2, AMP)

3

Season of Ordinary Time

Season of Ordinary Time Introduction

The Season of Ordinary Time is divided into two sections. One section occurs between the end of the Season of Christmas and the beginning of the Season of Lent; the other section occurs between the end of the Season of Easter and the beginning of the Season of Advent.

The first section of Ordinary Time begins in 2025 on January 13 and ends on March 4; in 2026 it begins on January 12 and ends on February 17; in 2027 it begins on January 11 and ends on February 9; in 2028 it begins on January 10 and ends on February 29; in 2029 it begins on January 9 and ends on February 13; in 2030 it begins on January 14 and ends on March 5; in 2031 it begins on January 13 and ends on February 25; in 2032 it begins on January 12 and ends on February 10; in 2033 it begins on January 10 and ends on March 1; in 2034 it begins on January 10 and ends on February 21; in 2035 it begins on January 9 and ends on February 6; in 2036 it begins on January 14 and ends on February 26; in 2037 it begins on January 12 and ends on February 17; in 2038 it begins on January 11 and ends on March 9; in 2039 it begins on January 10 and ends on February 22.

The second section of Ordinary Time begins in 2025 on June 9 and ends on November 29; in 2026 it begins on May 25 and ends on November 28; in 2027 it begins on May 17 and ends on November 27; in 2028 it begins on June 5 and ends on December 2; in 2029 it begins on May 21 and ends on December 1; in 2030 it begins on June 10 and ends on November 30; in 2031 it begins on June 2 and ends on November 29; in 2032 it begins on May 17 and ends on November 27; in 2033 it begins on June 6 and ends on November 26; in 2034 it begins on May 29 and ends on December 2; in 2035 it begins on May 14 and ends on December 1; in 2036 it begins on June 2 and ends on November 29; in 2037 it begins on May 25 and ends on November 28; in 2038 it begins on June 14 and ends on November 27; in 2039 it begins on May 30 and ends on November 26.

The last Sunday in Ordinary Time is the solemnity of Our Lord Jesus Christ, King of the Universe. In 2025 it occurs on November 23; in 2026 it occurs on November 22; in 2027 it occurs on November 21; in 2028 it occurs on November 26; in 2029 it occurs on November 25; in 2030 it occurs on November 24; in 2031 it occurs on November 23; in 2032 it occurs on November 21; in 2033 it occurs on November 20; in 2034 it occurs on November 26; in 2035 it occurs on November 25; in 2036 it occurs on November 23; in 2037 it occurs on November 22; in 2038 it occurs on November 21; in 2039 it occurs on November 20.

The Season of Ordinary Time is designed around the months of the year. Some months have thirty days, some have thirty-one days, and February has twenty-eight, or, in leap years, twenty-nine, days. The reader may use each month as often as he or she likes. If the reader uses the Seasons—Advent, Christmas, Lent, Holy Week, and Easter—then he or she can return to Ordinary Time when the season ends. For example, after finishing the Season of Christmas in 2025 on January 12, he or she can move to January 13 (Day 13) in Ordinary Time and follow and repeat it for February and use it up to March 4. After completing the Season of Lent, Holy Week, and the Season of Easter, the reader returns to Ordinary Time in 2025 on June 9 (Day 9) and repeats it during July, August, September, October, and November to November 29. Then, he or she switches to the Season of Advent on November 30. If one chooses not to observe the liturgical seasons, then Ordinary Time can be repeated every month of the year.

For the latter purpose, notations for Alternative Readings are provided. To employ the use of Alternative Readings for either Morning Prayer or Evening Prayer or both, the reader will need a Bible. After finding and reading the recommended passage, one can use one of the following prompts for deeper reflection. (1) Ask yourself what connection you might find between the Psalm and the Reading, and explore the meaning of the connection. Or (2) ask yourself what word got your attention in either the Psalm or the Reading, explain what the word means, and reflect on how it makes your aware of the divine presence. Or (3) reflect on how the Reading helps you interpret a similar event in your life. Or (4) pray for others (intercessions) who are like a (the) character(s) in the Psalm or Reading. Or (5) make a list of points you want to ponder. Or (6) sit quietly and silently with the Reading before (7) writing a response to it in your journal.

Other books by Mark G. Boyer that follow the same structure of Morning Prayer and Evening Prayer that can be used—in substitution for what is provided here—during the Season of Ordinary Time include: *Weekday Saints: Reflections on Their Scriptures* (Eugene, OR: Wipf & Stock, 2014); *Very Short Reflections—for Advent and Christmas, Lent and Easter, Ordinary Time, and Saints—through the Liturgical Year* (Eugene, OR: Wipf & Stock, 2020); *Nature Spirituality: Praying with Wind, Water, Earth, Fire* (Eugene, OR: Resource Publications, 2013); *An Abecedarian of Animal Spirit Guides: Spiritual Growth through Reflections on Creatures* (Eugene, OR: Wipf & Stock, 2016); *An Abecedarian of Sacred Trees: Spiritual Growth through Reflections on Woody Plants* (Eugene, OR: Wipf & Stock, 2016); *Biblical Names for God: An Abecedarian Anthology of Spiritual Reflections for Anytime* (Eugene, OR: Wipf & Stock, 2023); *Journey into God: Spiritual Reflections for Travelers* (Eugene, OR: Wipf & Stock, 2022); *The Spirit of the Lord God: Biblical Names and Images for the Holy Spirit; An Abecedarian Anthology of Spiritual Reflections for Anytime* (Eugene, OR: Resource Publications, 2024); *What is Born of the Spirit is Spirit: A Biblical Spirituality of Spirit* (Eugene, OR: Wipf & Stock, 2019); *From Contemplation to Action: The Spiritual Process of Divine Discernment Using Elijah and Elisha as Models* (Eugene, OR: Wipf & Stock, 2018); *Living Parables: Today's Versions* with Corbin Cole (Eugene, OR: Wipf & Stock, 2020); *Fruit of the Vine: A Biblical Spirituality of Wine* (Eugene, OR: Wipf & Stock, 2017); *All Things Mary: Honoring the Mother of God—An Anthology of Marian Reflections* (Eugene, OR: Wipf & Stock, 2018); *Monthly Entries for the Spiritual but not Religious through the Year: Texts, Reflections, Journal/Meditations, and Prayers for the SBNR* (Eugene, OR: Wipf and Stock, 2022); *His Mercy Endures Forever: Biblical Reflections on Divine Mercy for Anytime* (Eugene, OR: Wipf & Stock,

2024); and *Seasons of Biblical Spirituality: Spring, Summer, Autumn, and Winter* (Eugene, OR: Resource Publications, 2023).

Antiphons and Psalms for the Season of Ordinary Time are taken from *The Message* (TM) by Eugene H. Peterson (Chicago, IL: ACTA Publications, 2013) and Readings for the Season of Ordinary Time are taken from the *New International Version* (NIV) of the Bible (Grand Rapids, MI: Zondervan, 2023) except for Our Lord Jesus Christ, King of the Universe, whose Antiphons, Psalms, and Readings are taken from *The Amplified Holy Bible* (AMP) (Grand Rapids, MI: Zondervan, 2018).

Days in the Season of Ordinary Time

Day 1

Morning

Antiphon: "[I] announce your love each daybreak." (Ps 92:2a, TM)
Psalm: "How well God must like you—/ . . . [Y]ou thrill to GOD's Word, / you chew on Scripture day and night. / You're a tree replanted in Eden, / bearing fresh fruit every month, / Never dropping a leaf, / always in blossom. / GOD charts the road you take . . . ." / (Ps 1:1a, 2–3, 6a, TM)
Repeat Antiphon (above):
Reading: "After the death of Moses the servant of the LORD, the LORD said to Joshua son of Nun, Moses' aide: 'Moses my servant is dead. Now then, you and all these people, get ready to cross the Jordan River into the land I am about to give to them—to the Israelites.'" (Josh 1:1–2, NIV)
Reflection: In the HB (OT) book of Deuteronomy, Moses, after explaining why he was no longer to be the leader of the Israelites (Deut 31:1–6) summoned Joshua, told him to be strong and courageous, and named him his successor (Deut 31:7–8). Later, the LORD addresses Joshua (Deut 31:23). The HB (OT) book of Joshua continues the narrative. Moses led the Israelites to the east side of the Jordan River. The promised land was on the other side. As Israel's new leader, Joshua is commissioned to lead the crossing of the Jordan River, conquer the land's inhabitants, and settle the people on the land by tribe.

Evening
Antiphon: "The wise counsel GOD gives when I'm awake / is confirmed by my sleeping heart." (Ps 16:7, TM)

Psalm: "Day and night I'll stick with GOD; / I've got a good thing going and I'm not letting go. / I'm happy from the inside out, / and from the outside in, I'm firmly formed. / Now you've got my feet on the life path, / all radiant from the shining of your face. / I'm on the right way." (Ps 16:8–9, 11, TM)
Repeat Antiphon (above):
Reading: The LORD said to Joshua: "No one will be able to stand against you all the days of your life. As I was with Moses, so I will be with you; I will never leave you nor forsake you. Be strong and courageous, because you will lead these people to inherit the land I swore to their ancestors to give them." (Josh 1:5–6, NIV)
Meditation/Journal: What do you consider to be the characteristics of a good leader? Have you ever received the assurances from God or another person that Joshua received from the LORD? Explain.
Alternative Readings: Ruth 4:1–12; 4:13–22; Prov 1:1–19; 1:20–33; Jer 1:1–10; 1:11–19.

Day 2

Morning
Antiphon: "[I] thank GOD for his marvelous love, / for his miracle mercy to the children he loves." (Ps 107:8, TM)
Psalm: "Oh, thank GOD—he's so good! / His love never runs out. / All of you set free by GOD, tell the world! / Tell how he freed you from oppression, / Then rounded you up from all over the place, / from the four winds, from the seven seas. / Some of your wandered for years in the desert, / looking but not finding a good place to live, / Half-starved and parched with thirst, / staggering and stumbling, on the brink of exhaustion. / Then, in your desperate condition, you called out to GOD. / He got you out in the nick of time; / He put your feet on a wonderful road / that took you straight to a good place to live. / He poured great draughts of water down parched throats; / the starved and hungry got plenty to eat." (Ps 107:1–7, 9, TM)
Repeat Antiphon (above):
Reading: ". . . Joshua son of Nun secretly sent two spies . . . . 'Go, look over the land,' he said, 'especially Jericho.' So they went and entered the house of a prostitute named Rahab and stayed there. . . . [S]he had taken them up to the roof and hidden them under the stalks of flax she had laid out on the roof. Before the spies lay down for the night, she went up on

the roof and said to them, '... [P]lease swear to me by the LORD that you will show kindness to my family, because I have shown kindness to you. Give me a sure sign'" (Josh 2:1–2, 6, 8, 12, NIV)

Reflection: Rahab runs the best little whore house in Jericho! And that is where the two spies sent by Joshua find both shelter and protection. They find shelter because she takes them into her house. They find protection, because she hides them from the king of Jericho who has heard about the Israelites gathered on the other side of the Jordan River and knows they have sent spies to look over the land. From an Israelite perspective, Rahab does the right thing because it is the right thing to do; in other words, she is righteous. That interpretation is used by the author of Matthew's Gospel in the CB (NT). In his genealogy of Jesus the Messiah, he lists Rahab as the mother of Boaz (Matt 1:5). Rahab is one of five righteous women interspersed in the all-male Matthean genealogy (Matt 1:1–16). While all the women are righteous, like Rahab, all of them have issues.

Evening Prayer

Antiphon: "The God of gods—it's GOD!—speaks out, shouts, 'Earth!' / welcomes the sun in the east, / farewells the disappearing sun in the west." (Ps 50:1, TM)

Psalm: "... [Y]ou, GOD, shield me on all sides; / You ground my feet, you lift my head high; / With all my might I shout up to GOD, / He answers thunder from the holy mountain. / I stretch myself out. I sleep. / Then I'm up again—rested, tall and steady .... / Up GOD! My God, help me! Real help comes from GOD. / Your blessing clothes your people!" (Ps 3:3–5, 7a, 8, TM)

Repeat Antiphon (above):

Reading: "... [Rahab] let [the spies] down by a rope through the window, for the house she lived in was part of the city wall. So she sent them away, and they departed, and she tied the scarlet cord in the window [to identify her house for protection when the Israelites entered Jericho]. When they left, they went into the hills and stayed there three days, until the pursuers had searched all along the road and returned without finding them. Then the two men started back. They said to Joshua, 'The LORD has surely given the whole land into our hands ....'" (Josh 2:15, 21b–22, 24, NIV)

Points to Ponder: First, the Israelite spies are saved by the lie of a prostitute. Israel is dependent upon God for protection, and he often uses the most inappropriate persons to effect the divine will. Second, spy

stories appear frequently in biblical literature (Num 13:1–33; 21:32; Deut 1:22–25; Josh 7:2–3; Judg 18:2–10); the returning spies usually report that the land can be taken by Israel's forces. Third, the scarlet cord the spies told Rahab to hang in her window is a sign to the invaders of where they will find willing collaborators. Fourth, the taking of the land is an achievement of Israel's God, the LORD; through Israel's forces he keeps the promise he made to Abraham, Isaac, Jacob, and their descendants.
Alternate Readings: 1 Sam 1:1–8; 1:9–11; Prov 2:1–15; 2:16–22; Jer 27:1–22; 28:1–17

Day 3

Morning
Antiphon: Hallelujah! / Praise the name of GOD, / praise the works of GOD. (Ps 135:1, TM)
Psalm: "Shout 'Hallelujah!' because GOD's so good, / sing anthems to his beautiful name. / I, too, give witness to the greatness of GOD, / our Lord, high above all other gods. / He does just as he pleases—/ however, wherever, whenever. / He makes the weather—clouds and thunder, / lightning and rain, wind pouring out of the north. / GOD, your name is eternal, / GOD stands up for his people, / GOD holds the hands of his people. / Family of Israel, bless GOD! / Family of Aaron, bless GOD! / Family of Levi, bless GOD! / You who fear GOD, bless GOD!" (Ps 135:3, 5–7, 13–14, 19–20, TM)
Repeat Antiphon (above):
Reading: "Early in the morning Joshua and all the Israelites . . . went to the Jordan, where they camped before crossing over. After three days the officers went throughout the camp, giving orders to the people. 'When you see the ark of the covenant of the LORD your God, . . . you are to move out from your positions and follow it. But keep a distance . . . between you and the ark; do not go near it.' Joshua told the people, 'Consecrate yourselves, for tomorrow the LORD will do amazing things among you.'" (Josh 3:1–3, 4b–5, NIV)
Points to Ponder: First, the Israelites camp near the Jordan River for three days. Three is a biblical number signifying the divine presence. Second, the people are instructed to keep their eyes on the ark of the covenant, a small portable box or chest. The top was called the mercy seat, because God was thought to sit there to enact atonement; the mercy seat was flanked by cherubim, whose wings extended over the ark. Inside

the box were the two tablets of stone inscribed with the terms of the divine covenant. In the CB (NT), the author of the Letter to the Hebrews states, most unlikely, that there was also a jar of manna and Aaron's staff in the chest (Heb 9:4). Third, the ark of the covenant was carried before the people to indicate that it was their God, the LORD, who was leading them. Fourth, because the ark represented the presence of God with the people, they were forbidden from touching it. Fifth, Joshua is presented as a type of Moses, who told the people facing Mount Sinai (Horeb) to wash their clothes, to be consecrated, and be ready to witness the LORD on Mount Sinai (Horeb), which they were forbidden to touch (Exod 19:10-15).

Evening Prayer
Antiphon: "God, for your sake, help me! / Use your influence to clear me. / Listen, God—I'm desperate. / Don't be too busy to hear me." (Ps 54:1-2, TM)
Canticle: "Have mercy on [me], God of all; look kindly upon [me] and show [me] the light of your compassion. . . . There's no God but you, Lord. Create new signage; do new wonders. . . . [Y]our storied wonders need to be made known. Have mercy upon your people, who invoke your name . . . . Have mercy on the city you have made holy, Jerusalem, a residential place of peace and quiet. Reintroduce the prophets, who were your creations; breathe new life into the prophecies they spoke in your name. Reward those who've kept their faith intact; may they find your word still relevant. Hear the prayers of your servants; be gracious to us as your promised . . . . Lead us down Justice Road so that every last inhabitant on earth will know that you, and you alone, are the God of the Ages." (Sir 36:1, 5b-6a, 10b, 17a, 18, 20-22, TM)
Repeat Antiphon (above):
Reading: "Joshua said to the Israelites, 'Come here and listen to the words of the LORD your God. This is how you will know that the living God is among you . . . . See, the ark of the covenant of the Lord of all the earth will go into the Jordan ahead of you. And as soon as the priests who carry the ark of the LORD—the Lord of all the earth—set foot in the Jordan, its waters flowing downstream will be cut off and stand up in a heap.'" (Josh 3:9-11, 13, NIV)
Points to Ponder: First, like Moses, Joshua calls upon the Israelites to listen to the words of the LORD their God. Second, like God made his presence known on Mount Sinai (Horeb), the Israelites will recognize his

presence among them in the ark standing in parted waters. Third, the waters of the Jordan will part for Joshua, just like the waters of the Sea of Reeds parted for Moses. Fourth, Moses used his staff to call upon God to split the sea in two; Joshua uses the ark of the covenant to part the Jordan River. Fifth, the ancestors of the people standing before the Jordan River passed through the Sea of Reeds on dry ground, and the Israelites standing on the shore of the Jordan do the same.

Alternative Readings: 1 Sam 1:12–18; 1:19–20; Prov 3:1–12, 3:13–35; Jer 13:1–11; 19:1–12.

Day 4

Morning

Antiphon: "When I call, give me answers. God, take my side! (Ps 4:1, TM)

Psalm: "Look at this: look / Who got picked by GOD! / He listens the split second I call to him. / Complain if you must, but don't lash out. / Keep your mouth shut, and let your heart do the talking. / Build your case before God and wait for his verdict. / Why is everyone hungry for *more*? 'More, more' they say. / 'More, more.' / I have God's more-than-enough, / More joy in one ordinary day / Than they get in all their shopping sprees. / At days end I'm ready for sound sleep, / For you, GOD, have put my life back together." (Ps 4:3–8, TM)

Repeat Antiphon (above):

Reading: ". . . Joshua called together the twelve men he had appointed from the Israelites one from each tribe, and said to them, 'Go over before the ark of the LORD your God into the middle of the Jordan. Each of you is to take up a stone on his shoulder, according to the number of the tribes of the Israelites, to serve as a sign among you. In the future, when your children ask you, "What do these stones mean?" tell them that the flow of the Jordan was cut off before the ark of the covenant of the LORD. When it crossed the Jordan, the waters of the Jordan were cut off. These stones are to be a memorial to the people of Israel forever.' So the Israelites did as Joshua commanded them. They took twelve stones from the middle of the Jordan . . . and they carried them over with them to their camp, where they put them down. Joshua set up the twelve stones that had been in the middle of the Jordan at the spot where the priests who carried the ark of the covenant had stood." (Josh 4:4–9a, NIV)

Activity: Choose a word or phrase from the verses of Psalm 4 or Joshua 4:4–9a. What does the word or phrase mean? How does the word or phrase make you aware of God's presence?

Evening Prayer
Antiphon: "I call to God; / GOD will help me. / At dusk, dawn, and noon I sigh / deep sighs—he hears, he rescues." (Ps 55:16–17, TM)
Psalm: "Open your ears, God, to my prayer; / don't pretend you don't hear me knocking. / Come close and whisper your answer. / I really need you. / My inside are turned inside out; / specters of death have me down. / I shake with fear, / I shudder from head to foot. / 'Who will give me wings,' I ask—/ 'wings like a dove?' / Get me out of here on dove wings; / I want some peace and quiet. / I want a walk in the country, / I want a cabin in the woods. / I'm desperate for a change / from rage and stormy weather." (Ps 55:1–2a, 4–8, TM)
Repeat Antiphon (above):
Reading: "The people hurried over, and as soon as all of them had crossed, the ark of the LORD and the priests came to the other side while the people watched. And the priests came up out of the river carrying the ark of the covenant of the LORD. No sooner had they set their feet on the dry ground than the waters of the Jordan returned to their place.... [Joshua] said to the Israelites, 'In the future when your descendants ask their parents, "What do these stone mean?" tell them, "Israel crossed the Jordan on dry ground." For the LORD your God dried up the Jordan before you until you had crossed over. The LORD your God did to the Jordan what he had done to the Red Sea when he dried it up before us until we had crossed over.'" (Josh 4:11, 18, 21–23, NIV)
Meditation/Journal: What is the catechetical lesson to be taught to children who see the pile of twelve stones? What do you use as signs of catechetical lessons to be remembered or taught?
Alternative Readings: 1 Sam 1:21–28; 2:18–21; Prov 4:1–9; 4:10–27; Jer 32:6–15; 51:60–64.

Day 5

Morning
Antiphon: "Listen, GOD! Please, pay attention!" (Ps 5:1, TM)
Psalm: "Can you make sense of these ramblings, / my groans and cries? / Every morning [, GOD,] / You'll hear me at it again. / Every morning

/ I lay out the pieces of my life / on your altar / and watch for fire to descend. / And here I am, your invited guest—/ it's incredible! / I enter your house; here I am, / prostrate in your inner sanctum, / Waiting for directions / to get me safely through enemy lines. / . . . [Y]ou'll welcome [me] with open arms / when [I] run for cover to you. / Let the party last all night! / Stand guard over [the] celebration. / You are famous, GOD, for welcoming God-seekers, / for decking [me] out in delight." (Ps 5:2–3, 7–8, 11–12, TM)

Repeat Antiphon (above):

Reading: ". . . [T]he LORD said to Joshua, 'Make flint knives and circumcise the Israelites . . . .' So Joshua made flint knives and circumcised the Israelites . . . . [A]ll the people born in the wilderness during the journey from Egypt had not [been circumcised]. The Israelites had moved about in the wilderness forty years . . . . [T]hese were the ones Joshua circumcised. They were still uncircumcised because they had not been circumcised on the way. And after the whole nation had been circumcised, they remained where they were in camp until they were healed." (Josh 5:2–3, 5–6a, 7b–8, NIV)

Reflection: While other groups of people practiced circumcision, the Israelite practice went back to Abraham (Gen 17:1–14). Granted, it limited covenant participation only to males, but it was a sign of the covenant inscribed in human flesh. The removal of the foreskin from the penis is not the common procedure done on male babies in hospitals in some countries today. Many people consider it a remnant of barbarism. The covenant made with Abraham and all Israelite men after him was meant to remind them that just as God gave life in creation, the man gave life in intercourse with his wife or concubine. Ancient people thought that the man carried the seed in his sperm. The agricultural image dominates ancient biological understanding. Through intercourse, the man planted his seed in an incubator, a woman, who carried it while it grew nine to ten months, and then it was born. Ancient genealogies, thus, traced ancestors from one man to another, since the woman was not considered to hand on anything. Modern biology, of course, knows better. In a patriarchal culture, circumcision was about the transmission of life. After spending a lifetime (forty years) in the desert and crossing the Jordan River into the promised land, God instructs Joshua to circumcise all the men born during those forty years. The Israelites are in a new land, where they will transmit new life for their people. Of course, after circumcising hundreds with flint knives, the men stayed where they were camped until they healed!

Evening Prayer
Antiphon: "I found myself in trouble and went looking for my Lord; / my life was an open wound that wouldn't heal." (Ps 77:2, TM)
Psalm: "When friends said, 'Everything will turn out all right,' / I didn't believe a word they said. / I remember God—and shake my head. / I bow my head—then wring my hands. / I'm awake all night—not a wink of sleep; / I can't even say what's bothering me. / I go over the days one by one, / I ponder the years gone by. / I strum my lute all through the night, / wondering how to get my life together. / 'Just my luck,' I said. 'The High God goes out of business / just the moment I need him.' / Once again I'll go over what GOD has done, / lay out on the table the ancient wonders; / I'll ponder all the things you've accomplished, / and give a long-loving look at your acts." (Ps 77:3–6, 10–12, TM)
Repeat Antiphon (above):
Reading: "On the evening of the fourteenth day of the month . . . on the plains of Jericho, the Israelites celebrated the Passover. The day after the Passover, that very day, they ate some of the produce of the land: unleavened bread and roasted grain." (Josh 5:10–11, NIV)
Reflection: Before celebrating Passover, all the Israelite males needed to be circumcised, as is narrated above. After crossing the Jordan River into the land promised to Abraham and his descendants by God, the Israelites celebrated Passover, the remembrance of eating a roasted lamb and smearing its blood on the lintel and doorposts of their homes. That ritual engendered their escape from Egyptian slavery. They remember their passing over through the Sea of Reeds, where they faced imminent death and came out alive. Then, just as their ancestors passed over from imminent death to new life, the next generation of Israelites had just accomplished passing over the Jordan River and entered a new life in the land of promise. The forty-day journey through the desert—death—is contrasted with land flowing with milk and honey (bread and grain)—life.
Alternate Readings: 1 Sam 3:1–9; 10–21; Prov 5:1–14; 5:5–23; Jer 43:7–13; 16:1–4.

Day 6

Morning
Antiphon: "[God,] . . . you'll welcome [me] with open arms / when I run for cover to you." (Ps 5:11, TM)

SEASON OF ORDINARY TIME

Psalm: "GOD! God! I'm running to you for dear life; / the chase is wild. / If they catch me, I'm finished; / ripped to shreds by foes fierce as lions, / dragged into the forest and left / unlooked for, unremembered. / GOD, if I've done what they say—/ betrayed my friends, / ripped off my enemies—/ If my hands are really that dirty, / let them get me, walk all over me, / leave me flat on my face in the dirt. / Stand up, GOD; pit your holy fury / against my furious enemies. / Wake up, God. My accusers have packed / the courtroom; it's judgment time. / Take your place on the bench, reach for your gavel, / throw out the false charges against me. / I'm ready, confident in your verdict: / 'Innocent.'" (Ps 7:1–8, TM)
Repeat Antiphon (above):
Reading: ". . . [T]he gates of Jericho were securely barred . . . . Then the LORD said to Joshua, 'See, I have delivered Jericho into your hands . . . . March around the city once with all the armed men. Do this for six days. Have seven priests carry trumpets of rams' horns in front of the ark. On the seventh day, march around the city seven times, with the priests blowing the trumpets. When you hear them sound a long blast on the trumpets, have the whole army give a loud shout; then the wall of the city will collapse and the army will go up, everyone straight in.'" (Josh 6:1–5, NIV)
Points to Ponder: First, the conquest of Jericho is not by might; in fact the Israelites do nothing but march around the city walls with the priests blowing trumpets! Jericho is conquered by God. Second, the LORD instructs Joshua to have the army march around the walls once a day for six days followed by the priests blowing trumpets in front of the ark of the covenant. Because they engage in this processional march for six days, it is incomplete; six is the biblical number signifying incompleteness. Third, there are three sets of seven—seven priests with trumpets, seventh day, and seven times around the city. Three is a sacred number indicating the divinity. Seven is a sacred number—the sum of three for the divinity and four for the earth. Thus, both God and people are bringing down the wall. With a loud shout on the seventh day after seven laps around the city, the walls collapse. The LORD not only wills the collapse of the walls of Jericho, he also participates in the action, represented by the ark of the covenant.

Evening Prayer
Antiphon: "GOD, you're my last chance of the day. / I spend the night on my knees before you. Put me on your salvation agenda; / take notes on the trouble I'm in." (Ps 88:1–2, TM)

Psalm: "I've had my fill of trouble; / I'm camped on the edge of hell. / I'm written off as a lost cause, / one more statistic, a hopeless case. / Abandoned as already dead, / one more body in a stack of corpses. / And not so much as a gravestone—/ I'm in a black hole in oblivion. / I call to you, GOD; all day I call. / I wring my hands, I plead for help. / I'm standing my ground, GOD, shouting for help, / at my prayers every morning, on my knees each daybreak." (Ps 88:3–5, 9, 13, TM)
Repeat Antiphon (above):
Reading: "The armed guard marched ahead of the priests who blew the trumpets, and the rear guard followed the ark. But Joshua had commanded the army, 'Do not give a war cry, do not raise you voices, do not say a word until the day I tell you to shout. Then shout!' So he had the ark of the LORD carried around the city, circling it once. Then the army returned to camp and spent the night there." (Josh 6:9a, 10–11, NIV)
Reflection: While there are guards both before and behind the priests with trumpets and the ark of the LORD, God will win the city of Jericho with a liturgical procession! In other words, the conquest of Jericho is a divine gift to the Israelites. To be sure that they understand that the conquest of Jericho will not be at their hands, Joshua instructs the armed guard to process silently around the city. These directions come from God, relayed to Joshua. The message is that obedience always redounds to Israel's benefit; it brings blessings. No battle is necessary; all takes place in silence. For one week, a liturgical procession carries the ark around the city of Jericho. It is difficult not to imagine what the citizens of Jericho thought was going on every day!
Alternative Readings: 1 Sam 8:1–9; 9:1–10; Prov 6:1–11; 6:12–19; Ezek 1:1–14; 1:15–21.

Day 7

Morning
Antiphon: "GOD, brilliant Lord, / yours is a household name." (Ps 8:1, TM)
Psalm: "Nursing infants gurgle choruses about you [, GOD]; / toddlers shout the songs / That drown out enemy talk, / and silence atheist babble. / I look up at your macro-skies, dark and enormous, / your handmade sky-jewelry, / Moon and stars mounted in their settings. / Then I look at my micro-self and wonder, / Why do you bother with [me]? / Why take a second look [my] way? / Yet [I've] so narrowly missed being [a] god,

/ bright with Eden's dawn light. / You put [me] in charge of your handcrafted world, / repeated to [me] your Genesis-charge, / Made [me] lord of sheep and cattle, / even animals out in the wild. / Birds flying and fish swimming, / whales singing in the ocean deeps. / GOD, brilliant Lord, / your name echoes around the world." (Ps 8:2–9, TM)

Repeat Antiphon (above):

Reading: "Joshua got up early . . . and the priests took up the ark of the LORD. The seven priests carrying the seven trumpets went forward, marching before the ark of the LORD and blowing the trumpets. The armed men went ahead of them and the rear guard followed the ark of the LORD, while the trumpets kept sounding. So on the second day they marched around the city once and returned to the camp. They did this for six days." (Josh 6:12–14, NIV)

Activity: What word or phrase gets your attention in the verses from Psalm 8 or the HB (OT) book of Joshua 6:12–14? What does the word or phrase mean? How does the word or phrase make you aware of God's presence?

Evening Prayer

Antiphon: "What a beautiful thing, GOD, to give thanks, / to sing an anthem to you, the High God! / To announce your love each daybreak, / sing your faithful presence all through the night . . . ." (Ps 92:1–2, TM)

Psalm: "You made me so happy, GOD. / I saw your work and I shouted for joy. / How magnificent your work, GOD! / How profound your thoughts! / . . . [Y]ou've made me strong as a charging bison, / you've honored me with a festive parade. / My ears are filled with the sounds of promise; / 'Good people will prosper like palm trees, / Grow tall like Lebanon cedars; / transplanted to GOD's courtyard, / They'll grow tall in the presence of God, / lithe and green, virile still in old age.'" (Ps 92:4–5. 10, 12–14, TM)

Repeat Antiphon (above):

Reading: "On the seventh day, [the armed guard and the priests carrying the ark of the LORD] got up at daybreak and marched around the city [of Jericho] seven times . . . . The seventh time around, when the priests sounded the trumpet blast, Joshua commanded the army, 'Shout! For the LORD has given you the city! The city and all that is in it are to be devoted to the LORD. Only Rahab the prostitute and all who are with her in her house shall be spared, because she hid the spies we sent.' When the trumpets sounded, the army shouted, and at the sound of the trumpet, when the men gave a loud shout, the wall collapsed; . . . and they took the city. They devoted the city to the LORD and destroyed with the sword every living thing in it—men and women, young and old, cattle, sheep, and donkeys." (Josh 6:15a, 16–17, 20–21, NIV)

Points to Ponder: First, it is import to recognize the numerology at work in the above passage from Joshua. Six represents incompleteness; the liturgical procession with the armed guard, priests with trumpets, and priests carrying the ark of the LORD have marched around the city walls of Jericho in the morning for six incomplete days. Now, on the seventh day they march around the city seven time. Seven (the sum of three—God—and four—the earth) represents completeness. After seven circumambulations on the seventh day, the walls of Jericho fall. Second, while it seems harsh to modern readers that everyone and everything in the city is destroyed, Joshua follows Moses' directions in the HB (OT) book of Deuteronomy: ". . . [I]n the cities of the nations the LORD your God is giving you as an inheritance, do not leave alive anything that breathes" (Deut 20:16, NIV). Called the ban (Deut 7:1–2), the Israelites are instructed to destroy completely every person and animal because the Gentiles will teach them to follow "all the detestable things they do in worshiping their gods, and [the Israelites] will sin against the LORD [their] God" (Deut 20:18, NIV). Third, the city of Jericho is not conquered by the Israelites; God conquers it with a liturgical procession of guards, priests with trumpets, and priests with the ark of the LORD. Jericho is the first Gentile city claimed by the LORD in the promised land.

Alternative Readings: 1 Sam 9:15–21; 9:22–26; Prov 6:20–35; 7:1–9; 7:10–20; Ezek 1:22–28; 4:1–4.

Day 8

Morning
Antiphon: "I'm thanking you, GOD, from a full heart, / I'm writing the book on your wonders." (Ps 9:1, TM)
Psalm: "[High God, y]ou took over and set everything right; / when I needed you, you were there, taking charge. / God holds the high center, / he sees and sets the world's mess right. / He decides what is right for us earthlings, / gives people their just des[s]erts. / GOD's a safe-house for the battered, / a sanctuary during bad times. / The moment you arrive, you relax; / you're never sorry you knocked. / Be kind to me, GOD; / I've been kicked around long enough." (Ps 9:4, 7–10, 13a, TM)

Repeat Antiphon (above):

Reading: "Joshua said to the two men who had spied out the land, 'Go into the prostitute's house and bring her out and all who belong to her, in accordance with your oath to her.' So the young men who had done the spying went in and brought out Rahab, her father and mother, her brothers and sisters, and all who belonged to her. They brought out her entire family and put them in a place outside the camp of Israel. Then they burned the whole city and everything in it . . . . But Joshua spared Rahab the prostitute, with her family and all who belonged to her, because she hid the men Joshua had sent as spies to Jericho . . . ." (Josh 6:22–24a, 25a, NIV)

Points to Ponder: First, Rahab was promised by the Israelite spies that no harm would come to her nor to anyone else in her house of ill repute when Jericho was captured. While everyone and everything is destroyed, because it is God's property and unsafe for human use, Joshua makes an exception to the Deuteronomist's law. Joshua shows mercy to Rahab and her family, just like God has showed mercy to the Israelites. Second, Rahab, who told the spies that she believed that the LORD was giving the land to them (Josh 2:8), demonstrates that even peripheral faith in the LORD is sufficient to save a Gentile woman, who is also a prostitute! Third, the sign the spies gave her was a scarlet cord hung in a window of her home. The red rope signifies the character of her home! Third, the tale about Rahab in the HB (OT) book of Joshua will inspire Nathaniel Hawthorne to write and publish *The Scarlet Letter* in 1850; it is set in the Puritan Massachusetts Bay Colony 1642–49, telling the story about Hester Prynne, who conceives a daughter with a man to whom she is not married and is sentenced to wear on her dress the scarlet letter A (for adultery).

Evening Prayer

Antiphon: ". . . [C]ome, let us worship; bow before [GOD], / on your knees before GOD, who made us! Oh, yes, he's our God . . . ." (Ps 95:6–7a, TM)

Psalm: "Come, let's shout praises to GOD, / raise the roof for the Rock who saved us! / Let's march into his presence singing praises, / lifting the rafters with our hymns! / And why? Because GOD is the best, / High King over all the gods. / In one hand he holds deep caves and caverns, / in the other hand grasps the high mountains. / He made Ocean—he owns it! / His hands sculpted Earth! / . . . [W]e're the people he pastures, the flock he feeds." (Ps 95:1–5, 7b, TM)

Repeat Antiphon (above):

Reading: ". . . Joshua built on Mount Ebal an altar to the LORD, the God of Israel. He built it according to what is written in the Book of the Law of Moses—an altar of uncut stones, on which no iron tool had been used. Joshua wrote on stones a copy of the law of Moses. Afterward, Joshua read all the words of the law—the blessings and the curses—just as it is written in the Book of the Law." (Josh 8:30, 31b, 32, 34, NIV)
Meditation/Journal: For what do you need to praise God this evening? Where is your altar to the LORD? What are elements of your way of life—blessings and curses—in God's presence?
Alternative Readings: 1 Sam 10:1-8; 10:17-27; Prov 7:21-27; 8:1-18; Ezek 4:5-8; 4:9-18.

Day 9

Morning
Antiphon: "I'm whistling, laughing, and jumping for joy; / I'm singing your song, High God." (Ps 9:2, TM)
Psalm: "I've already run for dear life / straight to the arms of GOD. / So why would I run away now / when you say, / 'Run to the mountains; the evil / bows are bent, the wicked arrows / Aimed to shoot under cover of darkness / at every heart open to God. / The bottom's dropped out of the country; / good people don't have a chance'? / But GOD hasn't moved to the mountains; / his holy address hasn't changed. / He's in charge, as always, his eyes / taking everything in, his eyelids / Unblinking, examining Adam's unruly brood / inside and out, not missing a thing. / GOD's business is putting things right; / he loves getting the line straight, / Setting us straight. Once we're standing tall, / we can look him straight in the eye." (Ps 11:1-4, 7, TM)
Repeat Antiphon (above):
Reading: ". . . [T]he five kings of the Amorites . . . joined forces. The LORD said to Joshua, 'Do not be afraid of them; I have given them into your hand. Not one of them will be able to withstand you.' The LORD threw them into confusion before Israel, so Joshua and the Israelites defeated them completely . . . . [T]he LORD hurled large hailstones down on them, and more of them died from the hail than were killed by the swords of the Israelites. On the day the LORD gave the Amorites over to Israel, Joshua said to the LORD in the presence of Israel: 'Sun, stand still . . . , / and you, moon . . . .' So the sun stood still . . . , / the moon stopped . . . . The sun stopped in the middle of the sky and delayed going

down about a full day. There has never been a day like it before or since, a day when the LORD listened to a human being. Surely the LORD was fighting for Israel." (Josh 10:5a, 8, 10a, 11b–13ac–14, NIV)

Reflection: The HB (OT) book of Joshua features a few battles in which the Israelite army engaged to conquer the promised land. After hearing about the power of the Israelite army, the Amorite king of Jerusalem formed a coalition with four other Amorite kings to defeat the Israelite army. What none of the kings in the coalition know is that the LORD defeats the enemies of his people. In this particular battle, the LORD's presence and battle strategy is represented by two miracles. The first consists of hailstones; such a weather phenomenon is a weapon of the LORD as divine warrior. The second miracle is in response to Joshua's prayer that the LORD extend the hours of daylight so there is more time for the Israelites to defeat the Amorites. The author of the book of Joshua interprets the latter miracle as occasioned by the LORD listening to a human being, Joshua. He concludes that both miracles indicate that God was fighting for his people. The reader must keep in mind that the book of Joshua is written from the biased point of view of Israel; modern people do not think that God picks a side and wins the battle for that side.

Evening Prayer

Antiphon: "GOD, listen! Listen to my prayer, / listen to the pain in my cries." (Ps 102:1, TM)

Psalm: "Don't turn your back on me [, GOD,] / just when I need you so desperately. / Pay attention! This is a cry for *help*! / And hurry—this can't wait! / I'm wasting away to nothing, / I'm burning up with fever. / I'm a ghost of my former self, / half-consumed already by terminal illness. / My jaws ache from gritting my teeth; / I'm nothing but skin and bones. / I'm like a buzzard in the desert, / a crow perched on the rubble. / Insomniac, I twitter away, / mournful as a sparrow in the gutter. / All day long my enemies taunt me, / while others just curse. / They bring me meals—casseroles of ashes! / I draw drink from a barrel of my tears. / There's nothing left of me—/ a withered weed, swept clean from the path." (Ps 102:2–9, 11, TM)

Repeat Antiphon (above):

Reading: "After a long time had passed and the LORD had given Israel rest from all their enemies around them, Joshua, by then a very old man, summoned all Israel . . . and said to them: 'I am very old. You yourselves have seen everything the LORD your God has done to all these nations for your sake; it was the LORD you God who fought for you. Now I am about to go the way of all the earth. You know with all your heart and soul that not one of all the good promises the LORD your God gave you has failed. Every promise has been fulfilled; not one has failed.'" (Josh 23:1–3, 14, NIV)

Reflection: Israel is invincible when God takes its side. God fights holy wars to fulfill his promise of land to the people he chose. The holy war consists of defeating the people living in Canaan so that the Israelites can take possession of the land. The operative metaphor—even though the word is not used—is covenant, the solemn agreement between God, the superior party, and the Israelites, the inferior party. The LORD acts on Israel's behalf; he maintains the relationship he established with the Hebrews, then the Israelites, who are charged with keeping the lifestyle dictated by Torah (Law). In his last words, Joshua, Moses' successor, reminds his people that God has kept his part of the covenant (promise). Now it remains for Israel to keep her part of the deal.

Alternative Readings: 1 Sam 12:1–18; 12:19–25; Prov 8:19–39; 9:1–12; Ezekiel 4:16–17; 5:1–4.

Day 10

Morning

Antiphon: "Sing your songs to . . . GOD, / tell his stories to everyone you meet . . . ." (Ps 9:11, TM)

Canticle: "How blessed is God! And what a blessing he is! He's the Father of our Master, Jesus Christ, and takes us to the high places of blessing in him. Long before he laid down earth's foundations, he had us in mind, had settled on us as the focus of his love, to be made whole and holy by his love. Long, long ago he decided to adopt us into his family through Jesus Christ. Because of the sacrifice of the Messiah, his blood poured out on the altar of the Cross, we're a free people . . . . He thought of everything, provided for everything we could possibly need, letting us in on the plans he took such delight in making. He set it all out before us in Christ, a long-range plan in which everything would be brought together and summed up in him, everything in deepest heaven, everything on planet earth." (Eph 1:3–5, 7, 9–10, TM)

Repeat Antiphon (above):

Reading: ". . . Joshua assembled all the tribes of Israel at Shechem. Joshua said to all the people, 'This is what the LORD, the God of Israel, says:

"Long ago your ancestors, including Terah the father of Abraham and Nahor, lived beyond the Euphrates River and worshiped other gods. But I took your father Abraham from the land beyond the Euphrates and led him throughout Canaan and gave him many descendants. I gave him Isaac, and to Isaac I gave Jacob . . . [,] and [he] and his family went down to Egypt. Then I sent Moses and Aaron, and I afflicted the Egyptians by what I did there, and I brought you out. When I brought your people out of Egypt, you came to the sea, and the Egyptians pursued them with chariots and horsemen as far as the Red Sea. But they cried to the LORD for help, and he put darkness between you and the Egyptians; he brought the sea over them and covered them. You saw with your own eyes what I did to the Egyptians. Then you lived in the wilderness for a long time. Then you crossed the Jordan and came to Jericho. So I gave you a land on which you did not toil and cities you did not build; and you live in them and eat from vineyards and olive groves that you did not plant.'" (Josh 24:1a, 2–7, 11a, 13, NIV)

Points to Ponder: First, in his closing remarks Joshua reminds the Israelites of their history. Like Moses addressed all Israel before his death, so Joshua does the same. Second, the setting for Joshua's final address is Shechem, a city associated with the patriarchs Abram (Gen 12:6–7) and Jacob (Gen 33:18–20). Third, Joshua represents the people who escaped Egyptian slavery, but his audience did not experience that history; this is why he narrates their history to them. It is the author's attempt to explain how they got to where they were when the HB (OT) book of Joshua was written. Fourth, while it is not in the passage above, Joshua leads the people in a covenant renewal ceremony, which involves the casting away of idols, the promise to serve the LORD, and the setting of a stone under an oak tree as a witness (Josh 24:14–27). Fifth, Joshua can be understood as the founder of Israelite religion in Canaan; he leads the people in their exclusive commitment to the LORD; then, he records everything in a book, and under the oak near the holy place of the LORD at Shechem, he plants a witness stone (Josh 24:25–27)

Evening Prayer
Antiphon: "Blessed be GOD—/ he heard me praying." (Ps 28:6, TM)
Psalm: "Now, I'm jumping for joy, / and shouting and singing my thanks to [GOD]. / GOD is all strength for his chosen leader; / save your people / and bless your heritage. / Care for them; / carry them like a good shepherd." (Ps 28:7–9, TM)

Repeat Antiphon (above):
Reading: Joshua said to all the people: "'Now fear the LORD and serve him with all faithfulness. Throw away the gods your ancestors worshiped beyond the Euphrates River and in Egypt and serve the LORD. But if serving the LORD seems undesirable to you, then choose for yourselves this day whom you will serve . . . . But as for me and my household, we will serve the LORD.' Then the people answered, 'Far be it from us to forsake the LORD to serve other gods. We too will serve the LORD, because he is our God.'" (Josh 24:14–15ac, 16, 18b, NIV)
Meditation/Journal: Do you fear the LORD and serve him? Why? Explain.
Alternative Readings: 1 Sam 13:1–4; 13:8–15; Prov 9:13–18; 10:1–14; Ezekiel 12:1–7; 12:8–11.

Day 11

Morning
Antiphon: "I've thrown myself headlong into your arms [, GOD,] / I'm celebrating your rescue." (Ps 13:5, TM)
Psalm: "Long enough, GOD— / you've ignored me long enough. / I've looked at the back of your head / long enough. Long enough / I've carried this ton of trouble, / lived with a stomach full of pain. / Long enough my arrogant enemies / have looked down their noses at me. / Take a good look at me, GOD, my God; / I want to look life in the eye, / So no enemy can get the best of me / or laugh when I fall on my face." (Ps 13:1–4, TM)
Repeat Antiphon (above):
Reading: "Joshua said to the people [assembled at Shechem], 'You are not able to serve the LORD. He is a holy God; he is a jealous God.' But the people said to Joshua, 'No! We will serve the LORD.' 'Now then,' said Joshua, 'throw away the foreign gods that are among you and yield your hearts to the LORD, the God of Israel.' And the people said to Joshua, 'We will serve the LORD our God and obey him.'" (Josh 24:19ab, 21, 23–24, NIV)
Reflection: At the beginning of chapter 24 of the HB (OT) book of Joshua, Joshua had recounted God's beneficence to the Israelites. Now, Joshua solicits a response after narrating the people's response. While the LORD gave the land to the people's ancestors and brought the people into the land promised to Abraham and his descendants, it is the responsibility of the people to keep the land through undivided service to God. After the people indicate that they will serve the LORD, Joshua reminds them

they are not able to serve him unless he wills it and lets them. They will demonstrate that they want to serve him by throwing away the statues or other emblems of other gods that they have accumulated in Egypt and their forty years in the desert. Once all the idols are removed, the people demonstrate that desire to enter the LORD's service and cooperate in the work he began a long time ago. Up to this point (and in some ways even past it), the Israelites are henotheists; they believe in many gods with a greater emphasis placed on a particular god. Joshua urges them to be monotheists, to believe in only the LORD their God and serve him, whose image cannot be captured in stone, wood, or metal.

Evening
Antiphon: "I'm singing at the top of my lungs, / I'm so full of answered prayers." (Ps 13:6, TM)
Canticle: "Blessed are you, O Lord, God of our ancestors! You alone are praiseworthy and high above us, and your name will be blessed forever! Blessed are you in the Temple of your glory; you are praiseworthy and high above us forever. Blessed are you on the throne of your glory; you are praiseworthy and high above us forever. Blessed are you who take time to observe what is going on here below; you are praiseworthy and high above us forever. Blessed are you for always seeing the big picture; you are praiseworthy and high above us forever." (Dan 3:52–56 [Sg Three 1:29–34], TM)
Repeat Antiphon (above):
Reading: ". . . Joshua son of Nun, the servant of the LORD, died at the age of a hundred and ten. And Joseph's bones, which the Israelites had brought up from Egypt, were buried at Shechem . . . ." (Josh 24:29, 32a, NIV)
Points to Ponder: First, the title "servant of the LORD" which had been given by the author of the HB (OT) book of Joshua only to Moses (Josh 1:1, 7, 15) is, at the end of the book, allotted to Joshua. A servant of the LORD is a person who receives divine revelation, passes it on, and, if necessary, does something related to it. In other words, a servant of the LORD is a person who is faithful to God. Second. Joshua lived to be 110, while his predecessor, Moses, lived to be 120 (Deut 34:7). One hundred twenty is a multiple of forty multiplied by three; forty is a lifetime or a long time, and three is the number for God. Thus, Moses lived a long time in the divine presence. However, Joshua's 110 represents two multiples of 40 plus 30; while his life serving the LORD is less than Moses, he lives a long life in the divine presence. Third, during the exodus, the escape of

the Hebrews from the Egyptians, the Israelites carry the bones of Joseph with them (Exod 13:19). Nothing biblical is heard about Joseph's bones until the author of Joshua states that they were buried or entombed at Shechem. The bones of Joseph represent the movement of the Hebrews to Egypt and their exit from Egypt. Because Joseph saved his people from death by famine, he is treated as a holy man. Shechem is where his grandfather, Abraham, worshiped God (Gen 12:6), and where his father, Jacob, worshiped God (Gen 33:18), under an oak tree.
Alternative Readings: 1 Sam 15:1–9; 15:10–23; Prov 10:15–32; 11:1–15; Ezekiel 21:18–23; 24:1–8.

Day 12

Morning
Antiphon: "I love you, GOD— / you make me strong. / GOD is bedrock under my feet, / the castle in which I live, / my rescuing knight." (Ps 18:1–2a, TM)
Psalm: "My God—the high crag, / where I run for dear life, / hiding behind the boulders, / safe in the granite hideout. / I sing to GOD, the Praise-Lofty, / and find myself safe and saved. / . . . I call to GOD, / I cry to God to help me. / From his palace he hears my call; / my cry brings me right into his presence—/ a private audience! / . . . [M]e he caught— reached all the way / . . . he pulled me out . . . . / . . . GOD stuck by me. / He stood me up on a wide-open field; / I stood there saved—surprised to be loved! (Ps 18:2b–3, 6, 16, 18b–19, TM)
Repeat Antiphon (above):
Reading: "After [Joshua son of Nun's] whole generation had been gathered to their ancestors, another generation grew up who knew neither the LORD nor what he had done for Israel. Then the Israelites did evil in the eyes of the LORD . . . . They forsook the LORD, the God of their ancestors, who had brought them out of Egypt. They followed and worshiped various gods of the peoples around them. . . . [T]he LORD gave them into the hands of raiders who plundered them. Then the LORD raised up judges, who saved them out of the hands of these raiders. Whenever the LORD raised up a judge for them, he was with the judge and saved them out of the hands of their enemies as long as the judge lived . . . . But when the judge died, the people returned to ways even more corrupt than those of their ancestors, following other gods and serving and worshiping them." (Judg 2:10–14a, 16, 18–19, NIV)

SEASON OF ORDINARY TIME

Reflection: The author of the HB (OT) book of Judges presents his recurring thesis in chapter 2 of the book. The pattern he follows in arranging the material in the book consists of the following: (1) the Israelites sin; (2) the LORD allows his people to be oppressed by their neighbors; (3) the people repent; (4) God raises a judge, usually a military leader, to defeat enemies; (5) a period of peace ensues, usually noted in increments of twenty (one-half of a lifetime), forty (a lifetime), or eighty (two lifetimes or a very long time) years. Because Israel had not finished the acquisition of the land before Joshua's death, the people often adopted the ways of the Canaanites. From Israel's perspective, this was idolatry. However, the LORD's compassion always overcame his justice; he did not abandon his people. He sent them judges, a military leader who called the people to follow the lifestyle the LORD had established for them; the judge fills the leadership vacuum caused by Joshua's death. Some of the tales about judges originally circulated orally and locally. The author of the book of Judges, gathered them, wrote them, and placed them in one book following the pattern given above.

Evening Prayer
Antiphon: "GOD made my life complete / when I placed all the pieces before him." (Ps 18:20, TM)
Psalm: "When I got my act together, [GOD] gave me a fresh start. / Now I'm alert to GOD's ways; / I don't take God for granted. / Every day I review the ways he works; / I try not to miss a trick. / I feel put back together, / and I'm watching my step. / GOD rewrote the text of my life / when I opened the book of my heart to his eyes. / Suddenly, GOD, you floodlight my life; / I'm glazing with glory, God's glory! / What a God! His road / stretches straight and smooth. / Every GOD-direction is road-tested. / Everyone who runs toward him / Makes it." (Ps 18:21–24, 28, 30, TM)
Repeat Antiphon (above):
Reading: "The Israelites . . . forgot the LORD their God and . . . the LORD . . . sold them into the hands of . . . [the] king of Aram . . . , to whom the Israelites were subject for eight years. But when they cried out to the LORD, he raised up for them a deliverer, Othniel . . . , who saved them. The Spirit of the LORD came on him, so that he became Israel's judge and went to war. The LORD gave . . . [the] king of Aram into the hands of Othniel, who overpowered him. So the land had peace for forty years, until Othniel . . . died." (Judg 3:7–11, NIV)

Activity: Use the five-part pattern given in the Reflection for Morning Prayer above and apply it to Judges 3:7–11, Othniel, the first judge mentioned in the HB (OT) book of Judges. What do you discover?
Alternative Readings: 1 Sam 16:1–5; 16:6–13; Prov 11:16–31; 12:1–14; Ezek 24:9–13; 37:15–23.

Day 13

Morning
Antiphon: "God's glory is on tour in the skies, / God-craft on exhibit across the horizon. / Madame Day holds classes every morning." (Ps 19:1–2a, TM)
Psalm: "[Madame Day's] words aren't heard, / [her] voice [isn't] recorded. / But [her] silence fills the earth; / unspoken truth is spoken everywhere. / God makes a huge dome / for the sun—a superdome! / The morning sun's a new husband / leaping from his honeymoon bed, / The daybreaking sun an athlete / racing to the tape. / That's how God's Word vaults across the skies / from sunrise to sunset, / Melting ice, scorching deserts, / warming hearts to faith. / The revelation of GOD is whole / and pulls our lives together. The signposts of GOD are clear / and point out the right road. / The life-maps of GOD are right, / showing the way to joy. / The directions of GOD are plain / and easy on the eyes. / GOD's reputation is twenty-four-carat gold, / with a lifetime guarantee. / The decisions of GOD are accurate / down to the nth degree." (Ps 19:3–9, TM)
Repeat Antiphon (above):
Reading: "Again the Israelites did evil in the eyes of the LORD, and because they did this evil the LORD gave Eglon king of Moab power over Israel. The Israelites were subject to Eglon king of Moab for eighteen years. Again the Israelites cried out to the LORD, and he gave them a deliverer—Ehud, a left-handed man.... The Israelites sent him with tribute to Eglon king of Moab. Ehud ... approached him ... and said, 'I have a message from God for you.' As the king rose from his seat, Ehud reached with his left hand, drew the word from his right thigh, and plunged it into the king's belly. After he had gone, the servants came and found the doors of the upper room locked.... [T]hey took a key and unlocked them. There they saw their lord fallen to the floor, dead. 'Follow me,' [Ehud] ordered [the Israelites], 'for the LORD has given Moab, your enemy, into your hands.' So they followed him down and took possession of the fords of the Jordan that led to Moab. That day Moab was made subject to Israel,

and the land had peace for eighty years. After Ehud came Shamgar . . . , who struck down six hundred Philistines with an oxgoad. He too saved Israel." (Judg 3:12, 14-15, 20-21, 24, 25b, 28, 30-31, NIV)

Points to Ponder: First, Ehud is lefthanded; that means that he wears his sword on his right hip. From the ancient world to almost modern times, a lefthanded person was considered evil; the word for *left* in Latin is *sinister*, while the word for *right* is *dexter*. What the author of the HB (OT) book of Judges does is reverse that understanding. Lefthanded Ehud slays righthanded Eglon, king of Moab; the weak (evil) lefthand conquers the powerful righthand. Second, Ehud is not checked for a sword on his right hip, because everyone carried it on his left hip; thus Ehud enters Eglon's presence with a weapon. Third, Ehud tells Eglon that he brings him a message from God; the message is that the LORD is using Ehud to slay Eglon. Fourth, overweight Eglon's death implies the dissolution of his forces; relief has been brought to Israel's paying tribute. Fifth, Israel does not have to fight against Moab; in this holy war, all the Israelites do is station themselves at the fords of the Jordan River to eliminate the retreating Moabite forces. Nevertheless, Ehud is a deliverer raised up by the LORD to lead Israel to victory. Sixth, this tale about lefthanded Ehud contrasts the cleverness of the Israelites with the stupidity of the Moabites—they fail to check an enemy for a weapon! Seventh, Shamgar succeeds Ehud, but, because the author knows nothing about him, he is mentioned in only one verse!

Evening Prayer
Antiphon: "God's glory is on tour in the skies, / God-craft on exhibit across the horizon. / Professor Night lectures each evening." (Ps 19:1-2b, TM)
Psalm: "God's Word is better than a diamond, / better than a diamond set between emeralds. / You'll like it better than strawberries in spring, / better than red, ripe strawberries. / There's more: God's Word warns us of danger / and directs us to hidden treasure. / These are the words in my mouth; / these are what I chew on and pray. / Accept them when I place them / on the morning altar, / O God, my Altar-Rock, / God, Priest-of-My-Altar." (Ps 19:10-11, 14, TM)
Repeat Antiphon (above):
Reading: "Again the Israelites did evil in the eyes of the LORD, now that Ehud was dead. So the LORD sold them into the hands of [King] Jabin . . . . Sisera, the commander of his army, . . . had cruelly oppressed

the Israelites for twenty years; they cried to the LORD for help. Now Deborah, a prophet[ess], ... was leading Israel at that time. She sent for Barak ... and said to him, 'The LORD, the God of Israel, commands you: "Go, take with you ten thousand men ... and lead them up to Mount Tabor. I will lead Sisera, the commander of Jabin's army, with his chariots and his troops ... and give him into your hands." Barak said to her, 'If you go with me, I will go; but if you don't go with me, I won't go.' 'Certainly I will go with you,' said Deborah. 'But ... the honor will not be yours, but the LORD will deliver Sisera into the hands of a woman.' Then Deborah said to Barak, 'Go! This is the day the LORD has given Sisera into your hands.' Barak pursued the ... army ... , and all Sisera's troops fell by the sword; not a man was left. Sisera, meanwhile, fled on foot to the tent of Jael.... Jael ... picked up a tent peg and a hammer and went quietly to Sisera while he lay fast asleep, exhausted. She drove the peg through his temple into the ground, and he died. On that day God subdue Jabin ... before the Israelites. Then the land had peace forty years." (Judg 4:1-4, 6-9, 14a 16-17a, 21, 23; 5:31b, NIV)

Points to Ponder: First, the tale about a woman judge named Deborah begins with the pattern found throughout the book of Judges: (1) the Israelites sin; (2) the LORD allows the Israelites to be oppressed; (3) the Israelites repent and cry to the LORD for help; and (4) God raises a judge in answer to their prayers. Second, because the judge is a woman—Deborah—she enlists the help of Barak, an army commanded, who easily defeats King Jabin's forces led by Sisera, his army commander. Third, after Sisera's forces are defeated by Barak, another woman enters the picture. Sisera flees the battle scene to Jael's tent. After he falls asleep—because he is exhausted by the battle he just fought—she drives a tent peg through his temple to kill him. Fourth, then the usual pattern concludes with peace for forty years. Fifth, God uses two powerless women—Deborah and Jael—to defeat two powerful men—Jabin and Sisera! The LORD's victory is achieved through two women's actions.

Alternative Readings: 1 Sam 17:1-11; 17:12-27; Prov 12:15-28; 13:1-13; Hos 1:1-5; 1:6-9.

Day 14

Morning

Antiphon: "GOD answer you on the day your crash, / ... Give you what your heart desires, / Accomplish your plans." (Ps 20:1a, 4, TM)

Psalm: "When you win, we plan to raise the roof / and lead the parade with our banners. / May all your wishes come true! / That clinches it—help's coming, / an answer's on the way, / everything's going to work out. / See those people polishing their chariots, / and those others grooming their horses? / But we're making garlands for GOD our God. / The chariots will rust, / those horses pull up lame—/ and we'll be on our feet, standing tall." (Ps 20:5-8, TM)
Repeat Antiphon (above):
Reading: "The Israelites did evil in the eyes of the LORD, and for seven years he gave them into the hands of the Midianites. Whenever the Israelites planted their crops, the Midianites . . . and other eastern peoples invaded the country. They camped on the land and ruined the crops . . . and did not spare a living thing for Israel, neither sheep nor cattle nor donkeys. Midian so impoverished the Israelites that they cried out to the LORD for help. . . . [H]e sent them a prophet, who said, 'This is what the LORD, the God of Israel, says: I said to you, "I am the LORD your God; do not worship the gods of [others], in whose land you live." But you have not listened to me.'" (Judg 6:1, 3-4 6, 8, 10, NIV)
Meditation/Journal: What connection(s) do you find between the verses of Psalm 20 above and the verses from chapter 6 of the book of Joshua above?

Evening Prayer
Antiphon: "My God, don't turn a deaf ear to my hallelujah prayer." (Ps 109:1, TM)
Psalm: "Oh, GOD, my Lord, step in; / work a miracle for me—you can do it! / Get me out of here—your love is so great!—/ I'm at the end of my rope, my life in ruins, / I'm fading away to nothing, passing away, / my youth gone, old before my time. / Help me, oh help me, GOD, my God, / save me through your wonderful love . . . . / My mouth's full of great praise for GOD, / I'm singing his hallelujahs surrounded by crowds, / For he's always at hand to take the side of the needy, / to rescue a life from the unjust judge." (Ps 109:21-23, 26, 30-31, TM)
Repeat Antiphon (above):
Reading: "The angel of the LORD came and sat down under the oak in Ophrah . . . where . . . Gideon was threshing wheat in a winepress to keep it from the Midianites. When the angel of the LORD appeared to Gideon, he said, 'The Lord is with you, mighty warrior.' 'Pardon me, my lord,' Gideon replied, 'but if the LORD is with us, why has all this happened

to us?' The LORD turned to him and said, 'Go in the strength you have and save Israel out of Midian's hand. Am I not sending you? I will be with you, and you will strike down all the Midianites, leaving none alive.' Gideon replied, 'If now I have found favor in your eyes, give me a sign that it is really you talking to me. Please do not go away until I come back and bring my offering and set it before you.' And the LORD said, 'I will wait until you return.'" (Judg 6:11–13a, 14, 16–18, NIV)

Reflection: After the typical introduction to a new judge found in the HB (OT) book of Judges (6:1–10, the Reading for Morning Prayer), the author introduces the reader to Gideon. Chapters six through eight are an extended tale—one that circulated independently orally or in written form before it was incorporated into the book of Judges—about the judge Gideon, who needs a sign to convince him that it is the LORD who is calling him to lead Israel. Like the narrative about Moses and the burning bush (Exod 3:2–4), the angel (a biblical code for God) of the LORD quickly becomes the LORD talking with Gideon. Likewise, the LORD appeared to Abraham under trees as three visitors (Gen 18:1–15), and so the angel of the LORD appears as a visitor and sits under an oak before speaking with Gideon. The angel of the LORD is a visible manifestation of the LORD's presence. God finds Gideon beating wheat in the confined space of a winepress; wheat was usually beaten or threshed on a windy hilltop or breezy threshing floor. Gideon's reluctance to appear preparing food in public stresses the Midianite scourge.

Alternative Readings: 1 Sam 17:28–37; 17:38–47; Prov 13:14–25; 14:1–18; Hos 2:2–6; 2:7–15.

Day 15

Morning

Antiphon: "Show your strength, GOD, so no one can miss it. / I'm out singing the good news!" (Ps 21:13, TM)

Psalm: "God, God . . . my God! / Doubled up with pain, I call to God / all the day long. No answer. Nothing. / I keep at it all night, tossing and turning. / [I] know you were there for [my] parents; / they cried for your help and you gave it; / they trusted and lived a good life. / Everyone pokes fun at me; / they make faces at me, they shake their heads . . . . / . . . [Y]ou were midwife at my birth, / setting me at my mother's breasts! / When I left the womb, you cradled me; / since the moment of birth you've been my God. / You, GOD—don't put off my rescue! / Hurry and help me! / If you don't show up soon, / I'm done for . . . . / Here's the story I'll tell my friends when they come to worship, / and punctuate it with Hallelujahs: / Shout Hallelujah, you God-worshipers . . . . / He has never let you down, / never looked the other way / when you were being kicked around." (Ps 22:1a, 2, 4–5, 7, 9–10, 19, 21–23a, 24a, TM)

Repeat Antiphon (above):

Reading: "Gideon went inside, prepared a young goat, and from an ephah of flour he made bread without yeast. Putting the meat in a basket and its broth in a pot, he brought them out and offered them to [the LORD] under the oak. The angel of God said to him, 'Take the meat and the unleavened bread, place them on this rock, and pour out the broth.' And Gideon did so. Then the angel of the LORD touched the meat and the unleavened bread with the tip of the staff that was in his hand. Fire flared from the rock, consuming the meat and the bread. And the angel of the LORD disappeared. When Gideon realized that it was the angel of the LORD, he exclaimed, 'Alas, Sovereign LORD! I have seen the angel of the LORD face to face!' But the Lord said to him, 'Peace! Do not be afraid. You are not going to die.' So Gideon built an altar to the LORD there and called it The LORD is Peace." (Judg 6:19–24a, NIV)

Points to Ponder: First, Gideon is not yet a public person. He had been threshing wheat in a winepress when the angel of the LORD appeared to him. After getting the angel to wait for him to prepare an offering, he went inside his house to do so. Second, the preparation of the offering of a boiled young goat and baked unleavened bread would have taken a long time. Third, the elements of the offering are very significant. When preparing to celebrate the first Passover, the LORD tells Moses that the lamb can be taken from either the sheep or the goats (Exod 12:5). Also, unleavened bread (Exod 12:34; 13:6–8) is to be eaten; the bread must be unleavened because ancient people thought that some evil force caused it to rise. Fourth, it there was any doubt that the angel of God was the LORD, the touching of the meat and bread with the tip of the angel's staff so that fire flared and everything was consumed should confirm the divine presence, which quickly disappears, even though Gideon and the LORD continue their conversation. Fifth, there was an ancient understanding that no one could see the face of God and live; however, those called by God—like Moses and Gideon—see the face of God and live.

Evening Prayer

Antiphon: "Thank GOD because he's good, / because his love never quits." (Ps 118:1, TM)

Psalm: "Tell the world . . . , / '[GOD's] love never quits.' / And you who fear GOD, join in, / 'His love never quits.' / Pushed to the wall, I called to GOD; / from the wide-open spaces, he answered. / GOD's now at my side and I'm not afraid; / who would dare lay a hand on me? / GOD's my strong champion; / I flick off my enemies like flies. / Far better to take refuge in GOD / than trust in people; / Far better to take refuge in GOD / than trust in celebrities. / GOD's my strength, he's also my song, / and now he's my salvation. / Hear the shouts, hear the triumph songs / in the camp of the saved? / 'The hand of God has turned the tide! / The hand of God is raised in victory! / The hand of God has turned the tide!'" (Ps 118:2, 4–9, 14–16, TM)

Repeat Antiphon (above):

Reading: ". . . [T]he Spirit of the LORD came on Gideon . . . . Gideon said to God, 'If you will save Israel by my hand as you have promised—look, I will place a wool fleece on the threshing floor; if there is a dew only on the fleece and all the ground is dry, then I will know that you will save Israel by my hand, as you said. And that is what happened. Gideon rose early the next day; he squeezed the fleece and wrung out the dew—a bowlful of water. Then Gideon said to God, 'Do not be angry with me. Let me make just one more request. Allow me one more test with the fleece, but his time make the fleece dry and let the ground be covered with dew.' That night God did so. Only the fleece was dry; all the ground was covered with dew." (Judg 6:34a, 36–40, NIV)

Reflection: Gideon needs a sign that the venture he is taking is what the LORD wants. The tests with the fleece determine God's will. This process is known as divining; today it is better known as discerning. The supreme irony of Gideon's divining is that the HB (OT) book of Deuteronomy forbids such a practice (Deut 18:14). Thus, while Gideon wants to ensure the success of his leadership, he determines it through a technique forbidden by the LORD himself. In other words, the victory over Midian that Gideon will enact is the LORD's doing; that is why the LORD breaks his own rule! The double test using the fleece informs Gideon that what he is about to do is God's will, and he will succeed.

Alternative Readings: 1 Sam 17:48–58; 18:1–30; Prov 14:19–35; 15:1–17; Hos 3:1–5; 6:1–6.

Day 16

Morning

Antiphon: "From the four corners of the earth / people are coming to their senses, / are running back to GOD. / Long-lost families / are falling on their faces before him." (Ps 22:27, TM)

Psalm: "GOD, my shepherd! / I don't need a thing. / You have bedded me down in lush meadows, / you find me quiet pools to drink from. / True to your word, / you let me catch my breath / and send me in the right direction. / I'm not afraid / when you walk at my side. / You revive my drooping head; / my cup brims with blessing. / Your beauty and love chase after me / every day of my life. / I'm back home in the house of GOD / for the rest of my life."(Ps 23:1–3, 4b, 5b–6, TM)

Repeat Antiphon (above):

Reading: "Early in the morning . . . (Gideon) and all his men camped at [a] spring . . . . The camp of Midian was north of them . . . . The LORD said to Gideon, 'You have too many men. I cannot deliver Midian into their hands, or Israel would boast against me . . . . Now announce to the army, "Anyone who trembles with fear may turn back . . . ."' So twenty-two thousand men left, while ten thousand remained. But the LORD said to Gideon, 'There are still too many men. Take them down to the water, and I will thin them out for you there.' So Gideon took the men down to the water. There the LORD told him, 'Separate those who lap the water with their tongues as a dog laps from those who kneel down to drink.' Three hundred of them drank from cupped hands, lapping like dogs. All the rest got down on their knees to drink. The LORD said to Gideon, 'With the three hundred men that lapped I will save you and give the Midianites into your hands. Let the others go home.'" (Judg 7:1–4ab, 5–7, NIV)

Reflection: While Gideon leads the Israelite army, the LORD is the opponent of Midian. The LORD reduces the size of Gideon's army two times to be sure that the victory over Midian is credited to him and not to Gideon and the army. That is a basic feature of the holy war ideology; God is depicted as a super divine warrior, to whom belongs the victory. Gideon begins with a total of thirty-two thousand troops; twenty-two thousand were afraid of fighting and were dismissed to go home. That left ten thousand soldiers. However from the LORD's perspective, that is still too many. So, employing a test of how the ten thousand drank water from a stream, the troops are reduced to three hundred men. Three is a sacred number referring to the spiritual order; it gives divine order to chaos. In biblical literature, three indicates the divine presence. One hundred is a multiple of ten signifying totality. Thus, Gideon's three-hundred soldiers represent the divine warrior, the LORD, who will, under Gideon's leadership, defeat the chaos-causing Midianites.

Evening Prayer
Antiphon: "Thank GOD—he's so good. / His love never quits!" (Ps 118:29, TM)
Psalm: "I didn't die. I *lived*! / And now I'm telling the world what GOD did. / GOD tested me, he pushed me hard, / but he didn't hand me over to Death. / Swing wide the city gates—the *righteous* gates! / I'll walk right through and thank GOD! / Thank you for responding to me; / you've truly become my salvation! / This is GOD's work. / We rub our eyes—we can hardly believe it! / This is the very day GOD acted—/ let's celebrate and be festive! / Salvation now, GOD. Salvation now! / Oh yes, GOD—a free and full life!" (Ps 118:17–19, 21, 23–25, TM)
Repeat Antiphon (above):
Reading: "Now the camp of Midian lay below [Gideon] in the valley. During that night the LORD said to Gideon, 'Get up, go down against the camp, because I am going to give it into your hands.' Gideon arrived just as a man was telling a friend his dream. 'I had a dream,' he was saying. 'A round loaf of barley bread came tumbling into the Midianite camp. It struck the tent with such force that the tent overturned and collapsed.' His friend responded. 'This can be nothing other than the sword of Gideon . . . . God has given the Midianites and the whole camp into his hands.'" (Judg 7:8b–9, 13–14, NIV)
Points to Ponder: First, as he does frequently in biblical literature, the LORD speaks to Gideon during the night; the activities that take place in darkness reveal the light that is to come. Second, Gideon overhears one Midianite telling another about his dream. In the biblical world, a dream is considered a vehicle for divine-human communication; the best example of that is found in the narrative about Joseph, son of Jacob (Gen 37:5–11; 40:6—41:39), and in the CB (NT) another Joseph, son of Jacob (Matt 1:18—2:12). God works through his people's enemy! Second, the barley loaf in the dream represents the agrarian society that is Israel. When the barley loaf crushes the tent, it reveals that the Midianites are going to be beaten. Gideon has been assured of the LORD's victory.
Alternative Readings: 1 Sam 19:1–7; 19:8–24; Prov 15:18–33; 16:1–18; Hos 10:1–8; 11:1–7.

Day 17

Morning
Antiphon: "GOD has taken charge; / from now on he has the last word." (Ps 22:28, TM)
Canticle: "I'm bursting with GOD-news! / I'm walking on air. / Nothing and no one is holy like GOD, / no rock mountain like our God. / GOD brings death and GOD brings life, / brings down to the grave and raises up. / GOD brings poverty and GOD brings wealth; / he lowers, he also lifts up. / He puts poor people on their feet again; / he rekindles burned-out lives with fresh hope, / Restoring dignity and respect to their lives—/ a place in the sun. / For the very structures of earth are GOD's; / he has laid out his operations on a firm foundation." (1 Sam 2:1b, 2, 6–8, TM)
Repeat Antiphon (above):
Reading: ". . . Gideon . . . returned to the camp of Israel and called out, 'Get up! The LORD has given the Midianite camp into your hands. Watch me,' he told them. 'Follow my lead. When I get to the edge of the camp, do exactly as I do. When I and all who are with me blow our trumpets, then from all around the camp blow yours and shout, "For the LORD and for Gideon."'" (Judg 7:15, 17–18, NIV)
Meditation/Journal: How do the verses from the canticle from First Samuel illustrate the passage from Judges 7:15, 17–18? What message does that insight deliver to you? How can you apply it to your life? Explain.

Evening Prayer
Antiphon: "Thank GOD! He deserves your thanks. / *His love never quits.*" (Ps 136:1, TM)
Psalm: "Thank the miracle-working God, / *His love never quits.* / The God whose skill formed the cosmos, / *His love never quits.* / The God who laid out earth on ocean foundations, / *His love never quits.* / The God who filled the skies with light, / *His love never quits.* / The sun to watch over the day, / *His love never quits.* / Moon and stars as guardians of the night, / *His love never quits.*" (Ps 136:4–9, TM)
Repeat Antiphon (above):
Reading: "[Gideon] placed trumpets and empty jars in the hands of all [his troops], with torches inside. Gideon and the . . . men with him reached the edge of the camp at the beginning of the middle watch, just after they had changed the guard. They blew their trumpets and broke the jars that were in their hands. . . . Grasping the torches in their left

hands and holding in their right hands the trumpets they were to blow, they shouted, 'A sword for the LORD and for Gideon.' While each man held his position around the camp, all the Midianites ran, crying out as they fled. . . . [T]he LORD caused the men throughout the camp to turn on each other with their swords." (Judg 7:16, 19, 20b–22a, NIV)

Reflection: Because this is the LORD's battle against the Midianites, Gideon's army has little to do. After surrounding the Midianite camp during the night, Gideon's army carry the light of torches in ceramic jars both to hide the light from their enemies and to remind them that the LORD is the light winning this battle. While the activity takes place in the dark, the light in the clay vessels tells the reader who will win. The sleeping enemy is startled awake by the trumpet blasts—reminiscent of the Jericho story—and panics in the dark, while the Israelite army burns their camp with God's light! The LORD gets full credit for the victory over Midian!

Alternative Readings: 1 Sam 20:1–17; 28:3–25; Prov 16:19–33; 17:1–14; Joel 1:1–7; 3:1–8.

Day 18

Morning

Antiphon: "GOD claims Earth and everything in it, / GOD claims World and all who live on it." (Ps 24:1, TM)

Psalm: "[GOD] built [Earth] on Ocean foundations, / laid it out on River girders. / Who can climb Mount GOD? / Who can scale the holy north-face? / Only the clean-handed, / only the pure-hearted . . . . / GOD is at their side; / with GOD's help they make it. / Wake up, you sleepyhead city! / Wake up, your sleepyhead people! / King-Glory is ready to enter. / Who is this King-Glory? / God-of-the-Angel-Armies: he is King-Glory." (Ps 24:2–4a, 5, 7, 10, TM)

Repeat Antiphon (above):

Reading: "The Israelites said to Gideon, 'Rule over us—you, your son, and your grandson—because you have saved us from the hand of Midian.' But Gideon told them, 'I will not rule over you, nor will my son rule over you. The LORD will rule over you.'" (Judg 8:22–23, NIV)

Meditation/Journal: What light do the verses of Psalm 24 shed on Judges 8:22–23? Explain.

SEASON OF ORDINARY TIME

Evening Prayer
Antiphon: "Thank the God of all gods, *His love never quits.*" (Ps 136:2, TM)
Psalm: "Come, bless GOD, / all you servants of GOD! / You . . . posted to the nightwatch in GOD's shrine, / Lift your praising hands to the Holy Place, and bless GOD. / In turn, may GOD . . . bless you—/ GOD who made heaven and earth!" (Ps 134:1–3, TM)
Repeat Antiphon (above):
Reading: "[Gideon] went back home to live. He had seventy sons of his own, for he had many wives. His concubine, who lived in Shechem, also bore him a son, whom he named Abimelek. Gideon . . . died at a good old age and was buried in the tomb of his father . . . . No sooner had Gideon died than the Israelites again prostituted themselves to the Baals . . . and did not remember the LORD their God, who had rescued them from the hands of all their enemies on every side." (Judg 8:29–34, NIV)
Intercessions: For all your servants, I pray to you, LORD. For all who lead others in any way, I pray to you, LORD. For all people who lift praising hands to you, I pray to you, LORD. For all who live to a good old age, I pray to you, LORD. For all parents, who raise sons and daughters for you, I pray to you, LORD. For all who forget you, I pray to you, LORD.
Alternative Readings: 1 Sam 31:1–13; 2 Sam 1:1–10; Prov 17:15–28; 18:1–12; Amos 9:1–4; 9:5–10.

Day 19

Morning
Antiphon: "Wake up, you sleepyhead city! / Wake up, you sleepyhead people! / King-Glory is ready to enter." (Ps 24:7, TM)
Psalm: "GOD, investigate my life; / get all the facts firsthand. / I'm an open book to you; / even from a distance, you know what I'm thinking. . . / You know when I leave and when I get back; / I'm never out of your sight. / You know everything I'm going to say / before I start the first sentence. / I look behind me and you're there, / then up ahead and you're there, too—/ your reassuring presence, coming and going. / This is too much, too wonderful—/ I can't take it all in!" (Ps 139:1–6, TM)
Repeat Antiphon (above):
Reading: "Abimelek son of [Gideon] went to his mother's brothers in Shechem and said to them and to all his mother's clan, 'Ask all the citizens of Shechem, which is better for you; to have all seventy of [Gideon's] sons rule over you, or just one man?' When the brothers repeated all this

to the citizens of Shechem, they were inclined to follow Abimelek, for they said, 'He is related to us.' He went to his father's home . . . and on one stone murdered his seventy brothers . . . . But Jotham, the youngest son . . . escaped by hiding. Then all the citizens of Shechem . . . gathered beside the great tree at the pillar in Shechem to crown Abimelek king." (Judg 9:1–2a, 3, 5–6, NIV)

Reflection: Abimelek (also spelled Abimelech) is Gideon's son by the concubine. Not only did Gideon have many wives, but he had a least one concubine. His multiple wives gave him seventy sons. Because the biological understanding was that the man carried the seed and implanted it in a woman's womb, the woman had no biological contribution to make. Thus, Gideon died having seventy-one sons. The son of his concubine, Abimelek, plotted to play on some dissatisfaction at the possibility of one of his brothers becoming the ruler of Shechem. The seventy sons held some prominence because of their father, Gideon. Abimelek goes to his uncles, his mother's brothers, and gets them to convince Shechem's popular assembly to lead their resistance against Gideon's dominant clan. Abimelek's first action is to be sure that all seventy of Gideon's sons are killed, so that he will have no one with whom he must contend. However, the youngest of the seventy sons, Jotham, escapes the blood bath. Abimelek is named king of Shechem, but he is never biblically named king of Israel. Abimelek's actions demonstrate how the monarchic system works; the potential king must convince the citizenry that he is the best man for the job, and he must eliminate any rivals to his throne, like seventy brothers! The reader must keep in mind that one of Abimelek's brothers, Jotham, escapes the blood bath with his life intact.

Evening Prayer
Antiphon: "Thank the Lord of all lords. / *His love never quits.*" (Ps 136:3, TM)
Psalm: "[GOD,] Is there anyplace I can go to avoid your Spirit? / to be out of your sight? / If I climb to the sky, you're there! / If I go underground, you're there! / If I flew on morning's wings / to the far western horizon, / You'd find me in a minute—/ you're already there waiting! / Then I said to myself, 'Oh, he even sees me in the dark! / At night I'm immersed in the light!' / It's a fact: darkness isn't dark to you; / night and day, darkness and light, they're all the same to you." (Ps 139:7–12, TM)
Repeat Antiphon (above):

Reading: "When Jotham was told about [Abimelek becoming king of Shechem], he . . . shouted to [the citizens of Shechem], 'Listen to me, citizens of Shechem, so that God may listen to you. One day the trees went out to anoint a king for themselves. They said to the olive tree, "Be our king." But the olive tree answered, "Should I give up my oil, by which both gods and humans are honored, to hold sway over the tress?" Next the trees said to the fig tree, "Come and be our king." But the fig tree replied, "Should I give up my fruit, so good and sweet, to hold sway over the trees?" Then the trees said to the vine, "Come and be our king" But the vine answered, "Should I give up my wine, which cheers both gods and humans, to hold sway over the trees?" Finally all the trees said to the thornbush, "Come and be our king." The thornbush said to the trees, "If you really want to anoint me king over you, come and take refuge in my shade . . . ."'" (Judg 9:7–15, NIV)

Reflection: Only Jotham, one of Gideon's seventy sons, escaped his half-brother Abimelech's massacre of the other sixty-nine sons of Gideon. From a mountaintop, Jotham pronounces a fable or parable. In the fable, the trees are the citizens of Shechem. At first, they ask the most precious of trees—olive, fig, vine—to reign over them. In other words, they want a king from Gideon's line, like the other nations around them have kingly leaders. However, all the best trees decline, because all Gideon's sons are dead. The only son of Gideon to accept their offer is Abimelek, who is compared to a thornbush or bramble, which invites all to take refuge in its shade, when, in fact, it is completely useless as a shade tree! All fruitful trees decline the invitation. The fable or parable is a commentary by the author of Judges on what he thinks about monarchy. The question about monarchy is raised again in the First Book of Samuel.

Alternative Readings: 2 Sam 5:1–5; 5:6–10; Prov 18:13–24; 19:1–15; Mic 4:1–5; 5:2–5.

Day 20

Morning

Antiphon: "My head is high, GOD, held high; / I'm looking to you, GOD; / No hangdog skulking for me." (Ps 25:1–2, TM)

Psalm: "I've thrown in my lot with you [, GOD,]; / Forget that I sowed wild oats; / Mark me with your sign of love. / Plan only the best for me, GOD! / GOD is fair and just; / He corrects the misdirected, / Sends them in the right direction. / He gives the rejects his hand, / And leads them step-by-step. / From now on every road you travel / Will take you to GOD. / Follow the Covenant signs; / Read the charted directions." (Ps 25:2a, 7–10, TM)

Repeat Antiphon (above):

Reading: Jotham said to the citizens of Shechem: "'Have you acted honorably and in good faith by making Abimelek king? Have you been fair to [Gideon] and his family? Have you treated him as he deserves? Remember that my father fought for you and risked his life to rescue you from the hand of Midian. But today you have revolted against my father's family. You have murdered his [sixty-nine] sons on a single stone and have made Abimelek, the son of his female slave, king over the citizens of Shechem . . . . So have you acted honorably and in good faith toward [Gideon] and his family today? If you have, may Abimelek be your joy and may you be his, too. But if you have not, let fire come out from Abimelek and consume you, the citizens of Shechem . . . , and let fire come out from you, the citizens of Shechem, and consume Abimelek!' Then Jotham fled . . . because he was afraid of his brother Abimelek." (Judg 9:16–21, NIV)

Reflection: After telling the citizens of Shechem the fable or parable of the trees, Jotham, the one son of Gideon who was not killed by Abimelek, asks the citizens a series of questions about honor, faith, and fairness concerning his father, the judge Gideon. At the end of this questioning, he offers the Shechem citizens a choice, depending on the answers they give to his questions. If they have acted honorably, faithfully, and fairly, then he wishes them joy in their king. But if they have not acted honorably, faithfully, and fairly, then he wishes that fire will come from Abimelek to consume them and that fire will come from them to consume Abimelek. The material about fire is related to the thornbush or bramble in the fable or parable. Because thornbushes or brambles grew close to the ground, they easily caught on fire and burned the land. After he finishes his speech, Jotham flees the city; otherwise, Abimelek would find him and kill him.

Evening Prayer

Antiphon: "Thank you [, GOD]! Everything in me says, 'Thank You!' / Angels listen as I sing my thanks." (Ps 138:1, TM)

Psalm: "When they hear what you have to say, GOD, all earth's [leaders] will say, 'Thank You.' / They'll sing of what you've done: 'How great the glory of GOD!' / And here's why: GOD, high above, sees far below; / no matter the distance, he knows everything about us. / When I walk into the thick of trouble, / keep me alive in the angry turmoil. / . . . [S]ave me. / Finish what you started in me, GOD, / Your love is eternal—don't quit on me now." (Ps 138:4-6, 8, TM)

Repeat Antiphon (above):

Reading: "After Abimelek had governed Israel three years, God stirred up animosity between Abimelek and the citizens of Shechem so that they acted treacherously against Abimelek. God did this in order that the crime against [Gideon's sixty-nine] sons, the shedding of their blood, might be avenged on their brother Abimelek and on the citizens of Shechem, who had helped him murder his brothers. . . . Gaal [, son of Ebed, a clan that moved into Shechem,] led out the citizens of Shechem and fought Abimelek. Abimelek chased him all the way to the entrance of the gate, and many were killed as they fled. Then Abimelek . . . drove Gaal and his clan out of Shechem. The next day the people of Shechem went out to the fields, and this was reported to Abimelek. So he took his men . . . and set an ambush in the fields. Abimelek . . . rushed forward to a position at the entrance of the city gate . . . and struck them down. All that day Abimelek pressed his attack against the city until he had captured it and killed its people. Then he destroyed the city and scattered salt over it. . . . [When Abimelek heard that] the citizens in the tower of Shechem . . . had assembled there . . . , [h]e took an ax and cut off some branches, which he lifted to his shoulders. He ordered the men with him, 'Quick! Do what you have seen me do.' So all the men cut branches and followed Abimelek. They piled them against the stronghold and set it on fire with the people still inside. So all the people in the tower of Shechem . . . died. (Judg 9:22-24, 39-45, 47-49, NIV)

Points to Ponder: First, the author of the narrative begins it by indicating that God oversees what takes place in his world. The author attributes the stirring of animosity between Abimelek and the citizens of Shechem to God. Second, the reason God stirred animosity between King Abimelek and the citizens of Shechem is to avenge the death of Gideon's sixty-nine sons. Many people do not like a God who avenges, but the author of the HB (OT) book of Judges does! According to the author, God is going to get Abimelek and Shechem's citizens, holding them accountable for their crime. Third, the new clan of Ebed, with a son named Gaal, move into Shechem and stir the citizens to rise against Abimelek. However, Abimelek has more power and defeats Gaal and drives his clan out of the city. But Abimelek is not finished yet. As the citizens of Shechem go about their daily tasks, like going to work in the fields, Abimelek attacks them and kills them. The few who take refuge in the tower are burned alive. Fourth, the reader must remember that Jotham had predicted that fire would come from the thornbush or bramble; and it does, as Abimelek cuts branches and carries them to the tower and instructs his men to do the same and sets everything on fire. Fifth, the very people who had chosen Abimelek to be their king are killed by the king they chose at God's hand!

Alternative Readings: 2 Sam 6:1–11; 6:12–23; Prov 19:16–28; 29:1–15; Nah 2:10–13; 3:8–19.

Day 21

Morning

Antiphon: "Show me how you work, GOD; / School me in your ways." (Ps 25:4, TM)

Psalm: "Keep up your reputation, GOD; / Forgive my bad life; God-friendship is for God-worshipers; / They are the ones he confides in. / If I keep my eyes on GOD, / I won't trip over my own feet. / Look at me and help me! / I'm all alone and in big trouble. / Keep watch over me and keep me out of trouble; / Don't let me down when I run to you. / Use all your skill to put me together; / I wait to see your finished product." (Ps 25:11, 14–16, 20–21, TM)

Repeat Antiphon (above):

Reading: ". . . Abimelek went to Thebez [, a village dependent on Shechem,] and besieged it and captured it. Inside the city, however, was a strong tower, to which all the men and women—all the people of the city—had fled. They had locked themselves in and climbed up on the tower roof. Abimelek went to the tower and attacked it. But as he approached the entrance to the tower to set it on fire, a woman dropped an upper millstone on his head and cracked his skull. Hurriedly he called to his armor-bearer, 'Draw your sword and kill me, so that they can't say, "A woman killed him."' So his servant ran him through, and he died. Thus God repaid the wickedness that Abimelek had done to his father by murdering his [sixty-nine] brothers. God also made the people of Shechem pay for all their wickedness. The curse of Jotham son of [Gideon] came on them." (Judg 9:50–54, 56–57, NIV)

Points to Ponder: First, once Abimelek begins a course of destruction, he immerses himself in it totally. Evil begets evil; evil grows more evil.

His first dramatic act was the slaughter of his sixty-nine brothers; his last act was to direct his armor-bearer to kill him. Second, Abimelek's demise is begun by a woman, who drops a large stone from a tower onto his head. The author of the HB (OT) book of Judges has both a sense of humor and a sense of irony! Third, the author of the book is very clear that God repays Abimelek's wickedness with death and, likewise, the citizens of Shechem with death, too. Fourth, the cause of all deaths, according to the author, is the curse uttered by Jotham (Judg 9:19–20). A biblical curse is a solemn utterance which cannot be retracted or annulled. Jotham's spoken word is endowed with an ability to be fulfilled. In other words, a biblical curse is not the same as understood today, being the use of expletives or four-letter words!

Evening Prayer
Antiphon: "I kneel in worship facing your holy temple, [GOD,] / and say it again: 'Thank you!' / Thank you for your love, / thank you for your faithfulness; / Most holy is your name, / most holy is your Word." (Ps 138:2, TM)
Psalm: "Oh yes, you shaped me first inside, then out [, GOD]; / you formed me in my mother's womb. / I thank you, High God—you're breathtaking! / Body and [spirit], I am marvelously made! / I worship in adoration—what a creation! / You know me inside and out, / you know every bone in my body; / You know exactly how I was made, bit by bit, / how I was sculpted from nothing into something. / Like an open book, you watched me grow from conception to birth; / all the stages of my life were spread out before you, / The days of my life all prepared / before I'd even lived one day." (Ps 139: 13–16, TM)
Repeat Antiphon (above):
Reading: "After the time of Abimelek, . . . Tola . . . rose to save Israel. He led Israel twenty-three years; then he died . . . He was followed by Jair . . . , who lead Israel twenty-two years. . . . Jair died . . . . Again the Israelites did evil in the eyes of the LORD. And because the Israelites forsook the LORD and no longer served him, he became angry with them. He sold them into the hands of the Philistines . . . . For eighteen years they oppressed all the Israelites . . . . Then the Israelites cried out to the LORD, 'We have sinned against you, forsaking our God . . . . Do with us whatever you think best, but please rescue us now.'" (Judg 10:1–3, 5–8, 10, 15, NIV)
Meditation/Journal: What connection do you find between the verses of Psalm 139 and the passage from the book of Judges 10:1–3, 5–8, 10, 15? Explain.

Alternative Readings: 2 Sam 7:1–3; 7:4–17; Prov 20:16–30; 21:1–16; Hab 2:1–5; 2:6–20.

Day 22

Morning
Antiphon: [GOD,] "[t]ake me by the hand; / Lead me down the path of truth. /You are my Savior, aren't you? (Ps 25:5, TM)
Psalm: "Clear my name, GOD; / I've kept an honest shop. / I've thrown in my lot with you, GOD, and / I'm not budging. / Examine me, GOD, from head to foot, / order your battery of tests. / Make sure I'm fit / inside and out / So I never lose / sight of your love, / But keep in step with you, / never missing a beat. / GOD, I love living with you; your house glows with your glory. You know I've been aboveboard with you; / now be aboveboard with me. / I'm on the level with you, GOD; / I bless you every chance I get." (Ps 26:1–3, 8, 11–12, TM)
Repeat Antiphon (above):
Reading: "Jephthah . . . was a mighty warrior. His father was Gilead; his mother was a prostitute. Gilead's wife also bore him sons, and when they were gown up, they drove Jephthah away. Some time later, when the Ammonites were fighting against Israel, the elders . . . went to get Jephthah . . . . 'Come,' they said, 'be our commander, so we can fight the Ammonites. . . . [W]e are turning to you now; come with us to fight the Ammonites, and you will be head over all of us who live in Gilead.' Jephthah answered, 'Suppose you take me back to fight the Ammonites and the LORD gives them to me—will I really be your head?' The elders . . . replied, 'The LORD is our witness; we will certainly do as you say.' So Jephthah went with the elders . . , , and the people made him head and commander over them." (Judg 11:1–2a, 4–6, 8–11a, NIV)
Meditation/Journal: What connection do you find between the verses of Psalm 26 and the passage from the HB (OT) book of Judges introducing Jephthah? Explain.

Evening Prayer
Antiphon: "GOD, come close. Come quickly! / Open your ears—it's my voice you're hearing!" (Ps 141:1, TM)
Psalm: "Post a guard at my mouth, GOD, / set a watch at the door of my lips. / Don't let me so much as dream of evil / or thoughtlessly fall into bad company. / And these people who only do wrong—/ don't let them

lure me with their sweet talk! / May the Just One set me straight, / may the Kind One correct me. / Don't let sin anoint my head. / I'm praying hard against their evil ways!" (Ps 141:3–6, TM)

Repeat Antiphon (above):

Reading: ". . . Jephthah sent messengers to the Ammonite king with the question, 'What do you have against me that you have attacked my country?' The king of the Ammonites answered Jephthah's messengers, 'When Israel came up out of Egypt, they took away my land. . . . Now give it back peaceably.' Jephthah sent back messengers to the Ammonite king, saying: 'Israel took over all the land of the Amorites, who lived in that country. . . . [S]ince the LORD, the God of Israel, has driven the Amorites out before his people Israel, what right have you to take it over?' The king of Ammon, however, paid no attention to the message Jephthah sent him. (Judg 11:12–14, 21b, 23, 28, NIV)

Reflection: Like some of his predecessors, Jephthah's lineage—his father was Gilead and his mother was a prostitute—is not noteworthy! Furthermore, his half-brothers drive him away from his home so that they do not have to share the family inheritance with him. What marks Jephthah is his superior warrior status. The native Ammonites want to take back the land previously seized by the Israelites at God's direction. The offer to return and be the commander from the elders is one that the social outcast Jephthah cannot ignore. As soon as he accepts the elders' offer, he begins diplomacy. He sends the king of the Ammonites a long letter tracing the history of the LORD giving the land to the Israelites. In biblical understanding, land is a grant from God. The conquest and possession of it is a sure sign of the LORD's divine donation and favor. The Ammonite king does not accept Jephthah's diplomacy, and that means that war is inevitable.

Alternative Readings: 2 Sam 7:18–28; 11:1–5; Prov 21:17–31; 22:1–8; Zeph 1:2–6; 1:7–9.

Day 23

Morning

Antiphon: "Mark the milestones of your mercy and love, GOD; / Rebuild the ancient landmarks!" (Ps 25:6, TM)

Canticle: "Listen, Heavens, I have something to tell you. / Attention, Earth, I've got a mouth full of words. / My teaching, let it fall like a gentle rain, / my words arrive like morning dew, / Like a sprinkling rain on new grass, / like spring showers on the garden. / For it's GOD's Name

I'm preaching—/ respond to the greatness of our God! / The Rock: His works are perfect, / and the way he works is fair and just; / A God you can depend upon, no exceptions, / a straight-arrow God." (Deut 32:1–4, TM)
Repeat Antiphon (above):
Reading: ". . . [T]he Spirit of the LORD came on Jephthah. And Jephthah made a vow to the LORD: 'If you give the Ammonites into my hands, whatever comes out of the door of my house to meet me when I return in triumph from the Ammonites will be the LORD's, and I will sacrifice it as a burnt offering.' Then Jephthah went over to fight the Ammonites, and the LORD gave them into his hands. Thus Israel subdued Ammon. (Judg 11:29a, 30–32, 33b, NIV)
Reflection/Meditation/Journal: A vow is a deliberate promise to God of a good which is better than its opposite. The promise made by Jephthah to God for giving the Ammonites into his hands was to sacrifice whatever exited his house to meet him when he returned. In other words, his vow was an act of worship affirming the divinity of the LORD to whom his promise was made. What vow(s) have you made? Of what did it (they) consist? To whom did you make it (them)?

Evening Prayer
Antiphon: "Treat my prayer as sweet incensing rising [to you, GOD]; . my raised hands are my evening prayers." (Ps 141:2, TM)
Psalm: ". . . GOD, dear Lord, / I only have eyes for you. / Since I've run for dear life to you, / take good care of me. / Protect me from . . . evil scheming, / from all . . . demonic subterfuge. / Let the wicked fall flat on their faces, / while I walk off without a scratch." (Ps 141:8–10, TM)
Repeat Antiphon (above):
Reading: "When Jephthah returned to his home . . . , who should come out to meet him but his daughter, dancing to the sound of timbrels! She was an only child. Except for her he had neither son nor daughter. When he saw her, he tore his clothes and cried, 'Oh no, my daughter! You have brough me down and I am devastated. I have made a vow to the LORD that I cannot break.' 'My father,' she replied, 'you have given your word to the LORD. Do to me just as you promised . . . . But grant me this one request,' she said. 'Give me two months to roam the hills and weep with my friends, because I will never marry.' 'You may go,' he said. And he let her go for two months. She and her friends went into the hills and wept because she would never marry. After the two months, she returned to her father, and he did to her as he had vowed." (Judg 11:34–39a, NIV)

SEASON OF ORDINARY TIME

Reflection: Based on the plan of a biblical home, the first or ground floor housed animals acceptable for sacrifice. In making his vow to the LORD, Jephthah assumed that one of the animals would be the first to greet him. While there are a few exceptions, human sacrifice is not usually acceptable in HB (OT) religion. Imagine the surprise on Jephthah's face when he sees his daughter coming out of the house instead of an animal. Nevertheless, a vow made to the LORD must be fulfilled, so after two months, he offers his daughter as a sacrifice. The two months is a period of mourning for the dead. Anticipating her death, Jephthah's daughter and her friends mourn her imminent death at the hands of her father. "Jephthah led Israel six years. Then Jephthah . . . died . . ." (Judg 12:7, NIV).
Alternative Readings: 2 Sam 11:6–13; 11:14–21; Prov 22:9–16; 22:17–29; Zeph 1:10–13; 1:14–18.

Day 24

Morning
Antiphon: "God, listen to me shout, / bend an ear to my prayer." (Ps 61:1, TM)
Psalm: "When I'm far from anywhere, / down to my last gasp, / I call out [to you, God], 'Guide me / up High Rock Mountain!' / You've always given me breathing room, / a place to get away from it all, / A lifetime pass to your safe-house, / an open invitation as your guest. / You've always taken me seriously, God, / made me welcome among those who know and love you. / . . . [P]ost Steady Love and Good Faith as lookouts, / And I'll be the poet who sings your glory—/ and live what I sing every day." (Ps 61:2–5, 7b–8, TM)
Repeat Antiphon (above):
Reading: "Again the Israelites did evil in the eyes of the LORD, so the LORD delivered them into the hands of the Philistines for forty years. A certain man . . . , named Manoah, . . . had a wife who was childless, unable to give birth. The angel of the LORD appeared to her and said, 'You are barren and childless, but you are going to become pregnant and have a son whose head is never to be touched by a razor because the boy is to be a Nazirite, dedicated to God from the womb. He will take the lead in delivering Israel from the hands of the Philistines.'" (Judg 13:1–5, NIV)
Points to Ponder: First, the usual elements of a new section of the HB (OT) book of Judges begins with the author's typical formula: The Israelites did evil and God punished them for forty years with the Philistines.

Second, then the author uses a model he found in the HB (OT) book of Genesis: Abraham and Sarah. Both are very old, and Sarah is past the age of childbearing. But because God opens her womb, she becomes pregnant with Isaac and gives birth to him (Gen16:15–17; 18:10–12; 21:1–5). In the story in Judges, the couple is Manoah and his nameless wife. She is barren and childless. Third, in Israelite understanding, a woman's barrenness is because God has not opened her womb; there is no consideration given to the possibility that the man is impotent! Fourth, this is why the angel of the LORD—a code phrase for God—declares that Manoah's wife will become pregnant and have a son; God is opening her womb. Fifth, from the womb the son Manoah's wife will bear is to be dedicated as a Nazarite. A Nazarite was a person—man or woman—who lived according to Torah intensely! Nazarites did not cut their hair, they abstained from intoxicating beverages, and they avoided contact with dead bodies. The vow was a temporary act of devotion to God. In the case of Manoah's wife, she is instructed to drink no wine or other fermented drink and to eat nothing unclean, so as not to contaminate the child in her womb! Once her son is born, she is not to cut his hair, and he is not to cut his hair.

Evening Prayer
Antiphon: "I cry out loudly to GOD, / loudly I plead with GOD for mercy." (Ps 142:1, TM)
Psalm: "As I sink in despair, my spirit ebbing away, / you [, GOD,] know how I'm feeling, / Know the danger I'm in, / the traps hidden in my path. / Look right, look left—/ there's not a soul who cares what happens! / I'm up against it, with no exit—/ bereft, left alone. / I cry out, GOD, call out: / 'You're my last chance, my only hope for life!' / Oh listen, please listen; / I've never been this low. / Rescue me from those who are hunting me down; / I'm no match for them. / Get me out of this dungeon / so I can thank you in public." (Ps 142:3–7a, TM)
Repeat Antiphon (above):
Reading: "... Manoah prayed to the LORD: 'Pardon your servant, Lord. I beg you to let the man of God you sent to us come again to teach us how to bring up the boy who is to be born.' God heard Manoah, and the angel of God came again to the woman.... The woman hurried to tell her husband, 'He's here! The man who appeared to me the other day!' Manoah got up and followed his wife. When he came to the man, he said, 'Are you the man who talked to my wife?' 'I am,' he said. So Manoah asked him, 'When your words are fulfilled, what is to be the rule that governs the

SEASON OF ORDINARY TIME

boy's life and work?' The angel of the LORD answered, 'Your wife must do all that I have told her.'" (Judg 13:8–13, NIV)
Intercessions: For all who seek your presence, I pray to you, LORD. For all who have difficulty conceiving a child, I pray to you, LORD. For all who seek your way of life, I pray to you, LORD. For all who need your confirmation of a mighty deed, I pray to you, LORD. For all who hesitate to believe the words of women, I pray to you, LORD.
Alternative Readings: 2 Sam 11:26–27; 12:1–15; Prov 23:1–18; 23:19–35; Zeph 3:1–7; 3:8–13.

Day 25

Morning
Antiphon: "... I pray. / GOD, it's time for a break! / God, answer in love! / Answer with your sure salvation!" (Ps 69:13, TM)
Psalm: "God, God, save me! / I'm in over my head, / Quicksand under me, swamp water over me; / I'm going down for the third time. / I'm hoarse from calling for help, / Bleary-eyed from searching the sky for God. / God, you know every sin I've committed; / My life's a wide-open book before you. Don't let those who look to you in hope / Be discouraged by what happens to me, / Dear Lord! GOD of the armies! / Don't let those out looking for you / Come to a dead end by following me—/ Please, dear God of Israel! I love you more than I can say. / Because I'm madly in love with you, / [My enemies] blame me for everything they dislike about you." (Ps 69:1–3, 5–6, 9, TM)
Repeat Antiphon (above):
Reading: "Manoah said to the angel of the LORD, 'We would like you to stay until we prepare a young goat for you.' The angel of the LORD replied, ... '[I]f you prepare a burnt offering, offer it to the LORD.' Then Manoah inquired of the angel of the LORD, 'What is your name, so that we may honor you when your word comes true?' He replied, 'It is beyond understanding.' Then Manoah took a young goat, together with the grain offering, and sacrificed it on a rock to the LORD. As the flame blazed up from the altar toward heaven, the angel of the LORD ascended in the flame. 'We are doomed to die,' [Manoah] said to his wife. 'We have seen God!' The woman gave birth to a boy and named him Samson. He grew and the LORD blessed him, and the Spirit of the LORD began to stir him...." (Judg 13:15–16ab, 17–19a, 20a, 22, 24–25, NIV)

Points to Ponder: First, the scene featuring the angel of the LORD and Manoah is like Gideon's encounter with an angel (Judg 6:11–23). There is a divine message, although it is delivered to Manoah's wife first; usually men get divine messages. Then, there is an offer of food used for sacrifice, a standard practice of hospitality. And there is the fire that consumes the sacrifice on a rock/altar and in which the angel ascends to heaven; the fire is the sign of the divine presence. Second, Manoah knows that no one can see God and live (Exod 33:20)—and, yet, it happens occasionally in biblical literature, as Manoah and his wife see God and live. Third, the narrator notes that the Spirit of the LORD began to stir Samson to action; it gives him great strength. Fourth, like Moses, who wants to know God's name (Exod 3:13), Manoah wants to know the angel of the LORD's name, and like Moses who gets no specific answer (Exod 3:14), Manoah is told that God's name is beyond understanding! In the biblical world, knowing someone's name gives the knower power over the known; thus God does not reveal a name to anyone, because no one can have power over the LORD.

Evening Prayer
Antiphon: "I spill out all my complaints before [GOD], / and spell out my troubles in detail . . . ." (Ps 142:2, TM)
Canticle: "GOD is my strength, GOD is my song, / and, yes! GOD is my salvation. / *This* is the kind of God I have / and I'm telling the world! *This* is the God of my father—/ I'm spreading the news far and wide! / God is a fighter, / pure GOD, through and through. / Who compares with you / among gods, O GOD? / Who compares with you in power, / in holy majesty, / In awesome praises, / wonder-working God? (Exod 15:2–3, 6–7, TM)
Repeat Antiphon (above):
Reading: "Samson went down to Timnah together with his father and mother. As they approached the vineyards of Timnah, suddenly a young lion came roaring toward him. The Spirit of the LORD came powerfully upon him so that he tore the lion apart with his bare hands . . . . Some time later . . . he turned aside to look at the lion's carcass, and in it he saw a swarm of bees and some honey. He scooped out the honey with his hands and ate as he went along." (Judg 14:5–6a, 8–9a, NIV)
Meditation/Journal: What power is displayed by Samson's destruction of the young lion? Why is it a lion that he kills? Why do bees swarm into the lion's carcass and make honey?

SEASON OF ORDINARY TIME

Alternative Readings: 2 Sam 13:1–22; 13:23–39; Prov 24:1–16; 24:17–34; Zech 1:7–17; 1:18–21.

Day 26

Morning

Antiphon: "Let me shout God's name with a praising song, / Let me tell his greatness in a prayer of thanks." (Ps 69:30, TM)

Psalm: "The poor in spirit see and are glad—/ Oh, you God-seekers, take heart! / For GOD listens to the poor, / He doesn't walk out on the wretched. / You heavens, praise him; praise him, earth; / Also ocean and all things that swim in it. / . . . [T]he children of his servants will get [the land], / The lovers of his name will live in it." (Ps 69:32–34, 36, TM)

Repeat Antiphon (above):

Reading: "Samson went down to Timnah and saw there a young Philistine woman. When he returned, he said to his father and mother, 'I have seen a Philistine woman in Timnah; now get her for me as my wife.' His father and mother replied, 'Isn't there an acceptable woman among your relatives or among all our people? Must you got to the uncircumcised Philistines to get a wife?' But Samson said to his father, 'Get her for me. She's the right one for me.' Now his father went down to see the woman. And there Samson held a feast, as was customary for young men. 'Let me tell you a riddle,' Samson said to [his companions]. 'Tell us your riddle,' they said. 'Let's hear it.' He replied, 'Out of the eater, something to eat; / out of the strong, something sweet.'" (Judg 14:1–3, 10, 12a, 13b–14a, NIV)

Reflection: It is important to note that Samson's choice of a Philistine woman for a wife contrasts sharply with the piety of his parents, Manoah and his wife, who have entertained the angel of the LORD! The HB (OT) book of Genesis, while it doesn't forbid marriage outside the clan, presents an aversion to doing so (Gen 24:1–4; 26:34; 27:46—28:9). In other words, the marriage to a foreign woman is contrary to accepted Israelite practice. In this specific case, Samson is marrying into the enemy of his people! During the seven-day wedding feast, Samon presents a riddle to the attendants. The author has already informed the reader as to the meaning of the riddle, but that does not imply that those attending the feast know its meaning.

Evening Prayer
Antiphon: "My mouth is filled with GOD's praise. / Let everything living bless him, / bless his holy name from now to eternity!" (Ps 145:21, TM)
Psalm: "I'll bless you every day, [GOD,] / and keep it up from now to eternity. / GOD is magnificent; he can never be praised enough. / There are no boundaries to his greatness. / Generation after generation stands in awe of your work; / each one tells stories of your mighty acts. / Your beauty and splendor have everyone talking; / I compose songs on your wonders. / Your marvelous doings are headline news; / I could write a book full of the details of your greatness. / The fame of your goodness spreads across the country; / your righteousness is on everyone's lips. / GOD is all mercy and grace—/ not quick to anger, is rich in love." (Ps 145:2–8, TM)
Repeat Antiphon (above):
Reading: "For three days [the attendants at the wedding feast] could not give the answer [to Samson about the riddle]. On the fourth day, they said to Samson's wife, 'Coax your husband into explaining the riddle for us . . . .' Then Samson's wife threw herself on him, sobbing, 'You hate me! You don't really love me. You've given my people a riddle, but you haven't told me the answer.' She cried the whole seven days of the feast. So on the seventh day [Samson] finally told her, because she continued to press him. She in turn explained the riddle to her people. Before sunset on the seventh day the men of the town said to him, 'What is sweeter than honey? / What is stronger than a lion?' Then the Spirit of the LORD came powerfully upon [Samson]. Burning with anger, he returned to his father's home. And Samson's wife was given to one of his companions who had attended him at the feast." (Judg 14:14b–15a, 16ab, 17–18a, 19ac, 20, NIV)
Activity: Evaluate the role Samson's Philistine wife plays in the Judge's story. According to the author of the HB (OT) book of Judges, what are the Philistines (those attempting to solve Samson's riddle and his wife) like? Characterize them. Is Samson's anger warranted? Explain. Should Samson's Philistine wife have been given to one of his companions? Explain.
Alternative Readings: 2 Sam 14:33; 15:1–12; Prov 25:1–14; 25:15–28; Zech 2:1–5; 3:1–10.

SEASON OF ORDINARY TIME

Day 27

Morning

Antiphon: "All day long I'm chanting / about you [, God,] and your righteous ways, / While those who tried to do me in / slink off looking ashamed." (Ps 71:24, TM)

Psalm: "I run for dear life to GOD, / I'll never live to regret it. / Do what you do so well: / get me out of this mess and up on my feet. / Put your ear to the ground and listen, / give me space for salvation. / Be a guest room where I can retreat; / you said your door was always open! / You're my salvation—my vast, granite fortress. / You keep me going when times are tough—/ my bedrock, GOD, since my childhood. / I've hung on you from the day of my birth, / the day you took me from the cradle; / I'll never run out of praise." (Ps 71:1–3, 5–6, TM)

Repeat Antiphon (above):

Reading: ". . . [A]t the time of wheat harvest, Samson took a young goat and went to visit his wife. He said, 'I'm going to my wife's room.' But her father would not let him go in. 'I was so sure you hated her,' he said, 'that I gave her to your companion.' Samson said . . . , 'This time I have a right to get even with the Philistines . . . .' So he went out and caught three hundred foxes and tied them tail to tail in pairs. He then fastened a torch to every pair of tails, lit the torches and let the foxes loose in the standing grain of the Philistines. He burned up the shocks and standing grain, together with the vineyards and olive groves." (Judg 15:1–2a, 3–5, NIV)

Meditation/Journal: Based on the information provided by the author of the HB (OT) book of Judges, if you were an Israelite, what would you have thought about Samson? If you were an Israelite, what would you have thought about the Philistines?

Evening Prayer

Antiphon: "GOD is good to one and all; / everything he does is suffused with grace." (Ps 145:9, TM)

Psalm: "Creation and creatures applaud you, GOD; / your holy people bless you. / They talk about the glories of your rule, / they exclaim over your splendor, / Letting the world know of your power for good, / the lavish splendor of your kingdom. / Your kingdom is a kingdom eternal; / you never get voted out of office. / GOD always does what he says, / and is gracious in everything he does. / GOD gives a hand to those down on their luck, / gives a fresh start to those ready to quit. / All eyes are on you,

expectant; / you give them their meals on time. / Generous to a fault, / you lavish your favor on all creatures." (Ps 145:10–16, TM)
Repeat Antiphon (above):
Reading: "The Philistines went . . . and camped in Judah . . . . The people of Judah asked, 'Why have you come to fight us?' 'We have come to take Samson prisoner,' they answered, 'to do to him as he did to us.' Then three thousand men from Judah went . . . and said to Samson, 'Don't you realize that the Philistines are rulers over us? What have you done to us?' He answered, 'I merely did to them what they did to me.' They said to him, 'We've come to tie you up and hand you over to the Philistines. We will not kill you.' So they bound him with two new ropes . . . . The Spirit of the LORD came powerfully upon him. The ropes on his arms became like charred flax, and the bindings dropped from his hands. Finding a fresh jawbone of a donkey, he grabbed it and struck down a thousand men. / 'With a donkey's jawbone / I have made donkeys of them. / With a donkey's jawbone / I have killed a thousand men.' Because he was very thirsty, he cried out to the LORD, 'You have given your servant this great victory. Must I now die of thirst and fall into the hands of the uncircumcised?' Then God opened up the hollow place . . . , and water came out of it. When Samson drank, his strength returned and he revived. Samson led Israel for twenty years in the days of the Philistines." (Judg 15:9–12a, 13bc, 14b–16, 18–19b, 20, NIV)
Meditation/Journal: What do you think about the cycle of revenge found in the narrative about Samson and the Philistines?
Alternative Readings: 2 Sam 15:13–37; 16:1–14; Prov 26:1–14; 26:15–28; Zech 4:1–14; 5:1–4.

Day 28

Morning
Antiphon: ". . . I'm in the very presence of God—/ oh, how refreshing it is! / I've made Lord GOD my home. / God, I'm telling the world what you do." (Ps 73:28, TM)
Psalm: "No doubt about it! God is good—/ good to good people, good to the good-hearted. / When I was beleaguered and bitter, / totally consumed by envy, / I was totally ignorant, a dumb ox, in your very presence. / I'm still in your presence, / but you've taken my hand. / You wisely and tenderly lead me, / and then you bless me. / You're all I want in heaven! /

You're all I want on earth! / When my skin sags and my bones get brittle, / GOD is rock-firm and faithful." (Ps 73:1, 21–26, TM)

Repeat Antiphon (above):

Reading: "One day Samson . . . saw a prostitute. He went in to spend the night with her. But Samson lay there only until the middle of the night. Then he got up and took hold of the doors of the city gate, together with the two posts, and tore them loose, bar and all. He lifted them to his shoulders and carried them [away]. Some time later, he fell in love with a woman . . . whose name was Delilah. The rulers of the Philistines went to her and said, 'See if you can lure him into showing you the secret of his great strength and how we can overpower him so we may tie him up and subdue him.' So Delilah said to Samson, 'Tell me the secret of your great strength and how you can be tied up and subdued.' Samson answered her, 'If anyone ties me with seven fresh bowstrings that have not been dried, I'll become as weak as any other man.' Then the rulers of the Philistines brought her seven fresh bowstrings that had not been dried, and she tied him with them. With men hidden in the room, she called to him, 'Samson, the Philistines are upon you.' But he snapped the bowstrings as easily as a piece of string snaps when it comes close to a flame. So the secret of his strength was not discovered." (Judg 16:1, 3–5a, 6–9, NIV)

Reflection: Just when the reader things that the account about Samson is finished, another tale is presented in the HB (OT) book of Judges. Most likely, there were several versions of the Samson story in circulation—both orally and written—that the author of the book of Judges used to present the Samson narrative. This one illustrates his strength more deeply. After visiting a prostitute, the Philistines presume that he will spend the night with her, as that was the usual process. They could station themselves in the rooms within the city gates, which were shut for the night. In the morning, they would be in an ideal position to capture Samson. However, Samson has other plans. Instead of following the usual procedure with the prostitute, Samson gets up and leaves early. And on his way out, he removed the doors of the city gates and the posts to which they are attached. Thus, the Philistines are unable to capture him. Next, as in the first tale, Samson falls in love with a Philistine woman named Delilah, who is at the disposal of the Philistine leaders. Her first attempt to get Samson to disclose the source of his strength (as illustrated by his ability to remove the doors of the city gate and posts to which they were attached) fails. Delilah, whom he presumes loves him, is ready to betray him. The image painted by the story continues to contrast Samson, who repeatedly falls in love with Philistine women, with his devoted parents.

Evening Prayer

Antiphon: "Everything GOD does is right—/ the trademark on all his works is love." (Ps 145:17, TM)

Psalm: "GOD's there, listening for all who pray, / for all who pray and mean it. / He does what's best for those who fear him—/ hears them call out, and saves them. / GOD sticks by all who love him, / but it's all over for those who don't. / My mouth is filled with GOD's praise. / Let everything living bless him, / bless his holy name from now to eternity!" (Ps 146:18–21, TM)

Repeat Antiphon (above):

Reading: ". . . Delilah said to Samson, 'You have made a fool of me; you lied to me. Come now, tell me how you can be tied.' He said, 'If anyone ties me securely with new ropes that have never been used, I'll become as weak as any other man.' So Delilah took new ropes and tied him with them. Then, with men hidden in the room, she called to him, 'Samson the Philistine are upon you!' But he snapped the ropes off his arms as if they were threads. Delilah then said to Samson, 'All this time you have been making a fool of me and lying to me. Tell me how you can be tied.' He replied, 'If you weave the seven braids of my head into the fabric on the loom and tighten it with the pin, I'll become as weak as any other man.' So while he was sleeping, Delilah took the seven braids of his head, wove them into the fabric and tightened it with the pin. Again she called to him, 'Samson, the Philistines are upon you!' He awoke from his sleep and pulled up the pin and the loom, with the fabric." (Judg 16:10–14, NIV)

Reflection: This part of the Samson tale features two sacred numbers. The first number is three, which represents the spiritual world and the order that is given to chaos. Three times Delilah asks Samson to reveal to her the source of his strength, and three times he lies to her. At first, the reader finds himself or herself in a conundrum; however, Samson's lying is to protect the source of his strength. That source is revealed in another number. Samson wears seven braids of hair. His hair is braided because he was dedicated to God in the womb as a Nazarite, and Nazarites do not cut their hair. Seven, the sum of three (the divine order) and four (the created order) refers to completion. In other words, Samson is absolutely

strengthened by God. He is stronger than any other man; his mission has been to defend and defeat the enemy of Israel: the Philistines.
Alternative Readings: 2 Sam 18:1–8; 18:9–23; Prov 27:1–14; 27:15–27; Zech 5:5–11; 6:1–8.

Day 29

Morning
Antiphon: "GOD, don't shut me out; / don't give me the silent treatment, O God." (Ps 83:1, TM)
Canticle: "Blessed are you, GOD of Israel, our father / from of old and forever. / To you, O GOD, belong the greatness and the might, / the glory, the victory, the majesty, the splendor; / Yes! Everything in heaven, everything on earth; / the kingdom all yours! You've raised yourself high over all. / Riches and glory come from you, / you're ruler over all; / You hold strength and power in the palm of your hand / to build up and strengthen all. / And here [I am], O God, giving thanks to you, / praising your splendid Name." (1 Chr 29:10b–13, TM)
Repeat Antiphon (above):
Reading: "[Delilah] said to [Samson], 'How can you say, I love you,' when you won't confide in me? This is the third time you have made a fool of me and haven't told me the secret of your great strength.' So he told her everything. 'No razor has ever been used on my head,' he said, 'because I have been a Nazirite dedicated to God from my mother's womb. If my head were shaved, my strength would leave me, and I would become as weak as any other man.' After putting him to sleep on her lap, she called for someone to shave off the seven braids of his hair, and so began to subdue him. And his strength left him. Then the Philistines seized him [and] gouged out his eyes . . . . Binding him with bronze shackles, they set him to grinding grain in the prison. But the hair on his head began to grow again after it had been shaved." (Judg 16:15, 17, 19, 21–22, NIV)
Meditation/Journal: What connection do you find between the canticle from the HB (OT) First Book of Chronicles (29:10b–13) and the passage from the HB (OT) book of Judges (16:15, 17, 19, 21–22)? What (Who) is the source of your spiritual strength? Explain.

Evening Prayer
Antiphon: "Light, space, zest—/ that's GOD! / So, with him on my side I'm fearless, / afraid of no one and nothing." (Ps 27:1, TM)

Psalm: "Bravo, GOD, bravo! / Gods and all angels shout, 'Encore!' / In awe before the glory, / in awe before God's visible power. / Stand at attention! / Dress your best to honor him! / God thunders across the waters. / Brilliant, his voice and his face, streaming brightness—/ GOD, across the flood waters. / GOD's thunder tympanic, / God's thunder symphonic. / GOD's thunder smashes cedars, / God topples the northern cedars. / The mountain ranges skip like spring colts, / The high ridges jump like wild kid goats. / GOD's thunder spits fire. / GOD thunders, the wilderness quakes.... / GOD's thunder sets the oak trees dancing / A wild dance, whirling the pelting rain strips their branches. [I] fall to [my] knees—[I] call out, 'Glory!'" (Ps 29:1–9, TM)

Repeat Antiphon (above):

Reading: "Now the rulers of the Philistines assembled to offer a great sacrifice to Dagon their god and to celebrate, saying, 'Our god has delivered Samson, our enemy, into our hands.' While they were in high spirits, they shouted, 'Bring out Samson to entertain us.' So they called Samson out of the prison, and he performed for them. When they stood him among the pillars, Samson said to the servant who held his hand, 'Put me where I can feel the pillars that support the temple, so that I may lean against them.' Then Samson prayed to the LORD, 'Sovereign LORD, remember me. Please, God, strengthen me just once more, and let me with one blow get revenge on the Philistines for my two eyes.' Then Samson reached toward the two central pillars on which the temple stood. Samson said, 'Let me die with the Philistines!' Then he pushed with all his might, and down came the temple on the rulers and all the people in it. Thus he killed many more when he died than while he lived. Then his brothers and his father's whole family went ... to get him. They brought him back and buried him ... in the tomb of Manoah his father. He had led Israel twenty years." (Judg 16:23, 25–26, 28–29a, 30–31, NIV)

Points to Ponder: First, once Samson is captured by the Philistines, he is not treated as a prisoner of war nor like a slave. He becomes a beast of burden; his task is to work a treadmill grinding grain into flour. Second, Samson did not take his status as a Nazarite seriously; he abandoned God for foreign women. Third, even after Samson abandoned the LORD, God did not abandon him. Fourth, Samson is presented by the author of the HB (OT) book of Judges as an image of the Jews in exile. In Samson they can recognize their history of idolatry and unfaithfulness to the LORD's covenant. Fifth, once Samson's hair begins to grow again, he makes one final, heroic, suicidal move against the enemy Philistines. After praying

for strength from the LORD—returning to his God—he realizes that the LORD is greater than Dagon, and so Dagon's temple collapses, bringing death to a foreign god and his Philistine devotees.
Alternative Readings: 2 Sam 18:24–33; 19:1–10; Prov 28:1–14; 28:15–28; Mal 3:1–5; 4:1–5.

Day 30

Morning
Antiphon: "Pay attention, GOD, to my prayer; / bend down and listen to my cry for help." (Ps 86:6, TM)
Psalm: "Bend an ear, GOD; answer me. / Help your servant—I'm depending on you! / You're my God; have mercy on me. / I count on your from morning to night. / Give your servant a happy life; / I put myself in your hands! / You're well-known as good and forgiving, / highhearted to all who ask for help. / Train me, GOD, to walk straight; / then I'll follow your true path. / Put me together, one heart and mind; / then, undivided, I'll worship in joyful fear. / From the bottom of my heart I thank you, dear Lord; / I've never kept secret what you're up to. / You've always been great toward me—what love!" (Ps 86:1a, 2b–5, 11–13, TM)
Repeat Antiphon (above):
Reading: "In the days when the judges ruled, there was a famine in the land. So a man from Bethlehem in Judah, together with his wife and two sons, went to live for a while in the country of Moab. The man's name was Elimelek, his wife's name was Naomi, and the names of his two sons were Mahlon and Killion. Now Elimelek, Naomi's husband, died, and she was left with her two sons. They married Moabite women, one named Orpah and the other Ruth. After they had lived there about ten years, both Mahlon and Killion also died, and Naomi was left without her two sons and her husband. With her two daughters-in-law [Naomi] left the place where she had been living and set out on the road that would take them back to the land of Judah. Then Naomi said to her two daughters-in-law, 'Go back, each of you, to your mother's home. May the LORD show you kindness, as you have shown kindness to your dead husbands and to me.' Then Orpah kissed her mother-in-law goodbye, but Ruth clung to her.... Ruth replied, 'Don't urge me to leave you or to turn back from you. Where you go I will go, and where you stay I will stay. Your people will be my people and your God my God. Where you die I will die, and there I will be buried.' When Naomi realized that Ruth was determined

to go with her, she stopped urging her. So Naomi returned from Moab accompanied by Ruth the Moabite, her daughter-in-law, arriving in Bethlehem as the barley harvest was beginning." (Ruth 1:1–3a, 4–5, 7–8, 14b, 16–17a, 18, 22, NIV)

Points to Ponder: First, the story of Ruth is set during the time of the judges (around 1200–1025 BCE). Second, the main character in the book is Ruth, a Moabite, a non-Israelite, who is helped by the hidden LORD, the God of Israel. Third, the main characters, other than Ruth, are Elimelek (meaning *my god is king*), Naomi (Elimelek's wife, meaning *my delight*), Mahlon (Elimelek's and Naomi's son, meaning *disease, sick*, or *sickness*), and Killion (Elimelek's and Naomi's son, meaning *wasting* or *destruction*); just from the meaning of the sons' names, the reader can conclude that their demise is imminent. Fourth, each son marries a Moabite woman: Orpah (meaning *neck* or *fawn*) and Ruth (meaning *friend* or *friendship*). Fourth, tragedy follows tragedy: Elimelek's death is followed by Mahlon's and Killion's death. Three women are left, and all of them are widows, who, in ancient culture, needed a man (security) to take care of them. In other words, the three women are considered powerless. That is why Naomi attempts to send them back to their parents, who can take care of them. Fifth, the powerless widows are not as powerless as their society would think them to be. Sixth, after insisting that Orpah return to her Moabite family, Naomi and Ruth determine their own survival without husbands; they decide to return to the place from which Naomi came, Bethlehem, which means *house of bread*, and arrive, ironically, as the barley harvest is just getting underway.

Evening Prayer
Antiphon: "I'm asking GOD for one thing, / only one thing: / To live with him in his house / my whole life long. / I'll contemplate his beauty; / I'll study at his feet." (Ps 27:4, TM)
Psalm: "That's the only quiet, secure place / in a noisy world, / The perfect getaway, / far from the buzz of traffic. / God holds me head and shoulders / above all who try to pull me down. / I'm headed for his place to offer anthems / that will raise the roof! / Already I'm singing God-songs; / I'm making music to GOD." (Ps 27:5–6, TM)
Repeat Antiphon (above):
Reading: "Now Naomi had a relative on her husband's side, a man . . . , whose name was Boaz. [Ruth] went out, entered a field, and began to glean behind the harvesters. As it turned out, she was working in a field

belonging to Boaz. Boaz said to Ruth, '. . . Don't go and glean in another field and don't go away from here. Stay here with the women who work for me.' At this, she bowed down with her face to the ground. She asked him, 'Why have I found such favor in your eyes that you notice me—a foreigner?' Boaz replied, 'I've been told all about what you have done for your mother-in-law since the death of your husband—how you left your father and mother and your homeland and came to live with a people you did not know before.' 'May I continue to find favor in your eyes, my lord,' she said." (Ruth 2:1, 3, 8, 10–11, 13a, NIV)

Reflection: Boaz (meaning *strength*) now enters the picture of Naomi and Ruth. Boaz is a wealthy landowner, who meets Ruth, as she is gleaning or gathering the leftovers after the barley harvesters. The patriarchal character of Boaz takes an interest in Ruth. He offers her protection from the young men in the field. He investigates her origin and discovers that she is his kinswoman's (Naomi's) daughter-in law. Then, he shows hospitality to a foreigner; Ruth is amazed by the way he treats her, just as he is amazed by her action of leaving her Moabite relatives and traveling with her mother-in-law to Bethlehem to live with the Israelites.

Alternative Readings: 2 Sam 19:11–43; 23:1–7; Prov 29:1–14; 29:15–27; Zech 9:9 (Matt 21:1–11); Acts 21:10–11.

Day 31

Morning

Antiphon: "Your love, GOD, is my song, and I'll sing it! / I'm forever telling everyone how faithful you are. / I'll never quit telling the story of your love . . . ." (Ps 89:1, TM)

Psalm: "Your love [, God,] has always been [my life's] foundation, / your fidelity has been the roof over [the] world. / GOD! Let the cosmos praise your wonderful ways, / the choir of holy angels sing anthems to your faithful ways! / Search high and low, scan skies and land, / you'll find nothing and no one quite like GOD. / The holy angels are in awe before him; / he looms immense and august over everyone around him. You own the cosmos—you made everything in it, / everything from atom to archangel. / The Right and Justice are the roots of your rule; / Love and Truth are its fruits. / Blessed are the people who know the passwords of praise, / who shout on parade in the bright presence of God." (Ps 89:2, 5–7, 10–11, 14–15, TM)

Repeat Antiphon (above):

Reading: "At mealtime Boaz said to [Ruth], 'Come over here. Have some bread and dip it in the wine vinegar.' When she sat down with the harvesters, he offered her some roasted grain. She ate all she wanted and had some left over. . . . Ruth gleaned in the field until evening. Then she threshed the barley she had gathered . . . . She carried it back to town, and her mother-in-law saw how much she had gathered. Her mother-in-law asked her, 'Where did you glean today?' Then Ruth told her mother-in-law about the one at whose place she had been working 'The name of the man I worked with today is Boaz,' she said. 'The LORD bless him!' Naomi said to her daughter-in-law. 'That man is our close relative; he is one of our guardian-redeemers.' . . . Ruth stayed close to the women of Boaz to glean until the barley and wheat harvests were finished. And she lived with her mother-in-law." (Ruth 2:14, 17–18a, 19ad, 20ac, 23, NIV)

Reflection/Meditation/Journal: A guardian-redeemer is a man who has an obligation to redeem a relative in serious difficulty. In the account of Naomi and Ruth, Naomi's closest male relative must see to the widow's well-being, and, in this case, to her dependent, Ruth. Who is your guardian-redeemer? Explain.

Evening Prayer
Antiphon: "Listen, GOD, I'm calling at the top of my lungs; / 'Be good to me! Answer me!'" (Ps 27:7, TM)
Psalm: "When my heart whispered, 'Seek God,' / my whole being replied, 'I'm seeking him!' / Don't hide from me now! / You've always been right there for me; / don't turn your back on me now. / Don't throw me out, don't abandon me; / you've always kept the door open. / My father and mother walked out and left me, / but GOD took me in. / Point me down your highway, GOD; / direct me along a well-lighted street . . . . / I'm sure now I'll see God's goodness / in the exuberant earth. / Stay with GOD! / Take heart. Don't quit. / I'll say it again: / Stay with GOD." (Ps 27:8–11, 13–14, TM)
Repeat Antiphon (above):
Reading: "One day Ruth's mother-in-law Naomi said to her, 'My daughter, I must find a home for you, where you will be well provided for. Now Boaz, with whose women you have worked, is a relative of ours. Tonight he will be winnowing barley on the threshing floor. Wash, put on perfume, and get dressed in your best clothes. Then go down to the threshing floor, but don't let him know you are there until he has finished eating and drinking. When he lies down, note the place where he is lying. Then

go and uncover his feet and lie down. He will tell you what to do.' In the middle of the night something startled the man; he turned—and there was a woman lying at his feet. 'Who are you?' he asked. 'I am your servant Ruth,' she said. 'Spread the corner of your garment over me, since you are a guardian-redeemer of our family.' So she lay at his feet until morning, but got up before anyone could be recognized; and he said, 'No one must know that a woman came to the threshing floor.' When Ruth came to her mother-in-law, Naomi asked, 'How did it go my daughter?' Then she told her everything Boaz had done for her . . . . Then Naomi said, 'Wait, my daughter, until you find out what happens. For the man will not rest until the matter is settled . . . .'" (Ruth 3:1–4, 8–9, 14, 16, 18, NIV)

Points to Ponder: First, Naomi, meaning *my delight* or *pleasant*, decides that she needs to be sure that Ruth has care. The two of them are living in Bethlehem; Ruth is getting food for them by gleaning what is left after the barley harvesters have passed by. Second, Naomi's kinsman, Boaz, has been very kind to Ruth, making sure that she has food and is not harassed by young harvesters. Third, Naomi devises a plan to spur Boaz to action as their guardian-redeemer. She instructs Ruth to enter the threshing floor, an outdoor or indoor circular surface of stone, wood, or smooth floor of earth where grain was separated from straw for the purpose of exposing and collecting the grain. Boaz would be living there—eating meals and sleeping—to protect the grain. Fourth, Naomi's instructions to Ruth include uncovering Boaz's feet—a euphemism for sexual organs—and to tell Boaz to spread the corner of his garment over her—a euphemism for marriage. In other words, Naomi tells Ruth to go sleep with Boaz. Fifth, after investigating another relative, who has a previous claim on Naomi (and consequently on Ruth), and discovering that the other man is not interested, Boaz marries Ruth. Sixth, Boaz and Ruth conceive a son, whom they named Obed, who is the father of Jesse, who is the father of King David. Sixth, in the CB (NT), the author of Matthew's Gospel repeats the Davidic genealogy found in the HB (OT) book of Ruth (Ruth 4:18–22; Matt 1:2–6). In Matthew's genealogy of Jesus the Messiah, Matthew 1:2–6 contains the names of the first three of four women in the total list. Judah (son of Jacob [Israel]) was seduced by Tamar because he would not fulfill his levirate marriage duty. Boaz's mother was Rahab, the prostitute who ran the best little whorehouse in Jericho. Ruth, a foreign Moabite, had a sexually suggestive meeting with Boaz during the night on the threshing floor! The inclusion of the names of these women in Matthew's genealogy is interesting, to say the least, because women are usually not included in biblical genealogies (they are only incubators for male seed in Israelite understanding). However, these women have one thing in common: they are righteous (in their unrighteous behavior); they did the right thing because it was the right thing to do! Seventh, beginning with Perez, Boaz is the seventh name in the genealogical list; this indicates that he prepared the way for his great-grandson, King David, whose great-grandmother, Ruth, was a Moabite—not an Israelite!

Alternative Readings: 1 Kgs 1:22–37; 2:1–12; Prov 30:1–16; 30:17–33; Acts 5:34–39; 7:54—9:1.

Our Lord Jesus Christ, King of the Universe

Last Sunday in Ordinary Time
Morning
Antiphon: "The LORD reigns, He is clothed with majesty and splendor...." (Ps 93:1a, AMP)
Psalm: "The LORD has clothed and encircled Himself with strength; / the world is firmly established, it cannot be moved. / Your throne is established from of old; / You are from everlasting. / More than the sounds of many waters, / More than the mighty breakers of the sea, / The LORD on high is mighty. / ... Holiness adorns Your house, / O LORD, forever."(Ps 93:1b–2, 4, 5bc, AMP)
Repeat Antiphon (above):
Reading: "Grace [be granted] to you and peace [inner clam and spiritual well-being], from Him Who is [existing forever] and Who was [continually existing in the past] and Who is to come, and from the seven Spirits that are before His throne, and from Jesus Christ, the faithful and trustworthy Witness, the Firstborn of the dead, and the Ruler of the kings of the earth. To Him who [always] loves us and who [has once for all] freed us [or washed us] from our sins by His own blood (His sacrificial death)—and formed us into a kingdom [as His subjects], priests to His God and Father—to Him be the glory and the power and the majesty and the dominion forever and ever. Amen. 'I am the Alpha and the Omega [the Beginning and the End],' says the Lord God. 'Who is [existing forever] and Who was [continually existing in the past] and Who is to come, the Almighty [the Omnipotent, the Ruler of all].'" (Rev 1:4–6, 8, AMP)
Points to Ponder: First, celebrating a feast day in honor of a king in a democratic country is probably meaningless to most of its citizens.

Second, throughout the HB (OT), the LORD is king, as indicated in the verses from Psalm 93. Third, the feast of Jesus Christ, King, is derived from, first, the LORD being king, and, second, from the fact that God gave his people kings—Saul, David, Solomon—to rule them. Fourth, the anonymous author of the CB (NT) book of Revelation presents Jesus Christ as the universal king. (a) Jesus died and was raised; he is the King of kings (Rev 17:14; 19:16); (b) he has brought salvation in which people are washed or baptized; (c) he created a kingdom of new people, who worship and praise God. (d) While God is the beginning and end of all things, Jesus, makes all things new, shares in the all-encompassing God (Rev 21:6; 22:13).

Evening
Antiphon: "Unto You [, God,] I lift up my eyes. / O You who are enthroned in the heavens!" (Ps 123:1, AMP)
Psalm: "I was glad when they said to me, 'Let us go to the house of the LORD.' / To give thanks to the name of the LORD. / For there the thrones . . . were set, / The thrones of the house of David. / Pray for . . . peace . . . ; / 'May they prosper who love you . . . . / May peace be with [you] . . . / And prosperity within [you] . . . .' For the sake of my brothers [and sisters] and my friends, / I will now say, 'May peace be within you.' / For the sake of the house of the LORD our God . . . , / I will seek your . . . good." (Ps 122: 1, 4c–9, AMP)
Repeat Antiphon (above):
Reading: ". . . [A]ll the tribes of Israel came to David at Hebron and said, 'Behold, we are your bone and your flesh. In times past, when Saul was king over us, it was you who led Israel out [to war] and brought Israel in [from battle]. And the LORD told you, "You shall shepherd My people Israel and be ruler over them."' So all the elders (tribal leaders) of Israel came to the king at Hebron, and King David made a covenant with them at Hebron before the LORD; and they anointed him king over Israel. David was thirty years old when he became king, and he reigned forty years." (2 Sam 5:1–4, AMP)
Meditation/Journal: What does the anointing of David as King of Israel have to do with the feast of Jesus Christ, King of the Universe? What word or phrase from the verses of Psalm 122 gets most of your attention? How is that word of phrase connected to this feast? How does it help to make you aware of the divine presence?

4

Season of Advent

Season of Advent Introduction

The Season of Advent, which initiates a new liturgical year, begins with the First Sunday of Advent and lasts from three to four weeks, depending on what day of the week Christmas, December 25, falls on. Advent begins in 2025 on November 30; in 2026 on November 29; in 2027 on November 28; in 2028 on December 3; in 2029 on December 2; in 2030 on December 1; in 2031 on November 30; in 2032 on November 28; in 2033 on November 27; in 2034 on December 3; in 2035 on December 2; in 2036 on November 30; in 2037 on November 29; in 2038 on November 28; in 2039 on November 27. The last day of Advent is always December 24.

When the feast of St. Andrew, Apostle (November 30), falls on a Sunday, it is omitted that year. When the solemnity of the Immaculate Conception (December 8) falls on a Sunday, it is moved to December 9. When the feast of Our Lady of Guadalupe (December 12) falls on a Sunday, it is omitted that year.

Other books by Mark G. Boyer that follow the same structure of Morning Prayer and Evening Prayer that can be used—in substitution for what is provided here—during the Season of Advent include: *Weekday*

Saints: Reflections on Their Scriptures (Eugene, OR: Wipf & Stock, 2014); *Very Short Reflections—for Advent and Christmas, Lent and Easter, Ordinary Time, and Saints—through the Liturgical Year* (Eugene, OR: Wipf & Stock, 2020); *Names for Jesus: Reflections for Advent and Christmas* (Eugene, OR: Wipf & Stock, 2017); *Shhh! The Sound of Sheer Silence: A Biblical Spirituality that Transforms* (Eugene, OR: Wipf & Stock, 2019); and *Love Addict* with Matthew S. Ver Miller and Corbin S. Cole (Eugene, OR: Wipf & Stock, 2019).

Antiphons, Psalms, and Readings for the Season of Advent are taken from *The Contemporary English Version* (CEV) (Nashville, TN: Thomas Nelson Publishers, 1995).

Days in the Season of Advent

Day 1

Morning

Antiphon: "Do something, LORD God, / and use your powerful arm to help those in need." (Ps 10:12, CEV)
Psalm: ". . . [Y]ou see the trouble / and the distress, and you will do something, [LORD God]. / The poor can count on you, and so can orphans. / Our LORD, you will always rule, / but nations will vanish from the earth. / You listen to the longings of those who suffer. / You offer them hope, / and you pay attention to their cries for help. / You defend orphans and everyone else in need, / so that no one on earth can terrify others again." (Ps 10:14, 16–18, CEV)
Repeat Antiphon (above):
Reading: "The time is coming when the LORD will make his land fruitful and glorious again . . . . Then the LORD will cover the whole city and its meeting places with a thick cloud each day and with a flaming fire each night. God's own glory will be like a huge tent that covers everything. It will provide shade from the heat of the sun and a place of shelter and protection from storms and rain." (Isa 4:2, 5–6, CEV)
Reflection: The cloud and fire signify God's presence; in the HB (OT) book of Exodus, God is present as a pillar of cloud by day and a pillar of fire by night. According to Isaiah, God's presence will engulf everyone and everything, protecting all, like a tent shelters those under it from sun and rain. We discover God adventing as falling leaves, drifting snow, shorter days,

longer nights, family members, friends, and more. Wherever we find signs of divine presence, fruitfulness and gloriousness appear.

Evening
Antiphon: "The LORD is sitting / in his sacred temple on his throne in heaven. / He knows everything we do because he sees us all." (Ps 11:4, CEV)
Psalm: "Please help me, LORD! All who were faithful / and all who were loyal have disappeared. / But you, LORD, tell them, 'I will do something! / The poor are mistreated and helpless people moan. I'll rescue all who suffer.' Our LORD, you are true to your promises, / and your word is like silver heated seven times in a fiery furnace. / You will protect us / and always keep us safe . . . ." (Ps 12:1, 5–7, CEV)
Repeat Antiphon (above):
Reading: ". . . [A] sign will appear in the sky. And there will be the Son of Man . . . coming on the clouds of heaven with power and great glory. No one knows the day or hour. The angels in heaven don't know, and the Son himself doesn't know. Only the Father knows. Homeowners never know when a thief is coming, and they are always on guard to keep one from breaking in." (Matt 24:30, 36, 43, CEV)
Meditation/Journal: What are you like this Advent (for example, a homeowner awaiting a thief)?

Day 2

Morning
Antiphon: "Open the ancient gates, / so that the glorious king may come in." (Ps 24:9, CEV)
Psalm: "Our God approaches, but not silently; / a flaming fire comes first, and a storm surrounds him. / God comes to judge his people. / He shouts to the heavens and to the earth, / 'Call my followers together! / They offered me a sacrifice, and we made an agreement.' The heavens announce, / 'God is the judge, and he is always honest.' My people, I am God! / I am God Most High! The only sacrifice I want / is for you to be thankful and to keep your word. / Pray to me in time of trouble. / I will rescue you, and you will honor me." (Ps 50:3–7a, 14–15, CEV)
Repeat Antiphon (above):
Reading: "Night is almost over, and day will soon appear. We must stop behaving as people do in the dark and be ready to live in the light. Let the

SEASON OF ADVENT

Lord Jesus Christ be as near to you as the clothes you wear." (Rom 13:12, 14a, CEV)
Meditation/Journal: What metaphor do you use to describe the nearness of the Lord Jesus Christ to you?

Evening Prayer
Antiphon: "Trust the LORD! / Be brave and strong and trust the LORD." (Ps 27:14, CEV)
Psalm: "Only you, LORD, are a mighty rock! / Don't refuse to help me when I pray. / If you don't answer me, I will soon be dead. / Please listen to my prayer and my cry for help, / as I lift my hands toward your holy temple. / I praise you, LORD, for answering my prayers. / You are my strong shield, / and I trust your completely. / You have helped me, / and I will celebrate and thank you in song. / Come save us and bless us. / Be our shepherd and always carry us in your arms." (Ps 28:1–2, 6–7, 9, CEV)
Repeat Antiphon (above):
Reading: "Rip the heavens apart! / Come down, LORD; make the mountains tremble. / Be a spark that starts a fire causing water to boil. / You are the only God ever seen or heard of / who works miracles for his followers. / Only by your help can we ever be saved. / You, LORD, are our Father. We are nothing but clay, / but you are the potter who molded us." (Isa 64:1–2a, 4, 5b, 8, CEV)
Reflection: Isaiah's plea that the LORD rip apart the heavens and come down reflects a three-storied-universe understanding. God lived above the heavens; people lived on the flat plate-like surface of the earth; and the dead lived under the earth. Living in a sun-centered universe, modern people no longer look for ripped apart sky. The trembling mountains with fire refer to the eruption of a volcano or an earthquake, both were signs of God's presence. Because the HB (OT) book of Genesis portrays God as a male potter molding people from clay, the prophet asks him to work a miracle and save his people. During Advent, look for answered prayers.

Day 3

Morning
Antiphon: "You see everything, LORD! / Please don't keep silent or stay so far away." (Ps 35:22, CEV)
Psalm: "I will celebrate and be joyful / because you, LORD, have saved me. / You protect the helpless from those in power; / you save the poor

and needy from those who hurt them. / . . . [W]hen your people meet, I will praise you / and thank you, Lord, in front of them all. / . . . I will shout all day, / 'Praise the LORD God! He did what was right.'" (Ps 35:9, 10bc, 18, 28, CEV)

Repeat Antiphon (above):

Reading: "My prayer is that God our Father and the Lord Jesus Christ will be kind to you and will bless you with peace! You are not missing out on any blessings, as you wait for him to return. And until the day Christ does return, he will keep you completely innocent. God can be trusted, and he chose you to be partners with his Son, our Lord Jesus Christ." (1 Cor 1:3, 7–9, CEV)

Reflection: In his First Letter to the Corinthians, Paul reminds his readers of the early church belief that Jesus was returning soon. Over the course of time, that expectation got tempered and pushed into the far future. The return of the Lord Jesus is the only hoped-for biblical event that has never occurred. Those who believe in him spend Advent waiting for that day to come. In the meantime, they trust God, as Paul states, who has chosen Corinthians to be partners with Jesus. According to Paul, God is worthy of human trust, and Advent is good time to deepen it.

Evening Prayer

Antiphon: "Only God gives inward peace, and I depend on him. / God alone is the mighty rock that keeps me safe, / and he is the fortress where I feel secure." (Ps 61:5–6, CEV)

Psalm: "Only God can save me, and I calmly wait for him. / God alone is the mighty rock that keeps me safe / and the fortress where I am secure. / God saves me and honors me. / He is that mighty rock where I find safety. / We humans are only a breath; none of us are truly great. / All of us together weigh less than a puff of air." (Ps 62:1–2, 7, 9, CEV)

Repeat Antiphon (above):

Reading: "No one knows the day or the time [when the Son of Man will return]. It is like what happens when a man goes away for a while and places his servants in charge of everything. He tells each of them what to do, and he orders the guard to keep alert. So be alert! You don't know when the master of the house will come back. But if he comes suddenly, don't let him find you asleep." (Mark 13:32, 34–35ab, 36, CEV)

Meditation/Journal: To what can you compare waiting for the return of the Son of Man? What it is like?

Day 4

Morning

Antiphon: "Shepherd . . . , you sit on your throne above the winged creatures. / Listen to [my] prayer and let your light shine . . . . Save [me] by your power." (Ps 80:1ac, 2b, CEV)

Psalm: "Our God, make [me] strong again! Smile on [me] and save [me]. / God All-Powerful, please do something! / Look down from heaven / and see what's happening . . . . / Put new life into [me] and [I] will worship you. / LORD God All-Powerful, / make [me] strong again! Smile on [me] and save [me]. (Ps 80:3, 18b–19, CEV)

Repeat Antiphon (above):

Reading: ". . . [W]hen our Lord comes with all his people, I pray that he will make your hearts pure and innocent in the sight of God the Father. Remember the instructions we gave you as followers of the Lord Jesus. God wants you to be holy . . . ." (1 Thess 3:13; 4:2–3a, CEV)

Activity: Choose a word or phrase from either Psalm 80 or 1 Thessalonians. What does the word mean to you? What does the word mean in its context? How does the word apply to you?

Evening Prayer

Antiphon: "[The LORD] is coming to judge / all people on earth with fairness and truth." (Ps 96:13, CEV)

Psalm: "Sing a new song to the LORD! / Everyone on this earth, sing praises to the LORD, sing and praise his name. / Day after day announce, 'The LORD has saved us!' / Tell every nation on earth, 'The LORD is wonderful and does marvelous things! / The LORD is great and deserves our greatest praise! / He is the only God worthy of our worship. Give honor and praise to the LORD, / whose power and beauty fill his holy temple.' / Announce to the nations, 'The LORD is King! / The world stands firm, never to be shaken, / and he will judge its people with fairness.'" (Ps 96:1–4, 6, 10, CEV)

Repeat Antiphon (above):

Reading: Jesus said: "When you see a fig tree or any other tree putting out leaves, you know that summer will soon come. So, when you see [strange things happening to the sun, moon, stars, roaring seas, and tides], you know that God's kingdom will soon be here." (Luke 21:29–31, CEV)

Meditation/Journal: What are the modern signs that God's kingdom is here? Make a list.

Day 5

Morning
Antiphon: "I come to you, LORD, / for protection. / Listen to my prayer and hurry to save me." (Ps 31:1a, 2a, CEV)
Psalm: "Be my mighty rock / and the fortress where I am safe [, LORD]. / You, LORD God, / are my mighty rock and the fortress where I am safe. / Lead me and guide me, / so that your name will be honored. / You are faithful, / and I trust you because you rescued me. / You are wonderful, and while everyone watches, / you store up blessings for all who honor and trust you. / I will praise you, LORD, for showing great kindness.... / All who trust the LORD be cheerful and strong." (Ps 31:2b–3, 5, 19, 21a, 24, CEV)
Repeat Antiphon (above):
Reading: "Leopards will lie down with young goats, / and wolves will rest with lambs. / Calves and lions will eat together / and be cared for by little children. / Cows and bears will share the same pasture; / their young will rest side by side. / Lions and oxen will both eat straw. / Little children will play near snake holes. Nothing harmful will take place on the LORD's holy mountain." (Isa 11:6–8a, 9a, CEV)
Meditation/Journal: When the LORD shows great kindness (Psalm 31), what happens to animals who are enemies of each other (Isaiah 11)?

Evening Prayer
Antiphon: "Sing a new song. Shout! Play beautiful music. / The LORD is truthful; he can be trusted." (Ps 33:3–4, CEV)
Psalm: "Praise the LORD with harps! / Use harps with ten strings to make music for him. / He loves justice and fairness, / and he is kind to everyone everywhere on earth. / The LORD made the heavens / and everything in them by his word. / He scooped up the ocean and stored the water. / Everyone in this world / should worship and honor the LORD! / As soon as he spoke the world was created; / at his command, the earth was formed. / ... [W]hat the LORD has planned / still stand forever. His thoughts never change." (Ps 33:2, 5–9, 11, CEV)
Repeat Antiphon (above):
Reading: "... I was told: These words are true and can be trusted. The Lord God controls the spirits of his prophets, and he is the one who sent his angel to show his servants what must happen right away. Remember, I am coming soon! God will bless everyone who pays attention to the

message of this book. I am coming soon! And when I come, I will reward everyone for what [he or she has] done." (Rev 22:6–7, 12, CEV)

Meditation/Journal: What word or phrase gets your attention in Psalm 33 or Revelation 22:6–7, 12? What does the word or phrase mean? How does the word or phrase make you aware of God's presence? How does it connect to, inspire, affect your life?

Day 6

Morning

Antiphon: "Now the kingdom of this world / belongs to our Lord and to his Chosen One! / And he will rule forever and ever!" (Rev 11:15, CEV)

Canticle: "Lord God All-Powerful, / you are and you were, and we thank you. / You used your great power and started ruling. / It is time for you to reward your servants the prophets / and all of your people / who honor your name, no matter who they are. / Our God has shown / his saving power, and his kingdom has come! / God's own Chosen One has shown his authority. / The heavens should rejoice, / together with everyone who lives there." (Rev 11:17, 18cd; 12:10ab, 12a, CEV)

Repeat Antiphon (above):

Reading: ". . . John the Baptist started preaching in the desert . . . . He said, 'Turn back to God! The kingdom of heaven will soon be here.' John wore clothes made of camel's hair. He had a leather strap around his waist and ate grasshoppers and wild honey." (Matt 3:1–2, 4, CEV)

Meditation/Journal: In what specific ways do you need to turn back to God? How do John the Baptist's clothes and food illustrate his message?

Evening Prayer

Antiphon: "Praise the Lord!" (Rev 19:3a, CEV)

Canticle: "Praise the Lord! / To our God belongs the glorious power to save, / because his judgments are honest and fair. / If you worship and fear our God, / give praise to him, no matter who you are. / Praise the Lord! / Our Lord God All-Powerful now rules as king. / So we will be glad and happy and give him praise. / The wedding day of the Lamb is here, and his bride is ready. / She will be given a wedding dress / made of pure and shining linen. / This linen stands for / the good things God's people have done." (Rev 19:1b–2a, 5, 6b–8, CEV)

Repeat Antiphon (above):

Reading: "Our God has said: / 'Encourage my people! Give them comfort. / Speak kindly . . . and announce: / Your slavery is past; your punishment is over. / I, the LORD, made you pay double for your sins.' Someone is shouting: / 'Clear a path in the desert! / Make a straight road for the LORD our God.'" (Isa 40:1–3, CEV)

Meditation/Journal: What paths are your clearing in your life this Advent? Explain. What roads are you straightening in your life this Advent? Explain.

Day 7

Morning
Antiphon: "Have pity, LORD! Help!" (Ps 30:10, CEV)
Psalm: "I will always praise the LORD. / With all my heart, I will praise the LORD. / Let all who are helpless, listen and be glad. / Honor the LORD with me! Celebrate his great name. / I asked the LORD for help, / and he saved me from all my fears. / Keep your eyes on the LORD! / You will shine like the sun and never blush with shame. / I was a nobody, but I prayed, / and the LORD saved me from all my troubles." (Ps 34:1–6, CEV)
Repeat Antiphon (above):
Reading: ". . . [D]on't forget that for the Lord one day is the same as a thousand years, and a thousand years is the same as one day. The Lord isn't slow about keeping his promises, as some people think he is. The day of the Lord's return will surprise us like a thief." (2 Pet 3:8–9a, 10a, CEV)
Activity: The author of the Second Letter of Peter compares the day of the Lord's return to a surprise visit by a thief. What positive comparisons can you make?

Evening Prayer
Antiphon: "I will always praise the LORD" (Ps 34:1, CEV)
Psalm: "Discover for yourself that the LORD is kind. / Come to him for protection, and you will be glad. / Honor the LORD! You are his special people. / No one who honors the LORD will ever be in need. / If you obey the LORD, / he will watch over you and answer your prayers. / When his people pray for help, / he listens and rescues them from their troubles. / The LORD is there to rescue / all who are discouraged and have given up hope." (Ps 34:8–9, 15, 17–18, CEV)
Repeat Antiphon (above):

Reading: "This is the good news about Jesus Christ, the Son of God. It began just as God had said in the book written by Isaiah the prophet, 'I am sending my messenger / to get the way ready for you. / In the desert, someone is shouting, "Get the road ready for the Lord! / Make a straight path for him."'" (Mark 1:1–3, CEV)

Meditation/Journal: What do you consider the good news about Jesus Christ, the Son of God, to be? In what specific ways is the road (path) in your desert ready for the coming of the Lord?

Day 8

Morning

Antiphon: "Your love is faithful, LORD, / and even the clouds in the sky can depend on you." (Ps 36:5, CEV)

Canticle: "In the future, the mountain / with the LORD's temple will be the highest of all. / It will reach above the hills; every nation will rush to it. / Many people will come and say, 'Let's go to the mountain / of the LORD God . . . and worship in his temple.' They will pound their swords / and their spears into rakes and shovels; they will never make war or attack one another. / People . . . . , let's live by the light of the LORD." (Isa 2:2–3a, 4b–5, CEV)

Repeat Antiphon (above):

Reading: ". . . [W]henever I [, Paul,] mention you in my prayers, it makes me happy. This is because you have taken part with me in spreading the good news from the first day you heard about it. God is the one who began this good work in you, and I am certain that he won't stop before it is complete on the day that Christ Jesus returns." (Phil 1:4–6, CEV)

Intercessions: Pray for all those with whom you share the good news. Thank God by naming all the good work he does in you.

Evening Prayer

Antiphon: "Your love is a treasure, [LORD,] / and everyone finds shelter in the shadow of your wings." (Ps 36:7, CEV)

Psalm: "You give your guests a feast in your house, [LORD,] / and you serve a tasty drink that flows like a river. / The life-giving fountain belongs to you, / and your light gives light . . . . / Our LORD, keep showing love to everyone who knows you, / and use your power to save all whose thoughts please you." (Ps 36:8–10, CEV)

Repeat Antiphon (above):

Reading: "Thirsty deserts will be glad; / barren lands will celebrate and blossom with flowers. / Deserts will bloom everywhere and sing joyful songs. / Everyone will see / the wonderful splendor of the LORD our God. / Here is a message for all / who are weak, trembling, and worried: /Cheer up! Don't be afraid. / Your God is coming . . . .'" (Isa 35:1–2ad, 3–4ab, CEV)

Meditation/Journal: In what specific ways are you like a thirsty desert? What is God doing to satisfy your thirsts?

Day 9

Morning
Antiphon: "Be patient and trust the LORD." (Ps 37:7a, CEV)
Canticle: "'I thank you, LORD! / I trust you to save me, / LORD God, and I won't be afraid. / My power and my strength / come from you, and you have saved me.' / With great joy, you people / will get water from the well of victory. / At that time you will say, / 'Our LORD, we are thankful, and we worship only you. / We will tell the nations / how glorious you are and what you have done. / Because of your wonderful deeds / we will sing your praises everywhere on earth.' Sing . . . . / Celebrate the greatness of the holy LORD . . . . / God is here to help you." (Isa 12:1a, 2–6, CEV)
Repeat Antiphon (above):
Reading: ". . . [B]e patient until the Lord returns. Think of farmers who wait patiently for the spring and summer rains to make their valuable crops grow. Be patient like those farmers and don't give up. The Lord will soon be here!" (Jas 5:7–8, CEV)
Meditation/Journal: In what specific ways are you patient? Where do you need to cultivate patience in your life? To what can you compare being patient?

Evening Prayer:
Antiphon: "If you do what the LORD wants, / he will make certain each step you take is sure." (Ps 37:23, CEV)
Psalm: "The LORD will hold your hand, / and if you stumble, you still won't fall. / As long as I can remember, / good people have never been left helpless, / and their children have never gone begging for food. / They gladly give and lend, / and their children turn out good. / The LORD loves justice, / and he won't ever desert his faithful people. / He always protects them . . . . / Words of wisdom come / when good people speak

for justice. / They remember God's teachings, / and they never take a wrong step." (Ps 37:24–26, 28abc, 30–31, CEV)
Repeat Antiphon (above):
Reading: "Always be joyful and never stop praying. Whatever happens, keep thanking God because of Jesus Christ. This is what God wants you to do. I [, Paul,] pray that God, who gives peace, will make you completely holy. And may your spirit, soul, and body be kept healthy and faultless until our Lord Jesus Christ returns." (1 Thess 4:16–18, 23, CEV)
Intercessions: Make a list of what has happened to you today, and thank God for each item on your list.

Day 10

Morning
Antiphon: "You are the LORD God! / Stay nearby and don't' desert me. / You are the one who saves me; Please hurry and help." (Ps 38:21–22, CEV)
Canticle: "'The LORD is [my] fortress, and he gives [me] victory. / The LORD gives perfect peace to those whose faith is firm. / So always trust the LORD / because he is forever our mighty rock.' / Our LORD, you always do right, / and you make the path smooth for those who obey you. / You are the one we trust to bring about justice; / above all else we want your name to be honored. Throughout the night, my heart searches for you, / because your decisions / show everyone on this earth how to live right. / You will give us peace, LORD, / because everything we have done was by your power." (Isa 26:1d, 3–4, 7–9, 12, CEV)
Repeat Antiphon (above):
Reading: ". . . [T]he Scriptures were written to teach and encourage us by giving us hope. God is the one who makes us patient and cheerful. I [, Paul,] pray that he will help you live at peace with each other, as you follow Christ. Then all of you together will praise God, the Father of our Lord Jesus Christ." (Rom 15:4–6, CEV)
Meditation/Journal: Specifically, what hope have you discovered during this Advent? In what specific ways has God made you patient and cheerful? Specifically, for what do you need to praise God this morning?

Evening Prayer
Antiphon: "Listen, LORD, to my prayer! / My eyes are flooded with tears, as I pray to you. / I am merely a stranger / visiting in your home as my ancestors did." (Ps 39:12, CEV)

Psalm: "I patiently waited, LORD, for you to hear my prayer. You let me stand on a rock with my feet firm, / and you gave me a new song, a song of praise to you. / Many will see this, / and they will honor and trust you, the LORD God. / You bless all of those who trust you, LORD . . . . / You, LORD God, have done many wonderful things, / and you have planned marvelous things for us. / No one is like you! / I would never be able to tell all you have done." (Ps 40:1a, 2b–4a, 5, CEV)

Repeat Antiphon (above):

Reading: "From Paul, a servant of Christ Jesus. God chose me to be an apostle, and he appointed me to preach the good news that he promised long ago by what his prophets said in the holy Scriptures. This good news is about his Son, our Lord Jesus Christ! As a human, he was from the family of David. But the Holy Spirit proved that Jesus is the powerful Son of God, because he was raised from death. Jesus was kind to me and chose me to be an apostle, so that people of all nations would obey and have faith. You are some of those people chosen by Jesus Christ." (Rom 1:1–6, CEV)

Activity: What word or phrase in either Psalm 40 or Romans 1:1–6 gets your attention? What does the word or phrase mean? How does the word or phrase make you aware of God's presence?

Day 11

Morning

Antiphon: "You, LORD, never fail to have pity on me; / your love and faithfulness always keep me secure." (Ps 40:11, CEV)

Canticle: "Please, LORD, be kind to [me]! [I] depend on you. / Make [me] strong each morning, / and come to save [me] when [I am] in trouble. / You, LORD, are above all others, and you live in the heavens. / You have brought justice and fairness; / you are the foundation on which [I] stand today. / You always save [me] and give true wisdom and knowledge. / Nothing means more to [me] than obeying you. / . . . [T]here will be rewards / for those who live right and tell the truth . . . ." (Isa 33:2, 5–6, 15ab, CEV)

Repeat Antiphon (above):

Reading: ". . . [A]n angel from the Lord came to [Joseph] in a dream. The angel said, 'Joseph, the baby that Mary will have is from the Holy Spirit. Go ahead and marry her. Then after her baby is born, name him Jesus, because he will save his people from their sins.'" (Matt 1:20–21, CEV)

SEASON OF ADVENT

Reflection: Hebrew names, like Jesus, usually indicate the function of the person named. Yeshua (Joshua in English translation) was a common name among Jews. It means *Yahweh is salvation*. Thus, Joshua, who takes over leadership of the Israelites after Moses, guides his people into the land promised by God in order to save them. The author of Matthew's Gospel hints at the meaning of the name, when he writes that Mary's baby is to be named Jesus (Joshua) because he will lead his people from sin to salvation. A good exercise is to find out the meaning of one's name; this can be done using a dictionary, a book of names, or using the internet.

Evening Prayer
Antiphon: The LORD says, "Everyone, both far and near, / come look at what I have done. See my mighty power!" (Isa 33:13, CEV)
Psalm: "Please show that you care / and come to my rescue [, LORD]. Hurry and help me! / Our LORD, let your worshipers rejoice and be glad. / They love you for saving them, / so let them always say, 'The LORD is wonderful!' / I am poor and needy, / but, LORD God, you care about me, / and you come to my rescue. Please hurry and help. (Ps 40:13, 16–17, CEV)
Repeat Antiphon (above):
Reading: "Praise God! He can make you strong by means of my good news, which is the message about Jesus Christ. For ages and ages this message was kept secret, but now at last it has been told. The eternal God commanded his prophets to write about the good news, so that all nations would obey and have faith. And now because of Jesus Christ, we can praise the only wise God forever! Amen! (Rom 16:25–27, CEV)
Activity: Using the information found in the Reflection (above) for Morning Prayer, what is the good news or message about Jesus Christ? What application do you make to yourself?

Day 12

Morning
Antiphon: "In my heart, I am thirsty / for you, the living God. When will I see your face? (Ps 42:2, CEV)
Canticle: "There is good news.... / Shout it as loud as you can from the highest mountain. / Don't be afraid to shout..., 'Your God is here!' / Look! The powerful LORD God / is coming to rule with his mighty arm.

/ . . . [A]nd he rewards his people. / The LORD cares for his [people], / just as shepherds care for their flocks. / He carries the lambs in his arms, / while gently leading the mother sheep. / Who compares with God? Is anything like him? / Don't you know? Haven't you heard? / Isn't it clear that God created the world? / God is the one who rules the whole earth, / and we that live here are merely insects. / He spread out the heavens / like a curtain or an open tent." (Isa 40:9–11, 18, 21–22, CEV)

Repeat Antiphon (above):

Reading: "Bethlehem Ephrathah, / you're one of the smallest towns in the nation of Judah. / But the LORD will choose / one of your people to rule the nation—/ someone whose family goes back to ancient times. / Like a shepherd taking care of his sheep, / this ruler will lead and care for his people / by the power and glorious name of the LORD his God." (Mic 5:2, 4abc, CEV)

Reflection: King David was born in Bethlehem, which was also known as Ephrathah, the name of David's clan. The town was so small that the citizens could put the entering and leaving sign on the same pole! During the latter part of the eighth century BCE, Judah was being threatened by the Assyrian expansion and in the sixth century BCE by the Babylonian empire, which eliminated David's line. The prophet Micah offers hope that the Davidic dynasty will be restored from family members who trace their heritage to ancient times. To emphasize Jesus' importance and to connect him to David, the author of Matthew's Gospel states that he was born in the village of Bethlehem (Matt 2:1), while the author of Luke's Gospel presents a story about Joseph and Mary making a trip to Bethlehem to register for a census (Luke 2:1–7). The earliest gospel, Mark, does not indicate where he was born; neither does the latest gospel, John. The place of his birth is theological, not historical.

Evening

Antiphon: "As a deer gets thirsty for steams of water, / I truly am thirsty for you, my God." (Ps 42:1, CEV)

Psalm: "Day and night my tears are my only food, / as everyone keeps asking, 'Where is your God?' / Why am I discouraged? / Why am I restless? I trust you! / And I will praise you again / because you help me, / and you are my God. Every day, you are kind, and at night / you give me a song / as my prayer to you, the living LORD God. / You are my mighty rock. Why am I discouraged? / Why am I restless? I trust you! / And I will

praise you again / because you help me, and you are my God." (Ps 42:3, 5–6a, 8–9a, 11, CEV)
Repeat Antiphon (above):
Reading: "When Christ came into the world, he said to God, 'Sacrifices and offerings are not what you want, / but you have given me my body.' The Christ said, 'And so, my God, I have come to do / what you want, as the Scriptures say.'" (Heb 10:5, 7, CEV)
Reflection: Using verses 6 and 8 from Psalm 40, the author of the misnamed letter to the Hebrews—a mixture of exhortation and argument, like a sermon or homily—presents Jesus replacing the covenant of animal sacrifices and offerings for sin with a new covenant of doing God's will. Jesus is the model of faithfulness to God. "So we are made holy because Christ obeyed God and offered himself once for all" (Heb 10:10, CEV), concludes the author of Hebrews. "By his one sacrifice he has forever set free from sin the people he brings to God" (Heb 10:14, CEV).

Day 13

Morning
Antiphon: "[I] boast about you, [my] God, and [I am] always grateful." (Ps 44:8, CEV)
Psalm: "I run to you for protection. / Send your light and your truth to guide me. / Let them lead me to your house on your sacred mountain. / Then I will worship / at your altar because you make me joyful. / You are my God, and I will praise you. / Yes, I will praise you as I play my harp. / Why am I discouraged? / Why am I restless? I trust you! / And I will praise you again / because you help me, and you are my God." (Ps 43:2a, 3–5, CEV)
Repeat Antiphon (above):
Reading: "Like a branch that sprouts from a stump, / someone from David's family will someday be king. / The Spirit of the LORD will be with him / to give him understanding, wisdom, and insight. / He will be powerful, / and he will know and honor the LORD. / His greatest joy will be to obey the LORD." (Isa 11:1–3a, CEV)
Reflection: The prophet Isaiah compares the Davidic heir in Babylonian captivity to a stump! The last kings of Judah, Jehoiachin and Zedekiah, had been captured by the Babylonian king, Nebuchadnezzar, and taken as prisoners to Babylon. Like the stumps of some trees after they are felled sprout a new branch, Isaiah offers hope to a defeated nation that

God will raise a new king from David's line. The expectation is that the new king will be guided by God's Spirit and not by politics, as were the previous two. Instead of playing national politics, Isaiah declares that the new king's greatest joy will be to obey God. Sad to say, but Isaiah's hope was never fulfilled. By declaring Joseph to be of David's line, as does the author of Matthew's Gospel (Matt 1:1–16, 18), the unknown author presents Jesus as the new king, even though Joseph is not Jesus' father (Matt 1:20).

Evening Prayer
Antiphon: "The holy God asks, 'Who compares with me? Is anyone my equal?'" (Isa 40:25, CEV)
Canticle: "Look at the evening sky! Who created the stars? / Who gave them each a name? The LORD is so powerful / that none of the stars [is] ever missing. / Don't you know? Haven't you heard? / The LORD is the eternal God, Creator of the earth. / He never gets weary or tired; / his wisdom cannot be measured. / The LORD gives strength to those who are weary. / . . . [T]hose who trust the LORD will find new strength. / They will be strong like eagles soaring upward on wings; / they will walk and run without getting tired." (Isa 40:26, 28–29, 31, CEV)
Repeat Antiphon (above):
Reading: "On this mountain the LORD All-Powerful / will prepare for all nations a feast of the finest foods. / Choice wines and the best meats will be served. / Here the LORD will strip away / the burial clothes that cover the nations. / The LORD All-Powerful / will destroy the power of death and wipe away all tears. / The LORD has spoken." (Isa 25:6–8, CEV)
Meditation/Journal: Which of the three images—God as creator of the stars, God as cook, God as destroyer of death—from Isaiah 40 and 25 above gets most of your attention? After spending time with the image, ask yourself: How does the image nurture my spirituality?

Day 14

Morning
Antiphon: "Tell the whole world to sing a new song to the LORD! (Isa 42:10, CEV)
Canticle: "Tell those who sail the ocean / and those who live far away to join in the praise. / Tell . . . everyone in the mountains to celebrate and sing. / Let them announce his praises everywhere. / . . . I, the

LORD, . . . will scream and groan like a woman giving birth. / I will lead the blind on roads they have never known; / I will guide them on paths they have never traveled. / Their road is dark and rough, but I will give light / to keep them from stumbling. / This is my solemn promise. / You people are deaf and blind, / but the LORD commands you to listen and to see. (Isa 42:11–12, 14, 16, 18, CEV)
Repeat Antiphon (above):
Reading: Jesus said: "Anyone who hears and obeys these teachings of mine is like a wise person who built a house on solid rock. Rain poured down, rivers flooded, and winds beat against that house. But it did not fail, because it was built on solid rock." (Matt 7:24–25, CEV)
Meditation/Journal: To what do you listen and see (Isa 42) after reading Jesus' words (Matt 7:24–25)?

Evening Prayer
Antiphon: "The LORD All-Powerful is with us." (Ps 46:11a, CEV)
Psalm: "God is our mighty fortress, / always ready to help in times of trouble. / And so, we won't be afraid! Let the earth tremble / and the mountains tumble into the deepest sea. / Let the ocean roar and foam, / and its raging waves shake the mountains. / A river and its streams bring joy to the city, / which is the sacred home of God Most High. / God is in that city, / and it won't be shaken. / He will help it at dawn. / Nations rage! Kingdoms fall! / But at the voice of God the earth itself melts. / The LORD All-Powerful is with us. Come! See the fearsome things the LORD has done on earth." (Ps 46:1–7a, 8, CEV)
Repeat Antiphon (above):
Reading: "As Jesus was walking along, two blind men began following him and shouting, 'Son of David, have pity on us!' He asked them, 'Do you believe I can make you well?' 'Yes, Lord,' they answered. Jesus touched their eyes and said, 'Because of your faith, you will be healed.'" (Matt 9:27, 28ab–29, CEV)
Meditation/Journal: What does the story about Jesus healing two blind men in Matthew's Gospel illustrate in the verses from Psalm 46 above?

Day 15

Morning
Antiphon: "Our God says, 'Calm down, and learn that I am God! / All nations on earth will honor me.'" (Ps 46:10, CEV)

Canticle: "I have taken hold of your hand [, Cyrus, says the LORD,] / to help you capture nations and remove kings from power. / City gates will open for you; not one will stay closed. / As I lead you, I will level mountains / and break the iron bars on bronze gates of cities. / I will give you treasures / hidden in dark and secret places. / Then you will know that I, / the LORD God, . . . have called you by name. / Cyrus, you don't even know me! / But I have called you by name and highly honored you . . . . I have made you strong, though you don't know me (Isa 45:1b–4, 5b, CEV)

Repeat Antiphon (above):

Reading: "In the first year that Cyrus was king of Persia, the LORD had Cyrus send a message to all parts of his kingdom. The message said: I am King Cyrus of Persia. The LORD God of heaven has made me the ruler of every nation on earth. He has also chosen me to build a temple for him in Jerusalem, which is in Judah. The LORD God will watch over any of his people who want to go back to Judah." (2 Chr 36:22a, 23, CEV)

Meditation/Journal: The LORD God worked through the non-Jewish King Cyrus. Which non-believer do you know who has been an instrument for God's work in your world? Explain.

Evening

Antiphon: "I am the LORD, the Creator, the holy God . . . ." (Isa 45:11a, CEV)

Canticle: "I created the world and covered it with people. / I stretched out the sky and filled it with stars. / I have done the right thing by placing Cyrus in power, / and I will make the roads easy for him to follow. / I am the LORD All-Powerful! Cyrus will rebuild my city and set my people free without being paid a thing. / I, the LORD have spoken. / . . . [Y]our God is a mystery, though he alone can save. . . . I, the LORD, / will always keep your safe and free from shame." (Isa 45:12–13, 15b, CEV)

Repeat Antiphon (above):

Reading: ". . . [I]n the first year that Cyrus was king of Persia, the LORD kept his promise by having Cyrus send this official message to all parts of his kingdom: I am King Cyrus of Persia. The LORD God of heaven . . . has made me the ruler of all nations on earth. And he has chosen me to build a temple for him in Jerusalem, which is in Judah. The LORD God will watch over and encourage any of his people who want to go back to Jerusalem and help build the temple." (Ezra 1:1–3, CEV)

Reflection: King Cyrus had ruled Persia since 549 BCE. He captured Babylon, where the Jews had been deported earlier, in 539 BCE. The account about Cyrus found in the beginning of the HB (OT) book of Ezra presents the foreign king as a servant of God. Indeed, according to Ezra, God chose him to rebuild his temple in Jerusalem which had been destroyed by King Nebuchadnezzar of Babylon. Cyrus, according to Ezra, was also aware that God would both protect and encourage the captives Cyrus was releasing to return to Jerusalem and rebuild the temple. The prophet Isaiah refers to Cyrus as the LORD's anointed (Isa 45:1); in other words, Isaiah states that God has chosen Cyrus, just like he chose King David and his heirs. The LORD anointed Cyrus, who did not know or worship God, to be his agent in freeing his people and rebuilding his temple!

Day 16

Morning

Antiphon: ". . . I, the LORD, / will always keep you safe and free from shame." (Isa 45:17, CEV)

Canticle: "The LORD alone is God! / He created the heavens and made a world / where people can live . . . . / The LORD alone is God; there are no others. / The LORD did not speak in a dark secret place . . . . The LORD speaks the truth . . . . / I am the only God! There are no others. / I bring about justice, and have the power to save. / I invite the whole world to turn to me and be saved. / I alone am God! No others are real. / I have made a solemn promise, one that won't be broken: / Everyone will bow down and worship me. / They will admit that I alone can bring about justice." (Isa 45:18, 19ac, 22–24a, CEV)

Repeat Antiphon (above):

Reading: "The LORD God is waiting / to show how kind he is and to have pity on you. / The LORD always does right; / he blesses those who trust him." (Isa 30:18, CEV)

Meditation/Journal: For what is God waiting to show you kindness and to have pity on you? How does Isaiah 45 above, illustrate trust in God?

Evening

Antiphon: "All of you nations, / clap your hands and shout joyful praises to God." (Ps 47:1, CEV)

Psalm: "The LORD Most High is fearsome, the ruler of all the earth. / God goes up to his throne / as people shout and trumpets blast. / Sing praises to God our King, / the ruler of all the earth! Praise God with songs. / God rules the nations from his sacred throne. / Their leaders come together / and are now the people of Abraham's God." (Ps 47:2a, 5–9a, CEV)

Repeat Antiphon (above):

Reading: "A good road will be there, / and it will be named 'God's Sacred Highway.' / It will be for God's people; no one unfit to worship God will walk on that road. / And no fools can travel on that highway. / No lions or other wild animals will come near that road; / only those the LORD has saved will travel there." (Isa 35:8–9, CEV)

Meditation/Journal: What road have you been traveling during Advent? Explain. What has gotten in the way of your travels (wild animals)?

Day 17

Morning

Antiphon: "I am the LORD, / and when the time comes, I will quickly do all this." (Isa 60:22bc, CEV)

Canticle: "The Spirit of the LORD God has taken control of me! / The LORD has chosen and sent me / to tell the oppressed the good news, / to heal the brokenhearted, / and to announce freedom for prisoners and captives. / This is the year when the LORD God / will show kindness to us . . . . / The LORD has sent me / to comfort those who mourn . . . . / He sent me to give them flowers in place of their sorrow, / olive oil in place of tears, / and joyous praise in place of broken hearts. / They will be called 'Trees of Justice,' planted by the LORD to honor his name. / I celebrate and shout / because of my LORD God. / His saving power and justice are the very clothes I wear. / They are more beautiful / than the jewelry worn by a bride or a groom. / The LORD will bring about / justice and praise in every nation on earth / like flowers blooming in a garden." (Isa 61:1–3, 10–11, CEV)

Repeat Antiphon (above):

Reading: "Our God has said: / 'Encourage my people! Give them comfort.' Someone is shouting: 'Clear a path in the desert! Make a straight road for the LORD our God. / Fill in the valleys; / flatten every hill and mountain. / Level the rough and rugged ground. / Then the glory of the LORD / will appear for all to see. / The LORD has promised this!'" (Isa 40:1, 3–5, CEV)

Activity: Choose a word from either Isaiah 61 (above) or Isaiah 40 (above). What does the word mean? How does the word apply to your spiritual life right now during Advent?

SEASON OF ADVENT

Evening

Antiphon: "You are my God. I worship you. In my heart, I long for you, / as I would long for a stream in a scorching desert." (Ps 63:1, CEV)

Psalm: "I have seen your power / and your glory [, God,] in the place of worship. / Your love means more / than life to me, and I praise you. / As long as I live, I will pray to you. / I will sing joyful praises / and be filled with excitement like a guest at a banquet. / I think about you before I go to sleep, / and my thoughts turn to you during the night. / You have helped me, / and I sing happy songs in the shadow of your wings. / I stay close to you, / and your powerful arm supports me." (Ps 63:2–8, CEV)

Repeat Antiphon (above):

Reading: "Be silent and listen . . . . Who controls human events? I do! I am the LORD. / I was there at the beginning; I will be there at the end. Don't be afraid. I am with you. / Don't tremble with fear. I am your God. I will make you strong, / as I protect you with my arm and give you victories. I am the LORD your God. / I am holding your hand, so don't be afraid. / I am here to help you." (Isa 41:1a, 4bc, 10, 13, CEV)

Meditation/Journal: What power and glory of God have you witnessed during your life? In what specific situations of your life have you experienced God holding your hand? Explain.

Day 18

Morning

Antiphon: "Here is what the LORD has said for all the earth to hear: / 'Soon I will come to save . . . , and to reward you.'" (Isa 62:11, CEV)

Canticle: "Jerusalem, I will speak up for your good. / I will never be silent / till you are safe and secure, sparkling like a flame. / Your great victory will be seen by every nation and king; / the LORD will even give you a new name. / You will be a glorious crown, / a royal headband, / for the LORD your God. / You will please the LORD; your country will be his bride. / Your people will take the land, / just as a young man takes a bride. / The LORD will be pleased because of you, / just as a husband is pleased with his bride. / Jerusalem, on your walls / I have stationed guards, whose duty it is / to speak out day and night without resting. / They must remind the LORD and not let him rest / till he makes Jerusalem strong and famous everywhere." (Isa 62:1–3, 4b–7, CEV)

Repeat Antiphon (above):

Reading: Jesus said: "What sort of person did you go out into the desert to see? What did you really go out to see? Was he a prophet? He certainly was. I tell you that he was more than a prophet. I tell you that no one ever born on this earth is greater than John the Baptist. But whoever is least in the kingdom of heaven is greater than John." (Matt 11:7b, 9, 11, CEV)
Meditation/Journal: In what specific ways does John the Baptist make you aware of God's presence?

Evening
Antiphon: "Pray for [God's] blessings to continue / and for everyone on earth to worship our God." (Ps 67:7, CEV)
Psalm: "Our God, be kind and bless us! Be pleased and smile. / Then everyone on earth will learn to follow you, / and all nations will see your power to save us. / Make everyone praise you and shout your praises. / Let the nations celebrate with joyful songs, / because you judge fairly and guide all nations. / Make everyone praise you and shout your praises. / Our God has blessed the earth . . . ." (Ps 67:1–6, CEV)
Repeat Antiphon (above):
Reading: The LORD said: "Today I am doing something new, / something you cannot say you have heard before. / I, the LORD, am true to myself . . . . / I alone am the LORD, the first and the last. / Come closer and listen! / I have never kept secret the things I have said, / and I was here before time began." (Isa 48:7, 9a, 12b, 16, CEV)
Activity: During this Advent, what newness has God been doing in your life? Recite or write a psalm of praise to God for that newness.

Day 19

Morning
Antiphon: "Jerusalem is like a mother/ who gave birth to her children as soon as she was in labor." (Isa 66:8cd, CEV)
Canticle: "If you love Jerusalem, celebrate and shout! / If you were in sorrow / because of the city, you can now be glad. / She will nurse and comfort you, / just like your own mother, until you are satisfied. / You will fully enjoy her wonderful glory. / The LORD has promised: 'I will flood Jerusalem / with the wealth of nations and make the city prosper. / Zion will nurse you at her breast, / carry you in her arms, and hold you in her lap. / I will comfort you there / like a mother comforting her child.' / When you see this happen, you will celebrate; / your strength will return

faster than grass can sprout. / Then everyone will know / that the LORD is present with his servants . . . ." (Isa 66:10–14d, CEV)
Repeat Antiphon (above):
Reading: "The disciples asked Jesus, 'Don't the teachers of the Law of Moses say that Elijah must come before the Messiah does?' Jesus told them, 'Elijah certainly will come and get everything ready. In fact, he has already come. But the people did not recognize him and treated him just as they wanted to.' Then the disciples understood that Jesus was talking to them about John the Baptist." (Matt 17:10–12ab, 13, CEV)
Reflection: In the HB (OT), the prophet Malachi ends his book with the LORD saying that the day of judgment will certainly come. "I, the LORD, promise to send the prophet Elijah before that great and terrible day comes" (Mal 4:5). In Christian tradition, that verse from Malachi came to be understood as a prediction of the coming of the Messiah. The author of Matthew's Gospel, written for a Jewish audience, uses it uniquely to convince his readers that Jesus of Nazareth is the Messiah. He does that by having his Jesus character equate John the Baptist with Elijah. In other words, according to the Matthean Jesus, John the Baptist was Elijah, who returned to herald the arrival of the Messiah (Anointed).
Meditation/Journal: How is God a mother to you?

Evening
Antiphon: "[God,] . . . let your people be happy and celebrate because of you." (Ps 68:3, CEV)
Psalm: "Our God, you are the one / who rides on the clouds, and we praise you. / Your name is the LORD, / and we celebrate as we worship you. / Our God, from your sacred home / you take care of orphans and protect widows. / You find families for those who are lonely. / You set prisoners free and let them prosper . . . . / You set your people free, / and you led them through the desert. / God . . . , / the earth trembled and rain poured down. / You alone are the God who rules from Mount Sinai. / When your land was thirsty, / you sent showers to refresh it. / Your people settled there, / and you were generous to everyone in need." (Ps 68:4–6a, 7–10, CEV)
Repeat Antiphon (above):
Reading: "Jesus said: I will tell you a story about a man who had two sons. The father went to the older son and said, 'Go work in the vineyard today!' His son told him that he would not do it, but later he changed his mind and went. The man then told his younger son to go work in the

vineyard. The boy said he would, but he didn't go. Which one of the sons obeyed his father?" (Matt 21: 28ac, 29–31a, CEV)

Meditation/Journal: In what specific ways are you like (or have you been like) the older son? In what specific ways are you like (or have you been like) the younger son?

Day 20

Morning

Antiphon: "Come and rescue your people, LORD!" (Jer 31:7b CEV)

Canticle: "I, the LORD, will bring / my people back from . . . everywhere . . . on earth. / The blind and the lame will be there. / Expectant mothers and women about to give birth / will come and be part of that great crowd. / They will weep and pray as I bring them home. / I will lead them to streams of water. / They will walk on a level road and not stumble. / I am a father to . . . my favorite children. / I will protect them like a shepherd guarding a flock. / My people will come . . . and celebrate; / their faces will glow because of my blessings. / Young women and young men, together with the elderly, will celebrate and dance, / because I will comfort them / and turn their sorrow into happiness." (Jer 31:8–9, 10c, 12ab, 13, CEV)

Repeat Antiphon (above):

Reading: "Balaam was sure that the LORD would tell him to bless Israel. . . . Just then, God's Spirit took control of him, and Balaam said: ' . . . [M]y words are true, so listen to my message! / It comes from the LORD, the God All-powerful. / I bowed down to him and saw a vision of Israel. / People of Israel, your camp is lovely. Your king will rule with power / and be a [great] king . . . . But someday, a king of Israel will appear like a star.'" (Num 24:1a, 2b–5, 7b, 17b, CEV)

Reflection: In the HB (OT) book of Numbers, King Balak of Moab sees the Israelites conquering the land and hires Balaam, a known curser, to come and curse them. In the ancient world, a curse meant that Israel would fail to conquer the people who lived in the land. God, however, has a plan. Once Balaam arrives at Israel's camp, instead of cursing the Israelites, God inspires him to bless them four times! Every time Balaam opens his mouth to utter a curse, he ends up pronouncing a blessing of prosperity instead (Num 22:1—24:25). In Balaam's fourth blessing, he declares that a king of Israel will appear like a star. Those words of Balaam caught the attention of the author of Matthew's Gospel. Uniquely, he presents a story about wise men (magi) from the east (Gentiles) following a star and seeking a newborn king of the Jews (Matt 2:1–12). The wise men follow the star to the house where Mary and Jesus are living; after presenting gifts to the infant, they leave, and they are never heard of again. In other words, the child Jesus is the star, according to the author of Matthew's Gospel, whom Balaam had foreseen.

Evening

Antiphon: "[I] praise you, Lord God!" (Ps 68:19a, CEV)

Psalm: "You treat [me] with kindness day after day, and you rescue [me]. / You always protect [me] and save [me] from death. / [My] God, show your strength! Show [me] once again. / Now sing praises to God! / Every kingdom on earth, sing to the Lord! / Praise the one who rides across the ancient skies; / listen as he speaks with a mighty voice. / Tell about God's power! (Ps 68:19–20, 28, 32–34a, CEV)

Repeat Antiphon (above):

Reading: "John [the Baptist's] followers told John everything that was being said about Jesus. So he sent two of them to ask the Lord, 'Are you the one we should be look for? Or must we wait for someone else?' Jesus said to the messengers sent by John, 'Go and tell John what you have seen and heard. Blind people are now able to see, and the lame can walk. People who have leprosy are being healed, and the deaf can now hear. The dead are raised to life, and the poor are hearing the good news." (Luke 7:18–19, 22, CEV)

Reflection: In the earliest days of what came to be known as Christianity, there arose a controversy about who was greater: John the Baptist or Jesus? If John baptized Jesus as both the author of Mark's Gospel (1:9–11) and the author of Matthew's Gospel (3:13–17) state, then John must be greater! Both the author of Matthew's Gospel (11:1–19) and the author of Luke's Gospel (7:18–35) answer that question by portraying their Jesus character as superior to John. Uniquely, Matthew portrays John baptizing Jesus reluctantly (Matt 3:14–15). Earlier in his work, Luke had begun to answer the question by presenting John in jail (Luke 3:20) before Jesus was baptized (Luke 3:21–22); this unique scene left no doubt as to who was greater! Then, Luke—following the same source used by Matthew, called Q by biblical scholars—presents Jesus healing the blind, the lame, the diseased, raising the dead, and preaching the good news to the poor as proof that he is greater than John. Today, for most Christians the question is mute!

Day 21

Morning
Antiphon: "Save me, God!" (Ps 69:1a, CEV)
Psalm: ". . . I pray to you, LORD. So when the time is right, / answer me and help me with your wonderful love. / Answer me, LORD! You are kind and good. / Pay attention to me! You are truly merciful. / Don't turn away from me. / I am your servant, and I am in trouble. / Please hurry and help! / Come and save me . . . . / Protect me, God, and keep me safe! / I will praise the LORD God / with a song and a thankful heart. / This will please the LORD . . . ." (Ps 69:13, 16–18, 29b–31a, CEV)
Repeat Antiphon (above):
Reading: Jacob (Israel) said: "Judah, you will be praised by your brothers; / they will bow down to you . . . . / My son, you are a lion ready to eat your victim! / You are terribly fierce; no one will bother you. / You will have power and rule / until nations obey you and come bringing gifts." (Gen 49:8–10, CEV)
Reflection: King David was a descendant of the tribe of Judah. According to Matthew's Gospel, Jesus was a descendant of Judah and David. The author of the HB (OT) book of Genesis, written after David's reign, reflects kingly royalty in words attributed to Jacob (Israel), son of Isaac, son of Abraham. It is easy to predict that Judah will become a line of kings, because it had already happened, when Genesis was written.

Evening Prayer:
Antiphon: "Save me, LORD God! Hurry and help." (Ps 70:1, CEV)
Psalm: "Let your worshipers celebrate and be glad because of you [, God]. / They love your saving power, / so let them always say, 'God is wonderful!' / I am poor and needy, / but you, the LORD God, care about me. / You are the one who saves me. Please hurry and help!" (Ps 70:4–5, CEV)
Repeat Antiphon (above):
Reading: "Jesus Christ came from the family of King David and also from the family of Abraham. And this is a list of his ancestors. From Abraham to King David, his ancestors were: Abraham, Isaac, Jacob, Judah . . . ; Obed (his mother was Ruth), Jesse, and King David. . . . Jacob, and Joseph, the husband of Mary, the mother of Jesus, who is called the Messiah." (Matt 1:1–2, 5–6, 16, CEV)
Meditation/Journal: Why do you think it is important for the author of Matthew's Gospel to present Jesus' lineage going back to Abraham and David?

Day 22

Morning

Antiphon: "I run to you, LORD, / for protection. Don't disappoint me." (Ps 71:1, CEV)

Psalm: "[LORD, y]ou do what is right, so come to my rescue. / Listen to my prayer and keep me safe. / Be my mighty rock, the place / where I can always run for protection. / Save me by your command! / You are my mighty rock and my fortress. / Come and save me, LORD God.... I depend on you, / and I have trusted you since I was young. / I have relied on you from the day I was born. / You brought me safely / through birth, and I always praise you. / ... [Y]ou are my mighty protector, / and I praise and honor you all day long. / Don't throw me aside when I am old; / don't desert me when my strength is gone." (Ps 71:2–4a, 5–6, 7b–9, CEV)

Repeat Antiphon (above):

Reading: The LORD said: "Someday I will appoint / an honest king from the family of David, / a king who will be wise and rule with justice. / As long as he is king, / Israel will have peace, and Judah will be safe. / The name of this king will be 'The LORD Gives Justice.'" (Jer 23:5–6, CEV)

Meditation/Journal: For what do you praise God, like the author of Psalm 71? How do you interpret the above words of the prophet Jeremiah?

Evening

Antiphon: "Come closer, GOD! Please hurry and help." (Ps 71:12, CEV)

Psalm: "I will never give up hope or stop praising you [, God]. / All day long I will tell / the wonderful things you do to save your people. / But you have done much more than I could possibly know. / I will praise you, LORD God, / for your mighty deeds and your power to save. / You have taught me since I was a child, / and I never stop telling about your marvelous deeds. / Don't leave me when I am old and my hair turns gray. / Let me tell future generations about your mighty power. / Your deeds of kindness / are known in the heavens. No one is like you!" (Ps 71:14–19, CEV)

Repeat Antiphon (above):

Reading: "This is how Jesus Christ was born. A young woman named Mary was engaged to Joseph from King David's family. But before they were married, she learned that she was going to have a baby by God's Holy Spirit." (Matt 1:18, CEV)

Meditation/Journal: What parallels can you draw from the portion of Psalm 71 above for Morning Prayer and the portion of Psalm 71 above for Evening Prayer? What connection do you see between Psalm 71 and the passage from Matthew's Gospel?

Day 23

Morning

Antiphon: "Heaven and earth will praise our God, / and so will the oceans and everything in them." (Ps 70:34, CEV)

Psalm: "I will praise you, God, / the Holy One . . . . You are faithful. / I will play the harp and sing your praises. / You have rescued me! I will celebrate and shout, / singing praises to you with all my heart. / All day long I will announce your power to save." (Ps 71:22–24a, CEV)

Repeat Antiphon (above):

Reading: ". . . [A]n angel from the LORD appeared to [Manoah's wife] and said: You have never been able to have any children, but very soon you will be pregnant and have a son. He will belong to God from the day he is born. . . . Manoah's wife did give birth to a son, and she named him Samson. As the boy grew, the LORD blessed him." (Judg 13:2b–3, 24, CEV)

Intercessions: For women who are not able to have children, I pray to you, O LORD. For pregnant women to have safe deliveries, I pray to you, O LORD. For children who need your blessing, I pray to you, O LORD.

Evening

Antiphon: "Always pray for the [leader] and praise him (her) each day." (Ps 72:15b, CEV)

Psalm: "Please help the [leader] / to be honest and fair just like you, our God. / Let him (her) be honest and fair / with all your people, especially the poor. / Let peace and justice rule every mountain and hill. / Let the [leader] defend the poor, / rescue the homeless and crush everyone who hurts them. / Let the [leader] live forever like the sun and the moon. / Let him (her) be as helpful as rain / that refreshes the meadows and the ground. / Let the [leader] be fair with everyone, / and let there be peace until the moon falls from the sky." (Ps 72:1–7, CEV)

Repeat Antiphon (above):

Reading: "Both [Zechariah and Elizabth] were good people and pleased the Lord God by obeying all that he had commanded. But they did not have children. Elizabeth could not have any, and both Zechariah and Elizabth were already old. . . . [A]n angel from the Lord appeared to

SEASON OF ADVENT

Zechariah.... [T]he angel told him: Your wife Elizabeth will have a son and you must name him John." (Luke 1:6–7, 12–13, CEV)
Meditation/Journal: After rereading the passage from the HB (OT) book of Judges from Morning Prayer above, where do you think the author of Luke's Gospel found inspiration for his story about Zechariah and Elizabeth? What do both accounts illustrate?

Day 24

Morning
Antiphon: "Shout praises to the LORD, everyone on this earth. / Be joyful and sing / as you come in to worship the LORD!" (Ps 100:1–2, CEV)
Psalm: ". . . [The leader] rescues the homeless when they cry out, / and he (she) helps everyone who is poor and in need. / The [leader] has pity / on the weak and the helpless and protects those in need. / He (She) cares when they hurt, / and he (she) saves them from cruel and violent deaths. / Long live the [leader]! Let the people in the cities prosper like wild flowers. / May the glory of the [leader] / shine brightly forever like the sun in the sky. / Let him (her) make nations prosper and learn to praise him. / LORD God, . . . we praise you. Only you can work miracles. / We will always praise your glorious name. / Let your glory be seen / everywhere on earth. Amen and amen." (Ps 72:12–15a, 16b–19, CEV)
Repeat Antiphon (above):
Reading: ". . . [T]he LORD God spoke to King Ahaz. This time he said, 'Ask me for proof that my promise will come true.' 'No, LORD,' Ahaz answered. 'I won't test you!' Then I [, Isaiah,] said: [T]he LORD will still give you proof. A virgin is pregnant; she will have a son and will name him Immanuel." (Isa 7:10–11a, 12–13a, 14, CEV)
Activity: From a Bible, read Isaiah 7:1–25. What is the context for the above passage? How does knowing the context change the meaning of the passage?

Evening
Antiphon: "God is truly good . . . / to everyone with a pure heart." (Ps 73:1, CEV)
Psalm: "It was hard for me to understand . . . . / Then I went to [God's] temple, and there I understood / what will happen . . . . Once I was bitter and brokenhearted. / I was stupid and ignorant / and I treated you as a wild animal would. / But I never really left you, and you hold my right

hand. / Your advice has been my guide, / and later you will welcome me in glory. / In heaven I have only you, / and on this earth you are all I want. / My body and mind may fail, / but you are my strength and my choice forever. / It is good for me to be near you. / I choose you as my protector, / and I will tell about your wonderful deeds." (Ps 73:16–17, 21–26, 28, CEV)

Repeat Antiphon (above):

Reading: ". . . God sent the angel Gabriel to the town of Nazareth in Galilee with a message for a virgin named Mary. . . . [T]he angel told Mary: God is pleased with you, and you will have a son. His name will be Jesus. He will be great and will be called the Son of God Most High." (Luke 1:26–27, 30–32a, CEV)

Reflection: What connection do you find between the reading above from the prophet Isaiah for Morning Prayer and the reading above from Luke's Gospel for Evening Prayer?

Day 25

Morning

Antiphon: "Our God, we thank you for being so near to us! Everyone celebrates your wonderful deeds." (Ps 75:1, CEV)

Psalm: "You, our God, / are famous . . . and honored. / You are more glorious than the eternal mountains. / From heaven you announce your decisions as judge! / And all who live on this earth were terrified and silent / when you took over as judge, / ready to rescue everyone in need. / Everyone, make your promises / to the LORD your God and do what you promise. / I pray to you, Lord God, and beg you to listen. . . . I search for you. / And at night I tirelessly / lift my hands in prayer . . . ." (Pss 76:1, 4, 8–9, 11ab, 78:1–2, CEV)

Repeat Antiphon (above):

Reading: "Everyone . . . / celebrate and shout with all your heart! / Your LORD . . . stands at your side; / you don't have to worry about any more troubles. . . . / [T]he time is coming when it will be said to you: / 'Don't be discouraged or grow weak from fear! The LORD your God / wins victory after victory and is always with you. / He celebrates and sings because of you, / and he will refresh your life with his love.' / The LORD has promised; / Your sorrow has ended, and you can celebrate." (Zeph 3:14, 15c–18, CEV)

Meditation/Journal: In the above reading, what word gets your attention? What does it mean to you? How does it make you aware of God's presence?

Evening
Antiphon: "I will sing to you, LORD! / I will celebrate your kindness and your justice." (Ps 101:1, CEV)
Psalm: "I pray to you, LORD! Please listen. . . . / Pay attention to my prayer and quickly give an answer. / My days disappear like smoke, / and my bones are burning as though in a furnace. / I am wasting away like grass, and my appetite is gone. / My groaning never stops, / and my bones can be seen through my skin. / I am like a lonely owl in the desert / or a restless sparrow alone on a roof. / My life fades like a shadow / at the end of day and withers like grass. / You will live forever! / Years mean nothing to you. . . . / You are always the same. Years cannot change you." (Ps 102:1, 2b–7, 11, 24, 27, CEV)
Repeat Antiphon (above):
Reading: ". . . Mary hurried to a town in the hill country of Judea. She went into Zechariah's home, where she greeted Elizabeth. When Elizabeth heard Mary's greeting, her baby moved within her. The Holy Spirit came upon Elizabeth. Then in a loud voice she said to Mary: God has blessed you more than any other woman. He has also blessed the child you will have. Why should the mother of my Lord come to me?" (Luke 1:39–43, CEV)
Meditation/Journal: What connection do you find between evening and the experience of the psalmist in Psalm 102 above? What experience in your life does the psalmist illustrate? What parallel do you find between the reading for Morning Prayer and the reading for Evening Prayer? Explain.

Day 26

Morning
Antiphon: "With all my heart I praise the LORD, / and with all that I am I praise his holy name!" (Ps 103:1, CEV)
Canticle: "You make me strong and happy, LORD. / You rescued me. / Now I can be glad and laugh . . . . / No other god is like you. / We're safer with you than on a high mountain. / Nothing is hidden from the LORD, and he judges what we do. / Our LORD, . . . you give strength to everyone

who stumbles. / . . . [Y]ou give the hungry more than enough to eat. / A woman did not have a child, and you gave her seven. / You take away life, and you give life. / You send people down / to the world of the dead and bring them back again. / Our LORD, you are the one who makes us rich or poor." (1 Sam 2:1–2, 3b, 4b, 5cd, 6–7a, CEV)

Repeat Antiphon (above):

Reading: ". . . Hannah and Elkanah took Samuel to the LORD's house. They brought along a three-year-old bull, a twenty-pound sack of flour, and a clay jar full of wine. Hannah and Elkanah offered the bull as a sacrifice, then brought the little boy to Eli. 'Sir,' Hannah said, 'Here [is the child for whom I asked the LORD]. Now I am giving him to the LORD, and he will be the LORD's servant for as long as he lives.'" (1 Sam 1:24–28, CEV)

Reflection: In biblical understanding, it was the LORD who opened the womb; if the woman was barren, it was because God had not granted her request for a child. This biblical theme is found in the HB (OT) First Book of Samuel. Hannah, Elkanah's wife, is barren, but while making a trip to Shilo, where the ark was kept, Hannah prays for a child. After they go home, she conceives a son, whom they name Samuel, which means *name of God*. Samuel is the last of the judges, a prophet, a priest, and the anointer of Saul and David as kings of Israel.

Evening

Antiphon: "With all my heart I praise the LORD! / I will never forget how kind he has been." (Ps 103:2, CEV)

Canticle: "With all my heart I praise the Lord, / and I am glad because of God my Savior. / God cares for me, his humble servant. / From now on, / all people will say God has blessed me. / God All-Powerful has done / great things for me, and his name is holy. / He always shows mercy / to everyone who worships him. / God . . . / is always merciful to his people. / The Lord made this promise to our ancestors, / to Abraham and his family forever!" (Luke 1:46–50, 54–55, CEV)

Repeat Antiphon (above):

Reading: The angel said to Mary, "The Holy Spirit will come down to you, and God's power will come over you. So your child will be called the holy Son of God." (Luke 1:35, CEV)

Activity: Make a list of all the kindnesses (blessings) God has given to you. After you finish the list, recite them to yourself, and after each one, say, "With all my heart I praise you, LORD."

Day 27

Morning
Antiphon: "With all my heart I praise the LORD!" (Ps 103:22c, CEV)
Psalm: "Each day that we live, [the LORD] provides for our needs / and gives us the strength of a young eagle. The LORD is merciful! / He is kind and patient, and his love never fails. / How great is God's love for all who worship him? / Greater than the distance between heaven and earth! / Just as parents are kind to their children, / the LORD is kind to all who worship him, / because he knows we are made of dust. / We humans are like grass / or wild flowers that quickly bloom. / But a scorching wind blows, / and they quickly wither to be forever forgotten. / The LORD is always kind to those who worship him, / and he keeps his promises / to their descendants who faithfully obey him." (Ps 103:5, 8, 11, 13–18, CEV)
Repeat Antiphon (above):
Reading: "When Elizabeth's son was born, her neighbors and relatives heard how kind the Lord had been to her, and they too were glad.... Elizabeth said, '... His name is John.' Everyone was amazed. Everyone who heard about this wondered what this child would grow up to be. They knew that the Lord was with him." (Luke 1:57–58, 60, 63b, 66, CEV)
Meditation/Journal: How does the reading above illustrate the words of Psalm 103 above?

Evening
Antiphon: "Our LORD, let the heavens now praise your miracles, / and let all of your angels praise your faithfulness." (Ps 89:5, CEV)
Psalm: "None who live in the heavens can compare with you. / You are LORD God All-Powerful! / No one is as loving and faithful as you are. / The heavens and the earth belong to you. / And so does the world with all its people / because you created them and everything else. / You are strong and mighty! / Your kingdom is ruled by justice and faithfulness / with love and faithfulness leading the way." (Ps 89:6, 8, 11–12a, 13–14, CEV)
Repeat Antiphon (above):
Reading: "I, the LORD All-Powerful, / will send my messenger to prepare the way for me / Then suddenly the Lord / you are looking for will appear in his temple. / The messenger you desire / is coming with my promise, and he is on his way." (Mal 3:1, CEV)
Meditation/Journal: How does the above reading from the HB (OT) prophet Malachi illustrate Psalm 89? Who is the messenger?

Day 28

Morning

Antiphon: "Our LORD, you bless those who join in the festival / and walk in the brightness of your presence." (Ps 89:15, CEV)

Psalm: "We are happy all day because of you [, LORD], / and your saving power brings honor to us. / Your own glorious power makes us strong, / and because of your kindness, our strength increases. / Our LORD . . . , the Holy One . . . , you are truly our shield. / Remember, life is short! / Our LORD, where is the love you have always shown . . . ? / Remember your servant, Lord! / I am your chosen one . . . . / Our LORD, we praise you forever. Amen and amen." (Ps 89:16–18, 47a, 49a, 50a, 51a, 52, CEV)

Repeat Antiphon (above):

Reading: "The Holy Spirit came upon Zechariah, and he began to speak: Praise the Lord . . . . / He has come to save his people. / Our God has given us a mighty Savior . . . . / Long ago the Lord promised / by the words of his holy prophets / to save us . . . . / Then we could serve him without fear, / by being holy and good as long as we live." (Luke 1:67–69a, 70–71a 74b–75, CEV)

Meditation/Journal: In what specific ways have you experienced God's salvation? How have each of those experiences of salvation made you stronger spiritually?

Evening

Antiphon: "God has set up his kingdom / in heaven, and he rules the whole creation." (Ps 103:19, CEV)

Psalm: "Our LORD, I will sing of your love forever. / Everyone yet to be born / will hear me praise your faithfulness. / I will tell them, 'God's love can always be trusted, / and his faithfulness lasts as long as the heavens.' / You said, 'David, my servant, is my chosen one, / and this is the agreement I made with him: / David, one of your descendants will always be king. / I have chosen David as my first-born son, / and he will be the ruler of all kings on earth. / My love for him will last, / and my agreement with him will never be broken.'" (Ps 89:1–4, 27–28, CEV)

Repeat Antiphon (above):

Reading: "That night, the LORD told Nathan [the prophet] to go to David and give him this message: Now I promise that you and your descendants will be kings. I'll choose one of your sons to be king when you reach the end of your life and are buried in the tomb of your ancestors. I'll make him a strong ruler . . . ." (2 Sam 7:4–5a, 11b–12, CEV)

Meditation/Journal: How is God's love (Psalm 89) manifested in his promise to David (2 Samuel)? How is God's love manifested in your life?

5

Season of Christmas

Season of Christmas Introduction

The Season of Christmas begins with Christmas Day, December 25, and lasts from two to three weeks, depending on what day of the week Christmas falls. The Christmas Season ends with the feast of the Baptism of the Lord; the feast brings the Season of Christmas to an end in 2026 on January 11; in 2027 on January 10; in 2028 on January 9; in 2029 on January 8; in 2030 on January 13; in 2031 on January 12; in 2032 on January 11; in 2033 on January 9; in 2034 on January 9; in 2035 on January 8; in 2036 on January 13; in 2037 on January 11; in 2038 on January 10; in 2039 on January 9. Depending on the calendar year, the feast of the Baptism of the Lord may fall on a Monday (instead of a Sunday) and bring the Season of Christmas to an end. If there is no Sunday between December 25 and January 1, the Feast of the Holy Family is celebrated on December 30; see Day 6b. If the Feast of the Holy Family falls on a Sunday between December 25 and January 1, other than December 30, then on December 30 use Day 6a.

Other books by Mark G. Boyer that follow the same structure of Morning Prayer and Evening Prayer that can be used—in substitution for what is provided here—during the Season of Christmas include:

Very Short Reflections—for Advent and Christmas, Lent and Easter, Ordinary Time, and Saints—through the Liturgical Year (Eugene, OR: Wipf & Stock, 2020); *Names for Jesus: Reflections for Advent and Christmas* (Eugene, OR: Wipf & Stock, 2017); and *Seasons of Biblical Spirituality: Spring, Summer, Autumn, and Winter* (Eugene, OR: Resource Publications, 2023).

Antiphons, Psalms, and Readings for the Season of Christmas are taken from *The Contemporary English Version* (CEV) (Nashville, TN: Thomas Nelson Publishers, 1995).

Days in the Season of Christmas

Day 1: December 25

Christmas
Morning
Antiphon: "This very day in King David's hometown a Savior was born for you. He is Christ the Lord." (Luke 2:11, CEV)
Psalm: "Sing a new song to the LORD! / Everyone on this earth, sing praises to the LORD, sing and praise his name. / Tell everyone of every nation, / 'Praise the glorious power of the LORD. / He is wonderful! Praise him / and bring an offering into his temple. / Everyone on earth, now tremble / and worship the LORD, majestic and holy.' / Tell the heavens and the earth to be glad and celebrate! / Command the ocean to roar with all of its creatures / and the fields to rejoice with all of their crops. / Then every tree in the forest / will sing joyful songs to the LORD." (Ps 96:1–2a, 7–9, 11–13a, CEV)
Repeat Antiphon (above):
Reading: "A child has been born for us. / We have been given a son who will be our ruler. / His names will be / Wonderful Advisor and Mighty God, / Eternal Father and Prince of Peace. / His power will never end; peace will last forever. / He will rule David's kingdom and make it grow strong. / He will always rule with honesty and justice. / The LORD All-Powerful / will make certain that all this is done." (Isa 9:6–7, CEV)
Reflection: While the above text is applied to the birth of Jesus on Christmas Day, in its historical context it refers to King Hezekiah, successor to King Ahaz. Isaiah's words are part of a coronation hymn, which celebrates the presence of a new king, who would restore the honor, fame, and authority of David's royal house. Hezekiah's ascent to the throne marked

the beginning of a new royal policy, expected to bring a change in the nation's fortunes. Hezekiah's arrival is a royal, spiritual birth, assuring divine assistance for the royal dynasty. When the text is applied to Jesus, as the author of Luke's Gospel does, the angel Gabriel tells Mary, "The Lord God will make [her son] king, as his ancestor David was. He will rule the people of Israel forever, and his kingdom will never end" (Luke 1:32b–33, CEV).

Evening Prayer
Antiphon: ". . . [A] light will show you the way and fill you with happiness." (Ps 97:11b, CEV)
Psalm: "The LORD is King! / Tell the earth to celebrate . . . . / Dark clouds surround him, / and his throne is supported by justice and fairness. / Fire leaps from his throne . . . , / and his lightning is so bright / that the earth sees it and trembles. / Mountains melt away like wax / in the presence of the LORD of all the earth. / The heavens announce, / 'The LORD brings justice!' Everyone sees God's glory. / The LORD rules the whole earth, / and he is more glorious than all the false gods. / You are the LORD's people! / So celebrate and praise the only God." (Ps 97: 1–6, 9, 12, CEV)
Repeat Antiphon (above):
Reading: "God has shown us how kind he is by coming to save all people. We are filled with hope, as we wait for the glorious return of our great God and Savior Jesus Christ. He gave himself to rescue us from everything that is evil and to make our hearts pure. He wanted us to be his own people and to be eager to do right." (Titus 2:11, 13–14, CEV)
Meditation/Journal: In what specific ways has God been kind to you? With what hope has God filled you on Christmas Day? For what are you praising God today?

Day 2: December 26

Feast of St. Stephen
Morning
Antiphon: ". . . I trust you, LORD. / I celebrate and shout because you are kind." (Ps 31:6b–7, CEV)
Psalm: ". . . I trust you, LORD, and I claim you as my God. / My life is in your hands. / Save me . . . . / Smile on me, your servant. / Have pity and rescue me. / I pray only to you. / All who belong to the LORD, show

how you love him. / The LORD protects the faithful . . . ." (Ps 31:14–17a, 23ab, CEV)
Repeat Antiphon (above):
Reading: "The twelve apostles . . . said, '. . . [C]hoose seven men who are respected and wise and filled with God's Spirit.' This suggestion pleased everyone, and they began by choosing Stephen. He had great faith and was filled with the Holy Spirit. God gave Stephen the power to work great miracles and wonders among the people. . . . Stephen . . . spoke with the great wisdom that the Spirit gave him." (Acts 6:2a, 3a, 5ab, 8, 10, CEV)
Reflection: The second day of Christmas is the Feast of St. Stephen, a celebration much older than Christmas! That is why it is the day after Christmas. For the author of the Acts of the Apostles—the same person who wrote Luke's Gospel—Stephen, whose name means *crown*, is an example of how a follower of Jesus ought to imitate him. Like Jesus, who is filled with the Spirit (Luke 1:35; 3:22; 4:1), Stephen is filled with the Spirit. Jesus did miracles, and Stephen does miracles. And as you will see in Evening Prayer below, Stephen speaks the same words that Jesus spoke. Thus, the author of the Acts of the Apostles models his Stephen character after his Jesus character. Such modeling enables the author to tie volume 1 (Luke's Gospel) to volume 2 (Acts of the Apostles).

Evening
Antiphon: "Sing joyful songs to the LORD!" (Ps 95: 1a, CEV)
Psalm: "Sing a new song to the LORD! He has worked miracles, / and with his own powerful arm, he has won the victory. / The LORD has shown the nations / that he has the power to save and to bring justice. / God has been faithful in his love . . . . and his saving power is seen everywhere on earth. / Tell everyone on this earth / to sing happy songs in praise of the LORD." (Ps 98:1–4, CEV)
Repeat Antiphon (above):
Reading: ". . . Stephen was filled with the Holy Spirit. He looked toward heaven, where he saw our glorious God and Jesus standing at his right side. Then Stephen said, 'I see heaven open and the Son of Man standing at the right side of God!' As Stephen was being stoned to death, he called out, 'Lord Jesus, please welcome me!' He knelt down and shouted, 'Lord, don't blame them for what they have done.' Then he died." (Acts 7:55–56, 59–60, CEV)

Activity: Compare the details of the death of Jesus in Luke's Gospel (Luke 23:34, 46 or Luke 23:32–49) to the death of Stephen in the Acts of the Apostles (above). What do you discover?

Day 3: December 27

Feast of St. John
Morning
Antiphon: "You, LORD God, are my fortress, / that mighty rock where I am safe." (Ps 94:23, CEV)
Psalm: "Make music for [the LORD] on harps. Play beautiful melodies! / Sound the trumpets and horns / and celebrate with joyful songs for our LORD and King! / Command the ocean to roar with all of its creatures, / and the earth to shout with all of its people. / Order the rivers to clap their hands, / and all the hills to sing together. / Let them worship the LORD! (Ps 98:4–9a, CEV)
Repeat Antiphon (above):
Reading: "In the beginning was the one who is called the Word. / The Word was with God and was truly God. / From the very beginning the Word was with God. / And with this Word God created all things. / Nothing was made without the Word. / Everything that was created received its life from him, / and his life gave light to everyone." (John 1:1–4, CEV)
Reflection: Not only is the above passage appropriate for the Christmas Season, when celebrating the incarnation of the Son of God, but it comes from John's Gospel, whose author is identified traditionally as the apostle John, even though biblical scholars think that various parts of John's Gospel were written by different people at different times, until a final editor put all the pieces together in what became the Gospel of John. The celebration of the incarnation or enfleshing of God, as depicted in the opening words of John's Gospel, echoes the words of Psalm 98, especially the words about calling upon all creatures on the earth and in the oceans and all the rivers to clap their hands, because they were made through the Word to receive its (his) life. Therefore, in the words of Psalm 98, let everything and everyone worship the LORD God and his incarnate Son.

Evening
Antiphon: "Praise the mighty rock where we are safe. / Come to worship [the LORD] / with thankful hearts and songs of praise." (Ps 95:1b–2, CEV)
Psalm: "The LORD is the greatest God, king over all other gods. / He holds the deepest part of the earth in his hands, / and the mountain peaks

belong to him. / The ocean is the Lord's because he made it, / and with his own hands he formed the dry land. / Bow down and worship the LORD our Creator! / The LORD is our God, and we are his people, / the sheep he takes care of in his own pasture. / Listen to God's voice today." (Ps 95:3–7, CEV)

Repeat Antiphon (above):

Reading: "Jesus walked on and soon saw James and John, the sons of Zebedee. They were in a boat, mending their nets. At once Jesus asked them to come with him. They left their father in the boat with the hired workers and went with him." (Mark 1:19–20, CEV)

Reflection: In the oldest gospel, Mark's, John the Baptist appears preaching and baptizing (Mark 1:1–8), Jesus appears and is baptized by John and goes to the desert for forty days (Mark 1:9–13), John is imprisoned and Jesus begins preaching about God's kingdom (Mark 1:14–15), and Jesus calls fishermen to follow him (Mark 1:16–20). The first two fishermen called are Simon (Peter) and his brother Andrew; then, Jesus calls the brothers James and John to follow. The focus of the call narratives is dying. Fish that are caught die. Simon and Andrew drop their nets and follow Jesus; they leave behind their livelihood! James and John leave behind their father! Following Jesus, as the narratives suggest, involves change, transformation, embracing a new life. During the Christmas season, it is a good spiritual practice to acknowledge the changes, transformations, and new life that have occurred in the past years.

Day 4: December 28

Feast of the Holy Innocents
Morning
Antiphon: "The LORD was on our side!" (Ps 124:1a, CEV)

Psalm: "Let everyone . . . say: 'The LORD was on our side! / Otherwise, the enemy attack would have killed us all, because it was furious. / We would have been swept away in a violent flood of high and roaring waves.' / Let's praise the LORD! / He protected us from enemies who were like wild animals, / and we escaped like birds from a hunter's torn net. / The LORD made heaven and earth, / and he is the one who sends us help." (Ps 124:1b–8, CEV)

Repeat Antiphon (above):

Reading: "In Ramah a voice is heard, crying and weeping loudly. / Rachel mourns for her children / and refuses to be comforted, because they are dead. / But I, the LORD, say to dry your tears. / Someday your children / will come home from the enemy's land. / Then all you have done for them will be greatly rewarded. / So don't lose hope. I, the LORD, have spoken." (Jer 31:15–17, CEV)

Reflection: Rachel was one of the wives of Jacob, son of Isaac and ancestor of the nation of the northern Kingdom of Israel, destroyed by the Assyrians in 720 BCE and many of its people scattered throughout the Assyrian empire. Jeremiah's words mentions the town of Ramah, which was the name of several towns at the time. Rachel, mother of Jospeh and Benjamin, whose sons became the ancestors of the leading tribes of the northern Kingdom of Israel, is portrayed by Jeremiah as mourning the death of her many children. Through Jeremiah, God tells Jeremiah's readers not to lose hope that one day he will restore what had been destroyed. The passage from Jeremiah is quoted by the author of Matthew's Gospel, when he uniquely narrates the death of innocent children below. A biblical passage about one event in Jeremiah is employed to create a unique story about another event in Matthew's Gospel.

Evening
Antiphon: "When I think of you [, Lord God], I feel restless and weak." (Ps 77:3, CEV)
Psalm: "Because of you, Lord God, I can't sleep. / I am restless and can't even talk. / I think of times gone by, and those years long ago. / Each night my mind is flooded with questions . . . . / O LORD, I will remember / the things you have done, your miracles of long ago. / I will think about each one of your mighty deeds. / Everything you do is right, / and no other god compares with you. / You alone work miracles, / and you have let nations see your mighty power." (Ps 77:4–6, 11–14, CEV)
Repeat Antiphon (above):
Reading: "[Herod] gave orders for his men to kill all the boys who lived in or near Bethlehem and were two years old and younger. So the Lord's promise came true, just as the prophet Jeremiah had said, 'In Ramah a voice was heard crying and weeping loudly. / Rachel was mourning for her children, / and she refused / to be comforted, because they were dead.'" (Matt 2:16b, 17–18, CEV)
Reflection: The narrative about Herod ordering the killing of children in Bethlehem to eliminate the child identified by the wise men as "king of the Jews" (Matt 1:2) is unique to the first gospel. As the author makes clear, he has created it from the HB (OT) prophet Jeremiah. The way

he intends it be understood is as a fulfillment of what Jeremiah wrote. However, as noted in the Reflection above for Morning Prayer, Jeremiah narrates the destruction of the northern Kingdom of Israel, whose descendants were children of Rachel. It is a characteristic of the author of Matthew's Gospel to use HB (OT) texts as fulfilled by NT (CB) stories that the author created!

Day 5: December 29

Fifth Day in the Octave of Christmas
Morning
Antiphon: "We praise you, LORD God, and we worship you . . . . / Only you are God!" (Ps 99:9, CEV)
Psalm: "You know the LORD is God! / He created us, and we belong to him; / we are his people, the sheep in his pasture. / Be thankful and praise the LORD . . . . / The LORD is good! / His love and faithfulness will last forever." (Ps 100:3–5, CEV)
Repeat Antiphon (above):
Reading: "The Word that gives life was from the beginning, / and this is the one our message is about. / Our ears have heard, our own eyes have seen, / and our hands touched this Word. / The one who gives life appeared! We saw it happen, and we are witnesses to what we have seen. Now we are telling you about this eternal life that was with the Father and appeared to us. (1 John 1:1–2, CEV)
Meditation/Journal: What message has your ears heard and your eyes seen about the Word that gives life, the one who appeared?

Evening
Antiphon: ". . . God is light and doesn't have any darkness in him." (1 John 1:5, CEV)
Psalm: "You have looked deep / into my heart, LORD, and you know all about me. / You know when I am resting or when I am working, / and from heaven you discover my thoughts. / You notice everything I do and everywhere I go. / Before I even speak a word, you know what I will say, / and with your powerful arm / you protect me from every side. / I can't understand all of this! / Such wonderful knowledge is far above me. / Where could I go to escape / from your Spirit or from your sight? / . . . [S]uppose I said, 'I'll hide / in the dark until night comes to cover me over.' / But you see in the dark / because daylight and dark are all the same to you." (Ps 139:1–7, 11–12, CEV)

Repeat Antiphon (above):
Reading: "If we say that we share in life with God and keep on living in the dark, we are lying and are not living by the truth. But if we live in the light, as God does, we share in life with each other. And the blood of his Son Jesus washes all our sins away." (1 John 1:6–7, CEV)
Reflection: The NRSV translation of verse 12 of Psalm 139 states, "[E]ven the darkness is not dark to you [, O LORD]; the night is as bright as the day, for darkness is as light to you." Because Psalm 139 was not written by the same author who penned the First Letter of John, the biblical writers disagree with each other. "God is light and doesn't have any darkness in him," states First John in the antiphon above. Yet, the psalmist states that "darkness is as light" to God, which implies that God knows darkness. The point is that Bible readers need to be careful of the dark-light dichotomy. People tend to equate what is bad with darkness and what is good with light. However, in God there is no such dichotomy. Dark and light exist side by side. And if people reflect on that insight, they discover that the presumed dichotomy doesn't exist within themselves either. Dark and light exist side by side in all.

Day 6a: December 30

Sixth Day in the Octave of Christmas
Morning
Antiphon: "O Lord, in all generations you have been [my] home." (Ps 90:1, CEV)
Psalm: "You [, Lord,] have always been God—/ long before the birth of the mountains, / even before your created the earth and the world. / . . . [A] thousand years mean nothing to you! / They are merely a day gone by or a few hours in the night. / [I am] merely tender grass that sprouts and grows / in the morning, but dries up by evening. / [I] can expect seventy years, / or maybe eighty, if [I am] healthy . . . . / Help [me], LORD! Don't wait! / Pity your servant. / When morning comes, / let your love satisfy all [my] needs. Then [I] can celebrate / and be glad for what time [I] have left." (Ps 90:2, 4, 5b–6, 10ab, 13–14, CEV)
Repeat Antiphon (above):
Reading: "[Mary and Joseph] took Jesus to the temple in Jerusalem and presented him to the Lord . . . . At this time a man named Simeon was living in Jerusalem. Simeon was a good man. He loved God and was waiting for God to save the people . . . . [T]he Spirit told Simeon to go into

the temple. Simeon took the baby Jesus in his arms and praised God . . . , 'Lord, I am your servant, and now I can die in peace, / because you have kept your promise to me.'" (Luke 2:22b, 25, 27b–29, CEV)

Meditation/Journal: Answer either of the following questions: (1) In what specific ways has God been your home? (2) What does it mean for Jesus to be presented to God in the Jerusalem Temple by his parents, Mary and Joseph? (3) What connection do you find between Psalm 90 and the Reading?

Evening
Antiphon: "Live under the protection of God Most High / and stay in the shadow of God All-Powerful." (Ps 91:1, CEV)
Psalm: "Then you will say to the LORD, / 'You are my fortress, my place of safety; / you are my God, and I trust you.' [The Lord] will spread his wings / over you and keep your secure. / His faithfulness is like a shield or a city wall. / You won't need to worry / about dangers at night or arrows during the day. / The LORD Most High is your fortress. Run to him for safety . . . ." (Ps 91:2, 4–5, 9, CEV)
Repeat Antiphon (above):
Reading: "The prophet[ess] Anna was . . . in the temple. . . . [S]he was very old. . . . [S]he was eighty-four years old. Night and day she served God in the temple by praying . . . . At that time Anna came in and praised God. She spoke about the child Jesus to everyone . . . ." (Luke 2:36ab, 37–38, CEV)
Reflection: The narrative about the prophetess Anna being in the temple, when Mary and Joseph presented Jesus to the Lord, is unique to Luke's Gospel (Luke 2:36–38). The story serves several purposes. First, it serves to illustrate a theme of the author of Luke's Gospel; a story about a man is followed by a story about a woman, or vice-versa. In this case, the account about Simeon (above) is balanced by the account about Anna. Second, the author of Luke's Gospel does not know that women do not spend nights and days in the temple! Thus, his account betrays his Gentile origin. Third, Anna becomes an example of one who, in the words of Psalm 91, lives under the protection of God and claims him as a place of safety. She, like a chick takes refuge under its mother's wings, stands under the Lord's wings. Fourth, Anna is an example of a person who trusts God, as Psalm 91 states. Like Anna, you live in God's shadow!

Day 6b: Sunday between December 25 and January 1 or December 30, when there is no Sunday between December 25 and January 1

Feast of the Holy Family of Jesus, Mary, and Joseph
Morning
Antiphon: "Children are a blessing and a gift from the LORD." (Ps, 127:3, CEV)
Psalm: "The LORD will bless you / if you respect him and obey his laws. / Your fields will produce, / and you will be happy and all will go well. / Your wife will be as fruitful as a grapevine, / and just as an olive tree is rich with olives, / your home will be rich with healthy children. / That is how the LORD will bless everyone who respects him. / May you live long enough to see your grandchildren. " (Ps 128:1–4, 6a, CEV)
Repeat Antiphon (above):
Reading: ". . . [A]n angel from the Lord appeared to Joseph in a dream and said, 'Get up! Hurry and take the child and his mother to Egypt! Stay there until I tell you to return, because Herod is looking for the child and wants to kill him.' That night, Joseph got up and took his wife and the child to Egypt, where they stayed until Herod died." (Matt 2:13–15a, CEV)
Reflection: The Feast of the Holy Family of Jesus, Mary, and Joseph is celebrated on the Sunday between Christmas and January 1; when there is no Sunday—because both Christmas and January 1 fall on Sunday, the Feast of the Holy Family is marked on December 30. In the reading above, the author of Matthew's Gospel presents a unique narrative featuring an angel of the Lord, a dream, and a trip to Egypt. The angel of the Lord, used often in the HB (OT) is a code phrase for God. Matthew's Joseph is created from Jacob's son named Joseph, a dreamer and interpreter of dreams. And the holy family travels to Egypt, the place of slavery from which their ancestors had escaped, because the author of Matthew's Gospel understands Jesus to be a new Moses. Thus, like Moses led the Hebrews out of Egypt to God, Jesus will lead his people out of slavery to the Law to the freedom of being God's children.

Evening
Antiphon: "Praise the Lord and pray in his name! / Tell everyone what he has done." (Ps 105:1, CEV)
Psalm: "Without the help of the LORD / it is useless to build a home . . . . / It is useless to get up early / and stay up late in order to earn a living. / God takes care of his own, even while they sleep. / Having a lot of children /

to take care of you in your old age / is like a warrior with a lot of arrows. / The more you have the better off you will be, / because they will protect you...." (Ps 127:1–2, 4–5ab, CEV)

Repeat Antiphon (above):

Reading: Abram said, "LORD All-Powerful, you have given me everything I could ask for, except children.' The LORD replied, '... You will have a son of your own, and everything you have will be his.' The LORD took Abram outside and said, 'Look at the sky and see if you can count the stars. That's how many descendants you will have.' Abram believed the LORD, and the LORD was pleased with him." (Gen 15:2, 4–6, CEV)

Reflection: Abram, before the LORD changed his name to Abraham, had heard the LORD call him to leave his country and go to a land that God would show him. God told him, "I will bless you and make your descendants into a great nation. You will become famous and be a blessing to others." (Gen 12:2, CEV). Abram did as the LORD directed. However, the one thing that he kept asking the God in whom he placed his trust was about descendants, as he and his wife, Sarah, had no children. Repeatedly, through Genesis, God reassures Abram that his descendants will be countless. Finally, Isaac is conceived by Sarah, is born, grows up, marries, and becomes the father of Jacob and Esau. In turn, Jacob marries several wives, and gives birth to twelve sons, who become the tribes of Israel. God's promise to Abram (Abraham) was fulfilled with descendants as countless as the stars in the sky. According to the author of the HB (OT book of Genesis, Abram's (Abraham's) trust of God was fulfilled, when Moses led the Hebrew families out of Egypt to the land promised to Abram (Abraham) and his countless descendants. Abraham's family was the first holy family; Jesus, Mary, and Joseph is the second holy family.

Day 8: January 1

Eighth (Octave) Day of Christmas
Solemnity of the Blessed Virgin Mary, Mother of God
Morning

Antiphon: "Our God, be kind and bless us! Be pleased and smile." (Ps 67:1, CEV)

Psalm: "Then everyone on earth will learn to follow you, [God], / and all nations will see your power to save us. / Make everyone praise you and shout your praises. / Let the nations celebrate with joyful songs, / because you judge fairly and guide all nations. / Make everyone praise you and shout your praises. / Our God has blessed the earth . . . . / Pray for his blessings to continue / and for everyone on earth to worship our God." (Ps 67:2–7, CEV)

Repeat Antiphon (above):

Reading: ". . . [W]hen the time was right, God sent his Son, and a woman gave birth to him. His Son obeyed the Law, so he could set us free from the Law, we could become God's children. Now that we are his children, God has sent the Spirit of his Son into our hearts. And his Spirit tells us that God is our Father. You are no longer slaves. You are God's children, and you will be given what he has promised." (Gal 4:4–7, CEV)

Meditation/Journal: What word gets your attention in Psalm 67 or Galatians 4? What does the word mean? How does it make you aware of God's presence?

Evening

Antiphon: "Tell everyone on this earth to shout praises to God!" (Ps 66:1, CEV)

Psalm: "Sing about [God's] glorious name. Honor him with praises. / All of you people, / come praise our God! Let his praises be heard. / All who worship God, come here and listen; / I will tell you everything God has done for me. / I prayed to the Lord, and I praised him. / . . . God did listen and answered my prayer. / Let's praise God! / He listened when I prayed, and he is always kind." (Ps 66:2, 8, 16–17, 19–20, CEV)

Repeat Antiphon (above):

Reading: ". . . [M]any . . . angels came down from heaven and joined in praising God. They said: 'Praise God in heaven! / Peace on earth to everyone who pleases God.' After the angels had left and gone back to heaven, the shepherds said to each other, 'Let's go to Bethlehem and see what the Lord has told us about.' They hurried off and found Mary and Joseph, and they saw the baby lying on a bed of hay. But Mary kept thinking about all this and wondering what it meant." (Luke 2:13–16, 19, CEV)

Reflection: The author of Luke's Gospel presents the baby Jesus being visited by shepherds on the night of his birth. In the ancient world, a shepherd was a poor man or woman, who lived in the field with the sheep. Shepherds were often thought of as thieves, because they pastured their sheep on other's property. Poor shepherds receive the message of the angels and respond to it. Throughout the rest of Luke's Gospel, Jesus ministers to the poor, who listen, respond, and are cured. Jesus' mother, Mary, who was declared the Mother of God after Jesus was understood to be both God and the Son of God, ponders the events of her life. When thinking or pondering, a person gives meaning to an experience. For example, while pondering the wind, one person may realize that the wind is blowing, while another declares the presence of the Holy Spirit. The psalmist says that he will declare everything that God has done for him. It is important to note that he is interpreting the events of his life as experiences of God.

Day 9: January 2

Morning
Antiphon: "Our LORD, you are King!" (Ps 99:1a, CEV)
Psalm: "[Our LORD, y]ou rule from your throne / above the winged creatures, as people tremble and the earth shakes. / You are praised . . . and you control all nations. / Only you are God! And your power alone, / so great . . . , is worthy of praise. / You are our mighty King, a lover of fairness, / who sees that justice is done everywhere . . . . / Our LORD and our God, we praise you / and kneel down to worship you, the God of holiness!" (Ps 99:1b–5, CEV)
Repeat Antiphon (above):
Reading: "What a beautiful sight! / On the mountains a messenger announces . . . , / 'Good news! You're saved. / There will be peace. Your God is now King.' / Everyone on guard duty, sing and celebrate! / Look! You can see the LORD . . . . / [R]ise! Join in the singing. / The LORD has given comfort / to his people; he comes to your rescue. / The LORD has shown all nations his mighty strength; / now everyone will see the saving power of our God." (Isa 52:7–10, CEV)
Meditation/Journal: What good news have you heard during this Christmas Season? What comfort have you received from God? Where have you discovered the LORD's strength?

Evening
Antiphon: "Our LORD, you are King! (Ps 93:1a, CEV)
Psalm: "[Our LORD, m]ajesty and power are your royal robes. / You put the world in place, and it will never be moved. / You have always ruled, and you are eternal. / The ocean is roaring, LORD! The sea is pounding hard. / Its mighty waves are majestic, / but you are more majestic, and you rule over all. / Your decisions are firm, / and your temple will always be beautiful and holy." (Ps 93:1b–5, CEV)

Repeat Antiphon (above):
Reading: "Long ago in many ways and at many times God's prophets spoke his message to our ancestors. But now at last, God sent his Son to bring his message to us. God created the universe by his Son, and everything will someday belong to the Son. God's Son has all the brightness of God's own glory and is like him in every way. By his own mighty word, he holds the universe together." (Heb 1:1–3b, CEV)
Meditation/Journal: Recall from memory messages the prophets delivered; make a list. Recall from memory the message God's Son delivered; add it to your list. While reviewing your list of messages, what do you conclude?

Day 10: January 3

Morning
Antiphon: "Do wonderful things for us, your servants, [LORD], / and show your mighty power to our children." (Ps 90:16, CEV)
Psalm: "Good people will prosper like palm trees, / and they will grow strong like the cedars of Lebanon. / They will take root / in your house, LORD God, and they will do well. / They will be like trees / that stay healthy and fruitful, even when they are old. ' And they will say about you, / 'The LORD always does right! God is our mighty rock.'" (Ps 92:12–15, CEV)
Repeat Antiphon (above):
Reading: "Here is the great mystery of our religion: Christ came as a human. / The Spirit proved that he pleased God, / and he was seen by angels. / Christ was preached to the nations. / People in this world put their faith in him, / and he was taken up to glory." (1 Tim 3:16, CEV)
Reflection: The author of the First Letter to Timothy in the CB (NT) preserves a quotation from a hymn, which reflects a creed of early followers of Jesus. "Christ came as a human" refers both to Jesus pre-existence, incarnation, and human existence on earth. The natural (flesh) is contrasted to the spiritual (Spirit). "The Spirit proved that he pleased God" by raising Jesus from the dead. After he was raised from the dead, "he was seen by angels" in three of the four gospels (Luke 24:23; Matt 28:2; John 20:12). The risen Christ (Anointed One) "was preached to the nations," that is, to the Gentiles, recalling the Pauline mission and lending Pauline status to this pseudepigraphical letter. The result of preaching Jesus Anointed was people putting "their faith in him," which brings

eternal life. "This world" is the universal arena of Jesus' salvific efforts. In his glorified (resurrected/ascended) state, Jesus Anointed "was taken up to glory," from where he began before he was incarnated in the womb of his mother. The hymn fragment or creed provides a model. The human response of Jesus to the Spirit is a model for every Christian believer—"the great mystery of our religion."

Evening

Antiphon: "Love the LORD . . . / God protects his loyal people / and rescues them . . . ." (Ps 97:10, CEV)

Psalm: "You know the LORD is God! / He created us, and we belong to him; / we are his people, the sheep in his pasture. / Be thankful and praise the LORD as you enter his temple. / The LORD is good!/ His love and faithfulness will last forever." (Ps 100:3–5, CEV)

Repeat Antiphon (above):

Reading: "The Word became / a human being and lived here with us. / We saw his true glory, / the glory of the only Son of the Father. / From him all the kindness / and all the truth of God have come down to us. John [the Baptist] spoke about him and shouted, 'This is the one I told you would come! He is greater than I am, because he was alive before I was born.' Because of all that the Son is, we have been given one blessing after another." (John 1:14–16, CEV)

Activity: Compare and contrast the Morning Prayer reading from 1 Timothy 3:16 to the Evening Prayer reading from John 1:14–16; what are your results? What do your results tell you about two different biblical authors? What blessings have you received during this Christmas Season?

Day 11: January 4

Morning

Antiphon: "Our LORD, you are King forever and will always be famous." (Ps 102:12, CEV)

Psalm: "Our LORD, the nations will honor you . . . . / Your glory will be seen, / and the prayers of the homeless will be answered. / Future generations must also / praise the LORD, so write this for them: / 'From his holy temple, / the LORD looked down at the earth. / He listened to the groans of prisoners, / and he rescued everyone who was doomed to die.' / In the beginning, LORD, / you laid the earth's foundation and created the heavens. / They will all disappear and wear out like clothes. / You change them, / as you would a coat, but you last forever." (Ps 102:15a, 16b–20, 25–26, CEV)

Repeat Antiphon (above):

Reading: ". . . [L]et the peace that comes from Christ control your thoughts. And be grateful. Let the message about Christ completely fill your lives, while you use all your wisdom to teach and instruct each other. With thankful hearts sing psalms, hymns, and spiritual songs to God. Whatever you say or do should be done in the name of the Lord Jesus, as you give thanks to God the Father because of him." (Col 3:15b–17, CEV)

Activity: Choose a word or phrase from Psalm 102 or Colossians 3 that gets your attention. What does the word of phrase mean? How does the word or phrase make you aware of God's presence?

Evening

Antiphon: "Every generation of those / who serve you [, LORD,] will live in your presence." (Ps 102:28, CEV)

Canticle: "Lord God All-Powerful, / you have done great and marvelous things. / You are the ruler of all nations, / and you do what is right and fair. / Lord, who doesn't honor and praise your name? / You alone are holy, / and all nations will come and worship you, / because you have shown / that you judge with fairness." (Rev 15:3–4, CEV)

Repeat Antiphon (above):

Reading: ". . . John [the Baptist] saw Jesus coming toward him and said: Here is the Lamb of God who takes away the sin of the world! He is the one I told you about when I said, 'Someone else will come. He is greater than I am, because he was alive before I was born.' I didn't know who he was. But I came to baptize you with water, so that everyone . . . would see him." (John 1:29–31, CEV)

Reflection: By the time of the writing of John's Gospel—at the end of the first century CE or the beginning of the second century CE—the controversy about who was greater (John the Baptist or Jesus) had been resolved. In John's Gospel, there can be no doubt that Jesus is greater, as John declares him to have been alive before he was born! Unique to John's Gospel are the words of John the Baptist about Jesus being the Lamb of God (John 1:29, 36). Many people pass over that name for Jesus, but in John's Gospel it has particular significance. In John's Gospel, Jesus dies before Passover begins; in Mark, Matthew, and Luke he eats the Passover with his disciples and dies the next day. The author of John's

Gospel presents Jesus as the new Passover lamb; he dies at the same time as the lambs for Passover are being slaughtered in the Jerusalem Temple. The author writes that because Jesus had already died, his legs were not broken, as was the usual Roman crucifixion custom to hurry the deaths of the crucified, to fulfill a Scripture passage: "No bone of his body will be broken" (John 19:36). The reference is to the Passover lamb (Exod 12:36b; Num 9:12a).

Day 12: January 5

Morning

Antiphon: "I praise you, LORD God, with all my heart." (Ps 104:1a, CEV)
Psalm: [LORD God,] You are glorious and majestic, / dressed in royal robes and surrounded by light. / You spread out the sky like a tent, / and you built your home over the mighty ocean. / The clouds are your chariot with the wind as its wings. / The winds are your messengers, / and flames of fire are your servants. / You built foundations / for the earth, and it will never be shaken. / You covered the earth / with the ocean that rose above the mountains. / Then your voice thundered! / And the water flowed down the mountains / and through the valleys to the place you prepared. / Now you have set boundaries, / so that the water will never flood the earth again. But what about the ocean so big and wide? / It is alive with creatures large and small." (Ps 104:1b-9, 25, CEV)
Repeat Antiphon (above):
Reading: ". . . Jesus and his disciples went to Judea, where he stayed with them for a while and was baptizing people. John had not yet been put in jail. He was at Aenon near Salim, where there was a lot of water, and people were coming there for John to baptize them." (John 3:22-24, CEV)
Reflection: The author of John's Gospel cannot make up his mind if Jesus baptized people. He says that Jesus was baptizing people (John 3:22), but later says that it was his disciples baptizing (John 4:2). There is no doubt that John the Baptist baptized people. John enacted a ritual washing of purification so that people could make themselves fit to worship and be in the presence of God. Water was used for all kinds of purification ceremonies. For people who lived in desert lands water was a precious resource. Psalm 104 reflects this when it explains that God lives in a home located above the ocean above the sky. Ancient cosmology pictured flood gates in the sky; rain was the result of God opening the gates and letting water from the ocean above the sky fall on the earth. That water ran

down mountain sides and was collected in the ocean on earth. Water represented chaos, which only God could tame. Like other potentates of his time, God visited the earth in a winged chariot made of clouds pushed along by the wind. The author of Psalm 104 depicts the ocean on the earth; God has set boundaries for it to keep it from flooding the earth. In other words, just as God calmed the chaos of the water above the earth, he has tamed the chaos of the water on the earth. When ancient people washed (purified) themselves using water, they immersed themselves in the God who lived above it and controlled it.

Evening
Antiphon: "With all my heart / I praise you, LORD! I praise you! (Ps 104:35bc, CEV)
Psalm: "You [, LORD God,] provide steams of water in the hills and valleys . . . . Birds build their nests nearby and sing in the trees. / Our LORD, your trees always have water, / and so do the cedars you planted in Lebanon. / Birds nest in those trees, / and storks make their home in the fir trees. / Our LORD, by you wisdom you made so many things; / the whole earth is covered with your living creatures." (Ps 104:10, 12, 16–17, 24, CEV)
Repeat Antiphon (above):
Reading: "Someday, I, the LORD, / will cut a tender twig from the top of a cedar tree, / then plant it on the peak of [the] tallest mountain, / where it will grow / strong branches and produce large fruit. / All kinds of birds will find shelter under the tree, / and they will rest in the shade of its branches. / Every tree in the forest will know that I, the LORD, / can bring down tall trees and help short ones grow. / I dry up green trees and make dry ones green. / I, the LORD, have spoken, and I will keep my word." (Ezek 17:22–24, CEV)
Meditation/Journal: What connections do you notice between Psalm 104 and Ezekiel 17? What connections do Psalm 104 and Ezekiel 17 have to the Christmas Season?

Day 13: January 6a

When Epiphany is celebrated on January 7 or January 8, the following Morning Prayer and Evening Prayer are used on January 6.

Morning
Antiphon: "Tell everyone what [the LORD] has done" (Ps 105:1b, CEV)

Psalm: Our LORD, "You created the moon to tell us the seasons. / The sun knows when to set, and you made the darkness, / so the animals in the forest could come out at night. . . . [W]e go out to work until the end of day. / You created all . . . by your Spirit, / and you give new life to the earth. / Our LORD, we pray / that your glory will last forever / and that you will be pleased with what you have done. / As long as I live, / I will sing and praise you, the LORD God. / I hope my thoughts will please you, / because you are the one who makes me glad." (Ps 104:19–20, 23, 30–31, 33–34, CEV)

Repeat Antiphon (above):

Reading: "Water and blood came out from the side of Jesus Christ. It wasn't just water, but water and blood. The Spirit tells about this, because the Spirit is truthful. In fact, there are three who tell about it. They are the Spirit, the water, and the blood, and they all agree." (1 John 5:6–8, CEV)

Reflection/Meditation/Journal: The author of the First Letter of John knows the narrative of John's Gospel about Jesus' side being pierced with a lance and water and blood coming out (John 19:34). In other words, the author attests to the fact that Jesus was truly human and he died. But the Spirit also attests to the resurrection of Christ from the dead. In other words, the author is telling what God has done. What has God done for you this Christmas Season?

Evening

Antiphon: "The LORD will listen when [people] cry out, / and he will never forget his people . . . ." (Ps 69:33, CEV)

Psalm: "Our God and King, / you have ruled since ancient times; / you have won victories everywhere on this earth. / By your power you made a path through the sea . . . . You opened the ground / for streams and springs and dried up mighty rivers. / You rule the day and the night, / and you put the moon and the sun in place. / You made summer and winter and gave them to the earth." (Ps 74:12–13a, 15–17, CEV)

Repeat Antiphon (above):

Reading: "When Jesus began to teach, he was about thirty years old. Everyone thought he was the son of Joseph. But his family went back through Heli, . . . Enosh, and Seth. The family of Jesus went all the way back to Adam and then to God." (Luke 3:23, 38, CEV)

Reflection: In the CB (NT) there are two genealogies of Jesus. One is found in Matthew's Gospel (1:1–16); it traces Jesus' lineage from Abraham, through David, to Joseph, son of Jacob. The other genealogy is found in Luke's Gospel (3:23–38); it begins with Joseph, son of Heli, and ends with Seth, son of Adam, son of God. Ancient genealogies trace lineage from father to son. Not only do the two disagree about who Joseph's father was, but they disagree on the method of tracing the ancestors and the names of many of the ancestors. Furthermore, if the Spirit impregnates Mary (Matt 1:18, 20; Luke 1:35), then Joseph does not, and the question of genealogy becomes mute. Nevertheless, the author of Luke's genealogy presents Jesus as the Son of God (Luke 1:35), whose lineage is traced back to Adam, the first son of God! With this background, what do you think is the purpose of the authors of Matthew's Gospel and Luke's Gospel recording separate genealogies?

Day 13b: January 2–8

Epiphany

When Epiphany is celebrated on the Sunday between January 2 and January 8, the following Morning Prayer and Evening Prayer are used.

Morning

Antiphon: "The LORD protects everyone who follows him." (Ps 1:6a, CEV)

Psalm: "Why do the nations plot, / and why do their people make useless plans? / The kings of this earth have all joined together / to turn against the LORD and his chosen one. / In heaven the LORD laughs / as he sits on his throne, making fun of the nations. / . . . [H]e says, 'I've put my king on Zion, my sacred hill.' / I will tell the promise that the LORD made to me: / 'You are my son, because today / I've become your father.'" (Ps 2:1–2, 4, 6–7, CEV)

Repeat Antiphon (above):

Reading: ". . . [S]tand up! Shine! Your new day is dawning. / The glory of the LORD shines brightly on you. / The earth and its people are covered with darkness, / but the glory of the LORD is shining upon you. / Nations and kings / will come to the light of your dawning day. / When you see this, your faces will glow; / your hearts will pound and swell with pride. / Treasures from across the sea / and the wealth of nations will be brought to you. / Your country will be covered / with caravans of young camels . . . bring[ing] gold and spices in praise of me, the LORD." (Isa 60:1–3, 5–6, CEV)

Reflection: Today's celebration is named the Epiphany of the Lord. The word *epiphany* means *the manifestation of a divine being*. In Psalm 2, a royal coronation hymn, God declares the new king of be his son, as God becomes his Father. Thus, the king, the LORD's chosen one, the LORD's anointed (messiah) is the earthly agent of God's reign. In other words, the king becomes a manifestation of the LORD God. In the reading from the prophet Isaiah, the city of Jerusalem becomes a manifestation of God, whose glory shines upon the earth and its people in darkness. Such a manifestation of God sparks people to bring treasures and praises to God. In the reading for Evening Prayer below is found the unique narrative of the manifestation of Jesus to the wise men. All these epiphanies urge you to ask yourself: Where have I encountered an epiphany?

Evening
Antiphon: "Our God, I am faithful to you / with all my heart, and you can trust me. / I will sing / and play music for you with all that I am." (Ps 108:1, CEV)
Psalm: "The LORD said to my Lord, 'Sit at my right side, / until I make your enemies into a footstool for you.' / The LORD will let your power reach out from Zion, / and you will rule over your enemies. / Your glorious power / will be seen on the day you begin to rule. / You will wear the sacred robes / and shine like the morning sun in all of your strength. / The LORD has made a promise that will never be broken: / 'You will be a priest forever, just like Melchizedek.' / My Lord is at your right side . . . ." (Ps 110:1–5a, CEV)
Repeat Antiphon (above):
Reading: "When Jesus was born in the village of Bethlehem . . . some wise men from the east came to Jerusalem and said, 'Where is the child born to be king of the Jews? We saw his star in the east and have come to worship him.' And the star they had seen in the east went on ahead of them until it stopped over the place where the child was. When the men went into the house and saw the child with Mary, his mother, they knelt down and worshiped him. They took out their gifts of gold, frankincense, and myrrh and gave them to him." (Matt 2:1–2, 9b, 11, CEV)
Reflection: The author of Matthew's Gospel likes to use irony in his prose. Irony is found in the reading above. Wise men are magi or stargazers from the east, meaning Babylon, where the Jews were captives of war. Babylonians believed that a new king was heralded by a star. The wise men are Gentiles, non-Jews, who have come to worship the new-born

king of the Jews! However, they must find him, which they do in nowheresville, Bethlehem. Once he is found, they offer him gifts that would have been given at a funeral; gold coins would have been placed on the dead's eyes to keep them closed; frankincense would have been burned to squelch the stench of a dead body; and myrrh was a sweet-smelling perfume used to anoint a dead body. In other words, the gifts of the wise men indicate that they know how the story will end. The new-born king of the Jews will be crucified, die, and be buried. The epiphany or manifestation of Jesus to the Gentile wise men—enemies from the east—who bring funeral gifts to a baby shower couldn't contain any more irony. Irony reveals deep truth. By reflecting on the irony in your life, you may discover deep truth and the presence of God.

Day 14a: January 7

When the Epiphany is celebrated on January 8, the following Morning Prayer and Evening Prayer are used on January 7. When Epiphany is celebrated on January 6, Morning Prayer and Evening Prayer for January 7 are found at Day 14b: January 7.

Morning
Antiphon: "You are my God and protector. Please answer my prayer." (Ps 4:1a, CEV)
Psalm: "The LORD has chosen everyone who is faithful / to be his very own, and he answers my prayers. / Silently search your heart as you lie in bed. / There are some who ask, 'Who will be good to us?' / Let your kindness, LORD, shine brightly on us. / You are my King and my God. / Answer my cry for help because I pray to you. / Each morning you listen to my prayer, / as I bring my requests to you and wait for your reply." (Ps 4:3, 4c, 6; 5:2–3, CEV)
Repeat Antiphon (above):
Reading: "We know that Jesus Christ the Son of God has come and has shown us the true God. And because of Jesus, we now belong to the true God who gives eternal life." (1 John 5:20, CEV)
Intercessions: I ask God to listen to my prayers, as I bring the following requests to him and wait for his reply:

Evening
Antiphon: "Now have pity [, God,] and listen as I pray." (Ps 4:1b, CEV)

Psalm: ". . . [Y]ou are my shield [, LORD], / and you give me victory and great honor. / I pray to you, and you answer from your sacred hill. I sleep and wake up refreshed / because you, LORD, protect me. / Come and save me, LORD God! / because you protect and bless your people." (Ps 3:3–5, 7a, 8, CEV)
Repeat Antiphon (above):
Reading: "The light keeps shining in the dark, and darkness has never put it out. / God sent a man named John, / who came to tell about the light / and to lead all people to have faith. / John wasn't that light. / He came only to tell about the light. / The true light that shines on everyone was coming into the world." (John 1:6–9, CEV)
Intercessions: I ask God to have pity and listen as I pray for those who live in the light:

Day 14b: January 7

Monday after Epiphany
When the Epiphany is celebrated between January 2 and 6, the following Morning Prayer and Evening Prayer are used on January 7. When Epiphany is celebrated on January 8, Morning Prayer and Evening Prayer for January 7 are found at Day 14a: January 7.

Morning
Antiphon: "Listen, LORD, as I pray! Pay attention when I groan." (Ps 5:1, CEV)
Psalm: "Because of your great mercy, I come to your house, LORD, / and I am filled with wonder / as I bow down to worship at your holy temple. / You do what is right, and I ask you to guide me. / Make your teaching clear . . . . / Let all who run to you / for protection always sing joyful songs. / Provide shelter for those who truly love you and let them rejoice. / Our LORD, you bless those who live right, / and you shield them with your kindness." (Ps 5:7–8, 11–12, CEV)
Repeat Antiphon (above):
Reading: "Think how much the Father loves us. He loves us so much that he lets us be called his children, as we truly are. But since the people of this world did not know who Christ is, they don't know who we are. My dear friends, we are already God's children, though what we will be hasn't yet been seen. But we do know that when Christ returns, we will be

like him, because we will see him as he truly is. This hope makes us keep ourselves holy, just as Christ is holy." (1 John 3:1–3, CEV)

Meditation/Journal: How much does the Father love you? What do you think about being called a child of God? In what specific ways does the hope for Christ's return keep you holy?

Evening
Antiphon: "Your love is faithful, LORD, / and even the clouds in the sky can depend on you." (Ps 36:5, CEV)
Psalm: "Your decisions are always fair [, LORD]. / They are firm like mountains, deep like the sea, / and all people and animals are under your care. / Your love is a treasure, / and everyone finds shelter in the shadow of your wings. / You give your guests a feast in your house, / and you serve a tasty drink that flows like a river. / The life-giving fountain belongs to you, / and your light gives light to each of us." (Ps 36:6–9, CEV)
Repeat Antiphon (above):
Reading: "When Jesus heard that John [the Baptist] had been put in prison, he went to Galilee. But instead of staying in Nazareth, Jesus moved to Capernaum. This town was beside Lake Galilee in the territory of Zebulum and Naphtali. So God's promise came true, just as the prophet Isaiah [9:2] had said, . . . 'Although your people live in darkness, / they will see a bright light. / Although they live in the shadow of death, / a light will shine on them.' Then Jesus started preaching, 'Turn back to God! The kingdom of heaven will soon be here.'" (Matt 4:12–14, 16–17, CEV)

Day 15: January 8

Tuesday after Epiphany
Morning
Antiphon: "Our LORD, keep showing love to everyone who knows you, / and use your power to save all whose thoughts please you." (Ps 36:10, CEV)
Psalm: "How much longer, LORD, will you forget about me? / Will it be forever? How long will you hide? / Please listen, LORD God, and answer my prayers. / Make my eyes sparkle again, / or else I will fall into the sleep of death. / I trust your love, / and I feel like celebrating because you rescued me. / You have been good to me, LORD, and I will sing about you." (Ps 13:1, 3, 5–6, CEV)
Repeat Antiphon (above):

Reading: "My Dear friends, we must love each other. Love comes from God, and when we love each other, it shows that we have been given new life. We are now God's children, and we know him. God is love, and anyone who doesn't love others has never known him. God showed his love for us when he sent his only Son into the world to give us life. Real love isn't our love for God, but his love for us. God sent his Son to be the sacrifice by which our sins are forgiven. Dear friends, since God loved us this much, we must love each other." (1 John 4:7–11, CEV)

Reflection: Unlike English, which has only one word for love, CB (NT) Greek has four words for love. In the passage from First John above, the Greek word is *agape*, the most used word for love in the CB (NT). Agape is used to describe God's very nature (God is love); it is self-sacrificing love. The author of the First Letter of John declares that God, who loved people first, revealed his self-sacrificing nature in the person of Jesus, the Son he sent into the world and whose birth is continued to be celebrated during the Christmas Season. Agape is unconditional love; it seeks no reward; it desires only the good of the other. God delights in giving himself to people and making them his children; God never stops loving, because it is his very nature to do so. Real love, according to the author of the First Letter of John, is not our love for God—our response to God's love—but his love for people. As people realize they are loved by God, they desire to share that self-sacrificing love with each other. The God revealed as self-sacrificing love in the person of Jesus changes people, who see God's love incarnated in Jesus, and, consequently, in those they love in response.

Evening

Antiphon: "Shout praises to the LORD! / He is good to us, and his love never fails." (Ps 107:1, CEV)

Psalm: "Everyone the LORD has rescued / from trouble should praise him, / everyone he has brought / from the east and the west, the north and the south. / Some of you were lost / in the scorching desert, far from a town. / You were hungry and thirsty and about to give up. / You were in serious trouble, / but you prayed to the LORD, and he rescued you. / Right away he brought you to a town. / You should praise the LORD for his love / and for the wonderful things he does for all of us. / To everyone who is thirsty, he gives something to drink; / to everyone who is hungry he gives good things to eat." (Ps 107:2–9, CEV)

Repeat Antiphon (above):

Reading: One "evening the disciples came to Jesus and said, 'This place is like a desert, and it is already late. Let the crowds leave, so they can go to the farms and villages near here to buy something to eat.' Jesus replied, 'You give them something to eat. How much bread do you have? Go and see.' [The disciples] found out and answered, 'We have five small loaves of bread and two fish.' Jesus took the five loaves and the two fish. He looked up toward heaven and blessed the food. Then he broke the bread and handed it to his disciples to give to the people. He also divided the two fish, so that everyone could have some. There were five thousand men who ate the food." (Mark 6:35–37a, 38, 41, 44, CEV)

Meditation/Journal: How does the reading from Mark's Gospel illustrate Psalm 107? From what has God rescued you? With what food did he feed you?

Day 16: January 9

Wednesday after Epiphany
Morning
Antiphon: "You should praise the LORD for his love / and for the wonderful things he does for all of us." (Ps 107:15, CEV)
Psalm: "Our God, I am faithful to you / with all my heart, and you can trust me. / I will sing / and play music for you with all that I am. / I will start playing my harps before the sun rises. / I will praise you, LORD, for everyone to hear; / I will sing hymns to you in every nation. / Your love reaches higher than the heavens, / and your loyalty extends beyond the clouds. / Our God, may you be honored above the heavens; / may your glory be seen everywhere on earth. / Answer my prayers / and use your powerful arm to give us victory. / Then the people you love will be safe." (Ps 108:1–6, CEV)
Repeat Antiphon (above):
Reading: "God has given us his Spirit. That is how we know that we are one with him, just as he is one with us. God sent his Son to be the Savior of the world. We saw his Son and are now telling others about him. God stays one with everyone who openly says that Jesus is the Son of God. That's how we stay one with God." (1 John 4:13–15, CEV)
Activity: What do the psalmist words about God's love reaching higher than the heavens mean to you? Give examples of how you have experienced God's love reaching higher than the heavens. Out of the examples

of how you have experienced God's love, which ones help you stay one with God? Explain.

Evening
Antiphon: "You should praise the LORD for his love / and for the wonderful things he does for all of us." (Ps 107:21, CEV)
Psalm: "Some of you made a living by sailing the mighty sea, / and you saw the miracles the LORD performed there. / At his command a storm arose, and waves covered the sea. / You were tossed to the sky and to the ocean depths, / until things look so bad that you lost your courage. / You staggered like drunkards and gave up all hope. / You were in serious trouble, / but you prayed to the LORD, and he rescued you. / He made the storm stop and the sea be quiet. / You were happy because of this, / and he brought you to the port where you wanted to go." (Ps 107:23–30, CEV)
Repeat Antiphon (above):
Reading: ". . . [T]hat evening [Jesus] was still [on a mountain praying] by himself, and the boat [with his disciples] was somewhere in the middle of the lake. He could see that the disciples were struggling hard, because they were rowing against the wind. Not long before morning, Jesus came toward them. He was walking on the water . . . . He . . . got into the boat with them, and the wind died down. The disciples were completely confused." (Mark 6:47–48, 51, CEV)
Activity: Using Psalm 107 above, what would you tell Jesus' disciples in their confusion? What is the author of Mark's Gospel implying by narrating that Jesus was walking on the water? What does the story of Jesus walking on the water have to do with the Christmas Season, the days after Epiphany?

Day 17: January 10
Thursday after Epiphany
Morning
Antiphon: "Protect me, LORD God! I run to you for safety . . . ." (Ps 16:1, CEV)
Psalm: ". . . I have said, 'Only you are my Lord! / Every good thing I have is a gift from you [, LORD God]. / You, LORD, are all I want! / You are my choice, and you keep me safe. / You make my life pleasant, and my future is bright. / I praise you, LORD, for being my guide. / Even in the

darkest night, your teachings fill my mind. / I will always look to you, / as you stand beside me and protect me from fear. / With all my heart, / I will celebrate, and I can safely rest. / I am your chosen one." (Ps 16:2, 5–10a, CEV)

Repeat Antiphon (above):

Reading: "We love because God loved us first. But if we say we love God and don't love each other, we are liars. We cannot see God. So how can we love God, if we don't love the people we can see? The commandment that God has given us is: 'Love God and love each other!'" (1 John 4:19–21, CEV)

Meditation/Journal: How would you answer the author of the First Letter of John: How can we love the God we cannot see, if we don't love the people we can see? What connection do you note between Psalm 16 and 1 John 4:19–21?

Evening

Antiphon: "Our LORD and Ruler, / your name is wonderful everywhere on earth!" (Ps 8:9, CEV)

Psalm: "Our Lord and Ruler, / your name is wonderful everywhere on earth! / You let your glory be seen in the heavens above. / With praises from children / and from tiny infants, you have built a fortress. / I often think of the heavens your hands have made, / and the moon and stars you put in place. / Then I ask, 'Why do you care about us humans?' You made us a little lower than yourself, / and you have crowned us with glory and honor. / You let us rule everything your hands have made. / And you put all of it under our power . . . ." (Ps 8:1–2a, 3–4a, 5–6, CEV)

Repeat Antiphon (above):

Reading: "Jesus went . . to Nazareth, where he had been brought up, and as usual he went to the meeting place on the Sabbath. When he stood up to read from the Scriptures, he was given the book of Isaiah the prophet. He opened it and read, 'The Lord's Spirit has come to me, / because he has chosen me / to tell the good news to the poor. / The Lord has sent me / to announce freedom for prisoners, / to give sight to the blind, / to free everyone who suffers, / and to say, "This is the year the Lord has chosen [Isa 61:1–2]."' Jesus closed the book, then handed it back to the man in charge and sat down. Everyone in the meeting placed looked straight at Jesus. Then Jesus aid to them, 'What you have just heard me read has come true today.'" (Luke 4:16–21, CEV)

Reflection: As the Christmas Season comes quickly to a close, the author of Luke's Gospel presents a literate Jesus. The reading represents a portion of the Lukan Jesus' first sermon or discourse. Biblical scholars see it as a programmatic text; that is, the words of Isaiah represent the author's outline for the rest of the gospel. From the day of his conception, the Lukan Jesus has been designated a Spirit-child; he was conceived by the Spirit, anointed by the Spirit, and filled with the Spirit. From this point in the gospel, he will proclaim good news to the poor, announce freedom to prisoners, heal the blind, and cure many. In other words, the Lukan Jesus first sermon or discourse in the Nazareth synagogue launches his career. Beginning with where you are today, spend some time thinking about when, how, and who launched your career.

Day 18: January 11

Friday after Epiphany
Morning
Antiphon: "Shout praises to the LORD! Our God is kind, / and it is right and good to sing praises to him." (Ps 147:1, CEV)
Canticle: "Christ is exactly like God, who cannot be seen. / He is the first-born Son, superior to all creation. / Everything was created by him, / everything in heaven and on earth, / everything seen and unseen, / including all forces and powers, / and all rulers and authorities. / All things were created by God's Son, / and everything was made for him. / God's Son was before all else, / and by him everything is held together. / He is the head of his body, which is the church. / He is the very beginning, / the first to be raised from death, / so that he would be above all others. / God himself was pleased to live fully in his Son. / And God was pleased for him to make peace / by sacrificing his blood on the cross, / so that all beings in heaven and on earth / would be brought back to God." (Col 1:15–20, CEV)
Repeat Antiphon (above):
Reading: "After King Herod died, an angel from the Lord appeared in a dream to Joseph while he was still in Egypt. The angel said, 'Get up and take the child and his mother back to Israel. The people who wanted to kill him are now dead.' Joseph got up and left with them for Israel.... [I]n a dream he was told to go to Galilee, and they went to live there in the town of Nazareth. So the Lord's promise came true, just as the prophet had said, 'He will be called a Nazarene.'" (Matt 2:19–21, 22b–23, CEV)

Reflection: The pre-existent Son of God in the canticle from the Letter to the Colossians, a second-generation Pauline correspondence, is not the same Son whom Joseph took with his mother to Egypt to protect him from the infanticide of King Herod. Keeping in mind that the author of Matthew's Gospel conceives of Jesus as a new Moses, he must get Jesus to Egypt so that Jesus can leave that country to lead people to God. More specifically, the author of Matthew's Gospel must get his Jesus character to Nazareth, since that was his hometown—not Bethlehem. According to the author of Matthew's Gospel, Jesus went to live in Nazareth to fulfill an unknown prophet's words; there is no biblical prophet who said that the Messiah (Anointed One) would come from Nazareth; Matthew probably manufactured that quotation. Both the Colossians Canticle and the Matthean narrative about Joseph taking Jesus and Mary to Egypt and, then, bringing them back to Nazareth present theological truths in poetic story form. Both are designed to present the author's view of who he thinks Jesus was. In Colossians, he is the pre-existent Son of God; in Matthew's Gospel he is a new Moses.

Evening
Antiphon: Those who ponder the Law of the LORD "are like trees growing beside a stream, / trees that produce / fruit in season and always have leaves. / Those people succeed in everything they do." (Ps 1:3, CEV)
Canticle: "[I, the LORD] . . . will bless those who trust me. / They will be like trees growing beside a stream—/ trees with roots that reach down to the water, / and with leaves that are always green. / They bear fruit every year / and are never worried by a lack of rain." (Jer 17:7–8, CEV)
Repeat Antiphon (above):
Reading: "Jesus came to a town where there was a man who had leprosy. When the man saw Jesus, he knelt down to the ground in front of Jesus and begged, 'Lord, you have the power to make me well, if only you wanted to.' Jesus put his hand on him and said, 'I want to. Now you are well.' At once the man's leprosy disappeared." (Luke 5:12–13, CEV)
Meditation/Journal: What connection do you discover between the Antiphon from Psalm 1, the Canticle from the HB (OT) prophet Jeremiah, and the Gospel according to Luke? What connection do you discover between Epiphany and the Gospel according to Luke?

Day 19: January 12

Saturday after Epiphany
Morning
Antiphon: "We worship you, Lord, and we should always pray . . . ." (Ps 32:6a, CEV)
Psalm: "I felt a fire burning inside, and the more I thought, / the more it burned, until at last I said: / 'Please, LORD, / show me my future. Will I soon be gone? / You made my life short, / so brief that the time means nothing to you. / Human life is but a breath, / and it disappears like a shadow.' / Listen, LORD to my prayer! / My eyes are flooded with tears, as I pray to you. / I am merely a stranger / visiting in your home as my ancestors did." (Ps 39:3–6a, 12, CEV)
Repeat Antiphon (above):
Reading: "All of you have faith in the Son of God, and I have written to let you know that you have eternal life. We are certain that God will hear our prayers when we ask for what pleases him. And if we know that God listens when we pray, we are sure that our prayers have already been answered." (1 John 5:13–15, CEV)
Meditation/Journal: What prayer of yours did God hear recently and answer? What truth do you find in the psalmist's words (Psalm 39) about being a stranger visiting God's home?

Evening
Antiphon: "The heavens keep telling the wonders of God / and the skies declare what he has done." (Ps 19:1, CEV)
Psalm: "Each day informs the following day; / each night announces to the next. / They don't speak a word, / and there is never the sound of a voice. / Yet their message reaches all the earth, / and it travels around the world. / In the heavens a tent is set up for the sun. / It rises like a bridegroom / and gets ready like a hero eager to run a race. / It travels all the way / across the sky. Nothing hides from its heat." (Ps 19:2–6, CEV)
Repeat Antiphon (above):
Reading: John the Baptist said: "At a wedding the groom is the one who gets married. The best man is glad just to be there and to hear the groom's voice. That's why I am so glad. Jesus must become more important, while I become less important." (John 3:29–30, CEV)
Activity: To what is a bridegroom being compared in Psalm 19 (above)? To what is a bridegroom being compared in John 3:29–30? After exploring the use of both metaphors, what do you conclude?

Day 20: Feast of the Baptism of the Lord

Usually Sunday after January 6

Morning

Antiphon: "Honor the wonderful name of the LORD, / and worship the LORD most holy and glorious." (Ps 29:2, CEV)

Psalm: "The voice of the LORD echoes over the oceans. / The glorious LORD God / thunders above the roar of the raging sea, / and his voice is mighty and marvelous. / The voice of the LORD destroys the cedar trees; / the LORD shatters cedars . . . . / The voice of the LORD / makes lightning flash and the desert tremble. / The LORD rules on his throne, king of the flood forever." (Ps 29:3–5, 7, 10, CEV)

Repeat Antiphon (above):

Reading: "The LORD says: / 'My thoughts and my ways are not like yours. / Just as the heavens are higher than the earth, / my thoughts and my ways are higher than yours. / Rain and snow fall from the sky. / But they don't return without watering the earth / that produces seeds to plant and grain to eat. / That's how it is with my words. They don't return to me / without doing everything I send them to do.'" (Isa 55:8–11, CEV)

Activity: What natural phenomenon does the psalmist (Psalm 29) name "the voice of the LORD"? Why do you think the psalmist names that the voice of the Lord? After reflecting on Isaiah 55:8–11, what has the LORD's words produced in you?

Evening

Antiphon: "Our God, you deserve praise . . . ." (Ps 65:1a, CEV)

Psalm: "Our God, you save us . . . . You give hope to people / everywhere on earth, even those across the sea. / You are strong, / and your mighty power put the mountains in place. / You silence the roaring waves / and the noisy shouts of the nations. You take care of the earth / and send rain to help the soil grow all kinds of crops. / Your rivers never run dry, / and you prepare the earth to produce much grain. / You water all of its fields and level the lumpy ground. / You send showers of rain / to soften the soil and help the plants sprout. Wherever your footsteps / touch the earth, a rich harvest is gathered. Desert pastures blossom and mountains celebrate. / Meadows are filled with sheep and goats; / valleys overflow with grain and echo with joyful songs." (Ps 65:5acd–7, 9–13, CEV)

Repeat Antiphon (above):
Readings:
(a) "... Jesus came from Nazareth in Galilee, and John [the Baptist] baptized him in the Jordan River. As soon as Jesus came out of the water, he saw the sky open and the Holy Spirit coming down to him like a dove. A voice from heaven said, 'You are my own dear Son, and I am pleased with you.'" (Mark 1:9–11, CEV)
(b) "Jesus left Galilee and went to the Jordan River to be baptized by John [the Baptist]. But John kept objecting and said, 'I ought to be baptized by you. Why have you come to me?' Jesus answered, 'For now this is how it should be, because we must do all that God wants us to do.' Then John agreed. So Jesus was baptized. And as soon as he came out of the water, the sky opened, and he saw the Spirit of God coming down on him like a dove. Then a voice from heaven said, 'This is my own dear Son, and I am pleased with him.'" (Matt 3:13–17, CEV)
(c) "... Herod put John [the Baptist] in jail, and this was the worst thing he had done. While everyone else was being baptized, Jesus himself was baptized. Then as he prayed, the sky opened up, and the Holy Spirit came down upon him in the form of a dove. A voice from heaven said, 'You are my own dear Son, and I am pleased with you.'" (Luke 3:20–22, CEV)
(d) John the Baptist said: "... I came to baptize you with water.... I was there and saw the Spirit come down on [Jesus] like a dove from heaven. And the Spirit stayed on him. Before this I didn't know who he was. But the one who sent me to baptize with water had told me, 'You will see the Spirit come down and stay on someone. Then you will know that he is the one who will baptize with the Holy Spirit.' I saw this happen, and I tell you that he is the Son of God." (John 1:31–34, CEV)
(e) Peter said to Cornelius: "You surely know what happened.... It all began in Galilee after John had told everyone to be baptized. God gave the Holy Spirit and power to Jesus from Nazareth. He was with Jesus, as he went around doing good and healing everyone...." (Acts 10:37–38, CEV)
Activity: What do the five accounts of Jesus' baptism have in common? What is unique or different in each of the accounts of Jesus' baptism? What do the uniquenesses or differences mean? What conclusion do you reach about the five accounts of Jesus' baptism?

6

Season of Lent

Season of Lent Introduction

The Season of Lent, which consists of forty-three days, begins with Ash Wednesday and lasts six weeks; Lent ends on Holy Thursday evening of Holy Week. Lent begins with Ash Wednesday in 2025 on March 5; in 2026 on February 18; in 2027 on February 10; in 2028 on March 1; in 2029 on February 14; in 2030 on March 6; in 2031 on February 26; in 2032 on February 11; in 2033 on March 2; in 2034 on February 22; in 2035 on February 7; in 2036 on February 27; in 2037 on February 18; in 2038 on March 10; in 2039 on February 23.

Lent's varied beginning is due to the way Easter is calculated. Easter is the first Sunday after the first full moon after the Spring Equinox. Once Easter is calculated, Palm Sunday of the Passion of the Lord is set as the Sunday before Easter, and five and half weeks before that is Ash Wednesday.

When the celebration of St. Joseph, Spouse of the Blessed Virgin Mary, (March 19) falls on a Sunday, it is moved to Monday that year, unless that Monday is in Holy Week; then, it is moved to the Monday after the second Sunday of Easter. Likewise, when the celebration of the Annunciation of the Lord (March 25) falls on a Sunday, it is moved to

Monday that year, unless that Monday is in Holy Week; then it is moved to the Monday after the second Sunday of Easter. If, by chance, both St. Joseph and Annunciation fall during Holy Week, they are moved to the Monday and Tuesday, respectively, after the second Sunday of Easter. In 2027, the Annunciation of the Lord will be moved to April 5; in 2029 to April 9; in 2032 to April 5; in 2035 to April 3. In 2034, St. Joseph will be moved to March 20; in 2035 to April 2.

Other books by Mark G. Boyer that follow the same structure of Morning Prayer and Evening Prayer that can be used—in substitution for what is provided here—during the Season of Lent include: *Weekday Saints: Reflections on Their Scriptures* (Eugene, OR: Wipf & Stock, 2014); *Very Short Reflections—for Advent and Christmas, Lent and Easter, Ordinary Time, and Saints—through the Liturgical Year* (Eugene, OR: Wipf & Stock, 2020); *Overcome with Paschal Joy: Chanting through Lent and Easter, Daily Reflections with Familiar Hymns* (Eugene, OR: Wipf & Stock, 2016); *Christ Our Passover Has Been Sacrificed: A Guide through Paschal Mystery Spirituality, Mystical Theology in The Roman Missal* (Eugene, OR: Wipf & Stock, 2018); *Biblical Names for God: An Abecedarian Anthology of Spiritual Reflections for Anytime* (Eugene, OR: Wipf & Stock, 2023); *Journey into God: Spiritual Reflections for Travelers* (Eugene, OR: Wipf & Stock, 2022); and *Seasons of Biblical Spirituality: Spring, Summer, Autumn, and Winter* (Eugene, OR: Resource Publications, 2023).

Antiphons and Psalms for the Season of Lent are taken from the *New Revised Standard Version with the Apocrypha* (NRSV): *The Access Bible* (New York: Oxford University Press, 1999), and Readings for the Season of Lent are taken from *The New English Bible with the Apocrypha* (NEB) (New York: Oxford University Press, 1976).

Days in the Season of Lent

Day 1: Ash Wednesday

Morning

Antiphon: "Lord, you have been our dwelling place in all generations. (Ps 90: 1, NRSV)

Psalm: "Before the mountains were brought forth, / or ever you had formed the earth and the world, / from everlasting to everlasting you are God. / You turn us back to dust, / and say, 'Turn back, you mortals.' / For a thousand years in your sight / are like yesterday when it is past, / or like a watch in the night. / You sweep them away; they are like a dream, / like grass that is renewed in the morning; / in the morning it flourishes and is renewed; / in the evening it fades and withers. / The days of our life are seventy years, / or perhaps eighty, if we are strong; / even then their span is only toil and trouble; / they are soon gone, and we fly away." (Ps 90:2–6, 10, NRSV)

Repeat Antiphon (above):

Reading: ". . . [T]he LORD says, even now / turn back to me with your whole heart, / fast, and weep, and beat your breasts. / Rend your hearts and not your garments; / turn back to the LORD your God; / for he is gracious and compassionate, long-suffering and ever constant, / always ready to repent . . . . It may be he will turn back and repent / and leave a blessing behind him . . . ." (Joel 2:12–14a, NEB)

Activity: Choose a word from Psalm 90 that you associate with Ash Wednesday. Explain the association. Choose a word from the prophet Joel that you associate with Ash Wednesday. Explain the association.

Evening

Antiphon: "Have mercy on me, O God, / according to your steadfast love; / according to your abundant mercy / blot out my transgressions." (Ps 51:1, NRSV)

Psalm: "Wash me thoroughly from my iniquity, [O God,] / and cleanse me from my sin. / You desire truth in the inward being; / therefore teach me wisdom in my secret heart. / Create in me a clean heart, O God, / and put a new and right spirit within me. / Restore to me the joy of your salvation, / and sustain in me a willing spirit. / The sacrifice acceptable to God is a broken spirit; / a broken and contrite heart, O God, you will not despise." (Ps 51:2, 6, 10, 12, 17, NRSV)

Repeat Antiphon (above):

Reading: Jesus said to his disciples: ". . . [W]hen you do some act of charity, do not announce it with a flourish of trumpets, as the hypocrites do in synagogue and in the streets to win admiration from men. I tell you this: they have their reward already. No; when you do some act of charity, do not let your left hand know what your right is doing; your good deed must be secret, and your Father who sees what is done in secret will reward you." (Matt 6:2–4, NEB)

Reflection: An act of charity is otherwise known as almsgiving. In the Judaism of Jesus' day it was considered a special act, deserving of admiration from others. The Matthean Jesus, who specializes in righteousness—doing the right thing because it is the right thing to do—endorses the practice of almsgiving, but removes the announcement about it. He considers people who need immediate gratification to be hypocrites! Jesus' disciples are to give alms, but they are to do so so secretly that their left hands do not know what their right hands are doing! In other words, they are to give alms because it is the right thing to do, and not so others will take notice of their good deeds. The only one who needs to be impressed is their Father—God—who knows what is done in secret and rewards those who are righteous. During Lent it is a good practice to review one's almsgiving and the reason for giving alms.

Day 2

Thursday after Ash Wednesday
Morning
Antiphon: LORD, "[y]ou show me the path of life. / In your presence there is fullness of joy; / in your right hand are pleasures forevermore." (Ps 16:11, NRSV)
Psalm: "To you, O LORD, I lift up my soul / O my God, in you I trust.... / Make me to know your ways, O LORD; / teach me your paths. / Lead me in your truth, and teach me, / for you are the God of my salvation; / for you I wait all day long. / Be mindful of your mercy, O LORD, and of your steadfast love, / for they have been from of old. (Ps 25:1–2a, 4–6, NRSV)
Repeat Antiphon (above):
Reading: Moses said to the Israelites: "I summon heaven and earth to witness against you this day: I offer you the choice of life or death, blessing or curse. Choose life and then you and your descendants will live; love the LORD your God, obey him and hold fast to him: that is life for you and length of days in the land which the LORD swore to give to your forefathers, Abraham, Isaac, and Jacob." (Deut 30:19–20, NEB)
Meditation/Journal: How deep is your trust of God? What mercy has the LORD showed to you? Have you chosen life (blessing) or death (curse)? How do you know?

Evening
Antiphon: "The LORD is my light and my salvation; whom shall I fear? / The LORD is the stronghold of my life...." (Ps 27:1, NRSV)
Psalm: "One thing I asked of the LORD, that will I seek after; / to live in the house of the LORD all the days of my life, / to behold the beauty

of the LORD, and to inquire in his temple. / Hear, O LORD, when I cry aloud, be gracious to me and answer me! / Do not hide your face from me. / Teach me your way, O LORD, and lead me on a level path . . . ." (Ps 27:4, 7, 9a, 11, NRSV)
Repeat Antiphon (above):
Reading: ". . . [T]o all [Jesus] said, 'If anyone wishes to be a follower of mine, he [or she] must leave self behind; day after day he [or she] must take up his [or her] cross, and come with me. Whoever cares for his [or her] own safety is lost; but if a man [or woman] will let himself [or herself] be lost for my sake, that man [or woman] is safe. What will a man [or woman] gain by winning the whole world, at the cost of his [or her] true self?" (Luke 9:23–25, NEB)
Activity: Write a response to Jesus' question: "What will a man [or woman] gain by winning the whole world, at the cost of his [or her] true self?

Day 3

Friday after Ash Wednesday
Morning
Antiphon: "Happy are those whose transgression is forgiven, / whose sin is covered." (Ps 32:1, NRSV)
Psalm: "Happy are those to whom the LORD imputes no iniquity, / and in whose spirit there is no deceit. . . . I acknowledged my sin to you, / and I did not hide my iniquity; / I said, 'I will confess my transgressions to the LORD,' / and you forgave the guilt of my sin. / Therefore let all who are faithful offer prayer to you; / at a time of distress, the rush of mighty waters shall not reach them. / You are a hiding place for me; / you preserve me from trouble; / you surround me with glad cries of deliverance. / Be glad in the LORD and rejoice, O righteous, / and shout for joy, all you upright in heart." (Ps 32:2, 5–7, 11, NRSV)
Repeat Antiphon (above):
Reading: "Is this what you call a fast, / a day acceptable to the LORD? / Is not this what I require of you as a fast; / to loose the fetters of injustice, / to untie the knots of the yoke, to snap every yoke, / and set free those who have been crushed? / Is it not sharing your food with the hungry, / taking the homeless poor into your house, / clothing the naked when you meet them, / and never evading a duty to your kinsfolk? / Then shall your light break forth like the dawn / and soon you will grow healthy like a wound

newly healed.... Then, if you call, the LORD will answer; / if you cry to him, he will say, 'Here I am.'" (Isa 58:5c–8ab, 9ab, NEB)
Activity: According to the prophet Isaiah, what are the elements of fasting? Which do you fulfill? Which elements of fasting need your attention during Lent?

Evening
Antiphon: "Great is the LORD, / who delights in the welfare of his servant." (Ps 37:27b, NRSV)
Psalm: '... [M]y soul shall rejoice in the LORD, / exulting in his deliverance. / All my bones shall say, 'O LORD, who is like you? / You deliver the weak / from those too strong for them, / the weak and needy from those who despoil them.' / But as for me, when they were sick, / I wore sackcloth; / I afflicted myself with fasting. / I prayed with head bowed on my bosom, / as though I grieved for a friend or a brother; / I went about as one who laments for a mother, / bowed down and in mourning. / You have seen, O LORD; do not be silent! / O Lord, do not be far from me!" (Ps 35:9–10, 13–14, 22, NRSV)
Repeat Antiphon (above):
Reading: "... John's disciples came to [Jesus] with the question: 'Why do we and the Pharisees fast, but your disciples do not?' Jesus replied, 'Can you expect the bridegroom's friends to go mourning while the bridegroom is with them? The time will come when the bridegroom will be taken away from them; that will be the time for them to fast.'" (Matt 9:14–15, NEV)
Meditation/Journal: From the verses from Psalm 35 and the verses from Matthew 9 what do you conclude to be the purpose of fasting? What place does fasting have in your life?

Day 4: Saturday after Ash Wednesday
Morning
Antiphon: "For God alone my soul waits in silence; / from him comes my salvation." (Ps 62:1, NRSV)
Psalm: "[God] alone is my rock and my salvation, / my fortress; I shall never be shaken. / For God alone my soul waits in silence, / for my hope is from him. / He alone is my rock and my salvation, / my fortress; I shall not be shaken. / On God rests my deliverance and my honor; / my mighty rock, my refuge is in God. / Trust in him at all times, O people;

/ pour out your heart before him; / God is a refuge for us." (Ps 62:2, 5–8, NRSV)

Repeat Antiphon (above):

Reading: "If you cease to tread the sabbath underfoot, / and keep my holy day free from your own affairs, / if you call the sabbath a day of joy / and the LORD's holy day a day to be honored, / if you honor it by not plying your trade, / not seeking your own interest / or attending to your own affairs, / then you shall find your joy in the LORD, / and I will set you riding on the heights of the earth . . . ." (Isa 58:13–14ab, NEB)

Activity: According to verses from Isaiah 58, how is a person to observe the sabbath? Do you think that is possible in modern times? Explain.

Evening

Antiphon: "O LORD, be gracious to me; / heal me, for I have sinned against you." (Ps 41:4, NRSV)

Psalm: "Happy are those who consider the poor; / the LORD delivers them in the day of trouble. / The LORD protects them and keeps them alive . . . . / The LORD sustains them on their sickbed; / in their illness you heal all their infirmities. / But you, O LORD, be gracious to me, / and raise me up . . . . Blessed be the LORD . . . from everlasting to everlasting. Amen and Amen." (Ps 41:1–2a, 3, 10, 13, NRSV)

Repeat Antiphon (above):

Reading: ". . . Levi held a big reception in his house for Jesus; among the guests was a large party of tax-gathers and others. The Pharisees and the lawyers of their sect complained to his disciples: 'Why do you eat and drink,' they said, 'with tax-gathers and sinners?' Jesus answered them: 'It is not the healthy that need a doctor, but the sick; I have not come to invite virtuous people, but to call sinners to repentance.'" (Luke 5:29–32, NEB)

Reflection: Levi, known as Matthew in Matthew's Gospel, is a Jew who works for the Roman occupation forces in his home country. He serves them by collecting taxes from his fellow Jews. He makes his living by raising the set amount of the tax and pocketing the difference. His fellow Jews detest him because he costs them money and he works for the army that rules their land. Levi is considered a sinner. "Sinners" are prostitutes, who, like tax collectors are considered outsiders. Thus, Jesus dines with outsiders. Insider Pharisees want to know why a holy man shares food with tax-gatherers and prostitutes? The Lukan Jesus tells them that they are spiritually sick, and he, a spiritual doctor, calls them to repentance.

Jesus calls them to change their minds first; then, a change in their behavior will follow. Levi's behavior has already changed; he left his seat in the custom-house and everything behind and followed Jesus. While you may not be a tax collector or a prostitute, what change in your mind do you need to make during Lent that will result in a change in your behavior?

Day 5: First Sunday of Lent

Morning

Antiphon: "Restore us, O God, / let your face shine, that we may be saved." (Ps 80:3, NRSV)

Psalm: "I will call to mind the deeds of the LORD; / I will remember your wonders of old. / I will meditate on all your work, / and muse on your mighty deeds. / Your way, O God, is holy. / What god is so great as our God? / You are the God who works wonders; / you have displayed your might among the peoples. / With your strong arm you redeemed your people . . . ." (Ps 77:11–15a, NRSV)

Repeat Antiphon (above):

Readings:

(a) ". . . "[T]he Spirit sent [Jesus] away into the wilderness, and there he remained for forty days tempted by Satan. After John had been arrested, Jesus came into Galilee, proclaiming the Gospel of God: 'The time has come; the kingdom of God is upon you; repent, and believe the Gospel.'" (Mark 1: 12–13a, 14–15, NEB)

(b) "Jesus was . . . led away by the Spirit into the wilderness, to be tempted by the devil. For forty days and nights he fasted . . . . When he heard that John had been arrested, Jesus withdrew to Galilee; and leaving Nazareth he went and settled at Capernaum on the Sea of Galilee . . . . From that day Jesus began to proclaim the message: 'Repent; for the kingdom of Heaven is upon you.'" (Matt 4:1–2a, 12–13, 17, NEB)

(c) "Full of the Holy Spirit, Jesus returned from the Jordan, and for forty days was led by the Spirit up and down the wilderness and tempted by the devil. Then Jesus, armed with the power of the Spirit, returned to Galilee; and reports about him spread through the whole country-side. Coming down to Capernaum, a town in Galilee, he taught the people on the Sabbath, and they were astounded at his teaching, for what he said had the note of authority." (Luke 4:1, 14, 31–32, NEB)

Meditation/Journal: What are the signs of the kingdom of God (heaven)? From what do you need to repent? What role does the Spirit play in your Lenten repentance?

Evening
Antiphon: "I cry aloud to God, / aloud to God, that he may hear me." (Ps 77:1, NRSV)
Psalm: "In the day of my trouble I seek the Lord; / in the night my hand is stretched out without wearying; / my soul refuses to be comforted. / I think of God, and I moan: / I meditate, and my spirit faints. / You keep my eyelids from closing; / I am so troubled that I cannot speak. / I consider the days of old, / and remember the years of long ago. / I commune with my heart in the night; / I meditate and search my spirit . . . ." (Ps 77:2–6a, NRSV)
Repeat Antiphon (above):
Reading: "It was through one man [, Adam,] that sin entered the world, and through sin death , . . . and Adam foreshadows the Man who was to come. But God's act of grace is out of all proportion to Adam's wrongdoing . For if the wrongdoing of that one man brought death upon so many, its effect is vastly exceeded by the grace of God and the gift that came to so many by the grace of the one man, Jesus Christ. And again, the gift of God is not be compared in its effect with that one man's sin; for the judicial action, following upon the one offense, issued in a verdict of condemnation, but the act of grace, following upon so many misdeeds, issued in a verdict of acquittal. It follows, then, that as the issue of one misdeed was condemnation for all men [and women], so the issue of one just act is acquittal and life for all men [and women]." (Rom 5:12b, 14b–16, 18, NEB)
Reflection: The above passage from Paul's Letter to the Romans represents a basic tenant of Pauline thought. Paul's presupposition is that God oversees everything. The first man, Adam, did not obey God; his disobedience, according to Paul, brought both sin and death into the world for all people (original sin). Keeping in mind that Adam means *man*, Paul thinks that he foreshadows the new man, the new Adam, to come: Jesus Christ. The man Jesus was chosen by God and overwhelmed with grace, God's gift of himself; grace was so abundant that in the new man God's grace overwhelmed sin and death. Thus, one misdeed by Adam brought God's verdict of guilty of sin to all people, so one just act by the new man, Jesus, brought God's verdict of acquittal of sin to all people and

eternal life. In other words, Adam brought death; Jesus brough eternal life. During Lent, it is good to reflect on human choices that bring death and divine choices that bring life.

Day 6: Monday of the First Week of Lent

Morning
Antiphon: "Restore us, O God of hosts; / let your face shine, that we may be saved." (Ps 80:7, NRSV)
Psalm: "You [, God,] brought a vine out of Egypt; / you drove out the nations and planted it. / You cleared the ground for it; / it took deep root and filled the land. / The mountains were covered with its shade, / the mighty cedars with its branches; / it sent out its branches to the [Mediterranean] sea, / and its shoots to the River [Euphrates]. Turn again, O God of hosts; / look down from heaven, and see; / have regard for this vine, / the stock that your right hand planted." (Ps 80:8–11, 14–15, NRSV)
Repeat Antiphon (above):
Reading: "The LORD spoke to Moses and said, Speak to all the community of the Israelites in these words: You shall be holy, because I, the LORD your God, am holy." (Lev 19:1–2, NEB)
Reflection: The basic meaning of the Hebrew word translated into English as holy is separate. There is a difference between the LORD and the creatures he has made. Yet, he desires that that quality unique to himself be shared with people. Thus, the people he has chosen, the Israelites, are to be separate from all other people, just like the LORD is separate from all other gods. While holiness cannot be seen, God manifests his holiness as glory, often in forms of light and fire. Holiness is derived in creatures by some association or contact with the divine, such as Moses and the burning bush that is not consumed. Through Moses, the LORD tells his chosen people that he desires that they enter and share his sphere of divinity. Thus, they are to be holy, as he is holy. When someone first encounters a manifestation of the LORD's holiness, he or she recognizes his or her unworthiness as a creature, but with his grace, himself, God makes the person holy.

Evening
Antiphon: "Restore us again, O God of our salvation . . . ." (Ps 85:4a, NRSV)

Psalm: "Show us your steadfast love, O LORD, / and grant us your salvation. / Let me hear what God the LORD will speak, / for he will speak peace to his people, / to his faithful, to those who turn to him in their hearts. / Steadfast love and faithfulness will meet; / righteousness and peace will kiss each other. Faithfulness will spring up from the ground, / and righteousness will look down from the sky." (Ps 85:7–8, 10–11, NRSV)
Repeat Antiphon (above):
Reading: Jesus said: "When the Son of Man comes in his glory . . . , he will sit in state on his throne, with all the nations gathered before him. He will separate men [and women] into two groups, as a shepherd separates the sheep from the goats, and he will place the sheep on his right hand and the goats on his left." (Matt 25:31–33, NEB)
Reflection: The key word in the passage from Matthew's Gospel above is separate, the meaning of the word *holy*. In the unique parable, the Matthean Jesus declares holy those who fed the hungry, gave water to the thirsty, welcomed strangers, clothed the naked, helped the ill, and visited the imprisoned. He declares that whatever the holy did for others they did for him. The holy are separate from the unholy, who saw the hungry, the thirsty, strangers, the naked, the sick, and the imprisoned, but they did nothing. The Matthean Jesus concludes that whatever they didn't do for others they didn't do for him. The unholy go off to eternal punishment, but the holy enter eternal life. In other words, the separation the unholy created in this life also exists when the Son of Man comes in glory.

Day 7: Tuesday of the First Week of Lent

Morning
Antiphon: "Praise the LORD!" (Ps 106:1a, NRSV)
Psalm: "O give thanks to the LORD, for he is good; / for his steadfast love endures forever. / Remember me, O LORD, when you show favor to your people . . . . / . . . [H]e regarded their distress when he heard their cry. / Save us, O LORD our God, / and gather us from among the nations, / that we may give thanks to your holy name / and glory in your praise. / Blessed be the LORD . . . / from everlasting to everlasting. / And let all the people say, 'Amen.' Praise the LORD!" (Ps 106:1b, 4a, 44, 47–48, NRSV)
Repeat Antiphon (above):
Reading: "Come, all who are thirsty, come, fetch water; / come, you who have no food, buy corn and eat; / come and buy, not for money, not for

a price. / Why spend money and get what is not bread, / why give the price of your labor and go unsatisfied? / Only listen to me [, the LORD,] and you will have good food to eat / and you will enjoy the fat of the land. / Come to me and listen to my words, / hear me, and you shall have life . . . / Inquire of the LORD while he is present, / call upon him when he is close at hand." (Isa 55:1–3a, 6, NEB)
Meditation/Journal: For what do you hunger or thirst that money cannot buy? What words do you hear the LORD speaking to you now?

Evening
Antiphon: "O give thanks to the LORD, for he is good; / for his steadfast love endures forever." (Ps 107:1, NRSV)
Psalm: "Let the redeemed of the LORD say so, / those he redeemed from trouble . . . . / He turns rivers into a desert, / springs of water into thirsty ground, / a fruitful land into a salty waste . . . . / He turns a desert into pools of water, / a parched land into springs of water. / And there he lets the hungry live . . . . / By his blessing they multiply greatly . . . . / . . . [H]e raises up the needy out of distress, / and makes their families like flocks. / Let those who are wise give heed to these things, / and consider the steadfast love of the LORD." (Ps 107:2, 33–34a, 35–36a, 38a, 41, 43, NRSV)
Repeat Antiphon (above):
Reading: Jesus said: "In your prayers do not go babbling on like the heathen, who imagine that the more they say the more likely they are to be heard. Do not imitate them. Your Father knows what your needs are before you ask him." (Matt 6:7–8, NEB)
Activity: Choose a word or phrase from either Psalm 107 or Matthew 6:7–8. What does the word or phrase mean? How does the word or phrase make you aware of God's presence?

Day 8: Wednesday of the First Week of Lent

Morning
Antiphon: "My heart is steadfast, O God, my heart is steadfast; / I will sing and make melody. / Awake, my soul! (Ps 108:1, NRSV)
Psalm: "Awake, O harp and lyre!/ I will awake the dawn. / I will give thanks to you, O LORD, among the peoples, / and I will sing praises to you among the nations. / For your steadfast love is higher than the heavens, / and your faithfulness reaches to the clouds. / Be exalted, O God, above the heavens, / and let your glory be over all the earth." (Ps 108:2–5, NRSV)

Repeat Antiphon (above):
Reading: "The word of the LORD came to Jonah . . . : 'Go to the great city of Nineveh, go now and denounce it, for its wickedness stares me in the face.' But Jonah set out for Tarshish to escape from the LORD. He went down to Joppa, where he found a ship bound for Tarshish. He paid his fare and went on board, meaning to travel by it to Tarshish out of reach of the Lord." (Jonah 1:1–3, NEB)
Activity: What do you discover if you contrast the LORD's faithfulness in Psalm 108 with Jonah's unfaithfulness? What do you learn from your discovery?

Evening
Antiphon: "I called to the LORD out of my distress, / and he answered me; / out of the belly of Sheol I cried, / and you heard my voice." (Jonah 2:2, NRSV)
Canticle: "The waters closed in over me; / the deep surrounded me; / weeds were wrapped around my head / at the roots of the mountains. / I went down to the land / whose bars closed upon me forever; / yet you brought up my life from the Pit, / O LORD my God. As my life was ebbing away, / I remembered the LORD; / and my prayer came to you, / into your holy temple." (Jonah 2:5–7, NRSV)
Repeat Antiphon (above):
Reading: ". . . [T]he LORD ordained that a great fish should swallow Jonah, and for three days and three nights he remained in its belly. Then the LORD spoke to the fish and it spewed Jonah out on to dry land. The word of the LORD came to Jonah a second time: 'Go to the great city of Nineveh, go now and denounce it in the words I give you.' Jonah obeyed at once and went to Nineveh. He began by going a day's journey into the city, a vast city, three days' journey across, and then proclaimed: 'In forty days Nineveh shall be overthrown!' The people of Nineveh believed God's word. They ordered a public fast and put on sackcloth, high and low alike." (Jonah 1:17; 2:10—3:5, NEB)
Lessons to be Learned from Jonah: (a) Unlike the other prophets, the HB (OT) book of Jonah is a short story. (b) A person called by God cannot run away from the LORD. (c) Jonah often says the right things, but he does not often follow them. (d) Jonah cannot begin to think that God would care about any man, woman, or beast who is not an Israelite. (e) Jonah becomes very upset when Nineveh repents and God forgives its citizens. (f) Ironically, the Israelite Jonah is sent by God to the capital of the Assyrian

empire—Nineveh—which defeated the northern Kingdom of Israel; in other words, Jonah is sent to his enemy to call him to repentance.

Day 9: Thursday of the First Week of Lent

Morning
Antiphon: "Do not be silent, O God of my praise." (Ps 109:1, NRSV)
Psalm: ". . [Y]ou, O LORD my Lord, / act on my behalf for your name's sake; / because your steadfast love is good, deliver me. / For I am poor and needy, / and my heart is pierced within me. / I am gone like a shadow at evening; / I am shaken off like a locust. / My knees are weak through fasting; / my body has become gaunt. / Help me, O LORD my God! / Save me according to your steadfast love. / With my mouth I will give great thanks to the LORD; / I will praise him in the midst of the throng. / For he stands at the right hand of the needy, / to save them from those who would condemn them to death." (Ps 109:21–24, 26, 30–31, NRSV)
Repeat Antiphon (above):
Reading: ". . . [T]he king of Nineveh . . . rose from his throne, stripped off his robes of state, put on sackcloth, and sat in ashes. Then he had a proclamation made in Nineveh: 'This is a decree of the king and his nobles. No man or beast, herd, or flock, is to taste food, to graze, or to drink water. They are to clothe themselves in sackcloth and call on God with all their might. . . . It may be that God will repent and turn away from his anger; and so we shall not perish.' God saw what they did, . . . and repented and did not bring upon them the disaster he had threatened." (Jonah 3:6–8a, 9–10, NEB)
Meditation/Journal: What connection do you find between the verses of Psalm 109 above and the passage from the HB (OT) book of Jonah above? Who repents? Explain.

Evening
Antiphon: "Praise the LORD! / Praise the LORD, O my soul!" (Ps 146:1, NRSV)
Psalm: "I will praise the LORD as long as I live; / I will sing praises to my God all my life long. / Happy are those whose help is . . . God, / whose hope is in the LORD . . . , who made heaven and earth, / the sea, and all that is in them; / who keeps faith forever; / who executes justice for the oppressed; / who gives food to the hungry . . . . / . . . [T]he LORD opens the eyes of the blind. / The LORD lifts up those who are bowed down; /

the LORD loves the righteous. / The LORD watches over the strangers; / he upholds the orphan and the widow . . . ." (Ps 146:2, 5–9, NRSV)
Repeat Antiphon (above):
Reading: "Jonah was greatly displeased and angry, and he prayed to the LORD: 'This, O LORD, is what I feared when I was in my own country, and to forestall it I tried to escape to Tarshish; I knew that [you are] 'a god gracious and compassionate, long-suffering and ever constant, and always willing to repent of the disaster.' And now LORD, take my life: I should be better dead than alive.' 'Are you so angry?' said the LORD." (Jonah 4:1–4, NEB)
Meditation/Journal: Most recently, when have you been upset because God has helped someone you know?

Day 10: Friday of the First Week of Lent

Morning
Antiphon: "Praise the LORD! / How good it is to sing praises to our God; / for he is gracious, and a song of praise is fitting. (Ps 147:1, NRSV)
Psalm: "[The LORD] determines the number of the stars; / he gives to all of them their names. / Great is our Lord, and abundant in power; / his understanding is beyond measure. / Sing to the LORD with thanksgiving; / make melody to our God on the lyre. / He covers the heavens with clouds, / prepares rain for the earth, / makes grass grow on the hills. / He gives to the animals their food, / and to the young ravens when they cry. / His delight is not in the strength of the horse, / nor his pleasure in the speed of a runner, / but the LORD takes pleasure in those who fear him, / in those who hope in his steadfast love. (Ps 147:4–5, 7–11, NRSV)
Repeat Antiphon (above):
Reading: "Jonah went out and sat down on the east of the city. There he made himself a shelter and sat in its shade, waiting to see what would happen to the city. Then the LORD God ordained that a climbing gourd should grow up over his head to throw its shade over him and relieve his distress, and Jonah was grateful for the gourd. But at dawn the next day God ordained that a worm should attack the gourd, and it withered; and at sunrise God ordained that a scorching wind should blow up from the east. The sun beat down on Jonah's head till he grew faint. Then he prayed for death and said, 'I should be better dead than alive.'" (Jonah 4:5–8, NEB)

Reflection: Both the verses from Psalm 147 and the passage from the HB (OT) book of Jonah reflect a biblical understanding that God oversees everything. Psalm 147 states that God not only determines the number of the stars, but he also names them. He brings forth rain clouds, and he makes grass grow for animals to eat. Unlike people who take pleasure in speed, God gets excited by someone who fears him and hopes in his steadfast love. Jonah, who is upset because his preaching was effective, is under God's control. Just like God sent a large fish to rescue Jonah from the sea and spew him onto the road that led to Nineveh, so did God cause a gourd plant to sprout and grow to protect Jonah from the sun. Then, God sent a worm to cut the plant and cause it to wither. After thinking that he has been defeated by God—when he has been successful—Jonah prays for death. "I am better dead than alive," he tells God. After listening to Jonah's prayer, how would you reply to him?

Evening
Antiphon: "[The LORD] sends out his command to the earth; / his word runs swiftly." (Ps 147:15, NRSV)
Psalm: "[The LORD] gives snow like wool; / he scatters frost like ashes. / He hurls down hail like crumbs—/ who can stand before his cold? / He sends out his word, and melts them; / he makes his wind blow, and the waters flow." (Ps 147:16–18, NRSV)
Repeat Antiphon (above):
Reading: ". . . God said to Jonah, 'Are you so angry over the gourd?' 'Yes,' he answered, 'mortally angry.' The LORD said, 'You are sorry for the gourd, though you did not have the trouble of growing it, a plant which came up in a night and withered in a night. And should not I be sorry for the great city of Nineveh, with its hundred and twenty thousand who cannot tell their right hand from their left, and cattle without number?'" (Jonah 4:9–11, NEB)
Activity: Write an answer to God's final question to Jonah: "Should not I be sorry for the great city of Nineveh, with its citizens who cannot tell their right hand from their left?" Explain carefully.

Day 11: Saturday of the First Week of Lent

Morning
Antiphon: "Praise is due to you, / O God . . . ." (Ps 65: 1a, NRSV)

Psalm: "O you who answer prayer! / To you [O God,] all flesh shall come. / By awesome deeds you answer us with deliverance, / O God of our salvation; / you are the hope of all the ends of the earth / and of the farthest seas. / By your strength you established the mountains; / you are girded with might. / You silence the roaring of the seas, / the roaring of their waves.... / Those who live at earth's farthest bounds are awed by your signs; / you make the gateways of the morning and the evening shout for joy." (Ps 65:2, 5–8, NRSV)

Repeat Antiphon (above):

Reading: Jesus said: "This ... generation ... demands a sign, and the only sign that will be given it is the sign of Jonah. For just as Jonah was a sign to the Ninevites, so will the Son of Man be to this generation. The men [and women] of Nineveh will appear at the Judgement when this generation is on trial....; they repented at the preaching of Jonah; and what is here is greater than Jonah." (Luke 11:29–30, 32, NEB)

Reflection: The Lukan Jesus interprets the repentance of the enemy Ninevites to Jonah's preaching as a sign. The author of Luke's Gospel thinks that Jesus is a sign of his generation's need for repentance. The generation demanding a sign already has it; the Lukan Jesus has been preaching repentance—the need to change one's mind followed by the change in one's behavior—and the generation demanding a sign has only to recognize him, like the Ninevites recognized Jonah as a sign of their need to repent. The author of Matthew's Gospel interprets the sign of Jonah in a different way. The Matthean Jesus states, "... [T]he only sign that will be given [to this generation] is the sign of the prophet Jonah. Jonah was in the sea-monster's belly for three days and three nights, and in the same way the Son of Man will be three days and three nights in the bowels of the earth" (Matt 12:39–40, NEB). The author of Matthew's Gospel sees in Jonah's three days in the belly of the big fish a prediction of the three days (Friday, Saturday, Sunday) Jesus would spend in the grave before being raised from the dead. Thus, the HB (OT) prophet Jonah is interpreted in different ways by the CB (NT) authors of Luke's Gospel and Matthew's Gospel. The fact that both interpretations are correct means that biblical truth is plural and not singular, as some people like to present it. Jonah can be a sign of the need to repent, and he can be a prediction of the three days Jesus will spend in the tomb.

Evening

Antiphon: "O LORD, be gracious to me; / heal me, for I have sinned against you." (Ps 41:4, NRSV)

Psalm: "Our of the depths I cry to you, O LORD. / Lord, hear my voice! / Let your ears be attentive / to the voice of my supplications! / If you, O LORD, should mark iniquities, / Lord, who could stand? / But there is forgiveness with you, / so that you may be revered. / I wait for the LORD, my soul waits, / and in his word I hope; / my soul waits for the Lord / more than those who watch for the morning, / more than those who watch for the morning. . . . [H]ope in the LORD. / For with the LORD there is steadfast love, / and with him is great power to redeem." (Ps 130:1–7, NRSV)

Repeat Antiphon (above):

Reading: Jesus said: "Ask, you will receive; seek, and you will find; knock, and the door will be opened. For everyone who asks receives, he who seeks finds, and to him who knocks, the door will be opened. Always treat others as you would like them to treat you . . . ." (Matt 7:7–8, 12, NEB)

Meditation/Journal: For what have you asked God and received? For what have you sought and found? Upon what door have you knocked and it was opened? Most recently, whom have you treated the way you like to be treated? Explain. What connection do you find between Psalm 130 and the verses from Matthew's Gospel?

Day 12: Second Sunday of Lent

Morning

Antiphon: "Let your steadfast love, O LORD, be upon us, / even as we hope in you." (Ps 33:22, NRSV)

Psalm: "The LORD looks down from heaven; / he sees all humankind. / From where he sits enthroned he watches / all the inhabitants of the earth—/ he who fashions the hearts of them all, / and observes all their deeds. / Truly the eye of the LORD is on those who fear him, / on those who hope in his steadfast love. / Our soul waits for the LORD; / he is our help and shield. / Our heart is glad in him, / because we trust in his holy name." (Ps 33:13–15, 18, 20–21, NRSV)

Repeat Antiphon (above):

Reading: "[The LORD] took Abram outside and said, 'Look up into the sky, and count the stars if you can. So many,' he said, 'shall your descendants be.' Abram put his faith in the LORD, and the LORD counted that faith to him as righteousness; he said to him 'I am the LORD who brought you out from Ur of the Chaldees to give you this land to occupy.' Abram said, 'O Lord GOD, how can I be sure that I shall occupy it?'" (Gen 15:5–8, NEB)

Activity: Using the verses of Psalm 33 above, how do your answer Abram's question to the Lord GOD about being sure that he shall occupy the land?

Evening
Antiphon: ". . . I will rejoice forever / I will sing praises to . . . God . . . ." (Ps 75:9, NRSV)
Psalm: ". . . God my King is from of old, / working salvation in the earth. / Yours is the day [, God], yours also the night; / you established the luminaries and the sun. / You have fixed all the bounds of the earth; / you made summer and winter. / Have regard for your covenant, / for the dark places of the land are full of the haunts of violence." (Ps 74:12, 16–17, 20, NRSV)
Repeat Antiphon (above):
Reading: "The LORD answered [Abram], 'Bring me a heifer three years old, a she-goat three years old, a ram three years old, a turtle-dove, and a fledgling.' He brought him all these, halved the animals down the middle and placed each piece opposite its corresponding piece, but he did not halve the birds. Then, as the sun was going down, a trance came over Abram . . . . The sun went down and it was dusk, and there appeared a smoking brazier and a flaming torch passing between the divided pieces. That very day the LORD make a covenant with Abram, and he said, 'To your descendants I give this land from the River of Egypt to the Great River, the river Euphrates . . . .'" (Gen 15:9–10, 12a, 17–18, NEB)
Points to Ponder: First, Genesis 15:9–18 is the LORD's response to Abram's question at Genesis 15:8. Second, the LORD's presence to Abram is noted in the three, three-year old animals; three is the number indicating God's presence, and it does not indicate Trinity! Third, God, represented by fire, walks between the cut-in-two animals in an ancient covenant-making ceremony; the covenant-maker states that if he does not fulfill the terms of the covenant, Abram can do to him what he did to the animals! It is important to note that Abram does not walk between the cut-in-two animal pieces, as he is in a trace, a transfigured or transformed state. Fourth, the covenant is made in the dark, because

God owns both day and night, and it is easier to see the fire in the dark. Fifth, God repeats his promise to give the land to Abram's descendants; that is why it is called the promised land.

Day 13: Monday of the Second Week of Lent

Morning
Antiphon: "O give thanks to the LORD, call on his name, / make known his deeds among the peoples." (Ps 105:1, NRSV)
Psalm: "Sing to [the LORD], sing praises to him; / tell of all his wonderful works. / Glory in his holy name; / let the hearts of those who seek the LORD rejoice. / Seek the LORD and his strength; / seek his presence continually. / Remember the wonderful works he has done, / his miracles, and the judgments he has uttered, / O offspring of his servant Abraham . . . . / He is mindful of his covenant forever, of the word that he commanded, for a thousand generations, / the covenant that he made with Abraham . . . ." (Ps 105:2–6, 8–9, NRSV)
Repeat Antiphon (above):
Reading: "When Abram was ninety-nine years old, the LORD appeared to him and said, 'I am God Almighty. Live always in my presence and be perfect, so that I may set my covenant between myself and you and multiply your descendants.' Abram threw himself down on his face, and God spoke with him and said, 'I make this covenant, and I make it with you: you shall be the father of a host of nations. Your name shall no longer be Abram, your name shall be Abraham, for I make you father of a host of nations. I will make you exceedingly fruitful; I will make nations out of you, and kings shall spring from you.'" (Gen 17:1–6, NEB)
Points to Ponder: First, Abram's age of ninety-nine represents divine perfection. Thirty-three, a multiple sacred number for God (three), multiplied by three results in ninety-nine. In other words, God is all over Abram. Second, God tells Abram to live in his presence and be perfect—whole—as only the divine can be. Third, this is the second time that God mentions making a covenant with Abram; the covenant is that God will bring forth many descendants for Abram. Fourth, the mention that many nations and kings will descend from Abram gives a clue as to when this section of the HB (OT) book of Genesis was written—namely, after the twelve tribes chose a king for the united kingdom and after the ten tribes of Jacob in the north became the Kingdom of Israel and the two tribes of Jacob in the south became the Kingdom of Judah, each nation having its

own king. Fifth, the name Abram means *exalted ancestor*, while Abraham means *ancestor of a multitude*. The change in name indicates a change in function. The name Abraham further guarantees God's promise. The patriarch becomes a sign of God's promise.

Evening
Antiphon: "Praise the LORD! / I will give thanks to the LORD with my whole heart, / in the company of the upright, in the congregation." (Ps 111:1, NRSV)
Psalm: "Great are the works of the LORD, / studied by all who delight in them. / Full of honor and majesty is his work, / and his righteousness endures forever. / He has gained renown by his wonderful deeds; / the LORD is gracious and merciful. / He provides food for those who fear him; / he is ever mindful of his covenant. /He sent redemption to his people; / he has commanded his covenant forever. / Holy and awesome is his name." (Psalm 111:2–5, 9, NRSV)
Repeat Antiphon (above):
Reading: "God said to Abraham, 'For your part, you must keep my covenant, you and your descendants after you, generation by generation. This is how you shall keep my covenant between myself and you and your descendants after you; circumcise yourselves, every male among you. You shall circumcise the flesh of your foreskin, and it shall be the sign of the covenant between us. Every male among you in every generation shall be circumcised on the eighth day, . . . thus shall my covenant be marked in your flesh as an everlasting covenant." (Gen 17:9–12, 13b NEB)
Reflection: Because God has promised Abraham numerous descendants, the sign chosen for the covenant is the circumcised penis, the instrument used to transmit life in ancient biology. Ancient people thought that a child was contained in the man's semen (seed). The man planted the child, using his penis, in the incubator, the woman. Thus, the means of transferring the seed from the man to the woman was marked (circumcised); just like God gave life, so Abraham gives life. And every time Abraham—and his descendants after him—give life, they are to remember the covenant God made. In Abraham's case, the covenant is that his descendants will be numerous. Furthermore, ancient biology sheds a light on biblical genealogical lists which trace ancestors and descendants from one man to another. In the CB (NT) only the author of Luke's Gospel mentions that Jesus was circumcised eight days after his

birth (Luke 2:21). In Judaism today, eight days after birth, a male child is circumcised; the ritual celebration is called a bris.

Day 14: Tuesday of the Second Week of Lent

Morning
Antiphon: "O LORD my God, I will give thanks to you forever." (Ps 30:12b, NRSV)
Psalm: "Sing praises to the LORD, O you his faithful ones, / and give thanks to his holy name. / Weeping may linger for the night, / but joy comes with the morning. / You have turned my mourning into dancing; / you have taken off my sackcloth / and clothed me with joy, / so that my soul may praise you and not be silent." (Ps 30 4, 5a, 11–12a, NRSV)
Repeat Antiphon (above):
Reading: "God said to Abraham, 'As for Sarai your wife; you shall call her not Sarai, but Sarah. I will bless her and give you a son by her. I will bless her and she shall be the mother of nations; the kings of many people shall spring from her.' Abraham threw himself down on his face; he laughed and said to himself, 'Can a son be born to a man who is a hundred years old? Can Sarah bear a son when she is ninety?'" (Gen 17:15–17, NEB)
Reflection: Just like God changed Abram to Abraham to indicate Abraham's new function, he changes Sarai, meaning *palace, mistress*, or *releaser*, to Sarah, meaning *princess*, to indicate her new function. The author of the HB (OT) book of Genesis, meaning *beginning*, writes after the descendants of Abraham and Sarah had become nations and produced kings. The author knows ancient biology; men one hundred years old do not father children, and women ninety years old do not conceive children. People today must be careful not to impose upon an old HB (OT) text a modern understanding of barrenness, such as the woman's or the man's infertility. In ancient understanding, a woman was considered barren because God had not opened her womb. In a patriarchal culture, infertility could not be attributed to a man. Both the ages given to Abraham and Sarah and Sarah's barrenness serve to highlight the miracle that God all-powerful will bring about in the couple he has chosen to create a new dynasty of people.

Evening
Antiphon: "Praise the LORD!" (Ps 148:14b, NRSV)

Psalm: "Praise the LORD! Praise the LORD from the heavens; / praise him in the heights! / Praise him, sun and moon; / praise him, all you shining stars! / Praise him, you highest heavens, / and you waters above the heavens! / Let them praise the name of the LORD, / for he commanded and they were created. / Mountains and all hills, / fruit trees and all cedars! / Let them praise the name of the LORD, / for his name alone is exalted; / his glory is above earth and heaven." (Ps 148:1, 3–5, 9, 13, NRSV)

Repeat Antiphon (above):

Reading: "The LORD appeared to Abraham by the terebinths . . . . As Abraham was sitting at the opening of his tent in the heat of day, he looked up and saw three men standing in front of him. When he saw them, he ran from the opening of his tent to meet them and bowed low to the ground. . . . Abraham hurried into the tent to Sarah and said, 'Take three measures of flour quickly, knead it, and make some cakes.' Then Abraham ran to the cattle, chose a fine tender calf, and gave it to a servant, who hurriedly prepared it. The stranger said, 'About this time next year I will be sure to come back to you, and Sarah your wife shall have a son.' . . . Sarah laughed to herself and said, 'I am past bearing children now that I am out of my time, and my husband is old.' The LORD said to Abraham, 'Why did Sarah laugh and say, "Shall I indeed bear a child when I am old?" Is anything impossible for the LORD? In due season I will come back to you, about this time next year, and Sarah shall have a son.'" (Gen 18:1–2, 6–7, 10, 12–14, NEB)

Points to Ponder: First, a terebinth is an oak tree; many important biblical events occur under oak trees. Second, the number three indicates the divine presence; God appears to Abraham as three visitors. Third, Abraham is the epitome of hospitality; he welcomes the three visitors during the hottest part of the day, gives them water to wash their feet, lets them rest under the oak tree, and feeds them a steak dinner with cottage cheese and freshly-baked rolls! Fourth, one of the visitors (God) tells Abraham that Sarah will have a son. Like Abraham before her, Sarah knows that old women past menopause do not conceive; that is why she laughs after she overhears the visitor speak. Fifth, the most important question is posed by the LORD to Abraham: Is anything impossible for the LORD? Not only does Abraham have to answer that question, but readers today need to answer that question.

Day 15: Wednesday of the Second Week of Lent

Morning

Antiphon: "Be exalted, O God, above the heavens. / Let your glory be over all the earth." (Ps 57:5, NRSV)

Psalm: "Your throne, O God, endures forever and ever. / Your royal scepter is a scepter of equity; / you love righteousness and hate wickedness. / Therefore God, your God, has anointed you / with the oil of gladness beyond your companions; / your robes are all fragrant with myrrh and aloes and cassia." (Ps 45:6–8a, NRSV)

Repeat Antiphon (above):

Reading: "Six days later Jesus took Peter, James, and John with him and led them up a high mountain where they were alone; and in their presence he was transfigured; his clothes became dazzling white, with a whiteness no bleacher on earth could equal. They saw Elijah appear, and Moses with him, and there they were conversing with Jesus. Then a cloud appeared, casting its shadow over them and out of the cloud came a voice: 'This is my Son, my Beloved, listen to him.'" (Mark 9:2–4, 7, NEB)

Reflection: The word translated into English as *transfiguration* appears in Greek as *metamorphosis*; it means a change in form and appearance—of which the ancient gods were thought possible. Biblical scholars do not consider the transfiguration of Jesus to be an historical event; rather, it is a theological event, most likely a story that in its oral form was a post-resurrection narrative, since two dead people—Elijah and Moses—appear with Jesus. Because Jesus has not yet been raised from the dead in story (gospel) time, the narrator indicates that the theological event occurs six days after Jesus speaks about the kingdom of God; the number six represents incompleteness. The theological event is confirmed using the number three—three apostles, three dead people—indicating the divine presence of God. Because ancient gods were capable of transfiguration, this theological event also serves the purpose of placing Jesus in the category of divinity. Both the whiteness of Jesus' clothing and the presence of a cloud harken to signs of God's presence at Mount Horeb (Sinai) (Exod 19:9–11, 14–16). Thus, the voice coming from the cloud identifying Jesus as God's Son becomes a theophany, the appearance of God. The theological, theophanic purpose of the narrative is confirmed by the three sets of three—three apostles, three dead men, three shelters (tents). And like any other theophany, it ceases as quickly as it begins (Mark 9:8).

Evening
Antiphon: "O LORD God of hosts, hear my prayer; / give ear, O God . . . !" (Ps 84:8, NRSV)
Psalm: "How lovely is your dwelling place, / O LORD of hosts! / My soul longs, indeed it faints / for the courts of the LORD; / my heart and my flesh sing for joy to the living God. / Even the sparrow finds a home, / and the swallow a nest for herself, / where she may lay her young, / at your altars, O LORD of hosts, / my King and my God. / Happy are those who live in your house, / ever singing your praise. / For a day in your courts is better than a thousand elsewhere. / For the LORD God is a sun and shield; / he bestows favor and honor. / No good thing does the LORD withhold from those who walk uprightly." (Ps 84:1–4, 10a, 11, NRSV)
Repeat Antiphon (above):
Reading: "Six days later Jesus took Peter, James, and John the brother of James, and led them up a high mountain where they were alone; and in their presence he was transfigured; his face shone like the sun, and his clothes became white as the light. And they saw Moses and Elijah appear, conversing with him. . . . [A] bright cloud suddenly overshadowed them, and a voice called from the cloud: 'This is my Son, my Beloved, on whom my favor rests; listen to him.'" (Matt 17:1–3, 5, NEB)
Points to Ponder: The author of Matthew's Gospel copied and adapted the transfiguration account he found in Mark's Gospel. First, he kept the "six days later" to indicate the incompleteness of Jesus' death and resurrection at the mid-point of his story. Second, he kept the three sets of three—apostles, dead men, and shelters (tents)—that he found in Mark's version. Third, knowing the importance of describing God in terms of light, he changed Mark's description of Jesus' clothing from brighter than any bleacher could make them to white as light. Fourth, he kept the characteristics of a HB (OT) theophany: mountain, cloud, and voice. Fifth, the author of Matthew's Gospel changed the words of the heavenly voice, adding that God's favor rests upon Jesus. Sixth, in Matthew's version of the transfiguration, Jesus' face shined like the sun, like Moses' face did, after he spent time in the divine presence (Exod 34:29).

Day 16: Thursday of the Second Week of Lent

Morning
Antiphon: "Praise the LORD!" (Ps 113:1a, NRSV)

Psalm: "Praise, O servants of the LORD; / praise the name of the LORD. / Blessed be the name of the LORD / from this time on and forevermore. / From the rising of the sun to its setting / the name of the LORD is to be praised. / The LORD is high above all nations, / and his glory above the heavens. / Who is like the LORD our God, / who is seated on high . . . ?" (Ps 113:1b–5, NRSV)

Repeat Antiphon (above):

Reading: "About eight days [later, Jesus] took Peter, John, and James with him and went up into the hills to pray. And while he was praying the appearance of his face changed and his clothes became dazzling white. Suddenly there were two men talking with him; these were Moses and Elijah, who appeared in glory and spoke of his departure, the destiny he was to fulfill in Jerusalem. . . . [T]here came a cloud which cast a shadow over them; they were afraid as they entered the cloud, and from it came a voice: 'This is my Son, my Chosen; listen to him.'"(Luke 9:28–31, 34, NEB)

Points to Ponder: After looking at the narrative of the transfiguration found in Mark's Gospel and Matthew's Gospel yesterday, today begins with the account found in Luke's Gospel. The author of Luke's Gospel took the transfiguration story he found in Mark and adapted it to the needs of his account of the good news. First, the transfiguration occurred on the eighth day, a number signifying completion. Second, as in the author of Mark's Gospel narrative, the author of Luke's Gospel kept the three sets of three—apostles, dead men, and shelters (tents)—to indicate the presence of God. Third, Jesus goes into the hills to pray; Jesus at prayer is a favorite theme of the author of Luke's Gospel. Fourth, just as Mary was overshadowed by the Holy Spirit (Luke 1:35), the three apostles are overshadowed and, like Moses on Mount Horeb (Sinai), they enter the cloud and hear the divine voice identify Jesus as God's Son, the chosen one. Fifth, Moses and Elijah, long dead but who appear in glory, speak about Jesus' departure in Jerusalem. The word in Greek for *departure* is *exodus*, referring both to his exodus from the tomb (resurrection) and his exodus from the earth (ascension), unique to Luke's Gospel.

Evening

Antiphon: "Praise the Lord!" (Ps 112:1a, NRSV)

Psalm: "Happy are those who fear the LORD, / who greatly delight in his commandments. / They rise in the darkness as a light for the upright; / they are gracious, merciful, and righteous. / Their hearts are steady, they will not be afraid . . . . / They have distributed freely, they have given to

the poor; / their righteousness endures forever; / their horn is exalted in honor." (Ps 112:1b, 4, 8a, 9, NRSV)
Repeat Antiphon (above):
Reading: "We . . . are citizens of heaven, and from heaven we expect our deliverer to come, the Lord Jesus Christ. He will transfigure the body belonging to our humble state, and give it a form like that of his own resplendent body, by the very power which enables him to make all things subject to himself." (Phil 3:20–21, NEB)
Meditation/Journal: What does the passage from Paul's Letter to the Philippians have to do with the transfiguration narratives (above) from the gospels according to Mark, Matthew, and Luke? How do the verses from Psalm 112 illustrate the two-verse passage from the letter to the Philippians?

Day 17: Friday of the Second Week of Lent
Morning
Antiphon: ". . . [T]hey sow fields, and plant vineyards, / and get a fruitful yield." (Ps 107:37, NRSV)
Psalm: "You [, O God,] brought a vine out of Egypt; / you drove out the nations and planted it. / You cleared the ground for it; / it took root and filled the land. / The mountains were covered with its shade, / the mighty cedars with its branches; / it sent out its branches to the sea, / and its shoots to the River [Euphrates]. / Why then have you broken down its walls, / so that all who pass along the way pluck its fruit?" (Ps 80:8–12, NRSV)
Repeat Antiphon (above):
Reading: "I will sing for my beloved / my love-song about his vineyard: / My beloved had a vineyard / high up on a fertile hill-side. / He trenched it and cleared it of stones / and planted it with red vines; / he built a watchtower in the middle / and then hewed out a winepress in it. / He looked for it to yield grapes, / but it yielded wild grapes. / Now, you who live . . . , / judge between me and my vineyard. / What more could have been done for my vineyard / that I did not do in it? / Why when I looked for it to yield grapes, / did it yield wild grapes?" (Isa 5:1–4, NEB)
Meditation/Journal: For whom is the vineyard metaphor intended? Explain. How does Psalm 80's question to God—Why have you broken down its walls, so that all who pass along the way pluck its fruit?—answered in Isaiah's love-song about a vineyard (Isa 5:1–4)? How do you

answer God's questions: What more could have been done for the vineyard? Why did the vineyard yield wild (sour) grapes?

Evening
Antiphon: "Stir up your might, [O Shepherd,] / and come to save us!" (Ps 80:2b, NRSV)
Psalm: "Turn again, O God of hosts; / look down from heaven, and see, / have regard for this vine, / the stock that your right hand planted. / [Enemies] have burned it with fire, they have cut it down; / may they perish at the rebuke of your countenance. / But let your hand be upon the one at your right hand, / the one whom you made strong for yourself. / Then we will never turn back from you; / give us life, and we will call on your name. / Restore us, O LORD God of hosts; / let your face shine, that we may be saved." (Ps 80:14–19, NRSV)
Repeat Antiphon (above):
Readings:
(a) "A man planted a vineyard and put a wall round it, hewed out a winepress, and built a watch-tower; then he let it out to vine-growers and went abroad. When the season came, he sent a servant to the tenants to collect from them his share of the produce. But they took him, thrashed him, and sent him away empty-handed. Again he sent them another servant, whom they beat about the head and treated outrageously. So he sent another, and that one they killed; and many more besides, of whom they beast some, and killed others. He had now only one left to send, his own dear son. In the end he sent him. 'They will respect my son,' he said. But the tenants seized him and killed him, and flung his body out of the vineyard. What will the owner of the vineyard do?" (Mark 12:1b–6, 8–9a, NEB)
(b) "There was a landowner who planted a vineyard: he put a wall round it, hewed out a winepress, and built a watch-tower; then he let it out to vine-growers and went abroad. When the vintage season approached, he sent his servants to the tenants to collect the produce due to him. But they took his servants and thrashed one, killed another, and stoned a third. Again, he sent other servants, this time a larger number; and they did the same to them. At last he sent to them his son. 'They will respect my son,' he said. But when they saw the son the tenants . . . took him, flung him out of the vineyard, and killed him. When the owner of the vineyard comes, how do you think he will deal with those tenants?" (Matthew 21:33b–38a, 39–40, NEB)

(c) "A man planted a vineyard, let it out to vine-growers, and went abroad for a long time. When the season came, he sent a servant to the tenants to collect from them his share of the produce, but the tenants thrashed him and sent him away empty-handed. He tried again and sent a second servant; but he also was thrashed, outrageously treated, and sent away empty-handed. He tired once more with a third; this one too they wounded and flung out. Then the owner of the vineyard said, 'What am I to do? I will send my own dear son; perhaps they will respect him.' But when the tenants saw him . . . , they flung him out of the vineyard and killed him. What then will the owner of the vineyard do to them?" (Luke 20:9b–13, 14a, 15, NEB)

Activity: Make a list of the similarities in the three versions of the parable of the vineyard above. Make a list of the differences in the three versions of the parable above? What do you notice from your lists? Answer the question posed by the Markan Jesus: What will the owner of the vineyard do? Answer the question posed by the Matthean Jesus: When the owner of the vineyard comes, how do you think he will deal with those tenants? Answer the question posed by the Lukan Jesus: What will the owner of the vineyard do to the tenants?

Day 18: Saturday of the Second Week of Lent

Morning
Antiphon: "Bless the LORD, O my soul. / O LORD my God, you are very great. / You are clothed with honor and majesty, / wrapped in light as with a garment." (Ps 104:1–2a, NRSV)
Psalm: "You [, O LORD,] cause the grass to grow for the cattle, / and plants for people to use, / to bring forth food from the earth, / and wine to gladden the human heart, / oil to make the face shine, / and bread to strengthen the human heart. / O LORD, how manifold are your works! / In wisdom you have made them all; / the earth is full of your creatures. / May the glory of the LORD endure forever; / may the LORD rejoice in his works . . . . / May my meditation be pleasing to him, / for I rejoice in the LORD." (Ps 104:14–15, 24, 31, 34, NRSV)
Repeat Antiphon (above):
Reading: "Naboth of Jezreel had a vineyard near the palace of Ahab king of Samaria. One day Ahab made a proposal to Naboth: 'Your vineyard is close to my palace; let me have it for a garden; I will give you a better vineyard in exchange for it or, if you prefer, its value in silver.' But Naboth

answered, 'The LORD forbid that I should let you have land which has always been in my family.' His wife Jezebel came . . . to him and said, 'I will make you a gift of the vineyard of Naboth of Jezreel.' So she wrote a letter in Ahab's name, sealed it with his seal, and sent it to the elders and notables of Naboth's city, who sat in council with him. She wrote: 'Proclaim a fast and give Naboth the seat of honor among the people. And see that two scoundrels are seated opposite him to charge him with cursing God and the king, then take him out and stone him to death.' As soon as Jezebel heard that Naboth had been stoned and was dead, she said to Ahab, 'Get up and take possession of the vineyard which Naboth refused to sell you, for he is no longer alive; Naboth of Jezreel is dead.' Then the word of the LORD came to Elijah the Tishbite: 'Go down at once to Ahab king of Israel, who is in Samaria; you will find him in Naboth's vineyard, where he has gone to take possession. Say to him, "This is the word of the LORD: Have you killed your man, and taken his land as well?"' Ahab said to Elijah, 'Have you found me, my enemy?' 'I have found you,' he said, 'because you have sold yourself to do what is wrong in the eyes of the LORD.'" (1 Kgs 21:1–3, 5a, 7b–10, 15, 17–19b, 20, NEB)

Activity: In the passage from the HB (OT) First Book of Kings identify all the wrongs done in the eyes of the LORD. After reviewing your list, ask yourself this question: Where do you find the same kinds of wrongs being done today?

Evening
Antiphon: "May our sons in their youth / be like plants full grown, / our daughters like corner pillars, / cut for the building of a palace." (Ps 144:12, NRSV)

Psalm: "Sons are indeed a heritage from the LORD, / the fruit of the womb a reward. / Like arrows in the hand of a warrior / are the sons of one's youth. / Happy is the man who has / his quiver full of them." (Ps 127:3–5a, NRSV)

Repeat Antiphon (above):
Reading: Jesus said: "A man had two sons. He went to the first, and said, 'My boy, go and work today in the vineyard.' 'I will, sir,' the boy replied; but he never went. The father came to the second and said the same, 'I will not,' he replied, but afterwards he changed his mind and went. Which of these two did as his father wished?" (Matt 21:28–31a, NEB)

Activity: Answer this question: Which of the two sons did what his father wanted? Why is the parable about working in a vineyard? Where would the parable be set today? Who would the two sons be?

Day 19: Third Sunday of Lent

Morning
Antiphon: "O give thanks to the LORD, for he is good, / for his steadfast love endures forever." (Ps 136:1, NRSV)
Psalm: "O give thanks to the Lord of lords, / for his steadfast love endures forever; / who alone does great wonders, / for his steadfast love endures forever, / who by understanding made the heavens, / for his steadfast love endures forever; / who spread out the earth on the waters, / for his steadfast love endures forever . . . ." (Ps 136:3–6, NRSV)
Repeat Antiphon (above):
Reading: "In the beginning of creation, when God made heaven and earth, the earth was without form and void, with darkness over the face of the abyss, and a mighty wind that swept over the surface of the waters. God said, 'Let there be a vault between the waters, to separate water from water.' So God made the vault, and separated the water under the vault from the water above it, and so it was; and God called the vault heaven. Evening came, and morning came, a second day." (Gen 1:1–2, 6–8, NEB)
Points to Ponder: First, based on the cosmology of the verses from Psalm 136 and the words of the HB (OT) book of Genesis, rain falls from the heavens, because God separated the water, a sign of chaos, with a dome, placing some water above the dome and some water on the earth below the dome. When people wanted rain, they prayed to God, asking him to open the floodgates and let some out! Second, the mighty wind sweeping over the surface of the water can also be translated as the spirit of God, like a bird, hovering over the waters. In other words, God is ready to hatch creation. Third, in Hebrew understanding, a day lasted from sunset to sunset, not like our day from midnight to midnight.

Evening
Antiphon: "Rejoice in the LORD, O you righteous. / Praise befits the upright." (Ps 33:1, NRSV)
Psalm: "Praise the LORD with the lyre; / make melody to him with the harp of ten strings. / Sing to him a new song; / play skillfully on the strings, with loud shouts. / For the word of the LORD is upright, / and all

his work is done in faithfulness. / He loves righteousness and justice; / the earth is full of the steadfast love of the LORD. / By the word of the LORD the heavens were made, / and all their host by the breath of his mouth. / He gathered the waters of the sea as in a bottle; / he put the deeps in storehouses." (Psalm 33: 2–7, NRSV)

Repeat Antiphon (above):

Reading: "God said, 'Let the waters under heaven be gathered into one place, so that dry land may appear'; and so it was. God called the dry land earth, and the gathering of the waters he called seas; and God saw that it was good." (Gen 1:9–10, NEB)

Reflection: In the ancient world, water represented chaos, just like flood waters do today. In the HB (OT) book of Genesis, God is presented as the one who conquers the chaos. His mighty wind or spirit sweeps over the waters. He separates the waters with a dome—presuming a flat plate-like earth—that places water above the dome and water below the dome on the earth. Then, further order ensues, as God gathers the water on the earth into seas. In other words, God creates boundaries or order so that life can flourish on dry land. During Lent, it is useful to identify the chaos of one's life (usually named sin) and seek God's help to bring order to it. According to the author of the HB (OT) book of Genesis, God sees boundaries or order as a good to make life flourish.

Day 20: Monday of the Third Week of Lent

Morning

Antiphon: "The LORD is king, he is robed in majesty; / the LORD is robed, he is girded with strength. / He has established the world; it shall never be moved . . . ." (Ps 93:1, NRSV)

Psalm: "The floods have lifted up, O LORD, / the floods have lifted up their voice; / the floods lift up their roaring. / More majestic than the thunders of mighty waters, / more majestic than the waves of the sea, / majestic on high is the LORD!" (Ps 93:3–4, NRSV)

Repeat Antiphon (above):

Reading: ". . . Noah had won the LORD's favor. God said to Noah, 'The loathsomeness of all mankind has become plain to me, for through them the earth is full of violence. I intend to destroy them, and the earth with them. I intend to bring the waters of the flood over the earth to destroy every human being under heaven that has the spirit of life; everything on earth shall perish. But with you I will make a covenant, and you shall go into the ark, you and your sons, your wife, and your sons' wives with you." (Gen 6:8, 13, 17–18, NEB)

Reflection: Water represents chaos, and a flood represents the epitome of chaos. After God brought order to the chaos, according to the author of the HB (OT) book of Genesis, people brought chaotic violence, and God's response is to use flood chaos to wash clean the earth again. The only exception to the cleansing is Noah, who found favor with God, because he did not add to or participate in the chaos. The Noah narrative in Genesis (6:5—9:29) is a composition of two versions of the same story of Noah and the ark. Biblical scholars identify the versions or sources as the Yahwist version and priestly version; the Yahwist version names God LORD, while the priestly version names God God. In written (or oral) form, the two versions were woven into one, but not edited enough to remove the traces remaining of each of the original versions. In the priestly version presented above, the flood lasts for forty days and nights; the number forty represents a lifetime of an average human generation, a long period of time, or a period of testing, trial, or temptation, which occurs during an average human generation. In other words, forty represents a human lifetime of trial. In Noah's case, the lifetime of trial lasts forty days and nights before God, again, brings the watery chaos under control. Lent is considered a forty-day period of each person's attempt, with God's help, to bring order to some of the chaos in his or her life.

Evening

Antiphon: "I lift up my eyes to the hills—/ from where will my help come? (Ps 121:1, NRSV)

Psalm: "If it had not been the LORD who was on our side . . . / if it had not been the LORD who was on our side, . . . / then the flood would have swept us away, / the torrent would have gone over us; / then over us would have gone / the raging waters. Blessed be the LORD . . . . / Our help is in the name of the LORD, / who made heaven and earth." (Ps 124:1a, 2a, 4–6a, 8, NRSV)

Repeat Antiphon (above):

Reading: ". . . God waited patiently in the days of Noah and the building of the ark, and in the ark a few persons, eight in all, were brought to safety through the water. This water prefigured the water of baptism through which you are now brought to safety. Baptism is not the washing away of bodily pollution, but the appeal made to God by a good conscience; and it brings salvation through the resurrection of Jesus Christ . . . ." (1 Pet 3:20–21, NEB)

Meditation/Journal: If you have been baptized, what safety has it brought you? If you have not been baptism, what do you think about the interpretation of the Noah story by the author of the CB (NT) book of First Peter?

Day 21: Tuesday of the Third Week of Lent

Morning

Antiphon: "Praise is due to you / O God . . . ." (Ps 65:1a, NRSV)

Psalm: "You visit the earth [, O God,] and water it, / you greatly enrich it; / the river of God is full of water; / you provide the people with grain, / for so you have prepared it. / You water its furrows abundantly, / settling its ridges, / softening it with showers, / and blessing its growth. / The pastures of the wilderness overflow, / the hills gird themselves with joy, / the meadows clothe themselves with flocks, / the valleys deck themselves with grain, / they shout and sing together for joy." (Ps 65:9–10, 12–13, NRSV)

Repeat Antiphon (above):

Reading: "There was a river flowing from Eden to water the garden, and when it left the garden, it branched into four streams. The name of the first is Pishon . . . . The name of the second river is Gihon . . . . The name of the third is Tigris . . . . The fourth river is the Euphrates." (Gen 2:10–11a, 13a, 14, NEB)

Reflection: The verses from Psalm 65 prepare the reader for the passage from the HB (OT) book of Genesis about an unnamed river flowing out of the Garden of Eden and branching into four rivers. This passage from Genesis is seldom read, but it is full of significance. The garden of life produces the river of life: "A flood used to rise out of the earth and water all the surface of the ground" (Gen 2:6). The four rivers which flowed from the life-giving water indicate that the whole earth has become a place of life. Four is the number for the earth; we still use it today with the four cardinal directions of North, South, East, and West. In ancient cosmology, the earth was a plate-like structure, supported by seven columns. Over the earth was a dome, which kept the waters above from the waters gathered into the seas on the earth. As Psalm 65 states, God's river is full of water, which fills the furrows of fields and settles the ridges. When it falls as rain from the water above the dome, it softens the earth with showers, and grain grows for people to eat. The water flows into the pastures and meadows, where it grows grass for the flocks of sheep. Even the meadows shout and sing about the abundance of water, the abundance of God.

Evening
Antiphon: "[The LORD] divided the sea and let [the Hebrews] pass through it, / and made the waters stand like a heap." (Ps 78:13, NRSV)
Psalm: "I will call to mind the deeds of the LORD; / I will remember your wonders of old. / When the waters saw you, O God, / when the waters saw you, they were afraid; / the very deep trembled. / The clouds poured out water; the skies thundered . . . . The crash of your thunder was in the whirlwind; / your lightnings lit up the world; / the earth trembled and shook. / Your way was through the sea, / your path, through the mighty waters; / yet your footprints were unseen." (Ps 77:11, 16–19, NRSV)
Repeat Antiphon (above):
Reading: ". . . Moses stretched out his hand over the sea, and the LORD drove the sea away all night with a strong east wind and turned the seabed into dry land. The waters were torn apart, and the Israelites went through the sea on the dry ground, while the waters made a wall for them to right and to left." (Exod 14:21–22, NEB)
Reflection: Keeping in mind that water signifies chaos, after their escape from Egypt, the Israelites find themselves camped opposite the Sea of Reeds, otherwise called the Red Sea. In the distance they can see the clouds of dust raised by Pharaoh's army of chariots pulled by horses with men riding in them ready to attack their run-away slaves. While it looks like the Israelites are trapped in the chaos, God, who turns chaos to order, splits the sea into two parts so that the Israelites can pass over. And that is what they do on the dry ground of the sea bed. Through the ordered waters walled on the right and the left, the Israelites pass from slavery to freedom and from impending death to life. After all Israel has passed over, God instructs Moses to return the sea to chaos. Pharaoh and his army of chariots have gotten mired in the mud, and they cannot outrun the return of the sea. Thus, they are drowned in the chaos, while the band of slaves escapes to an ordered life on the other side of the sea.

Day 22: Wednesday of the Third Week of Lent

Morning
Antiphon: "Tremble, O earth, at the presence of the LORD . . . ." (Ps 114:7a, NRSV)

Psalm: "When Israel went out from Egypt, / The sea looked and fled; / Jordan turned back. / The mountains skipped like rams, / the hills like lambs. / Why is it, O sea, that you flee? / O Jordan, that you turn back? / O mountains, that you skip like rams? / O hills, like lambs? Tremble, O earth, at the presence of the LORD, who turns the rock into a pool of water, / the flint into a spring of water." (Ps 114:1a, 3–7a, 8, NRSV)
Repeat Antiphon (above):
Reading: "... [T]he Jordan is in full flood in all its reaches throughout the time of harvest. When the priests reached the Jordan and dipped their feet in the water at the edge, the water coming down from upstream was brought to a standstill; it piled up like a bank for a long way back.... The waters coming down to the ... Dead Sea were completely cut off, and the people crossed over.... The priests carrying the Ark of the Covenant of the LORD stood firm on the dry bed in the middle of the Jordan; and all Israel passed over on dry ground until the whole nation had crossed the river." (Josh 3:15–17, NEB)
Points to Ponder: First, in the HB (OT) Joshua is presented as a type of Moses; his character is modeled on Moses. Thus, just like Moses stretched out his hands over the Sea of Reeds and the water parted for the Hebrews to pass through it on dry ground, Joshua instructs the priests carrying the Ark of the Covenant to step into the Jordan River, which parts so that the Israelites can cross into the Promised Land on dry ground. Second, both biblical events are commemorated in Psalm 114. Using poetic language, the psalmist personifies the Red Sea; it looks at the Hebrews and divides; the Jordan, too, divides. The water trembles at the presence of God, who in the beginning brought order to the chaotic waters, and who, while the Israelites were in the desert, brought water out of a rock. Third, crossing water indicates change. Once the Hebrews passed through the Sea of Reeds, they became the Israelites, who spent forty years in the desert of change. Once the Israelites crossed the Jordan, they inherited the Promised Land; under Joshua's leadership the land was divided and given to the tribes. The desert wanderers became farmers and city-dwellers. During the Season of Lent, it is good to name the waters we have crossed and the changes that ensued.

Evening
Antiphon: "Blessed be the LORD, my rock." (Ps 144:1a, NRSV)
Psalm: "Blessed be the LORD, my rock, ... / my rock and my fortress, / my stronghold and my deliverer, / my shield, in whom I take refuge.... /

Bow your heavens, O LORD, and come down; / touch the mountains so that they smoke. / Make the lightning flash and scatter them . . . . / Send out your hand from on high; / set me free and rescue me from the mighty waters . . . . (Ps 144: 1a, 2, 5–6a, 7, NRSV)
Repeat Antiphon (above):
Reading: "Elijah took his cloak, rolled it up and struck the water [of the Jordan River] with it. The water divided to right and left, and [he and Elisha] both crossed over on dry ground. [Elisha] picked up the cloak which had fallen from Elijah [as he was carried up in a whirlwind to heaven], and came back and stood on the bank of the Jordan. There he too struck the water with Elijah's cloak . . . . When he struck the water, it was again divided to right and left, and he crossed over." (2 Kgs 2:8, 13–14, NEB)
Reflection: In the narrative about the prophets Elijah and Elisha imbedded in the First and Second Books of Kings, both prophets are modeled on Moses. Elijah travels to Mount Horeb (Sinai) and ascends the mountain to speak to God, just like Moses did. Moses opened a path on dry ground through the Red Sea so the Hebrews could escape their Egyptian enemies; Elijah opened a way through the Jordan River so that he could leave the earth in a whirlwind. Elijah is to Moses like Elisha is to Joshua. Thus, after Elijah disappears, Elisha takes his cloak and strikes the Jordan River, which divides for him like it did for Joshua. All the biblical crossings of a sea and a river are the ways God, in the words of Psalm 144, rescues people from mighty waters. Moreover, each of those crossings is a passover; some kind of imminent death results in abundant life, signified by the water itself. The Hebrews face imminent death at the hands of the Egyptian army, but they passover to new life. Elijah faces imminent death after defeating the prophets of Baal, but he not only passes over the Jordan; he passes over from earthly to heavenly life. Likewise, Elisha, who has been chosen as Elijah's successor, discovers the water supply of Jericho to be polluted; after he crosses the Jordan River, he pours salt into it to purify it. Like the HB (OT) characters of the past, daily people face various kinds of situations that have some kind of death attached to them; by crossing over or through, by passing over them, they can discover new life.

Day 23: Thursday of the Third Week of Lent
Morning
Antiphon: "I love you, O LORD, my strength." (Ps 18:1, NRSV)

SEASON OF LENT

Psalm: "I call upon the LORD, who is worthy to be praised .... / In my distress I called upon the LORD; / to my God I cried for help. / He bowed the heavens, and came down; / thick darkness was under his feet. / He rode on a cherub, and flew; / he came swiftly upon the wings of the wind. / He made darkness his covering around him, / his canopy thick clouds dark with water. / He reached down from on high, he took me; / he drew me out of mighty waters." (Ps 18:3a, 6a, 9–11, 16, NRSV)
Repeat Antiphon (above):
Reading: "... [I]n baptism you were buried with [Christ], in baptism also you were raised to life with him through your faith in the active power of God who raised him from the dead." (Col 2:12, NEB)
Meditation/Journal: In what specific experiences of your life have you been buried with Christ? In what specific experiences of your life has the LORD drawn you out of the mighty waters?

Evening
Antiphon: "Our help is in the name of the LORD, / who made heaven and earth." (Ps 124:8, NRSV)
Psalm: "[The LORD] sends out his command to the earth; / his word runs swiftly. / He gives snow like wool; / he scatters frost like ashes. / He hurls down hail like crumbs—/ who can stand before his cold? / He sends out his word, and melts them; / he makes his wind blow, and the waters flow." (Ps 147:15–18, NRSV)
Repeat Antiphon (above):
Reading: "Have you forgotten that when we were baptized into union with Christ Jesus we were baptized into his death? By baptism we were buried with him and lay dead, in order that, as Christ was raised from the dead in the splendor of the Father, so also we might set our feet upon the new path of life. For if we have become incorporated with him in a death like his, we shall also be one with him in a resurrection like his." (Rom 6:3–5, NEB)
Intercessions: For all who are preparing for baptism, I pray to you, O LORD. For all who have been baptized into the death and resurrection of Christ, I pray to you, O LORD. For all who receive God's word and ponder it, I pray to you, O LORD. For all whose feet have been set upon a new path of life, I pray to you, O LORD. For all who lie dead, I pray to you, O LORD. For all who await resurrection, I pray to you, O LORD.

Day 24: Friday of the Third Week of Lent

Morning
Antiphon: "Have mercy upon us, O LORD, have mercy upon us." (Ps 123:3a, NRSV)
Psalm: "The LORD is my shepherd. I shall not want. / He makes me lie down in green pastures; / he leads me beside still waters; / he restores my soul. / He leads me in right paths / for his name's sake. / Even though I walk through the darkest valley, / I fear no evil; / for you are with me; / your rod and your staff—/ they comfort me. / Surely goodness and mercy shall follow me / all the days of my life, / and I shall dwell in the house of the LORD / my whole life long." (Ps 23:1-4, 6, NRSV)
Repeat Antiphon (above):
Reading: "Pharaoh's daughter . . . noticed the basket [with the three-month old Hebrew baby boy in it] among the reeds and sent her slave-girl for it. She took it from her and when she opened it, she saw the child. It was crying, and she was filled with pity for it. . . . Pharaoh's daughter . . . adopted him and called him Moses, 'because,' she said, 'I drew him out of the water.'" (Exod 2:5-6, 10, NEB)
Points to Ponder: First, the Hebrew word translated into English as basket is used only one other time in the Bible: Genesis 6:14, where it is translated into English as *ark*. Second, the narrative about Moses' rescue from a basket-ark is like God's rescue of Noah and his family in an ark; both are water rescues. Second, Pharaoh's daughter contradicts her father's decree about killing Hebrew baby boys after they were born (Exod 1:16). Third, biblical scholars differ as to the meaning of the name *Moses*; some think it is a play on a Hebrew verb meaning *to draw out*; others think it was originally joined to that of the Egyptian deity *Ra* to become *Ra-moses* or *Rameses* (Exod 1:11); thus, Pharaoh's unnamed daughter names the baby in the basket using one-half of a divine name.

Evening
Antiphon: "[God] made streams come out of the rock, / and caused waters to flow down like rivers." (Ps 78:16, NRSV)
Psalm: "[The LORD] brought Israel out [of Egypt] / and there was no one among [the Hebrew] tribes who stumbled. / He spread a cloud for a covering, / and fire to give light by night. / He opened the rock, and water gushed out; / it flowed through the desert like a river. / For he remembered his holy promise, / and Abraham, his servant." (Ps 105:37, 39, 41-42, NRSV)

Repeat Antiphon (above):

Reading: "[T]he [Israelites] became so thirsty that they raised an outcry against Moses: 'Why have you brought us out of Egypt with our children and our herds to let us all die of thirst?' Moses cried to the LORD, 'What shall I do with these people?' The LORD answered, 'Go forward ahead of the people; take with you . . . the staff with which you struck the Nile, and go. You will find me waiting for you there, by a rock in Horeb. Strike the rock; water will pour out of it, and the people shall drink.'" (Exod 17:3–6a, NEB)

Meditation/Journal: Recently, when have you found yourself in some type of wilderness needing some kind of refreshment? Explain. What rock did God instruct you to strike so that what you needed flowed out of it?

Day 25: Saturday of the Third Week of Lent

Antiphon: "Hear my prayer, O LORD; / give ear to my supplications in your faithfulness; / answer me in your righteousness." (Ps 143:1, NRSV)

Psalm: "O God, you are my God, I seek you, / my soul thirsts for you; / my flesh faints for you, / as in a dry and weary land where there is no water. / So I have looked upon you in the sanctuary, / beholding your power and glory. / Because your steadfast love is better than life, / my lips will praise you. / So I will bless you as long as I live; / I will lift up my hands and call on your name." (Ps 63:1–4, NRSV)

Repeat Antiphon (above):

Reading: "There was one of the Pharisees named Nicodemus, a member of the Jewish Council, who came to Jesus by night. 'Rabbi,' he said, 'we know that you are a teacher sent by God . . . .' Jesus answered, 'In truth, in very truth I tell you, unless a man has been born over again he cannot see the kingdom of God. In truth I tell you, no one can enter the kingdom of God without being born from water and spirit.'" (John 3:1–3, 5a, NEB)

Meditation/Journal: In what specific ways does your spirit thirst for God? In what specific ways have you been born over again? In what specific ways have you been born from water and spirit?

Evening

Antiphon: "Out of the depths I cry to you, O LORD." (Ps 130:1, NRSV)

Psalm: "Lord, hear my voice! / Let your ears be attentive / to the voice of my supplications! / If you, O LORD, should mark iniquities, / Lord, who could stand? / But there is forgiveness with you, / so that you may be revered. / I wait for the LORD, my soul waits, / and in his word I hope; / my soul waits for the Lord / more than those who watch for the morning, / more than those who watch for the morning. / For with the LORD there is steadfast love, / and with him is great power to redeem." (Ps 130:2–6, 7b, NRSV)

Repeat Antiphon (above):

Reading: "... [A] Samaritan woman came to draw water [from the spring called Jacob's well]. Jesus said to her, 'Give me a drink. If only you knew what God gives and who it is that is asking you for a drink, you would have asked him and he would have given you living water. Everyone who drinks this water will be thirsty again, but whoever drinks the water that I shall give him [or her] will never suffer thirst any more. The water that I shall give him [or her] will be an inner spring always welling up for eternal life.' 'Sir,' said the woman, 'give me that water, and then I shall not be thirsty, nor have to come all this way to draw.'" (John 4:7, 10, 13–15, NEB)

Meditation/Journal: In the passage from chapter 4 of John's Gospel, to what is the Johannine Jesus comparing water? Explain.

Day 26: Fourth Sunday of Lent

Morning

Antiphon: "My foot stands on level ground, / in the great congregation I will bless the LORD." (Ps 26:12, NRSV)

Psalm: "Vindicate me, O LORD, / for I have walked in my integrity, / and I have trusted in the LORD without wavering. / Prove me, O LORD, and try me; / test my heart and mind. / For your steadfast love is before my eyes, / and I walk in faithfulness to you. / I wash my hands in innocence, / and go around your altar, O LORD, / singing aloud a song of thanksgiving, / and telling all your wondrous deeds. / O LORD, I love the house in which you dwell, / and the place where your glory abides." (Ps 26:1–3, 6–8, NRSV)

Repeat Antiphon (above):

Reading: "Naaman, commander of the King of Aram's army, was a great man highly esteemed by his master, . . . but he was a leper. Elisha, the man of God, . . . sent [word to the king of Israel, saying,] 'Let the man come to me, and he will know that there is a prophet in Israel.' So Naaman came with his horses and chariots and stood at the entrance to Elisha's house.

Elisha sent out a messenger to say to him, 'If you will go and wash seven times in the Jordan, your flesh will be restored and you will be clean.' So he went down and dipped himself in the Jordan seven times as the man of God had told him, and his flesh was restored as a little child's and he was clean. Then he and his retinue went back to the man of God and stood before him; and he said, 'Now I know that there is no god anywhere on earth except in Israel.... [L]et me, sir, have two mules' load of earth.'" (2 Kgs 5:1, 8b–10, 14–15ab, 17a, NEB)

Points to Ponder: First, Naaman, the army commander for the king of Aram, represents one of Israel's enemies; in fact, the Arameans had been raiding Israel, capturing Israelites, and enslaving them. Second, there is obvious irony in that Naaman seeks a cure for his leprosy from his enemy. Third, Elisha, successor of Elijah, will not leave his house to speak to the great man Naaman. Fourth, Elisha sends Naaman to the Jordan River; he is to immerse himself in it seven times. Fifth, seven is a sacred number: it is the sum of three (God) and four (earth). In other words, Naaman is sent by the man of God to plunge himself into everything. Sixth, Naaman's cure results in that religious enemy's declaration that there is no god except Israel's LORD God. Seventh, Naaman wants a wagon-full of Israelite soil to take back with him to Aram; then he will be able to worship the LORD on God's own dirt. The story of Naaman imbedded in the HB (OT) Second Book of Kings indicates that God shows no partiality in curing. If the enemy army commanded can be cured of his leprosy, who can't be cured?

Evening
Antiphon: "O LORD my God, I cried to you for help, / and you have healed me." (Ps 30:2, NRSV)
Psalm: "To you, O LORD, I cried, / and to the LORD I made supplication. / Hear, O LORD, and be gracious to me! / O LORD, be my helper! / You have turned my mourning into dancing; / you have taken off my sackcloth / and clothed me with joy, / so that my soul may praise you and not be silent. / O LORD my God, I will give thanks to you forever." (Ps 30:8, 10–12, NRSV)
Repeat Antiphon (above):
Reading: "[Jesus] came to Nazareth, where he had been brought up, and went to synagogue on the Sabbath day as he regularly did. He stood up to read the lesson and was handed the scroll of the prophet Isaiah. He rolled up the scroll, gave it back to the attendant, and sat down; and all eyes in

the synagogue were fixed on him. He began to speak: 'I tell you this,' he [said]: 'no prophet is recognized in his own country. . . . [I]n the time of the prophet Elisha there were many lepers in Israel, and not one of them was healed, but only Naaman, the Syrian.' At these words the whole congregation [was] infuriated." (Luke 4:16, 20–21a, 24, 27–28, NEB)
Points to Ponder: First, the Lukan Jesus delivers his first sermon in his hometown of Nazareth. Second, only the author of Luke's Gospel presents a literate Jesus. Third, Jesus reminds his hearers that there is a history among his people of not recognizing the prophets God sends them. In so doing, Jesus is indicating that he, another prophet, will not be recognized; in other words, he is informing the reader of the end of the story. Fourth, one of the examples of the Israelites not recognizing their prophets is Elisha. At the time Elisha lived, there were many lepers in Israel. No Israelite leper was healed because they did not recognize him as a prophet. However, the commander of the army of Aram, a non-believer and an enemy, was healed by Elisha. Fifth, after Jesus rubbed salt into their wounds, his hometown crowd become infuriated; they did not like being reminded of their unfaithful past and the non-recognition of the prophet God sent them.

Day 27: Monday of the Fourth Week of Lent

Morning

Antiphon: "Do not be far from me, [God,] / for trouble is near / and there is no one to help." (Ps 22:11, NRSV)

Psalm: "[God,] I am poured out like water, / and all my bones are out of joint; / my heart is like wax; / it is melted within my breast; / my mouth is dried up like a potsherd; / and my tongue sticks to my jaws; / you lay me in the dust of death. I can count all my bones. / [Evildoers] divide my clothes among themselves, / and for my clothing they cast lots." (Ps 22:14–15, 17a, 18, NRSV)

Repeat Antiphon (above):

Reading: ". . . Israel [Jacob] loved Joseph more than any other of his sons, and he made him a long, sleeved robe. When his brothers saw that their father loved him more than any of them, they hated him and could not say a kind word to him." (Gen 37:3–4, NEB)

Meditation/Journal: Have you ever been in the position of Joseph? Explain. Have you ever been in the position of Joseph's eleven brothers? Explain.

Evening
Antiphon: "The LORD has done great things for us, / and we rejoiced." (Ps 126:3, NRSV)
Psalm: "May those who sow in tears / reap with shouts of joy. / Those who go out weeping, / bearing the seed for sowing, / shall come home with shouts of joy, carrying their sheaves." (Ps 126:5–6, NRSV)
Repeat Antiphon (above):
Reading: "[Joseph had a dream, which he told to his brothers:] 'Listen to this dream I have had. We were in the field binding sheaves, and my sheaf rose on end and stood upright, and your sheaves gathered round and bowed low before my sheaf!" (Gen 37:6–7, NEB)
Meditation/Journal: What connection do you find between the verses of Psalm 126 and the passage from the HB (OT) book of Genesis 37:6–7? What do you think Joseph's dream means?

Day 28: Tuesday of the Fourth Week of Lent

Morning
Antiphon: "Truly God is good to the upright, / to those who are pure in heart." (Ps 73:1, NRSV)
Psalm: ". . . I was envious of the arrogant; / I saw the prosperity of the wicked. / All in vain I have kept my heart clean / and washed my hands in innocence. / For all day long I have been plagued . . . . / They are like a dream when one awakes; / on awakening you despise their phantoms." (Ps 73:3, 13–14a, 20, NRSV)
Repeat Antiphon (above):
Reading: "[Joseph] had another dream, which he told to his father and his brothers. He said, 'Listen: I have had another dream. The sun and moon and eleven stars were bowing down to me.' When he told it to his father and his brothers, his father took him to task: 'What is this dream of yours?' he said. 'Must we come and bow low to the ground before you, I and your mother and your brothers?' His brothers were jealous of him, but his father did not forget." (Gen 37:9–11, NEB)
Journal/Meditation: What connection do you find between the verses of Psalm 73 and the passage from the HB (OT) book of Genesis 37:9–11? What do you think Joseph's dream means?

Evening

Antiphon: "Give ear, O Shepherd..., / you who lead Joseph like a flock!" (Ps 80:1a, NRSV)

Psalm: "Stir up your might, / and come to save us! / Restore us, O God; / let your face shine, that we may be saved. / Turn again, O God of hosts; / look down from heaven, and see; / have regard for this vine, / the stock that your right hand planted." (Ps 80:2b–3, 14–15, NRSV)

Repeat Antiphon (above):

Reading: "Joseph's brothers went to mind their father's flock.... Israel [Jacob] said to him, 'Go and see if all is well with your brothers and the sheep, and bring me back word.' They saw him in the distance, and before he reached them, they plotted to kill him. They said to each other, 'Here comes that dreamer. Now is our chance; let us kill him.... Then we shall see what will come of his dreams.' When Joseph came up to his brothers, they stripped him of the long, sleeved robe which he was wearing, took him, and threw him into [a] pit. Then they sat down to eat some food and, looking up, they saw an Ishmaelite caravan coming in from Gilead on the way down to Egypt.... Judah said to his brothers, 'Why not sell him to the Ishmaelites?' They sold him for twenty pieces of silver to the Ishmaelites and they brought Joseph to Egypt. Joseph's brothers took his robe, killed a goat, and dipped it in the goat's blood. Then they tore the robe, the long, sleeved robe, brought it to their father and said, 'A wild beast has devoured him. Joseph has been torn to pieces.'" (Gen 37:12–13a, 14, 18–20, 23, 25, 27a, 28b, 31–32a, 33b, NEB)

Intercessions: For all who need to be saved from violence, I pray to you, O Lord. For all who are sold into slavery, I pray to you, O Lord. For all who plot to kill others, I pray to you, O Lord. For all who lie to others, I pray to you, O Lord. For all in families who deceive each other, I pray to you, O Lord. For all (add your own intentions), I pray to you, O Lord.

Day 29: Wednesday of the Fourth Week of Lent

Morning

Antiphon: "Sing aloud to God our strength; / shout for joy to ... God. (Ps 81:1, NRSV)

Psalm: "Raise a song, sound the tambourine, / the sweet lyre with the harp. / Blow the trumpet at the new moon, / at the full moon, on our festal day. / For it is a statute..., an ordinance of... God.... / He made it a decree in Joseph, / when he went out over the land of Egypt. / O that

my people would listen to me, / that [they] would walk in my ways! / I would feed [them] with the finest of the wheat, / and with honey from the rock I would satisfy [them]." (Ps 81:2–5, 13, 16, NRSV)
Repeat Antiphon (above):
Reading: "When Joseph was taken down to Egypt, he was bought by Potiphar, one of Pharaoh's eunuchs, the captain of the guard, an Egyptian. Potiphar bought him from the Ishmaelites who had brought him there. The LORD was with Joseph and he prospered. He lived in the house of his Egyptian master, who saw that the LORD was with him and was giving him success in all that he undertook. Thus Joseph found favor with his master, and he became his personal servant. Indeed, his master put him in charge of his household and entrusted him with all that he had.... [T]he LORD blessed the Egyptian's household for Joseph's sake. (Gen 39:1–4ab, 5a, NEB)
Meditation/Journal: What has been your experience of taking a bad situation (like Joseph sold into slavery) and making it good (like Joseph in Potiphar's house)? What role did God play in your turning a bad situation into a good one?

Evening
Antiphon: "Protect me, O God, for in you I take refuge." (Ps 16:1, NRSV)
Psalm: "I say to the LORD, 'You are my Lord, / I have no good apart from you.' The LORD is my chosen portion and my cup; you hold my lot. / The boundary lines have fallen for me / in pleasant places; / I have a goodly heritage. / I bless the LORD who gives me counsel; / in the night also my heart instructs me. / I keep the LORD always before me; / because he is at my right hand, I shall not be moved." (Ps 16:2, 5–8, NRSV)
Repeat Antiphon (above):
Reading: "It happened ... that the king's butler ... offended [his] master [Pharaoh of Egypt].... [H]e put [him] in custody in the house of the captain of the guard, ... where Joseph was imprisoned. The captain of the guard appointed Joseph as [his] attendant .... One night [he] ... had [a] dream .... When Joseph came to [him] in the morning, ... Joseph said to [him], 'Does not interpretation belong to God? Tell me your dream.' So the chief butler told Joseph his dream: 'In my dream,' he said, 'there was a vine in front of me. On the vine there were three branches, and as soon as it budded, it blossomed, and its clusters ripened into grapes. Now I had Pharaoh's cup in my hand, and I plucked the grapes, crushed them into Pharaoh's cup, and put the cup into Pharaoh's hand.' Joseph said to

him, 'This is the interpretation. The three branches are three days; within three days Pharaoh will raise you and restore you to your post, and then you will put the cup into Pharaoh's hand as you used to do, when you were his butler.'"(Gen 40:1, 3–6, 8–13, NEB)

Points to Ponder: First, Joseph is in prison because Pharaoh's wife tried to get him to sleep with her, and, after he refused, she accused him of having done so. His master believed his wife, and had Joseph put in prison. Second, the whole narrative of Joseph imbedded in the HB (OT) book of Genesis reflects ancient people's belief that dreams foretold the future. All that was needed was an interpreter, a role played by Joseph. Third, while in prison, Joseph discovers that Pharoah's cupbearer has been put in prison for some offense; a cupbearer was one who tasted the wine to be sure it wasn't poisoned before giving it to his master. The butler (cupbearer) relates a dream he had to Joseph, who interprets it to mean that the butler (cupbearer) will be restored to his position within three days. Fourth, Joseph asks the butler (cupbearer) to remember him to Pharaoh, should the occasion present itself. Instead of thinking about dreams as visions during the night, it is good to think of dreams as plans for the future; a dream or plan helps a person hope for what can be, instead of being stuck in what is.

Day 30: Thursday of the Fourth Week of Lent

Morning

Antiphon: ". . . [W]e will tell to the coming generation / the glorious deeds of the LORD, and his might, / and the wonders that he has done." (Ps 78:4b, NRSV)

Psalm: "[The LORD] commanded the skies above, / and opened the doors of heaven; / he rained down on them manna to eat, / and gave them the grain of heaven. / Mortals ate of the bread of angels; / he sent the east wind to blow in the heavens, / and by his power he led out the south wind; / he rained flesh upon them like dust, / winged birds like the sand of the seas; / he let them fall within their camp, / all around their dwellings. / And they ate and were well filled, / for he gave them what they craved." (Ps 78:23–29, NRSV)

Repeat Antiphon (above):

Reading: "When the chief baker saw that Joseph had given a favorable interpretation, he said to him, 'I too had a dream, and in my dream, there were three baskets of white bread on my head. In the top basket there was every kind of food which the baker prepares for Pharaoh, and the birds were eating out of the top basket on my head.' Joseph answered, 'This is the interpretation. The three baskets are three days; within three days Pharaoh will raise you and hang you up on a tree, and the birds of the air will eat your flesh.'" (Gen 40:16–19, NEB)

Meditation/Journal: What connection to you find between the verses of Psalm 78 and the HB (OT) book of Genesis 40:16–19? Explain.

Evening

Antiphon: "Restore us, O God of hosts; / let your face shine, that we may be saved." (Ps 80:7, NRSV)

Psalm: "Give ear, O Shepherd . . . , / you who lead Joseph like a flock! / You who are enthroned upon the cherubim, shine forth . . . . / Stir up your might, / and come to save us! / Restore us, O God; / let your face shine, that we may be saved." (Ps 80:1–3, NRSV)

Repeat Antiphon (above):

Reading: ". . . Pharaoh had a dream: he was standing by the Nile, and there came up from the river seven cows, sleek and fat, and they grazed on the reeds. After them seven other cows came up from the river, gaunt and lean, and stood on the river-bank beside the first cows. The cows that were gaunt and lean devoured the cows that were sleek and fat. Then Pharaoh woke up. He fell asleep again and had a second dream: he saw seven ears of corn, full and ripe, growing on one stalk. Growing up after them were seven other ears, thin and shriveled by the east wind. The thin ears swallowed up the ears that were full and ripe. Then Pharaoh woke up and knew that it was a dream. Pharaoh thereupon sent for Joseph, and they hurriedly brought him out of the dungeon." (Gen 41:1–7, 14, NEB)

Reflection: Unknown to Pharaoh is Joseph's God. The narrator of the story of Joseph imbedded in the HB (OT) book of Genesis makes God present to Pharaoh by using the number seven. In the biblical world, seven is the sum of three and four. Three is the number for God; four is the number for the earth. Fullness is expressed by seven. The fullness of seven sleek and fat cows is set opposite the fullness of seven gaunt and lean cows. The fullness of seven ears of full and ripe corn on one stalk is set opposite the fullness of seven thin and shriveled ears of corn. Just like the seven gaunt and lean cows devour the seven fat and lean ones, so the seven ears of thin and shriveled ears swallow the seven ears of full and ripe corn. The dream interpreter named Joseph is needed to explain what Pharaoh's nighttime vision means. Joseph will do so because God reveals to him what God intends to do. God often reveals his intentions in dreams during the night; many people awaken in the morning and know what they need to do.

Day 31: Friday of the Fourth Week of Lent

Morning
Antiphon: "Let the favor of the Lord our God be upon us, / and prosper for us the work of our hands—/ O prosper the work of our hands!" (Ps 90:17, NRSV)
Psalm: "You sweep [mortals] away [, Lord]; they are like a dream, / like grass that is renewed in the morning; / in the morning it flourishes and is renewed; / in the evening it fades and withers. / So teach us to count our days / that we may gain a wise heart. / Satisfy us in the morning with your steadfast love, / so that we may rejoice and be glad all our days." (Ps 90:5–6, 12, 14, NRSV)
Repeat Antiphon (above):
Reading: "Joseph said to Pharaoh, 'Pharaoh's dreams are one dream. God has told Pharaoh what he is going to do. The seven good cows are seven years, and the seven good ears of corn are seven years. It is all one dream. The seven lean and gaunt cows that came up after them are seven years, and the empty ears of corn blighted by the east wind will be seven years of famine. There are to be seven years of great plenty throughout the land. After them will come seven years of famine . . . . This is what Pharaoh should do; appoint controllers over the land, and take one fifth of the produce of Egypt during the seven years of plenty. They should collect all this food produced in the good years that are coming and put the corn under Pharaoh's control in store in the cities, and keep it under guard. This food will be a reserve for the country against the seven years of famine which will come upon Egypt.'" (Gen 41:25–27, 29–30a, 34–36a, NEB)
Reflection/Meditation/Journal: The biblical character of Joseph represents the person who plans ahead, the person who is able to read the signs of the times, the person who pays attention to what is going on around him or her. Joseph, who has been in prison, does not bury his head in the sand. Once he is summoned to Pharaoh's presence, he interprets the king's dream as God's message about what is going to happen. Joseph is a self-starter, a self-motivated person, who knows what needs to be done and does it. He does not shy away from authority; he tells Pharaoh what

he ought to do. This Hebrew leader explains how the leader of Egypt needs to save non-Hebrews. Two possible applications of this story are true: (1) God has a sense of humor in using a Hebrew leader to save non-Hebrews (who will later enslave the Hebrews)! (2) God cares for all people: Hebrews and Egyptians. Which is more true? Explain. What other truths do you find?

Evening
Antiphon: "O give thanks to the LORD, call on his name, / make known his deeds among the peoples. (Ps 105:2, NRSV)
Psalm: "When [the LORD] summoned famine against the land [of Egypt], / and broke every staff of bread, / he had sent a man ahead . . . , / Joseph, who was sold as a slave. / His feet were hurt with fetters, / his neck was put in a collar of iron; / until what he had said came to pass, / the word of the LORD kept testing him. / The king sent and released him; / the ruler of the [Egyptian] peoples set him free. / He made him lord of his house, / and ruler of all his possessions, / to instruct his officials at his pleasure, / and teach his elders wisdom." (Ps 105:16–22, NRSV)
Repeat Antiphon (above):
Reading: "[Pharaoh said to his courtiers,] 'Can we find a man like [Joseph], one who has the spirit of a god in him?' He said to Joseph, 'Since a god has made all this known to you, there is no one so shrewd and intelligent as you. You shall be in charge of my household, and all my people will depend on your every word. I hereby give you authority over the whole land of Egypt.' He took off his signet-ring and put it on Joseph's finger, he had him dressed in fine linen, and hung a gold chain round his neck. Thus Pharaoh made him ruler over all Egypt. . . . During the seven years of plenty there were abundant harvests, and Joseph gathered all the food produced in Egypt during those years and stored it in the cities, putting in each the food from the surrounding country." (Gen 41:38–40a, 41–42, 43b, 47–48, NEB)
Intercessions: For all starving people around the world, I pray to you, Lord. For all who work to alleviate hunger, I pray to you, Lord. For all who work in soup kitchens, I pray to you, Lord. For all who work in food pantries, I pray to you, Lord. For all who support food pantries, I pray to you, Lord. For all who lead others in eradicating hunger in the world, I pray to you, Lord.

Day 32: Saturday of the Fourth Week of Lent

Morning

Antiphon: "Praise the LORD. / O give thanks to the LORD for he is good; / for his steadfast love endures forever." (Ps 106:1, NRSV)

Psalm: "Who can utter the mighty doings of the LORD, / or declare all his praise? / Happy are those who observe justice, / who do righteousness at all times. / Remember me, O LORD, when you show favor to your people, / help me when you deliver them . . . . / Our ancestors, when they were in Egypt, / did not consider your wonderful works; / they did not remember the abundance of your steadfast love . . . . / Yet [you] saved them for [your] name's sake, / so that [you] might make known [your] mighty power." (Ps 106, 2–4, 7–8, NRSV)

Repeat Antiphon (above):

Reading: "When the seven years of plenty in Egypt came to an end, seven years of famine began, as Joseph had foretold. There was famine in every country, but throughout Egypt there was bread. So when the famine spread through all Egypt the people appealed to Pharaoh for bread, and he ordered them to go to Joseph and do as he told them. In every region there was famine, and Joseph opened all the granaries and sold corn to the Egyptians, for the famine was severe. The whole world came to Egypt to buy corn from Joseph, so severe was the famine everywhere." (Gen 41:53–57, NEB)

Intercessions: For those who suffer from famine, I pray to you, O Lord. For those who cannot find justice, I pray to you, O Lord. For those who cannot buy fresh vegetables, I pray to you, O Lord. For those who cannot buy fresh fruits, I pray to you, O Lord. For those who have not experienced your steadfast love, I pray to you, O Lord. For those who feed the world out of their own resources, I pray to you, O Lord.

Evening

Antiphon: "By awesome deeds you answer us with deliverance, / O God of our salvation; / you are the hope of all the ends of the earth / and of the farthest seas." (Ps 65:5, NRSV)

Psalm: "You [, God,] visit the earth and water it, / you greatly enrich it; / the river of God is full of water; / you provide the people with grain, / for so you have prepared it. / You water its furrows abundantly, / settling its ridges, / softening it with showers, / and blessing its growth. [T]he meadows clothe themselves with flocks, / the valleys deck themselves with grain, / they shout and sing together for joy." (Ps 65:9–10, 13, NRSV)

Repeat Antiphon (above):

Reading: "When Jacob saw that there was corn in Egypt, he said to his sons, 'I have heard that there is corn in Egypt. Go down and buy some so that we may keep ourselves alive and not starve.' So Joseph's brothers, ten of them, went down to buy grain from Egypt. Joseph's brothers came and bowed to the ground before [Joseph], and when he saw his brothers, he recognized them but pretended not to know them . . . . Although Joseph had recognized his brothers, they did not recognize him. They did not know that Joseph understood, because he had used an interpreter. Joseph . . . took Simeon and bound him before their yes; then he gave orders to fill their bags with grain, to return each man's silver, putting it in his sack, and to give them supplies for the journey. All this was done; and they loaded the corn on to their asses and went away. When they came to their father Jacob in Canaan, they told him all that had happened to them. They said, 'This man, the lord of the country, said to us, "This is how I shall find out if you are honest men. Leave one of your brothers with me, take food for your hungry households, and go. Bring your youngest brother to me, and I shall know that you are not spies, but honest men. Then I will restore your brother to you, and you can move about the country freely."'" (Gen 42:1–3, 6b–7a, 8, 23–26, 29, 33–34, NEB)

Meditation/Journal: What connection do you find between the verse of Psalm 65 and the passage from the HB (OT) book of Genesis 42? What are your reflections on Joseph not revealing himself to his brothers?

Day 33: Fifth Sunday of Lent

Morning

Antiphon: "Blessed be the Lord, / who daily bears us up; / God is our salvation." (Ps 68:19, NRSV)

Psalm: "Your solemn processions are seen, O God, / the processions of my God, my King, into the sanctuary—/ the singers in front, the musicians last, / between them girls playing tambourines: 'Bless God in the great congregation . . . .' / There is Benjamin, the least of them, in the lead . . . . / Summon your might, O God; / show your strength, O God, as you have done for us before." (Ps 68:24–26a, 27a, 28, NRSV)

Repeat Antiphon (above):

Reading: "The famine was still severe in the country. When [Jacob and his sons] had used up the corn they had brought from Egypt, their father said to them, 'Go back and buy a little more corn for us to eat.' But Judah replied, 'The man plainly warned us that we must not go into his presence unless our brother was with us.' Their father Israel [Jacob] said to them, 'If it must be so, then do this; take in your baggage, as a gift for the man, some of the produce for which our country is famous: a little balsam, a little honey, gum tragacanth, myrrh, pistachio nuts, and almonds. Take double the amount of silver and restore what was returned to you in your packs; perhaps it was a mistake. Take your brother with you and go straight back to the man. May God Almighty make him kindly disposed to you, and may he send back the one whom you left behind, and Benjamin too.' . . . [T]hey approached Joseph's steward and spoke to him at the door of the house. He answered, 'Set your minds at rest; do not be afraid. It was your God, the God of your father, who hid treasure for you in your packs.' When Joseph came into the house, they presented him with the gifts which they had brought, bowing to the ground before him. 'Is this your youngest brother, of whom you told me? [he asked,] and to Benjamin he said, 'May God be gracious to you, my son!' Joseph was overcome; his feelings for his brothers mastered him, and he was near to tears. So he went into the inner room and wept." (Gen 43:1–3, 11–14, 19, 23, 26, 29–30, NEB)

Meditation/Journal: How have you experienced the providence of God, like Joseph's servant explains to Joseph's brothers? What connection do you find between the verses of Psalm 68 and the passage from the HB (OT) book of Genesis 43?

Evening
Antiphon: "All the ends of the earth shall remember / and turn to the LORD; / and all the families of the nations / shall worship before him." (Ps 22:27, NRSV)
Psalm: ". . . O LORD, do not be far away! / O my help, come quickly to my aid! / I will tell of your name to my brothers and sisters; / in the midst of the congregation I will praise you: / You who fear the LORD, praise him! / All you offspring of Jacob glorify him; / stand in awe of him, all you offspring of Israel!" (Ps 22:19, 22–23, NRSV)
Repeat Antiphon (above):
Reading: "Joseph said to his brothers, 'I am Joseph; can my father be still alive?' He said, 'I am your brother Joseph whom you sold into Egypt. Now do not be distressed or take it amiss that you sold me into slavery here; it was God who sent me ahead of you to save men's [and women's] lives. So it was not you who sent me here, but God, and he has made me a

father to Pharaoh, and lord over all his household and ruler of all Egypt. Make haste and go back to my father and give him this message from his son Joseph: "Come down to me; do not delay."'" (Gen 45:3a, 4b–5, 8–9, NEB)

Meditation/Journal: What connection do you find between the verses of Psalm 22 and the passage from the HB (OT) book of Genesis, chapter 45? In what specific ways have you experienced God sending you somewhere to help or save others? Explain.

Day 34: Monday of the Fifth Week of Lent

Morning
Antiphon: "Sing to [the LORD], sing praise to him; / tell of all his wonderful works." (Ps 105:2, NRSV)
Psalm: ". . . Israel came to Egypt; / Jacob lived as an alien in the land of Ham. / And the LORD made his people very fruitful, / and made them stronger than their foes, / whose hearts he then turned to hate his people, / to deal craftily with his servants." (Ps 105:23–25, NRSV)
Repeat Antiphon (above):
Reading: "When the report that Joseph's brothers had come reached Pharaoh's house, . . . Pharaoh said to Joseph, 'Say to your brothers: "Load your beasts and go to Canaan. Fetch your father and your households and bring them to me. I will give you the best that there is in the land. Take wagons from Egypt for your dependents and your wives and fetch your father and come."'" (Gen 45:16–19, NEB)
Activity: If you were invited to another country to escape famine, earthquake, or some other type of disturbance, would you go to the other country? Why? Why not?

Evening
Antiphon: "Long ago you [, LORD,] laid the foundation of the earth, / and the heavens are the work of your hands." (Ps 102:25, NRSV)
Psalm: "Let this be recorded for a generation to come, / so that a people yet unborn may praise the LORD: / that he looked down from his holy height, / from heaven the LORD looked at the earth . . . . / The children of your servants shall live secure; / their offspring shall be established in your presence." (Ps 102:18–19, 28, NRSV)
Repeat Antiphon (above):

Reading: "The sons of Israel [Jacob] did as they were told, and Joseph gave them wagons, according to Pharaoh's orders, and food for the journey. Thus they went up from Egypt and came to their father Jacob in Canaan. There they gave him the news that Joseph was still alive and that he was ruler of all Egypt. Israel said, 'It is enough. Joseph my son is still alive; I will go and see him before I die.'" (Gen 45:21, 25–26a, 28, NEB)

Meditation/Journal: What must it have been like for Jacob to hear that his favorite son, Joseph, was still alive after thinking that he was dead for many years? What must it had been like for Joseph's brothers, who had sold Joseph into slavery and told their father that he had been killed by a wild beast, to report to their father that Joseph was alive? What experience(s) of your life are comparable to either of those experiences narrated in the Bible?

Day 35: Tuesday of the Fifth Week of Lent

Morning

Antiphon: "I will sing of your steadfast love, O LORD, forever; / with my mouth I will proclaim your faithfulness to all generations." (Ps 89:1, NRSV)

Psalm: "I declare that your steadfast love is established forever [, O LORD]; / your faithfulness is as firm as the heavens. / Let the heavens praise your wonders, O LORD, / your faithfulness in the assembly of the holy ones. / For who in the skies can be compared to the LORD? / Who among the heavenly beings is like the LORD, / a God feared in the council of the holy ones, / great and awesome above all that are around him? / O LORD God of hosts, / who is as mighty as you, O LORD? / Your faithfulness surrounds you." (Ps 89:2, 5–8, NRSV)

Repeat Antiphon (above):

Reading: "God said to Israel in a vision by night, 'Jacob, Jacob,' and he answered, 'I am here.' God said, 'I am God, the God of your father. Do not be afraid to go down to Egypt, for there I will make you a great nation. I will go down with you to Egypt, and I myself will bring you back again without fail; and Joseph shall close your eyes.'" (Gen 46:2–4, NEB)

Meditation/Journal: How do the verses of Psalm 89 illustrate the passage from the HB (OT) book of Genesis, chapter 46? In what specific ways does your meditation/journal response make you aware of God's presence in your life?

SEASON OF LENT

Evening
Antiphon: "Let the favor of the Lord our God be upon us, / and prosper for us the work of our hands—/ O prosper the work of our hands!" (Ps 90:17, NRSV)
Psalm: "You who live in the shelter of the Most High, / who abide in the shadow of the Almighty, / will say to the LORD, 'My refuge and my fortress; / my God, in whom I trust.' / [H]e will cover you with his pinions, / and under his wings you will find refuge; / his faithfulness is a shield and buckler. / Because you have made the LORD your refuge, / the Most High your dwelling place, / no evil shall befall you, no scourge come near your tent." (Ps 91:1–2, 4, 9–10, NRSV)
Repeat Antiphon (above):
Reading: "Joseph came and told Pharaoh, 'My father and my brothers have arrived from Canaan, with their flocks and their cattle and all that they have, and they are now in Goshen.' Pharaoh said to Joseph, 'So your father and your brothers have come to you. The land of Egypt is yours; settle them in the best part of it.' Then Joseph brought his father in and presented him to Pharaoh, and Jacob gave Pharaoh his blessing. Pharaoh asked Jacob his age, and he answered, 'The years of my earthly sojourn are one hundred and thirty . . . .' Jacob then blessed Pharaoh and went out from his presence. So Joseph settled his father and his brothers, and gave them land in Egypt, in the best part of the country . . . ." (Gen 47:1, 5–6a, 7–11, NEB)
Points to Ponder: First, now that Jacob, his eleven sons, and his grandchildren have migrated to Egypt, all the Hebrews, including Joseph, his wife, and his two sons, are there. They are aliens in a foreign land. Second, the Pharaoh who made Joseph his second in command is gracious to the Hebrews, welcoming them to Egypt and giving them some of the best land in the country. Third, Jacob's age when he arrives in Egypt—130—needs to be decoded. One hundred thirty is a multiple of forty, a lifetime in the ancient world; forty represents the life of an average human generation. Thus, forty multiplied by three, the number for God, the spiritual order, indicates that Jacob has lived a divine, blessed life. Moreover the additional ten (120 + 10 = 130) signifies totality; Jacob has lived a total divine, blessed life by the time he gets to Egypt. Fourth, the author of Genesis states that Jacob lived in Egypt for seventeen years and lived to be a hundred and forty-seven years old (Gen 47:28). One hundred forty-seven displays that more deciphering is necessary. Contained in 147 is 144 (12 x 12 = 144). Twelve is a sacred number indicating the sons of

Jacob. Add three, the number for God, the spiritual order, and the total is 147. The sons of Jacob are a divine gift from God; Jacob himself has been blessed by God. Fifth, that is why the author of the book of Genesis states that Jacob blessed Pharaoh (Gen 47:7, 10); a blessing is a wish that God will bless with life, abundance, prosperity, and fertility. Near the end of Lent, a person might make a list of the blessings he or she has received during the past five weeks.

Day 36: Wednesday of the Fifth Week of Lent

Morning
Antiphon: "The LORD is my shepherd. I shall not want." (Ps 23:1, NRSV)
Psalm: "[The LORD] makes me lie down in green pastures; / he leads me beside still waters; / he restores my soul. / He leads me in right paths / for his name's sake. / Even though I walk through the darkest valley, / I fear no evil; / for you are with me; / your rod and your staff—/ they comfort me." (Ps 23:2–4, NRSV)
Repeat Antiphon (above):
Reading: "[Jacob] gave [the twelve tribes] his last charge and said, 'I shall soon be gathered to my father's kin; bury me with my forefathers in . . . the cave on the plot of land at Machpelah . . . , the field which Abraham bought . . . for a burial-place.' When Jacob had finished giving his last charge to his sons, he drew his feet up on to the bed, breathed his last, and was gathered to his father's kin." (Gen 49:29–30, 33, NEB)
Intercessions: For your mercy upon all who will die today, I pray to you, Lord. For your mercy upon all who have died in the past, I pray to you, Lord. For your mercy upon all the members of my immediate family who have died, I pray to you, Lord. For your mercy upon my grandparents, uncles, and aunts who have died, I pray to you, Lord. For your mercy upon me, when the day of my death comes, I pray to you, Lord.

Evening
Antiphon: "Let God rise up, let his enemies be scattered . . . ." (Ps 68:1a, NRSV)
Psalm: ". . . [L]et the righteous be joyful, / let them exult before God; / let them be jubilant with joy. / Sing to God, sing praises to his name; / lift up a song to him who rides upon the clouds—/ his name is the LORD—/ be exultant before him. / Blessed be the Lord, / who daily bears us up; / God

is our salvation. / Our God is a God of salvation, / and to GOD, the Lord, belongs escape from death." (Ps 68:3–4, 19–20, NRSV)
Repeat Antiphon (above):
Reading: "[Joseph] ordered the physicians in his service to embalm his father Israel [Jacob], and they did so, finishing the task in forty days . . . . Pharoah [said to Joseph], 'Go and bury your father, as he has made you swear to do.' So Joseph went to bury his father, accompanied by . . . his brothers, and his father's household . . . . Thus Jacob's sons did what he had told them to do. They took him to Canaan and buried him in the cave on the plot of land at Machpelah, the land which Abraham had bought as a burial-place . . . . Then, after he had buried his father, Joseph returned to Egypt with his brothers and all who had gone up with him. Joseph remained in Egypt, he and his father's household. He lived there to be a hundred and ten years old . . . . He said to his brothers, 'I am dying; but God will not fail to come to your aid and take you from here to the land which he promised on oath to Abraham, Isaac, and Jacob. When God thus comes to your aid, you must take my bones with you from here.' So Joseph died at the age of a hundred and ten. He was embalmed and laid in a coffin in Egypt." (Gen 50:1–2, 6–7a, 8b, 12–14, 22, 24, 25b–26, NEB)
Meditation/Journal: In what specific ways did Israel (Jacob), in the words of Psalm 68:20, "escape from death"? In what specific ways did Joseph, in the words of Psalm 68:20, "escape from death"? If you decode Joseph's age—110—what do you discover it means?

Day 37: Thursday of the Fifth Week of Lent

Morning
Antiphon: "If you try my heart [, O LORD], if you visit me by night, / if you test me, you will find no wickedness in me; / my mouth does not transgress." (Ps 17:3, NRSV)
Psalm: "Fools say in their hearts, 'There is no God.' / They are corrupt, they do abominable deeds; / there is no one who does good. / The LORD looks down from heaven on humankind / to see if there are any who are wise, / who seek after God. / They have all gone astray, they are all alike perverse; / there is no one who does good, / no, not one. / [They] would confound the plans of the poor, / but the LORD is their refuge." (Ps 14:1–3, 6, NRSV)
Repeat Antiphon (above):

Reading: "... [A] new king ascended the throne of Egypt, one who knew nothing of Joseph. He said to his people, 'These Israelites have become too many and too strong for us.' So they were made to work in gangs with officers set over them, to break their spirit with heavy labor. So they treated their Israelite slaves with ruthless severity, and made life bitter for them with cruel servitude, setting them to work on clay and brick-making, and all sorts of work in the fields. In short, they made ruthless use of them as slaves in every kind of hard labor." (Exod 1:8–9, 11, 13–14, NEB)
Intercessions: For those who foolishly think that there is no God, I pray to you, Lord. For all who are wise and seek after God, I pray to you, Lord. For all who do good deeds, I pray to you Lord. For all who find you to be their refuge, I pray to you, Lord. For all who enslave others, I pray to you, Lord. For all who reduce others to servitude of any kind, I pray to you, Lord. For all who toil laboriously for minimum wage, I pray to you, Lord.

Evening
Antiphon: "I think of God, and I moan; / I meditate, and my spirit faints." (Ps 77:3, NRSV)
Psalm: "I will call to mind the deeds of the LORD; / I will remember your wonders of old. / I will meditate on all your work, / and muse on your mighty deeds. / Your way, O God is holy. / What god is so great as our God? / You are the God who works wonders; / you have displayed your might among the peoples. / With your strong arm you redeemed your people, / the descendants of Jacob and Joseph. / You led your people like a flock / by the hand of Moses . . . ." (Ps 77:11–15, 20, NRSV)
Repeat Antiphon (above):
Reading: "Moses was minding the flock of his father-in-law . . . . He led the flock along the side of the wilderness and came to Horeb, the mountain of God. There the angel of the LORD appeared to him in the flame of a burning bush. Moses noticed that, although the bush was on fire, it was not being burnt up; so he said to himself, 'I must go across to see this wonderful sight. Why does not the bush burn away?' When the LORD saw that Moses had turned aside to look, he called to him out of the bush, 'Moses, Moses,' and Moses answered, 'Yes, I am here.' [God said,] 'I am the God of your forefathers, the God of Abraham, the God of Isaac, the God of Jacob. I have indeed seen the misery of my people in Egypt. I have heard their outcry against their slave-masters. I have taken heed of their sufferings, and have come down to rescue them from the power of Egypt, and to bring them up out of that country into a fine, broad land; it is a

land flowing with milk and honey.... I will send you to Pharaoh and you shall bring my people Israel out of Egypt.' Then Moses said to God, 'If I go to the Israelites and tell them that the God of their forefathers has sent me to them and they ask me his name, what shall I say?' God answered, 'I AM; that is who I am. [Go to the king of Egypt.] I know well that the king of Egypt will not give you leave unless he is compelled. I shall then stretch out my hand and assail the Egyptians with all the miracles I shall work among them After that he will send you away.'" (Exod 3:1–4, 6a, 7–8, 10, 13, 19–20, NEB)

Reflection: Moses, the son of Levite, was rescued from drowning by Pharaoh's daughter and raised as an Egyptian. After killing an Egyptian for beating a Hebrew slave, Moses fled Egypt and went to Midian, where he found a wife, who bore him a son. While tending the sheep of his father-in-law, he received a call from God. The call narrative becomes the biblical pattern for others throughout the Bible. First, there is an appearance of a divine being; God appears to Moses as fire burning a bush that is not consumed. Second, there is an excuse made by the person who is called to serve; Moses doesn't think that the Hebrews will believe him, and he has a speech impediment. Third, there is an empowering event that sets aside all excuses; Moses is given a staff that turns into a snake and several other signs. Aaron, his brother, is made Moses' spokesman. And fourth, there is a charge for mission with explicit instructions; Moses goes back to Egypt to gather the Hebrews and to convince Pharaoh to let the people go. This four-part pattern can be found in the call of Isaiah, Jeremiah, and Ezekiel. If applied carefully, it can be found in the reader's life, too.

Day 38: Friday of the Fifth Week of Lent

Morning

Antiphon: "[The LORD] sent his servant Moses, / and Aaron whom he had chosen. / They performed his signs among [the Egyptians] / and miracles in the land of Ham." (Ps 105:26–27, NRSV)

Psalm: "When the waters saw you, O God, / when the waters saw you, they were afraid; / the very deep trembled. / The clouds poured out water; / the skies thundered; / your arrows flashed on every side. / The crash of your thunder was in the whirlwind; / your lightnings lit up the world; / the earth trembled and shook. / Your way was through the sea, / your path through the mighty waters; / yet your footprints were unseen. /

You led your people like a flock / by the hand of Moses and Aaron." (Ps 77:16–20, NRSV)

Repeat Antiphon (above):

Reading: The LORD spoke to Moses: "You must tell your brother Aaron all I bid you say, and he will tell Pharaoh, and Pharaoh will let the Israelites go out of his country; but I will make him stubborn. Then will I show sign after sign and portent after portent in the land of Egypt. But Pharaoh will not listen to you, so I will assert my power in Egypt, and with mighty acts of judgment I will bring my people, the Israelites, out of Egypt. If Pharaoh demands some portent from you, then you, Moses, must say to Aaron, 'Take your staff and throw it down in front of Pharaoh, and it will turn into a serpent.' When Moses and Aaron came to Pharaoh, they did as the LORD had told them. Aaron threw down his staff in front of Pharaoh . . . , and it turned into a serpent." (Exod 7:2–4, 9–10, NEB)

Reflection: At this point in the HB (OT) book of Exodus narrative, the reader is drawn into the contest between Moses' and Aaron's God and Pharaoh's gods. It is easily pictured as one group on one side of a line taunting another group on the other side of a line, saying, "Our god is greater than your god!" and hearing in reply, "No, our god is greater than your god." The first incident in the taunt is the thrown-down staff that turns into a snake. While not mentioned above in the reading, Pharaoh's sorcerers, magicians, and wise men are able to toss their staffs, which become serpents. The only difference is that Aaron's staff swallows all the staff-turned serpents of Pharaoh's court. Thus, Moses' and Aaron's God is greater than Pharaoh's gods. In other words, Moses and Aaron have scored one point; Pharaoh has scored no points. This narrative also introduces the theme that God makes Pharaoh stubborn; other translations state that God hardens Pharaoh's heart. This theme recurs throughout the Exodus story, because ancient Israel understood the heart as the point of intersection between human intellect and will—not as the emotional center of a person, as is understood today. The stubbornness of Pharaoh or the hardening of his heart emphasizes that God is in control of what is going on; God's control ensures that the Hebrews will leave Egypt and acknowledge God's power. During these last days of Lent, it is wise to reflect on the control God has manifested in each person's life.

Evening

Antiphon: "[The LORD] turned [the Egyptians'] waters into blood." (Ps 105:29a, NRSV)

Psalm: "I will open my mouth in a parable; / I will utter dark sayings from of old, / things that we have heard and known, / that our ancestors have told us. [The Hebrews] did not keep in mind [God's] power, / or the day when he redeemed them from the foe; / when he displayed his signs in Egypt, / and his miracles in the fields. . . . / He turned their rivers to blood, / so that they could not drink of their streams." (Ps 78:2-3, 42-44, NRSV)

Repeat Antiphon (above):

Reading: "The LORD then told Moses to say to Aaron, 'Take your staff and stretch your hand out over the waters of Egypt, its rivers and its streams, and over every pool and cistern, to turn them into blood.' So Moses and Aaron did as the LORD had commanded. He lifted up his staff and struck the water of the Nile in the sight of Pharaoh . . . and all the water was changed into blood. But the Egyptian magicians did the same thing by their spells . . . . This lasted for seven days from the time when the LORD struck the Nile." (Exod 7:19a, 20, 22a, 25, NEB)

Reflection: The contest between the Hebrews' God and the Pharaoh's gods continues. This first plague is directed against the deified Nile, upon which all life in Egypt depends; the Nile's annual flooding replenishes and fertilizes the soil. Even though the Egyptians dig new wells for potable water, the narrative makes it clear that the water of life is God. In the last verse of the narrative, the reader is told that the Nile remained as blood for seven days; seven, signifying completeness—the sum of three, signifying God, and four, signifying the earth—indicates that the portent is complete, that the LORD struck the Nile, and that God both gives and takes life!

Day 39: Saturday of the Fifth Week of Lent

Morning

Antiphon: "[The Egyptians'] land swarmed with frogs, / even in the chambers of their kings." (Ps 105:30, NRSV)

Psalm: "We will not hide [sayings from of old] from [our] children; / we will tell to the coming generation / the glorious deeds of the LORD, and his might, / and the wonders that he has done. / He established a decree in Jacob, / and appointed a law in Israel, / which he commanded our ancestors / to teach their children; / that the next generation might know them, / the children yet unborn, / and rise up and tell them to their children, / so that they should set their hope in God, / and not forget the works of God, . . . / and that they should not be like their ancestors, / a

stubborn and rebellious generation / a generation whose heart was not steadfast, / whose spirit was not faithful to God. / He sent among [the Egyptians] . . . / frogs, which destroyed them." (Ps 78:4–8, 45b, NRSV)
Repeat Antiphon (above):
Reading: "The LORD then told Moses to go into Pharaoh's presence and say to him, 'These are the words of the LORD: "Let my people go in order to worship me."' Then the LORD told Moses to say to Aaron, 'Take your staff in your hand and stretch it out over the rivers, streams, and pools, to bring up frogs upon the land of Egypt.' So Aaron stretched out his hand over the waters of Egypt, and the frogs came up and covered all the land. The magicians did the same thing by their spells; they too brought up frogs upon the land of Egypt." (Exod 8:1, 5–7, NEB)
Reflection: The battle between the gods continues with the second plague of frogs. In Egypt there was a frog-goddess named Heqet or Heket; she was a goddess of fertility pictured with the head of a frog, which to the Egyptians was a sign of fertility related to the annual flooding of the Nile River. From the HB (OT) book of Genesis perspective, the plague of frogs involves a rupture of the order of creation. The boundary separating creatures of the water (frogs) and the dry land of Egypt has been violated by Moses' God. It is not Heqet who is responsible for fertility; it is the LORD God who gives fertility. Thus, the God of the Hebrews wins this battle.

Evening
Antiphon: "[The LORD] spoke, and there came . . . gnats throughout [the Egyptians'] country." (Ps 105:31, NRSV)
Psalm: "[The Hebrews] forgot what [God] had done, / and the miracles that he had shown them. / In the sight of their ancestors he worked marvels / in the land of Egypt . . . . / In the daytime he led them with a cloud, / and all night long with a fiery light. / He split rocks open in the wilderness, / and gave them drink abundantly as from the deep. / He made steams come out of the rock, / and caused waters to flow down like rivers." (Ps 78:11–12, 14–16, NRSV)
Repeat Antiphon (above):
Reading: "Aaron stretched out his staff and stuck the dust, and it turned into maggots on man and beast. All the dust turned into maggots through the land of Egypt. The magicians tried to produce maggots in the same way by their spells, but they failed. The maggots were everywhere, on man and beast. 'It is the finger of God,' said the magicians to Pharaoh, but

Pharaoh remained obstinate; as the LORD had foretold, he did not listen to them." (Exod 8:17–19, NEB)

Reflection: Biblical translations differ when describing the third plague. NEB states Aaron staff turns the dust of Egypt into maggots. NRSV declares that the dust turns into gnats. Either way, the third plague follows naturally from the second; maggots, gnats, or vermin would breed on decaying frog carcasses. What is important to note in the description of the third plague is the inability of the Egyptian magicians to duplicate it. In the story, which describes the third—the number for God—plague, the magicians' failure heightens the drama and anticipates the LORD's ultimate victory. Furthermore, the magicians tell Pharaoh that the maggots or gnats come from the finger of God, an idiom for a manifestation of divine power. Even in the face of divine power, potent Pharaoh remains obstinate; he cannot self-reflect and acknowledge that even he is under the LORD's command.

The Season of Lent continues with Day 40 in chapter 7, Holy Week.

7

Holy Week

Holy Week Introduction

The Season of Lent consists of forty-three days, with the last four days falling in Holy Week. Holy Week begins with Palm Sunday of the Passion of the Lord. Holy Week begins in 2025 on April 13; in 2026 on March 29; in 2027 on March 21; in 2028 on April 9; in 2029 on March 25; in 2030 on April 14; in 2031 on April 6; in 2032 on March 21; in 2033 on April 10; in 2034 on April 2; in 2035 on March 18; in 2036 on April 6; in 2037 on March 29; in 2038 on April 18; in 2039 on April 3.

When the solemnity of St. Joseph, Spouse of the Blessed Virgin Mary (March 19), falls during Holy Week, it is moved to the second Monday after Easter (Monday of the Second Week of Easter) that year. Likewise, when the solemnity of the Annunciation of the Lord (March 25) falls during Holy Week, it is moved to the second Monday or Tuesday after Easter (Monday of the Second Week of Easter or Tuesday of the Second Week of Easter) that year.

Other books by Mark G. Boyer that follow the same structure of Morning Prayer and Evening Prayer that can be used—in substitution for what is provided here—during Holy Week include: *Weekday Saints: Reflections on Their Scriptures* (Eugene, OR: Wipf & Stock, 2014); *Very*

Short Reflections—for Advent and Christmas, Lent and Easter, Ordinary Time, and Saints—through the Liturgical Year (Eugene, OR: Wipf & Stock, 2020); *Overcome with Paschal Joy: Chanting through Lent and Easter, Daily Reflections with Familiar Hymns* (Eugene, OR: Wipf & Stock, 2016); *Christ Our Passover Has Been Sacrificed: A Guide through Paschal Mystery Spirituality, Mystical Theology in The Roman Missal* (Eugene, OR: Wipf & Stock, 2018); *Biblical Names for God: An Abecedarian Anthology of Spiritual Reflections for Anytime* (Eugene, OR: Wipf & Stock, 2023); *Journey into God: Spiritual Reflections for Travelers* (Eugene, OR: Wipf & Stock, 2022); and *Seasons of Biblical Spirituality: Spring, Summer, Autumn, and Winter* (Eugene, OR: Resource Publications, 2023).

Antiphons and Psalms for Holy Week are taken from the *New Revised Standard Version with the Apocrypha* (NRSV): *The Access Bible* (New York: Oxford University Press, 1999) except for Holy Saturday Morning, when they are taken from *The New English Bible with the Apocrypha* (NEB) (New York: Oxford University Press, 1976), and Readings for Holy Week are taken from *The New English Bible with the Apocrypha* (NEB) (New York: Oxford University Press, 1976).

Days in Holy Week

The Season of Lent

Day 40: Palm Sunday of the Passion of the Lord

Morning

Antiphon: "O give thanks to the LORD, for he is good, / for his steadfast love endures forever." (Ps 18:29 NRSV)
Psalm: "The LORD is my strength and my might; / he has become my salvation. / I shall not die, but I shall live, / and recount the deeds of the LORD. / I thank you that you have answered me / and have become my salvation. / Blessed is the one who comes in the name of the LORD. / We bless you from the house of the LORD. / The LORD is God, / and he has given us light. / Bind the festal procession with branches, / up to the horns of the altar." (Ps 18:14, 17, 21, 26–27, NRSV)
Repeat Antiphon (above):
Readings:
(a) "[Two of Jesus' disciples] brought [a] colt to Jesus and spread their cloaks on it, and he mounted. And people carpeted the road with their

cloaks, while others spread brushwood which they had cut in the fields; and those who went ahead and the others who came behind shouted, 'Hosanna! Blessings on him who comes in the name of the Lord! Blessings on the coming kingdom of our father David! Hosanna in the heavens!'" (Mark 11:7–10, NEB)

(b) "The [two] disciples . . . brought the donkey and her foal; they laid their cloaks on them and Jesus mounted. Crowds of people carpeted the road with their cloaks, and some cut branches from the trees to spread in his path. Then the crowd that went ahead and the others that came behind raised this shout: 'Hosanna to the Son of David! Blessings on him who comes in the name of the Lord! Hosanna in the heavens!'" (Matt 21:6–9, NEB)

(c) "[Two of Jesus' disciples] brought [a] colt to Jesus. Then they threw their cloaks on the colt, for Jesus to mount, and they carpeted the road with them as he went on his way. And now, as he approached the descent from the Mount of Olives, the whole company of his disciples in their joy began to sing aloud the praise of God for all the great things they had seen: 'Blessings on him who comes as king / in the name of the Lord! / Peace in heaven, glory in highest heaven!'" (Luke 19:34b–38, NEB)

(d) ". . . [T[he great body of pilgrims who had come to the [Passover] festival, hearing that Jesus was on the way to Jerusalem, took palm branches and went out to meet him, shouting 'Hosanna! Blessings on him who comes in the name of the Lord! God bless the king of Israel!' Jesus found a donkey and mounted it, in accordance with the text of Scripture: 'Fear no more, daughter of Zion; see your king is coming, mounted on an ass's colt.'" (John 12:12–15, NEB)

Points to Ponder: First, this day would be better named Cloak Sunday, because only the author of John's Gospel mentions that the crowd took palm branches, a sign of victory, to greet Jesus. Second, the author of Matthew's Gospel is known for copying stories featuring one person or thing in Mark's Gospel and doubling them. In his account of Jesus' parade, he states that Jesus rode a donkey and her colt, making two out of Mark's singular colt. Third, the author of Luke's Gospel presents several hymns in the first two chapters of his narrative. The hymn he presents in his narrative about Jesus' parade echoes that of the one the heavenly host sang at his birth: "Glory to God in highest heaven, / and on earth his peace for men [and women] on whom his favor rests" (Luke 2:14, NEB). Fourth, the perspective of the author of the John's Gospel is that Jesus replaces all Jewish festivals, especially Passover. Thus, Jesus enters Jerusalem a few days before Passover begins. Fifth, also, it is only in John's Gospel that pilgrims—those Jews who traveled to Jerusalem for Passover—took palm branches to wave before Jesus. Only the author of John's Gospel sees Jesus' parade as fulfilling the prophet Zechariah: "Rejoice, rejoice, daughter of Zion, / shout aloud, daughter of Jerusalem; / for see, your king is coming to you, his cause won, his victory gained, / humble and mounted on an ass, / on a foal, the young of a she-ass" (Zech 9:9, NEB). The author of John's Gospel has taken the verse from the prophet Zechariah about a future Jewish king riding into town on a beast of burden—instead of on a war horse—and applied it to Jesus! Sixth, all the gospel writers use verse 26a from Psalm 118 as the basis for the crowds shouting: "Blessed in the name of the LORD are all who come" (Ps 118:26a, NEB). From that verse, each gospel writer adds other lyrics to emphasize his themes. Seventh, all the gospel writers use the word *Hosanna*! Literally, it means *O save*; it can be understood as an appeal for divine help or as a cry of praise.

Evening
Antiphon: "My God, my God, why have you forsaken Me? / Why are you so far from helping Me, from the words of my groaning?" (Ps 22:1, NRSV)
Psalm: ". . . I am . . . scorned by others, and despised by the people. / All who see me mock at me; / they make mouths at me, they shake their heads; / 'Commit your cause to the LORD; let him deliver—/ let him rescue the one in whom he delights!' / Do not be far from me, / for trouble is near / and there is no one to help. / I am poured out like water, / and all my bones are out of joint; / my heart is like wax; / it is melted within my breast; / my mouth is dried up like a potsherd, / and my tongue sticks to my jaws; / you lay me in the dust of death." (Ps 22:6–8, 11, 14–15, NRSV)
Repeat Antiphon (above):
Reading: ". . . [T]he divine nature was [Christ Jesus'] from the first; yet he did not think to snatch at equality with God, but made himself nothing, assuming the nature of a slave. Bearing the human likeness, revealed in human shape, he humbled himself, and in obedience accepted even death—death on a cross. Therefore God raised him to the heights and bestowed on him the name above all names, that at the name of Jesus every knee should bow—in heaven, on earth, and in the depths—and every tongue confess, 'Jesus Christ is Lord,' to the glory of God the Father." (Phil 2:6–11, NEB)

Activity: What word of phrase gets your attention in either the verses of Psalm 22 or the passage from the CB (NT) letter of Paul to the Philippians 2:6–11? What does the word of phrase mean? How does the word of phrase help you celebrate Palm Sunday? How does the word of phrase make you aware of God's presence?

Day 41: Monday of Holy Week

Morning
Antiphon: "[The LORD] spoke, and there came swarms of flies . . . ." (Ps 105:31a, NRSV)
Psalm: "[The Israelites] remembered that God was their rock, / the Most High God their redeemer. / Their heart was not steadfast toward him; / they were not true to his covenant. / Yet he, being compassionate, / forgave their iniquity, / and did not destroy them . . . . / He remembered that they were but flesh, / a wind that passes and does not come again. / He sent among them swarms of flies, / which devoured them . . . ." (Ps 78:35, 37–38a, 39, 45a, NRSV)
Repeat Antiphon (above):
Reading: "The LORD told Moses to rise early in the morning and stand in Pharaoh's path as he went out to the river and to say to him, 'These are the words of the LORD: "Let my people go in order to worship me. If you do not let my people go, I will send swarms of flies upon you, your courtiers, your people, and your houses. The houses of the Egyptians shall be filled with the swarms and so shall all the land they live in, but on that day I will make an exception of Goshen, the land where my people live: there shall be no swarms there. Thus you shall know that I, the LORD, am here in the land."' The LORD did this; dense swarms of flies infested Pharaoh's house and those of his courtiers; throughout Egypt the land was threatened with ruin by the swarms." (Exod 8:20–22, 24, NEB)
Reflection/Meditation/Journal: The swarms of flies, the fourth plague on Egypt, represent the natural mature larvae from the previous two plagues. What is added in this plague is the separation of the Hebrews from the Egyptians. The Hebrews, since the days of Joseph, lived in Goshen, a fertile area of the Nile River. They lived there because the Egyptians were offended by their way of life. Their separation from the Egyptians proves to be their favor from their God. While the Egyptians are afflicted with flies, the Hebrews are untouched. What application can you make of this separation in neighborhoods of modern cities and towns? Explain.

Evening

Antiphon: "Help us, O God of our salvation, / for the glory of your name; / deliver us, and forgive our sins, / for your name's sake." (Ps 79:9, NRSV)

Psalm: "[The Israelites] did not keep in mind [the Most High God's] power, / or the day when he redeemed them from the foe; / when he displayed his signs in Egypt, / and his miracles in the fields . . . . / . . . [H]e led out his people like sheep, / and guided them in the wilderness like a flock. / He led them in safety, so that they were not afraid . . . . / And he brought them to his holy hill, / to the mountain that his right hand had won." (Ps 78:42–43, 52–53a, 54, NRSV)

Repeat Antiphon (above):

Reading: "The LORD said to Moses, 'Go into Pharaoh's presence and say to him, "These are the words of the LORD the God of the Hebrews: 'Let my people go in order to worship me. If you refuse to let them go and still keep your hold on them, the LORD will strike your grazing herds, your horses and asses, your camels, cattle, and sheep with a terrible pestilence. But the LORD will make a distinction between Israel's herds and those of the Egyptians.'"' The next day the LORD struck. All the herds of Egypt died, but from the herds of the Israelites not one single beast died. Pharaoh . . . remained obdurate and did not let the people go." (Exod 9:1–4a, 6, 7b, NEB)

Reflection: The LORD continues to win battles, but Pharaoh continues to remain stubborn or hardened of heart. Some biblical translations refer to this fifth plague as pestilence, while others refer to it as a disease that kills animals; by killing the herds of Egypt, the LORD is removing some of the food supply of meat. By protecting the herds of the Hebrews, the LORD is preserving their lives. Furthermore, this plague is partially against the bovine deities of Hathor and Apis. Hathor, a major Egyptian goddess, was often depicted as a cow or as a woman wearing a headdress of cow horns and a sun disk. Apis or Hapis was a sacred bull, the son of Hathor, who was sacrificed and reborn. The gods of Egypt are no match for the God of the Hebrews.

Day 42: Tuesday of Holy Week

Morning

Antiphon: ". . . [God] did not spare [the Egyptians] from death, / but gave their lives over to the plague." (Ps 78:50bc, NRSV)

Psalm: "Bless the LORD, O my soul, / and all that is within me, / bless his holy name. / Bless the LORD, O my soul, / and do not forget all his benefits—/ who forgives all your iniquity, / who heals all your diseases, / who redeems your life from the Pit, / who crowns you with steadfast love and mercy, / who satisfies you with good as long as you live / so that your youth is renewed like the eagle's." (Ps 103:1–5, NRSV)

Repeat Antiphon (above):

Reading: "[Moses and Aaron] took ... soot from [a] kiln and stood before Pharaoh. Moses tossed it into the air and it produced festering boils on man [, woman,] and beast. The LORD then told Moses to rise early in the morning, present himself before Pharaoh, and say to him, 'These are the words of the LORD the God of the Hebrews: "Let my people go in order to worship me. This time I will strike home with all my plagues against you, your courtiers, and your people, so that you may know that there is none like me in all the earth. By now I could have stretched out my hand, and struck you and your people with pestilence, and you would have vanished from the earth. I have let you live only to show you my power and to spread my fame throughout the land."'" (Exod 9:10, 13–16, NEB)

Reflection: With the sixth plague of boils on man, woman, and beast, this is the first time that humans are directly afflicted. The LORD has won the contest of whose God is greater. The author of the HB (OT) book of Exodus makes that clear; God tells Moses to relay to Pharaoh the message that he could have afflicted him and his people with pestilence, which would have caused all to die. However, God, who has won the contest, let the Egyptians live to show Pharaoh that he is more powerful than all the gods of Egypt and, thus, to spread his fame, his reputation, throughout the land. The sixth plague is a turning point. It and the plagues that follow are all death-dealing is some way. One might spend some time reflecting on the sicknesses he or she has endured during his or her life and the methods used to achieve cures. Also, reflection can center on how God was involved in the cures.

Evening

Antiphon: "[The LORD] gave [the Egyptians] hail for rain, / and lightning that flashed through their land. / He struck their vines and fig trees, / and shattered the trees of their country." (Ps 105:32–33, NRSV)

Psalm: "[The Most High God] destroyed [the Egyptians'] vines with hail, / and their sycamores with frost. / He gave over their cattle to the hail, / and their flocks to thunderbolts." (Ps 78:47–48, NRSV)

Repeat Antiphon (above):
Reading: "Moses stretched out his staff towards the sky, and the LORD sent thunder and hail, with fire flashing down to the ground. Throughout Egypt the hail struck everything in the fields, both man [, woman,] and beast; it beat down every growing thing and shattered every tree. Only in the land of Goshen, where the Israelites lived, was there no hail." (Exod 9:23, 25–26, NEB)
Reflection: The seventh plague of the hail and fire indicates that the account of the plagues found in the HB (OT) book of Exodus is not a unified chronicle of consecutive historical events. The herds of Egypt were attacked in the previous plague. Therefore, there are no herds left for the hail to strike. Likewise, the next plague of locusts have nothing to eat after the hail beat down every growing thing and shattered every tree. Such biblical inconsistency is the result of oral story-telling being recorded in written form or from variant written stories being merged into one. Biblical truth is plural; various oral stories were told repeatedly, and in every telling they change—some things are added and some things are removed. Once they are written and collected, similar accounts are merged to form a new narrative. Some writers or editors are better at smoothing the wrinkles, disagreements, and conflicts than others. A good way to understand this phenomenon is to pay attention to the stories told by the elders during Thanksgiving dinner, even recording the basics of the various accounts. Then, the next year repeating the process, noting how different the versions are from person to person and from year to year. Several factors are at play here. First, we do not hear what another person says; we hear what we think the other person says. Second, a story continues to change as people change. Third, the only way to kill a good story is to record it; however, even written accounts can be changed by a good editor and manipulated to fit with other written versions of the same story.

Day 43: Wednesday of Holy Week

Morning
Antiphon: "[God] gave [the Egyptians'] crops to the caterpillar, / and the fruit of their labor to the locust." (Ps 78:46, NRSV)
Psalm: "[The LORD] spoke, and the locusts came, / and young locusts without number; / they devoured all the vegetation in their land, / and ate up the fruit of their ground." (Ps 105:34–35, NRSV)

Repeat Antiphon (above):
Reading: ". . . [T]he LORD said to Moses, 'Stretch out your hand over Egypt so that the locusts may come and invade the land and devour all the vegetation in it.' When morning came, the east wind had brought the locusts. They covered the surface of the whole land till it was black with them. They devoured all the vegetation and all the fruit of the trees. . . . There was no green left on tree or plant throughout all Egypt." (Exod 10:12, 13b, 15, NEB)
Reflection/Meditation/Journal: As they are today, swarms of locusts were known and feared throughout the ancient world. That was so because the locusts ate both vegetation and fruit. In other words, when the annual cycle of locusts produced adults, the food supply was attacked. In your world today, what can you compare to a swarm of locusts? Explain.

Evening
Antiphon: "The LORD] sent darkness, and made the land dark; / [the Egyptians] rebelled against his words." (Ps 105:28, NRSV)
Psalm: "Hear my prayer, O LORD; / give ear to my supplications in your faithfulness; / answer me in your righteousness. / Do not enter into judgment with you servant, / for no one living is righteous before you. / For the enemy has pursued me, / crushing my life to the ground, / making me sit in darkness like those long dead. / Therefore my spirit faints within me; / my heart within me is appalled. / I remember the days of old, / I think about all your deeds, / I meditate on the works of your hands. / I stretch out my hands to you; / my soul thirsts for you like a parched land." (Ps 143:1–6, NRSV)
Repeat Antiphon (above):
Reading: ". . . [T]he LORD said to Moses, 'Stretch out your hand towards the sky so that there may be darkness over the land of Egypt, darkness that can be felt.' Moses stretched out his hand towards the sky, and it became pitch dark throughout the land of Egypt for three days. . . . [T]here was no darkness wherever the Israelites lived. The LORD made Pharaoh obstinate, and he refused to let them go." (Exod 10:21–22, 23b, 27, NEB)
Points to Ponder: First, the author of the HB (OT) book of Exodus describes the ninth plague as if it were directed against the Egyptian sun-god, Re or Ra. Such darkness is caused by hot, dust-laden wind from the desert which covers the land with an eerie gloom; breathing becomes difficult. Second, as in past plagues, no darkness invades the places where the Hebrews live. The fact that something supernatural is taking place is

confirmed by the statement that the darkness lasts for three days; three is the number for God. While the Egyptians are in darkness, his people are in his light. Third, nevertheless, the LORD makes Pharaoh obstinate or hardens his heart even harder than before. Pharaoh tells Moses never to appear in his presence again; if he does so, he will die.

The Sacred Paschal Triduum

Holy Thursday

Morning

Antiphon: "Tremble, O earth, at the presence of the LORD . . . ." (Ps 114:7a, NRSV)

Psalm: "When Israel went out from Egypt, . . . / The sea looked and fled; / Jordan turned back. The mountains skipped like rams, / the hills like lambs. / Why is it, O sea, that you flee? / O Jordan, that you turn back? / O mountains, that you skip like rams? / O hills like lambs? Tremble, O earth, at the presence of the LORD, / . . . who turns the rock into a pool of water, / the flint into a spring of water." (Ps 114:1a, 3–7a, 8, NRSV)

Repeat Antiphon (above):

Reading: "The LORD said to Moses and Aaron in Egypt: Speak to the whole community of Israel and say to them: On the tenth day of this month let each man [and woman] take a lamb or a kid for his [and her] family, one for each household. You must have it in safe keeping until the fourteenth day of this month, and then all the assembled community of Israel shall slaughter the victim between dusk and dark. They must take some of the blood and smear it on the two doorposts and on the lintel of every house in which they eat the lamb. On that night they shall eat the flesh roast[ed] on the fire; they shall eat it with unleavened cakes and bitter herbs. It is the LORD's Passover. On that night I shall pass through the land of Egypt and kill every first-born of man [, woman,] and beast Thus will I execute judgment, I the LORD, against all the gods of Egypt. And as for you, the blood will be a sign on the houses in which you are: when I see the blood I will pass over you; the mortal blow shall not touch you, when I strike the land of Egypt." (Exod 12:1, 3, 6–8, 11b–13, NEB)

Points to Ponder: First, the HB (OT) book of Exodus pauses for a moment in identifying plagues to present the origin of Passover, which is the introduction to the last plague. Second, the author of the book of Exodus identifies the ritual choosing, slaughtering, and eating of a roasted lamb or kid as the LORD's Passover, because the LORD will pass over the houses that are marked with blood on the doorposts and lintels. Third, without lamb's blood or kid's blood smeared on the doorposts and lintels, the people inside the homes face death; those with blood smeared on the doorposts and lintels face death, but they will live. Fourth, why? Because blood represents life, and all life belongs to God. The Passover ritual will later be altered after the Temple is built in Jerusalem; the blood of the slaughtered animal will then be splashed onto the altar. This first Passover is one of many. Fifth, the verses of Psalm 114 above refer to three more Passovers. One occurs at the Sea of Reeds, where the people face death when trapped by Pharaoh's army and passover the sea to new life. Another Passover occurs at the Jordan River before the people enter the Promised Land; they face death, but passover the river to a land flowing with milk and honey. And the third Passover mentioned in Psalm 114 occurs in the desert; they face death because they have no water, but God provides water flowing from a rock for them to drink. Passover celebrates imminent death that becomes life, when God is involved.

Evening
Antiphon: "[The LORD] struck down all the firstborn in [the Egyptians'] land, / the first issue of all their strength." (Ps 105:36, NRSV)
Psalm: "O give thanks to the LORD, for he is good, / for his steadfast love endures forever. / O give thanks to the Lord of lords, / for his steadfast love endures forever; / who struck Egypt through their firstborn, / for his steadfast love endures forever; / and brought Israel out from among them, / for his steadfast love endures forever; / who divided the Red Sea in two, / for his steadfast love endures forever; / and made Israel pass through the midst of it, / for his steadfast love endures forever; / but overthrew Pharaoh and his army in the Red Sea, / for his steadfast love endures forever." (Ps 136:1, 3, 10–15, NRSV)
Repeat Antiphon (above):
Reading: ". . . [B]y midnight the LORD had stuck down every first-born in Egypt, from the first-born of Pharaoh on his throne to the first-born of the captive in the dungeon, and the first-born of cattle. . . . [A] great cry of anguish went up, because not a house in Egypt was without its dead. Pharaoh summoned Moses and Aaron while it was still night and said, 'Up with you! Be off, and leave my people, you and your Israelites. Go and worship the LORD, as you ask; take your sheep and cattle, and go; and ask God's blessing on me also.'" (Exod 12:29, 30b-32, NEB)

Reflection/Meditation/Journal: The verses of Psalm 136 along with the passage from Exodus 12 celebrate the death of the first-born of people and beasts in Egypt. The refrain of Psalm 136—God's steadfast love endures forever—was composed by an Israelite, whose perspective was Hebraic. In other words, the author of Psalm 136 views the death of the first-born as a demonstration of God's enduring love. Furthermore, the psalmist adds other demonstrations of God's steadfast love: the escape of the Israelite slaves from their master Egyptians; the dividing of the Red Sea; and the drowning of Pharaoh and his army in the Red Sea. Which of those biblical events would you not attribute to a demonstration of God's steadfast love? Why not?

Alternate Readings for Morning or Evening
Alternate 1
(a) "... [T]he tradition which I [, Paul,] handed on .... came to me from the Lord himself: that the Lord Jesus, on the night of his arrest, took bread and after giving thanks to God, broke it and said: 'This is my body, which is for you; do this as a memorial of me.' In the same way, he took the cup after supper, and said: 'This cup is the new covenant sealed by my blood. Whenever you drink it, do this as a memorial of me.' For every time you eat this bread and drink the cup, you proclaim the death of the Lord, until he comes." (1 Cor 11:23-26, NEB)
Reflection: The oldest narrative about the institution of the Lord's Supper is found in Paul's First Letter to the Corinthians. Written in the early 50s of the first century, the apostle indicates that the tradition of remembering Jesus with bread and wine was already in place. However, it is important to note that the remembrance of Jesus with bread and wine—a memorial—marked his absence; in other words, the idea of his presence in bread and wine had not yet developed. While marking his absence, according to Paul, the Corinthians were awaiting his return. It must be remembered that Paul thought that he would see the day of Jesus' return in glory. However, that never occurred. With that realization, the focus shifted from the absence of Jesus to his presence in bread and wine, and the waiting, while still remembered, passed into the limelight.
Alternate 2
(b) "... [W]hen the Passover lambs were being slaughtered, [i]n the evening [Jesus] came ... with the Twelve [and] they sat at supper. During supper he took bread, and having said the blessing he broke it and gave it to them, with the words: 'Take this; this is my body.' Then he took a cup,

and having offered thanks to God he gave it to them; and they all drank from it. And he said, 'This is my blood, the blood of the covenant, shed for many.'" (Mark 14:12, 18, 22–24, NEB)

(c) "In the evening [Jesus] sat down with the twelve disciples.... During [Passover] supper Jesus took bread, and having said the blessing he broke it and gave it to the disciples with the words: 'Take this and eat; this is my body.' Then he took a cup and having offered thanks to God he gave it to them with the words: 'Drink from it all of you. For this is my blood, the blood of the covenant, shed for many for the forgiveness of sins.'" (Matt 26:20, 26–28, NEB)

(d) "When the time came [to celebrate the festival of Unleavened Bread, known as Passover, Jesus] took his place at table, and the apostles with him.... Then he took a cup, and after giving thanks he said, 'Take this and share it among yourselves....' And he took bread, gave thanks, and broke it; and he gave it to them, with words: 'This is my body.' (Luke 22:1, 14, 17, 19, NEB) "And he did the same with the cup after supper, saying, 'This cup that is poured out for you is the new covenant in my blood.'" (Luke 22:20, NRSV)

Reflection: Above are the accounts of Jesus' last supper with the Twelve, the disciples, or the apostles, depending on what each gospel writer names them. All three of the accounts situate Jesus' last meal as a Passover supper. During the Passover meal, bread is broken and shared, and several cups of wine are poured and consumed. The oldest account of the last supper is found in Mark's Gospel, where the author mentions a part of the Passover supper, namely, the breaking and sharing of bread and the pouring of a cup of wine. According to the author of Mark's Gospel, Jesus adds a new interpretation to the bread and cup. While they once commemorated the escape of the Hebrews from Egyptian slavery, the Markan Jesus declares them to represent his body, which will be broken on the cross, and his blood, which will be shed on the cross. The author of Mark's Gospel does not understand the cup to represent a new covenant; rather, it represents the continuation of the covenant sealed in blood before Mount Horeb (Sinai). The author of Matthew's Gospel copies and alters the account he found in Mark's Gospel. While the cup continues the covenant sealed in blood before Mount Horeb (Sinai), it also represents the forgiveness of sins, the meaning of the name *Jesus* given to Joseph when he discovers Mary's pregnancy. The author of Luke's Gospel took Mark's Gospel's account of the last supper and conforms it more to the usual Passover meal. Jesus takes a cup, then he takes the bread, then he takes another cup, which is omitted by the NEB, but which is supplied from the NRSV above. Also, it is important to note that the author of Luke's Gospel understands Jesus to be inaugurating a new covenant in his blood, like the old one sealed in blood on Mount Horeb (Sinai). Thus, in the synoptic gospels (Mark, Matthew, and Luke), there are three versions of what Jesus did when he celebrated his last Passover supper with his followers.

Alternate 3

(e) "[B]efore the Passover festival... [d]uring supper, Jesus... rose from table, laid aside his garments, and taking a towel, tied it round him. Then he poured water into a basin, and began to wash his disciples' feet and to wipe them with the towel. After washing their feet and taking his garments again, he sat down. 'Do you understand what I have done for you?' he asked. 'You call me "Master" and "Lord", and rightly so, for that is what I am. Then if I, your Lord and Master, have washed your feet, you also ought to wash one another's feet. I have set you an example; you are to do as I have done for you.'" (John 13:1, 3, 4–5, 12–14, NEB)

Points to Ponder: First, according to John's Gospel, Jesus does not eat the Passover supper with his disciples; he eat a last supper with them, but it is before Passover begins. This is because the author of John's Gospel presents Jesus as the replacement for the Passover lamb. The Johannine Jesus dies on the cross at the same time the Passover lambs were being slaughtered in the Temple in preparation for the Passover supper. Thus, in John's Gospel, Jesus eats a last supper with his disciples, but it is not a Passover last supper, as it is in Mark, Matthew, and Luke. Second, unique to John's Gospel is the scene of Jesus washing the feet of his disciples. In Jesus' world, no one—not even a slave—could be made to wash a person's feet. After walking the dusty streets of any town, before entering their homes, people stopped at the door, removed their sandals, and washed their feet in a basin by pouring water over them, and dried them with towels. According to the author of John's Gospel, Jesus does what no slave could be made to do: he washes others' feet. Then, he teaches his followers the meaning of servanthood. If he, their Master and Lord, washed their feet, they must wash each other's feet. The Johannine Jesus tells them to imitate his extreme, servant humility. Thus, in John's Gospel in which there is no Passover supper, there is a last supper with the service of washed feet.

Good Friday

Morning
Antiphon: "Save us, O LORD our God . . . ." (Ps 106:47a, NRSV)
Psalm: "[O LORD,] you have seen my affliction; / you have taken heed of my adversities, and have not delivered me into the hand of the enemy; / you have set my feet in a broad place. / Be gracious to me, O LORD, for I am in distress; / my eye wastes away from grief, / my soul and body also. / For my life is spent with sorrow, / and my years with sighing; / my strength fails because of my misery, / and my bones waste away. / I have passed out of mind like one who is dead; / I have become like a broken vessel." (Ps 31:7b–10, 12, NRSV)
Repeat Antiphon (above):
Reading: "[The LORD's servant] was despised, he shrank from the sight of men, / tormented and humbled by suffering; / we despised him, we held him of no account, / a thing from which men [and women] turn away their eyes. / Yet on himself he bore our sufferings, / our torments he endured, / while we counted him smitten by God, / struck down by disease and misery; / but he was pierced for our transgressions, / tortured for our iniquities; / the chastisement he bore is health for us / and by his scourging we are healed. / We had all strayed like sheep, / each of us had gone his own way; / but the LORD laid upon him the guilt of us all. / He was afflicted, he submitted to be struck down / and did not open his mouth; he was led like a sheep to the slaughter, / like a[n] ewe that is dumb before the shearers." (Isa 53:3–7, NEB)
Meditation/Journal: Choose one of the following questions: (a) In what specific ways have you experienced yourself, in the words of Psalm 31, passing out of mind, like one who is dead? (b) In what specific ways have you experienced yourself, in the words of Psalm 31, becoming like a broken vessel? (c) In what specific ways have you experienced yourself, in the words of Isaiah 53, being like the LORD's servant? (d) In what specific ways have you experienced yourself, in the words of Isaiah 53, being like a sheep led to the slaughter? (e) In what specific ways have you experienced yourself, in the words of Isaiah 53, being like an ewe that is dumb before the shearers?

Evening
Antiphon: "Be gracious to me, O LORD, for I am languishing . . . ." (Ps 6:2a, NRSV)

HOLY WEEK

Psalm: "O LORD, heal me, for my bones are shaking with terror. / My soul also is struck with terror, / while you, O LORD—how long? / Turn, O LORD, save my life; / deliver me for the sake of your steadfast love. / For in death there is no remembrance of you; / in Sheol who can give you praise? / The LORD has heard my supplication, / the LORD accepts my prayer." (Ps 6:2b–5, 9, NRSV)

Repeat Antiphon (above):

Reading: "It was the eve of Passover, about noon. Pilate said to the Jews, 'Here is your king.' They shouted, 'Away with him! Away with him!' 'Crucify your king?' said Pilate. 'We have no king but Caesar,' the Jews replied. Then at last, to satisfy them, he handed Jesus over to be crucified. Jesus was not taken in charge and, carrying his own cross, went out to the Place of the Skull, as it is called (or, in the Jews' language, "Golgotha") where they crucified him and with him two others, one on the right, one on the left, and Jesus between them." (John 19:14–18, NEB)

Reflection: In Psalm 6, there is mentioned *Sheol*. Sheol is the Hebrew name for the first level of a three-storied universe. Sheol, on the first level, is where the dead live. Earth, a plate-like surface, the second level, is where people live. And above the dome of the sky, level three, is where God lives. Basically, the psalmist, who looks like he is dying, tells God to heal him and save his life. He presents two reasons why the LORD should save his life. God should save his life to demonstrate divine steadfast love; and God should save his life since no one in Sheol can praise God, and God will be missing praise if the psalmist dies. The psalmist lives; God hears his prayer, and saves him from death. Psalm 6 is contrasted with the passage from John's Gospel. Pilate attempts to save Jesus' life, but he is unable to do so. So, Jesus goes ironically to the Place of the Skull—a hill strewn with the bones of formerly crucified criminals—and dies between two criminals. Because we know the end of the story, God raises him after Passover. He dies on the eve of Passover and passes over to new life. In the imagery of Psalm 6, he goes to Sheol, but he is raised from there to earth, and from earth to heaven.

Alternate Readings for Morning or Evening

(a) "When [the soldiers] had finished their mockery, they stripped [Jesus] of the purple and dressed him in his own clothes. Then they took him out to crucify him. A man called Simon, from Cyrene, . . . was passing by on his way in from the country, and they pressed him into service to carry [Jesus'] cross. They brought him to the place called Golgotha, which

means 'Place of a skull.' He was offered drugged wine, but he would not take it. Then they fastened him to the cross." (Mark 15:20–24a, NEB)
(b) "When [the soldiers] had finished their mockery, they took off the [scarlet] mantle and dressed [Jesus] in his own clothes. Then they led him away to be crucified. On their way out they met a man from Cyrene, Simon by name, and pressed him into service to carry his cross. So they came to a place called Golgotha (which means 'place of a skull') and there he was offered a draught of wine mixed with gall; but when he had tasted it he would not drink. After fastening him to the cross they divided his clothes among them by casting lots, and then sat down there to keep watch." (Matt 27:31–35, NEB)
(c) "As [the soldiers] led [Jesus] away to execution they seized upon a man called Simon, from Cyrene, on his way in from the country, put the cross on his back, and made him walk behind Jesus carrying it. There were two others with him, criminals who were being led away to execution; and when they reached the place called The Skull, they crucified him there, and the criminals with him, one on his right and the other on his left." (Luke 23:26, 32–33, NEB)
Reflection/Activity: There are similarities in the four accounts of Jesus' crucifixion, like the place of crucifixion. However, each account is used by the gospel author to portray his definition of discipleship. In Mark's Gospel, discipleship is defined as helping Jesus carry his cross (Simon), as it is in Matthew's Gospel (Simon). In Luke's Gospel, discipleship is carrying the cross and following behind Jesus (Simon). In John's Gospel, Jesus, who is the Son of God, carries his cross by himself. Make a list of other differences and explain why you think they are there. Make a list of similarities and explain why they are there? Then, after reviewing the four accounts of Jesus' crucifixion, ask yourself this question: How do I better understand Jesus?

Holy Saturday

Morning
Antiphon: "Sing to the LORD, for he has risen up in triumph; / the horse and his rider he has hurled into the sea." (Exod 15:21, NEB)
Canticle: "At the blast of [your nostrils, LORD,] the sea piled up, / the waters stood up like a bank; / out at sea the great deep congealed. / [You blew] with your blast; the sea covered [Pharaoh's chariots and his army]. / They sank like lead in the swelling waves. / [You stretched] out [your]

right hand, / earth engulfed them. / In [your] constant love [you have] led the people / whom [you ransomed; / [you] guided them by your strength / to [your] holy dwelling-place." (Exod 15:8, 10, 12–13, NEB)
Repeat Antiphon (above):
Reading: "The LORD said to Moses, . . . 'Tell the Israelites to strike camp. And you shall raise high your staff, stretch out your hand over the [Red] [S]ea and cleave it in two, so that the Israelites can pass through the sea on dry ground. For my part I will make the Egyptians obstinate and they will come after you; thus will I win glory for myself at the expense of Pharaoh and his army, chariots, and cavalry all together.'" (Exod 14:15–17, NEB)
Activity: Specifically, what connections do you find between the verses from the canticle in Exodus 15 and the narrative in verses from Exodus 14? What do you think is the message to be heard from the parting of the Sea of Reeds? What do you think is the message to be heard from the death of Pharaoh, his army, chariots, and cavalry?

Evening
Antiphon: "I will sing to the LORD, for he has triumphed gloriously; / horse and rider he has thrown into the sea." (Exod 15:1, NRSV)
Canticle: "The LORD is my strength and my might, / and he has become my salvation; / this is my God, and I will praise him, / my father's God, and I will exalt him. / The LORD is a warrior; / the LORD is his name. / Pharaoh's chariots and his army he cast into the sea; / his picked officers were sunk in the Red Sea. / The floods covered them; / they went down into the depths like a stone. / Your right hand, O LORD, glorious in power—/ your right hand, O LORD, shattered the enemy." (Exod 15:2–6, NRSV)
Repeat Antiphon (above):
Reading: ". . . Moses stretched out his hand over the sea, and the LORD drove the sea away all night with a strong east wind and turned the seabed into dry land. The waters were torn apart, and the Israelites went through the sea on the dry ground, while the waters made a wall for them to right and to left. The Egyptians went in pursuit of them far into the sea, all Pharaoh's horse, his chariots, and his cavalry. [The LORD] clogged their chariot wheels and made them lumber along heavily . . . . Moses stretched out his hand over the sea, and at daybreak the water returned to its accustomed place; but the Egyptians were in flight as it advanced, and the LORD swept them out into the sea. The water flowed back and

covered all Pharaoh's army, the chariots, and cavalry, which had pressed the pursuit into the sea." (Exod 14:21–23, 25, 27–28, NEB)

Reflection: Biblical water represents chaos; dry land represents order. Just as in the creation account at the beginning of the HB (OT) book of Genesis, God makes dry land appear by parting the Sea of Reeds. As the story is told, Pharaoh, his horses, chariots, and cavalry attempt to take advantage of the order, but they are plunged into the chaos, as the sea returns to its normal depth. Furthermore, the Pharaoh who had tried to drown all Hebrew sons in the Nile River is drowned with his army in the Red Sea. The escape of the Hebrew slaves is the central event of the HB (OT). It names the book in which it occurs as the exodus, meaning a departure or going away from a place; the Greek word literally means *way out*. And the way out of Egypt for the Israelites is through the chaos on either side while traveling the order of the sea bed. In the canticle, the LORD is presented as a single, divine warrior, who not only fights for his people, but defeats their enemy with the very chaos (water) their enemy had inflicted upon them (drowning of baby boys).

8

Season of Easter

Season of Easter Introduction

The Season of Easter consists of fifty days. Easter begins in 2025 on April 20; in 2026 on April 5; in 2027 on March 28; in 2028 on April 16; in 2029 on April 1; in 2030 on April 21; in 2031 on April 13; in 2032 on March 28; in 2033 on April 17; in 2034 on April 9; in 2035 on March 25; in 2036 on April 13; in 2037 on April 5; in 2038 on April 25; in 2039 on April 10.

The change in the date for Easter Sunday every year is due to the way Easter is calculated. It is always the first Sunday after the first full moon after the Spring Equinox. Therefore, it cannot be any earlier than March 20, and it cannot be any later than April 25.

The traditional date for the solemnity of the Ascension of the Lord on the fortieth day of Easter, always a Thursday, occurs in 2025 on May 29; in 2026 on May 14; in 2027 on May 6; in 2028 on May 25; in 2029 on May 10; in 2030 on May 30; in 2031 on May 22; in 2032 on May 6; in 2033 on May 26; in 2034 on May 18; in 2035 on May 3; in 2036 on May 22; in 2037 on May 14; in 2038 on June 3; in 2039 on May 19. In many places, the solemnity of Ascension is moved to the following Sunday and takes the place of the Seventh Sunday of Easter.

The fifty-day Season of Easter ends with the solemnity of Pentecost, which occurs in 2025 on June 8; in 2026 on May 24; in 2027 on May 16; in 2028 on June 4; in 2029 on May 20; in 2030 on June 9; in 2031 on June 1; in 2032 on May 16; in 2033 on June 5; in 2034 on May 28; in 2035 on May 13; in 2036 on June 1; in 2037 on May 24; in 2038 on June 13; in 2039 on May 29.

The first Sunday after Pentecost is The Most Holy Trinity, which occurs in 2025 on June 15; in 2026 on May 31; in 2027 on May 23; in 2028 on June 11; in 2029 on May 27; in 2030 on June 16; in 2031 on June 8; in 2032 on May 23; in 2033 on June 12; in 2034 on June 4; in 2035 on May 20; in 2036 on June 8; in 2037 on May 31; in 2038 on June 20; in 2039 on June 5.

The second Sunday after Pentecost is The Most Holy Body and Blood of Christ (Corpus Christi), which occurs in 2025 on June 22; in 2026 on June 7; in 2027 on May 30; in 2028 on June 18; in 2029 on June 3; in 2030 on June 23; in 2031 on June 15; in 2032 on May 30; in 2033 on June 19; in 2034 on June 11; in 2035 on May 27; in 2036 on June 15; in 2037 on June 7; in 2038 on June 27; in 2039 on June 12.

The second Friday after Pentecost (or the Friday after The Most Holy Body and Blood of Christ [Corpus Christi]) is The Most Sacred Heart of Jesus, which occurs in 2025 on June 27; in 2026 on June 12; in 2027 on June 4; in 2028 on June 23; in 2029 on June 8; in 2030 on June 28; in 2031 on June 20; in 2032 on June 4; in 2033 on June 24; in 2034 on June 16; in 2035 on June 1; in 2036 on June 20; in 2037 on June 12; in 2038 on July 2; in 2039 on June 17.

Except for the first Week of Easter, the following may be celebrated, unless they fall on a Sunday: St. Mark, Evangelist (April 25); Sts. Philip and James, Apostles (May 3); St. Matthias, Apostle (May 14); The Visitation of the Blessed Virgin Mary (May 31); St. Barnabas, Apostle (June 11)

Other books by Mark G. Boyer that follow the same structure of Morning Prayer and Evening Prayer that can be used—in substitution for what is provided here—during the Season of Easter include: *Weekday Saints: Reflections on Their Scriptures* (Eugene, OR: Wipf & Stock, 2014); *Very Short Reflections—for Advent and Christmas, Lent and Easter, Ordinary Time, and Saints—through the Liturgical Year* (Eugene, OR: Wipf & Stock, 2020); *Overcome with Paschal Joy: Chanting through Lent and Easter, Daily Reflections with Familiar Hymns* (Eugene, OR: Wipf & Stock, 2016); *Christ Our Passover Has Been Sacrificed: A Guide through Paschal Mystery Spirituality, Mystical Theology in The Roman Missal* (Eugene, OR:

Wipf & Stock, 2018); *Biblical Names for God: An Abecedarian Anthology of Spiritual Reflections for Anytime* (Eugene, OR: Wipf & Stock, 2023); *Journey into God: Spiritual Reflections for Travelers* (Eugene, OR: Wipf & Stock, 2022); *The Spirit of the Lord God: Biblical Names and Images for the Holy Spirit; An Abecedarian Anthology of Spiritual Reflections for Anytime* (Eugene, OR: Resource Publications, 2024); *What is Born of the Spirit is Spirit: A Biblical Spirituality of Spirit* (Eugene, OR: Wipf & Stock, 2019); and *Seasons of Biblical Spirituality: Spring, Summer, Autumn, and Winter* (Eugene, OR: Resource Publications, 2023).

Antiphons, Psalms and Readings for the Season of Easter are taken from the *Christian Standard Bible* (CSB) (Nashville, TN: Holman Bible Publisher, 2018) except for Days 37 through Day 44, where the Antiphons and Canticles are taken from *The New American Bible* (NAB) (New York: Catholic Book Publishing Co., 1970, 1986) and except for The Most Holy Trinity, The Most Holy Body and Blood of Christ (Corpus Christi), and The Most Sacred Heart of Jesus, where Antiphons, Psalms, and Readings are taken from the *Amplified Holy Bible* (AMP) (Grand Rapids, MI: Zondervan, 2018); Readings for The Most Holy Trinity are taken from the *Catechism of the Catholic Church* (CCC) (Washington, DC: United States Catholic Conference, 1994).

Days in the Season of Easter

Day 1: Easter Sunday

Morning
Antiphon: "I am the First and the Last, and the Living One. I was dead, but look—I am alive forever and ever . . . ," said the Son of Man. (Rev 1:17–18, CSB) Alleluia!
Psalm: "The LORD is my shepherd; / I have what I need. / He lets me lie down in green pastures; / he leads me beside quiet waters. / He renews my life; / he leads me along the right paths / for his name's sake. / Even when I go through the darkest valley, / I fear no danger, / for you are with me; / your rod and your staff—they comfort me." (Ps 23:1–4, CSB)
Repeat Antiphon (above):
Reading: "On the first day of the week Mary Magdalene came to the tomb early, while it was still dark. She saw that the stone had been removed from the tomb. So she went running to Simon Peter and to the other disciple, the one Jesus loved, and said to them, 'They've taken the

Lord out of the tomb, and we don't know where they've put him!'" (John 20:1-2, CSB)
Activity: What word appears in both the verses of Psalm 23 and the passage from John's Gospel? What does that word have to do with Easter Sunday? How does that word make you aware of God's presence?

Evening
Antiphon: "I will praise you, Lord, among the peoples; / I will sing praises to you among the nations." (Ps 57:9, CSB) Alleluia!
Psalm: "Hear this, all you peoples; / listen, all who inhabit the world, / both low and high, / rich and poor together. / My mouth speaks wisdom; / my heart's meditation brings understanding. [Riches] cannot redeem a person / or pay his [or her] ransom to God—/ since the price of redeeming him [or her] is too costly, / one should forever stop trying—/ so that he [or she] may live forever / and not see the Pit. [The] graves [of the wise, foolish, and stupid] are their permanent homes, / their dwellings from generation to generation . . . . ." (Ps 49:1-3, 7-9, 11a CSB)
Repeat Antiphon (above):
Reading: "[Simon Peter] entered the tomb and saw the linen cloths lying there. The other disciple, who had reached the tomb first, then also went in, saw, and believed. For they did not yet understand the Scripture that he must rise from the dead." (John 20:6, 8-9, CSB)
Reflection: While John's Gospel is not the oldest account of the empty tomb story—the account in Mark's Gospel is the oldest empty-tomb account—it is the most theological. The other disciple mentioned in John's Gospel is the beloved disciple or the disciple Jesus loved. Like other important people in John's Gospel, he makes three appearances. He is reclining close to Jesus, when Jesus predicts Judas' betrayal (John 13:23). His second appearance is in the empty tomb story (John 20:2). And he identifies Jesus during the fishing story in the chapter added after the book had already been written (John 21:7), where he is also identified as the disciple who had leaned against Jesus at the supper (John 21:20). The disciple Jesus loved is presented as a character who illustrates the Johannine theme of seeing and believing. He enters the empty tomb, sees the grave cloths, and believes. The author of the gospel doesn't tell the reader what he believes, but he does state that those two disciples did not yet understand that Jesus must rise from the dead. Since no one knows what resurrection from the dead is, the empty tomb becomes a metaphor to attempt to describe it. In John's narrative of events, the risen Jesus has not

yet appeared to anyone. Because the empty tomb story is so well known, people do not often spend time with it. The last verse of Psalm 49 above presents the contrast the use of the empty tomb metaphor conveys: The grave or tomb is a permanent home.

Day 2: Monday in the Octave of Easter

Morning
Antiphon: "Let the whole earth shout joyfully to God! / Sing about the glory of his name; / make his praise glorious." (Ps 66:1–2, CSB) Alleluia!
Psalm: "This is my comfort in my affliction: / Your promise [, LORD,] has given me life. / I am severely afflicted; / LORD, give me life according to your word. / In keeping with your faithful love, hear my voice. / LORD, give me life in keeping with your justice. / Champion my cause and redeem me; / give me life as you promised. / Your compassions are many, LORD; / give me life according to your judgments." (Ps 119:50, 107, 149, 154, 156, CSB)
Repeat Antiphon (above):
Reading: ". . . Mary [Magdalene] stood outside the tomb, crying. As she was crying, she stooped to look into the tomb. She saw two angels in white sitting where Jesus's body had been lying, one at the head and the other at the feet. . . . [S]he turned around and saw Jesus standing there, but she did not know it was Jesus. Jesus said to her, 'Mary.' Turning around, she said to him in Aramaic, 'Rabboni!'—which means 'Teacher.'" (John 20:11–12, 14, 16, CSB)
Reflection: In John's Gospel, Mary Magdalene is the first to recognize an appearance of the risen Christ. Her love for Jesus is demonstrated by her presence at the tomb in which he was placed after he died on the cross. Only the author of John's Gospel mentions that the tomb was in a garden; that detail is meant to echo the Garden of Eden in Genesis (2:8–9). A garden is a place of life. So, while the tomb represents death, the garden represents life. And Mary Magdalene is the first person in John's Gospel to recognize the truth of that contradiction. First, she sees creatures that live in heavenly realms: angels. Then, she sees the risen Jesus, whom she does not recognize—because the living do not live in cemeteries—until he says her name. His voice reveals to her his living presence. And she responds by naming him Teacher. Once Mary recognizes him, she concludes that he is alive in the garden of life, and that is why his tomb is empty.

Evening

Antiphon: "The whole earth will worship you, [God,] / and sing praise to you. / They will sing praise to your name." (Ps 66:4, CSB) Alleluia!

Psalm: "[God,] I will bless you every day; / I will praise your name forever and ever. / The LORD is great and is highly praised; / his greatness is unsearchable. / All you have made will thank you, LORD; / the faithful will bless you. / They will speak of the glory of your kingdom / and will declare your might. / My mouth will declare the LORD's praise; / let every living thing / bless his holy name forever and ever." (Ps 145:2–3, 10–11, 21, CSB)

Repeat Antiphon (above):

Reading: "[Jesus told Mary Magdalene:] '. . . Go to my brothers and tell them that I am ascending to my Father and your Father, to my God and your God.' Mary Magdalene went and announced to the disciples, 'I have seen the Lord!' And she told them what he had said to her." (John 20:17b–18, CSB)

Reflection: The noun *apostle*, comes from a Greek verb meaning *to send forth*. In John's Gospel, Mary Magdalene is portrayed as an apostle. Once she recognizes Jesus alive, he sends her to his disciples to tell them the good news. The Johannine Jesus had already told his disciples that he was going away (John 8:21; 14:28), but this is the first time the word *ascend* is used in John's Gospel. The operative cosmology at the time John's Gospel was written was a three-story universe. Jesus, the Word, who was God and who was with God in the beginning (John 1:1–2)—living on the top story—became flesh (John 1:14) on the middle story of the earth, where people live. Thus, the movement of John's Gospel is that the one who came from the top story (descend) to live with people on the middle story will return (ascend) to the top story. The apostle Mary Magdalene is sent to Jesus' disciples, who are locked in a single room (John 20:19), to tell them that he is returning to the Father, who sent him.

Day 3: Tuesday in the Octave of Easter

Morning

Antiphon: "Return to us, God of our salvation . . . ." (Ps 85:4a, CSB) Alleluia!

Psalm: "Show us your faithful love, LORD, / and give us your salvation. / I will listen to what God will say; / surely the LORD will declare peace / to his people, his faithful ones, / and not let them go back to foolish

ways. / His salvation is very near those who fear him, / so that glory may dwell in our land. / Faithful love and truth will join together, / righteousness and peace will embrace. / Truth will spring up from the earth, / and righteousness will look down from heaven." (Ps 85:7–11, CSB)
Repeat Antiphon (above):
Reading: "When it was evening on that first day of the week, the disciples were gathered together with the doors locked . . . . Jesus came, stood among them, and said to them, 'Peace be with you.' Having said this, he showed them his hands and his side. So the disciples rejoiced when they saw the Lord." (John 20:19–20, CSB)
Reflection: Earlier in John's Gospel, Jesus told his disciples that he was giving them peace and leaving it with them (John 14:26). When he appears the first time to his disciples, who are in a room behind locked doors, he offers them peace. This peace is not the opposite of war; this peace is the opposite of fear. Peace quiets the disciples from their fear of seeing a ghost; after all, Jesus entered the room without opening the locked doors. So, he must be some kind of spirit. Thus, as presented by the author of John's Gospel, resurrection is not physical. After calming their fear, he shows them the wounds on his hands, where he had been nailed to the cross, and the wound in his side, where, after he was dead, a soldier had pierced his side. They recognize his non-physical body and rejoice to see him. In the narrative of John's Gospel, Mary Magdalene had seen him and told his disciples that she had seen him. Now, his disciples have seen him. The theme of seeing is believing continues in John's Gospel. Earlier in the Johannine narrative, Jesus performed signs—like changing water into wine, healing an official's son, feeding in Galilee, etc.—and after seeing the sign people believed in him. Now, Jesus shows his disciples the sign of his non-physical risen body. They, who have been believers, rejoice now that they have a sign that he is risen indeed. Seeing is believing.

Evening
Antiphon: "[The LORD] has shown his people the power of his works . . . ." (Ps 111:6a, CSB) Alleluia!
Psalm: "The works of [the LORD's] hands are truth and justice; / all his instructions are trustworthy. / They are established forever and ever, / enacted in truth and in uprightness. / He has sent redemption to his people. / He has ordained his covenant forever. / His name is holy and awe-inspiring." (Ps 111:7–9, CSB)

Repeat Antiphon (above):
Reading: "Jesus said to [his disciples] again, 'Peace be with you. As the Father has sent me, I also send you.'" (John 20:21, CSB)
Meditation/Journal: What fear does Jesus or God calm in you? What has Jesus sent you to do? What connection do you find between the verses of Psalm 111 and the verse from John's Gospel? Explain.

Day 4: Wednesday in the Octave of Easter

Morning
Antiphon: "Bless our God, you peoples; / let the sound of his praise be heard. / He keeps us alive / and does not allow our feet to slip." (Ps 66:8-9, CSB) Alleluia!
Psalm: "[LORD,] what is a human being that you remember him [or her], / a son [or daughter] of man that you look after him [or her]? / You made him [or her] little less than God / and crowned him [or her] with glory and honor. / You made him [and her] ruler[s] over the works of your hands; / you put everything under his [and her] feet: / all the sheep and oxen, / as well as the animals in the wild, / the birds of the sky, / and the fish of the sea / that pass through the currents of the seas." (Ps 8:4-8, CSB)
Repeat Antiphon (above):
Reading: ". . . Jesus revealed himself again to his disciples by the Sea of Tiberias. He revealed himself in this way: Simon Peter, Thomas (called 'Twin'), Nathanael from Cana of Galilee, Zebedee's sons, and two others of his disciples were together. 'I'm going fishing,' Simon Peter said to them. 'We're coming with you,' they told him. They went out and got into the boat, but that night they caught nothing." (John 21:1-3), CSB
Points to Ponder: First, it is important to note how many disciples there are. Simon Peter, Thomas, and Nathanael are three; add two sons of Zebedee, and two others and the total is seven. Seven is a sacred number—formed from the sum of three, the number for God, and four, the number for the earth—indicating completeness. Add in Jesus, and there are eight, the number for fullness. Second, the disciples are fishermen by trade, but they cannot catch a single fish, as will be seen below. Third, they are camped near the shore of the Sea of Tiberias, another name for the Sea of Galilee and the Sea of Gennesaret. Even though it is called a sea, it is a lake. In other words, nothing is the way it ought to be in this story in a chapter added to John's Gospel.

SEASON OF EASTER

Evening

Antiphon: "Hallelujah! / I will praise the LORD with all my heart . . . ." (Ps 111:1a, CSB) Alleluia!

Psalm: "The heavens declare the glory of God, / and the expanse proclaims the work of his hands. / Day after day they pour out speech; / night after night they communicate knowledge. / There is no speech; there are no words; / their voice is not heard. / Their message has gone out to the whole earth, / and their words to the ends of the world. / May the words of my mouth / and the meditation of my heart / be acceptable to you, / LORD, my rock and my Redeemer." (Ps 19:1–4ab, 14, CSB)

Repeat Antiphon (above):

Reading: "When daybreak came, Jesus stood on the shore, but the disciples did not know it was Jesus. 'Friends,' Jesus called to them, 'you don't have any fish, do you?' 'No,' they answered. 'Cast the net on the right side of the boat,' he told them, 'and you'll find some.' So they did and they were unable to haul it in because of the large number of fish." (John 21:4–6, CSB)

Reflection: The author of the chapter added onto John's Gospel indicates that the story he is narrating is a post-resurrection account of an appearance of Jesus after his death. The word used to indicate this is *daybreak*. Daybreak is the time when light first appears in the sky at the beginning of the day. In CB (NT) empty-tomb accounts, it is "very early in the morning" (Mark 16:2; Luke 24:1), or as the "first day of the week was dawning (Matt 28:1; John 20:1). Thus, daybreak indicates that this story is like the empty-tomb accounts; it is a post-resurrection appearance of Jesus, whom the disciples do not recognize until later. Furthermore, the account of the great catch of fish recorded here originally circulated orally, also finding a home in Luke's Gospel (5:4–6), where it is part of the call of Jesus' first disciples: Simon Peter, James, and John. It becomes the occasion for the Lukan Jesus to tell them, "From now on you will be catching people" (Luke 5:10b). In John's Gospel, the author states that the seven disciples caught 153 fish (John 21:11). At the time this chapter was written, it was thought that there were 153 people of the world that the net of the church encompassed without having its unity broken.

Day 5: Thursday in the Octave of Easter

Morning

Antiphon: "Hallelujah! / Give praise, servants of the LORD; / praise the name of the LORD." (Ps 113:1, CSB) Alleluia!
Psalm: "In the morning, LORD, you hear my voice; / in the morning I plead my case to you and watch expectantly. / . . . I enter your house / by the abundance of your faithful love . . . . / . . . [L]et all who take refuge in you rejoice ; / let them shout for joy forever. / May you shelter them, / and may those who love your name boast about you." (Ps 5:3, 7a, 11, CSB)
Repeat Antiphon (above):
Reading: "The disciple, the one Jesus loved, said to Peter [in the boat], 'It is the Lord!' When Simon Peter heard that it was the Lord [on the shore], he tied his outer clothing around him (for he had taken it off) and plunged into the sea. Since they were not far from land (about a hundred yards away), the other disciples came in the boat dragging the net full of fish." (John 21:7–8, CSB)
Reflection: According to the author of the chapter added to John's Gospel, the disciple Jesus loved—who is never given a name—identifies the man standing on the shore who just told the unsuccessful fishermen in a boat on the Sea of Tiberias (Galilee) where the fish were. The man on the shore is the risen Lord. Peter's response is emotionally sudden and seemingly funny. He puts on clothes to jump into the water and swim to shore, while the other six disciples bring the boat and the net of fish to shore. It was Simon Peter, who had decided to go fishing (John 21:3) with no reason given. However, it is not Peter who acknowledges the risen Jesus on the shore; it is the disciple Jesus loved, who makes his first appearance in John's Gospel (13:23) during the meal when Jesus predicts Judas' betrayal. And like other characters in John's Gospel, he makes two more appearance (19:26; 20:2); he also appears in 21:7, a chapter added later to the original gospel.

Evening
Antiphon: "Hallelujah! / My soul, praise the LORD." (Ps 146:1, CSB) Alleluia!
Psalm: "I remember the days of old; / I meditate on all you [, LORD,] have done; / I reflect on the work of your hands. / Let me experience / your faithful love in the morning, / for I trust in you. / Reveal to me the way I should go / because I appeal to you. / Teach me to do your will, / for you are my God. / May your gracious Spirit / lead me on level ground." (Ps 143:5, 8, 19, CSB)
Repeat Antiphon (above):

Reading: "When [the six disciples] got out [of the boat] on land, they saw a charcoal fire there with fish lying on it, and bread. 'Come and have breakfast,' Jesus told them. None of the disciples dared to ask him, 'Who are you?' because they knew it was the Lord. Jesus came, took the bread, and gave it to them. He did the same with the fish. This was now the third time Jesus appeared to the disciples after he was raised from the dead." (John 21:9, 12–14, CSB)

Points to Ponder: First, this scene with the risen Jesus is eucharistic in tone. He has a fire with fish and bread; he is feeding his disciples. Second, he is serving them breakfast; while the meals Jesus shares with his disciples are usually dinner or evening meals, this one begins their day; they feast with the risen Jesus on the shore at the beginning of the day. Third, the narrator has in mind the taking, breaking, and sharing that Jesus has done with his disciples at other meals; here Jesus takes the bread; it is implied that he breaks it to give it to them; and he shares fish with them. These are not the fish they caught, as the fire and fish are ready on shore before the disciples arrive with the net full of fish. Fourth, they know who it is who invites them to breakfast. The disciple Jesus loved has announced that the man serving them is the Lord, the risen Jesus. And fifth, the narrator either did not count accurately or he didn't have a copy of John's Gospel, when he was writing this additional chapter. This is the not the third time Jesus appeared to his disciples; this is the fourth in the Johannine narrative. The first appearance is to Mary Magdalene (John 20:15–17); the second appearance is to the disciples without Thomas (John 20:19–23); the third appearance is to the disciples with Thomas (John 20:24–29). Thus, the appearance in John 21:14 is the fourth. The author of chapter 21 may be using the number three to indicate the divine, since three is the number for God.

Day 6: Friday in the Octave of Easter

Morning

Antiphon: "Not to us, LORD, not to us, / but to your name give glory / because of your faithful love, because of your truth." (Ps 115:1, CSB) Alleluia!

Psalm: "Remember, LORD, you compassion / and your faithful love / for they have existed from antiquity. / All the LORD's ways show faithful love and truth / to those who keep his covenant and decrees. / The secret

counsel of the LORD / is for those who fear him. / Guard me and rescue me; . . . for I take refuge in you." (Ps 25:6, 10, 14, 20, CSB)
Repeat Antiphon (above):
Reading: ". . Jesus asked Simon Peter, 'Simon, son of John, do you love me more than these?' 'Yes, Lord,' he said to him, 'you know that I love you.' 'Feed my lambs,' he told him. A second time he asked him, 'Simon, son of John, do you love me?' 'Yes, Lord,' he said to him, 'you know that I love you.' 'Shepherd my sheep,' he told him. He asked him the third time, 'Simon, son of John, do you love me?' He said, 'Lord, you know everything; you know that I love you.' 'Feed my sheep,' Jesus said." (John 21:15–17acd, CSB)
Activity: Read John 18:15–18, 25–26. Considering John 18:15–18, 25–26, what is John 21:15–17 doing? Explain.

Evening
Antiphon: "Hallelujah! / Praise the name of the LORD. / Give praise, you servants of the Lord . . . ." (Ps 135:1, CSB) Alleluia!
Psalm: "[LORD, l]isten to the sound of my pleading / when I cry to you for help, / when I lift up my hands / toward your holy sanctuary. / Blessed be the LORD, / for he has heard the sound of my pleading. / The LORD is my strength and my shield; / my heart trusts in him, and I am helped. / Therefore my heart celebrates, / and I give thanks to him with my song." (Ps 28:2, 6–7, CSB)
Repeat Antiphon (above):
Reading: Jesus said to Peter: "'Truly I tell you, when you were younger, you would tie your belt and walk wherever you wanted. But when you grow old, you will stretch out your hands and someone else will tie you and carry you where you don't want to go.' He said this to indicate by what kind of death Peter would glorify God. After saying this, he told him, 'Follow me.'" (John 21:18–19, CSB)
Reflection: There is no doubt that the author of chapter 21 of John's Gospel has heard the rest of the original text. For example, he presents a story about Peter professing his threefold love for Jesus (John 21:15–17) to undo Peter's threefold denial of him (John 18:15–18, 25–26). Also, he portrays Jesus indicating how Peter will die (John 21:18–19) based on John 12:33, where the Johannine Jesus states, ". . . [I]f I am lifted up from the earth I will draw all people to myself." Then, the narrator adds, "He said this to indicate what kind of death he was about to die" (John 12:32–33). "Lifted up" is a reference to Jesus being lifted on the cross

and to his ascent to the Father. The author knows that Peter was crucified—tradition states upside down—but an account is not found in the Bible. After Peter has been rehabilitated and told how he will die with stretched-out hands (crucifixion), the author of chapter 21 of John's Gospel portrays Jesus telling him, "Follow me." In John's Gospel, Jesus tells Philip, "Follow me" (John 1:43), and in monologues he uses the phrase several time (John 10:27; 12:26; and 13:36), but nowhere does Jesus call Peter to follow him. Thus, the author of chapter 21 presents Jesus telling Peter to follow him twice (John 21:19, 22). There is a double meaning to Jesus' words "follow me" to Peter at the end of the second ending of John's Gospel. The "follow me" renews his call to follow Jesus after his threefold profession of love. Also, "follow me" is a call to Peter to follow Jesus to death and resurrection (John 13:26).

Day 7: Saturday in the Octave of Easter

Morning

Antiphon: "Those who live far away are awed by your signs [, God]; / you make east and west shout for joy." (Ps 65:8, CSB) Alleluia!

Psalm: "I call on you, God, / because you will answer me; / listen closely to me; hear what I say. / Display the wonders of your faithful love, / Savior of all who seek refuge / from those who rebel against your right hand. / Protect me as the pupil of your eye; / hide me in the shadow of your wings . . . ." (Ps 17:6–8, CSB)

Repeat Antiphon (above):

Reading: "Jesus performed many other signs in the presence of his disciples that are not written in this book. But these are written so that you may believe that Jesus is the Messiah, the Son of God, and that by believing you may have life in his name." (John 20:30–31, CSB)

Reflection: The two verses above (John 20:30–31) are the last sentences in the original edition of John's Gospel. It is clear that the author is concluding his narrative. In other words, the book is not a complete story of all the signs Jesus gave with his disciples witnessing them. John's Gospel is built on seven signs: water into wine (John 2:1–11), curing of an official's son (John 4:46–54), curing of a paralytic (John 5:1–15), feeding in Galilee (John 6:1–15), walking on water (John 6:16–21), curing a man born blind (John 9:1–41), and the raising of Lazarus from the dead (John 11:1–44). In some English translations of Psalm 17, "Display the wonders of your faithful love" becomes "Display the signs of your faithful love."

In John's Gospel, Jesus' disciples respond to seeing a sign with faith; they believe in Jesus (John 2:11; 4:53; 5:15; 6:14; 9:38). The author's hope is that readers of his book will respond like his characters with faith that Jesus is the Messiah, the Hebrew word for *Anointed*, and the Son of God. The result of such faith is eternal life in his name. As will be seen below, having faith because of seeing a sign could easily lead to readers wanting to see a sign in order to believe. Thus, the author will have to end the plot structure of seeing a sign and believing.

Evening
Antiphon: "Search me, God, and know my heart; / test me and know my concerns." (Ps 139:23, CEB) Alleluia!
Psalm: ". . . [I]t was you, [LORD,] who created my inward parts; / you knit me together in my mother's womb. / I will praise you / because I have been remarkably and wondrously made. / Your works are wondrous, / and I know this very well. / My bones were not hidden from you / when I was made in secret, / when I was formed in the depths of the earth. / Your eyes saw me when I was formless; / all my days were written in your book and planned / before a single one of them began. / God, how precious your thoughts are to me; / how vast the sum is!" (Ps 139:13–17, CSB)
Repeat Antiphon (above):
Reading: ". . . [T]here are also many other things that Jesus did, which, if every one of them were written down, I suppose not even the world itself could contain the books that would be written." (John 21:25, CSB)
Reflection: If one adds a chapter to a finished written book, an ending must follow. After ignoring the original ending to John's Gospel (John 20:30–31), the author of chapter 21 narrates Jesus' appearance to seven disciples camping near the Sea of Tiberias, their going fishing and inability to catch fish, his insight as to where to drop their nets for a catch, his preparation of breakfast on the shore for them, his threefold restoration of Peter, and more, he must write another conclusion to the book, stating that the world would not hold the library of books that would have to be written in order to narrate all the other things Jesus did. Certainly, that is an exaggeration! However, what the second ending of John's Gospel teaches is that biblical truth is plural. If it were singular, there would be only one ending to John's Gospel. The same truth is found in the three endings of Mark's Gospel. In the HB (OT), the same truth is found in two accounts of creation in the first two chapters of the book of Genesis. Also, First and Second Chronicles, which represent the cleaned version of First

and Second Samuel and First and Second Kings, present other versions of the same stories. The plurality of biblical truth opens perspectives. As stated in the verses of Psalm 139, God's works are wondrous, his thoughts are vast, and his perspective is plural!

Day 8: Second Sunday of Easter (Octave of Easter)

Morning

Antiphon: "The LORD will protect you from all harm; / he will protect your life." (Ps 120:7, CSB) Alleluia!

Psalm: "I rejoiced with those who said to me, / 'Let's go to the house of the LORD.' / Our feet were standing / within your gates, Jerusalem. / Pray for the well-being of Jerusalem: / 'May those who love you be secure; / may there be peace within your walls; / security within your fortresses.' / Because of my brothers [, sisters,] and friends, / I will say, 'May peace be in you.'" (Ps 122:1-2, 6-8, CSB)

Repeat Antiphon (above):

Reading: ". . . Thomas (called 'Twin'), one of the Twelve, was not with [the disciples] when Jesus came [the first time]. So the other disciples were telling him, 'We have seen the Lord!' But he said to them, 'If I don't see the mark of the nails in his hands, put my finger into the mark of the nails, and put my hand into his side, I will never believe.' A week later his disciples were indoors again, and Thomas was with them. Even though the doors were locked, Jesus came and stood among them and said, 'Peace be with you.'" (John 20:24-26, CSB)

Reflection: Thomas, whose name means *twin*—although no biblical twin is ever mentioned—is not present the first time the risen Jesus appears to his disciples. They explain that they had seen the risen Lord, but, of course, Thomas had not. To believe—seeing is believing—Thomas declares that he needs to touch the risen Jesus. In other words, he needs to touch a bodiless body, who can enter a room without opening the door! In the Johannine time schedule, a week later the bodiless body of the risen Jesus reappears. As he had done before, he offers them peace, which is the opposite of fear. His "Peace be with you" echoes words spoken earlier: "Peace I leave with you. My peace I give to you. I do not give to you as the world gives. Don't let your heart be troubled or fearful" (John 14:27, CSB). The peace Jesus offers is like that in the verses from Psalm 122; it consists of security within a fortified city, like Jerusalem. All the disciples except Thomas possess that security from fear; Thomas needs it. Thomas represents thenext generation of believers in Jesus' resurrection. There is no proof of resurrection; there is no verifying experience which can convince a person of God's reality or Jesus' resurrection with objective certainty. Thomas represents a common attitude of those who cannot believe without seeing. That is why he demands to touch the bodiless body! Touching was the surest means of ascertaining the reality of the phenomenon of the resurrection. The generation after Thomas and the disciples never saw the earthly Jesus nor the risen Jesus; all they had was the message, the word, transmitted to them, and that is how they should come to faith, according to the author of John's Gospel.

Evening
Antiphon: "Praise the LORD, all nations! / Glorify him, all peoples! / For his faithful love to us is great; / the LORD's faithfulness endures forever. / Hallelujah! (Ps 117:1–2, CSB)
Psalm: "My heart says this about you [, LORD]: / 'Seek his face.' / LORD, I will seek your face. / I am certain that I will see the LORD's goodness / in the land of the living. / Wait for the LORD; / be strong, and let your heart be courageous. / Wait for the LORD." (Ps 27:8, 13–14, CSB)
Repeat Antiphon (above):
Reading: "[Jesus] said to Thomas, 'Put your finger here and look at my hands. Reach out your hand and put it into my side. Don't be faithless, but believe.' Thomas responded to him, 'My Lord and my God!' Jesus said, 'Because you have seen me, you have believed. Blessed are those who have not seen and yet believe.'" (John 20:27–29, CSB)
Reflection: Since seeing signs and believing has been a theme in John's Gospel, the author must bring the theme to an end. Otherwise, the next generation of potential believers will be saying that they need to see a sign to believe. Thomas is a character who represents the next generation of potential believers. Thomas, who had declared that he would not believe that Jesus had been raised from the dead, is invited by Jesus to experience his bodiless body by putting his finger into Jesus' hands and putting his hand into Jesus' side. The reader is not told what Thomas did; the presumption is that he refrained from seeing (touching) to believe. The words of the Johannine Jesus to Thomas bring an end to the theme of seeing to believe. When he says that those who have not seen but believe are blessed, he has moved the gospel from the first generation to the next generation of potential believers. Thus, the reader is challenged to reflect upon how much or less seeing does he or she engage to believe, or, in

the words of Psalm 28, seek the face of the Lord. In the original gospel—before chapter 21 was added—this was the last scene in the gospel. The writer added two verses about Jesus performing many other signs that were not recorded by the author, but those in the book were narrated so others could believe that Jesus is the Anointed, the Son of God, who gave eternal life to all who believe.

Day 9: Monday of the Second Week of Easter

Morning
Antiphon: "Hallelujah! / Praise the name of the LORD. / Give praise, you servants of the LORD . . . ." (Ps 135:1, CSB) Alleluia!
Psalm: "[LORD, y]ou turn mankind to the dust, / saying, 'Return, descendants of Adam.' / For in your sight a thousand years / are like yesterday that passes by, / like a few hours of the night. / You end their lives, they sleep. / They are like grass that grows in the morning—/ in the morning it sprouts and grows; / by evening it withers and dries up." (Ps 90:3–6, CSB)
Repeat Antiphon (above):
Reading: "When the Sabbath was over, Mary Magdalene, Mary the mother of James, and Salome brought spices, so that they could go and anoint [Jesus]. Very early in the morning on the first day of the week, they went to the tomb at sunrise. They were saying to one another, 'Who will roll away the stone from the entrance to the tomb for us?' Looking up, they noticed that the stone—which was very large—had been rolled away." (Mark 16:1–4, CSB)
Reflection: Today, when the word *tomb* is heard, most people picture a grave. At the time of Jesus, a tomb was a cave-like structure hewed out of rock; the best picture would be the entrance to a mine. Inside the cave-like structure were shelves, upon which the dead were placed after their bodies had been wrapped in linen—think shroud—and anointed with spices and myrrh or some other sweet-smelling oil. After the body had been laid to rest, a large round stone was rolled or levered across the opening of the tomb. And since most tombs were owned by families, people hoped that they would not need to open the tomb for a long time because of the stench of the decaying bodies within. After years passed and one of the multiple shelves in the tomb was needed for a dead member of the family, the tomb was opened, the bones were gathered off a shelf and placed in a box, called an ossuary (bone box), and set under the shelf. The usual picture on Easter greeting cards with a stone sarcophagus

and a lid pushed to the side is a modern imagining of a tomb. The oldest empty-tomb story is the one found in the Mark's Gospel, which reflects the use of an ancient tomb with its focus on the large stone rolled across the entrance by several men after Jesus' body had been placed on a shelf inside it. The detail that there were three women—not men—discussing the rolling away of the large stone—reveals that this is a story featuring God. On the first day of the week, which would have been Sunday, very early in the morning—sunrise—the glory of God appears. The three women are too late; the resurrection, which is like an empty tomb, has already occurred. An empty tomb does not prove resurrection; it is a metaphor for it. If you were walking through a cemetery and saw a large hole in the ground, you would conclude that someone was going to be buried there or that someone had been exhumed. You would not fall on your knees and shout, "Alleluia! God raised another one." The author of Mark's Gospel does not tell the reader what resurrection is, because it is on the other side of the grave, where no one other than Jesus has ever gone.

Evening
Antiphon: "I will exalt you, LORD, / because you have lifted me up / and have not allowed my enemies / to triumph over me." (Ps 30:1, CSB) Alleluia!
Psalm: "LORD, you brought me up from Sheol; / you spared me from among those / going down to the Pit. / 'What gain is there in my death, / if I go down to the Pit? / Will the dust praise you? / Will it proclaim your truth?' / You turned my lament into dancing . . . ." (Ps 30:3, 9, 11a, CSB)
Repeat Antiphon (above):
Reading: "When [the three women] entered the tomb, they saw a young man dressed in a white robe sitting on the right side; they were alarmed. 'Don't be alarmed,' he said them. 'You are looking for Jesus of Nazareth, who was crucified. He has risen! He is not here. See the place where they put him.'" (Mark 16:5–6, CSB)
Points to Ponder: First, because the large, round stone covering the entrance to the cave-like tomb with shelves inside has been rolled away, the three women, upon entering the tomb, find a young man dressed in a white robe sitting on the right side in the tomb. It is important to note that this is not an angel; it is a young man. Second, the astute reader will ask: Who is the young man sitting in Jesus' tomb? Biblical scholars think he could be the Gerasene demoniac, who lived in tombs (Mark 5:2). After

he was healed by Jesus, he appeared "sitting there, dressed, and in his right mind" (Mark 5:15, CSB). He could also be the "certain young man, wearing nothing but a linen cloth" who was following Jesus. The soldiers who arrested Jesus "caught hold of him, but he left the linen cloth behind and ran away naked" (Mark 14:51–52, CSB). He could be Jesus, who is described as wearing dazzling white clothes at his transfiguration (Mark 9:3, CSB). Third, whoever the young man is, he is sitting in the position of power, the right side. Fourth, the women are alarmed for two reasons. They were looking for a dead body, and they found a young man in the place where the dead body was supposed to be! Fifth, the young man announces the resurrection to the women, but he is careful to identify Jesus as a person from Nazareth and as one who was crucified (dead). Sixth, Jesus is not there; the shelf where his body had been placed is empty. The tomb is empty. All the young man says is that Jesus has risen. Then, he invites the women to see for themselves the empty shelf where the body of Jesus had been. Seventh, the verses of Psalm 30 help shed light on all this. God has raised Jesus from Sheol, the first level of a three-leveled universe; sometimes Sheol is called the Pit. Usually, the dead tend to stay dead! However, as the psalmist states, there is no gain in death, because dust does not praise God. Thus, the living praise God. And so the young man in Jesus' tomb praises God for raising Jesus from Sheol.

Day 10: Tuesday of the Second Week of Easter

Morning
Antiphon: "Let everything that breathes praise the LORD. / Hallelujah! (Ps 150:6, CSB)
Psalm: "You [, God,] have kept me from closing my eyes; / I am troubled and cannot speak. / I consider days of old, / years long past. / At night I remember my music; / I meditate in my heart, and my spirit ponders. / Has [the Lord's] faithful love ceased forever? / Is his promise at an end for all generations? / Has God forgotten to be gracious? So I say, 'I am grieved / that the right hand of the Most High has changed.'" (Ps 77:4–6, 8–9a, 10, CSB)
Repeat Antiphon (above):
Reading: The young man in Jesus' tomb said to the thee women, "... [G]o, tell [Jesus'] disciples and Peter, 'He is going ahead of you to Galilee; you will see him there just as he told you.' They went out and ran from the

tomb, because trembling and astonishment overwhelmed them. And they said nothing to anyone, since they were afraid." (Mark 16:7–8, CSB)
Reflection: The two verses above represent the original end of Mark's Gospel. After the young man in the tomb commissions the three women to find Jesus' disciples and tell them to go to Galilee, where they will see him, they leave the tomb and say nothing to anyone. This, of course, leads to the question: From where did this (and other) information about Jesus' resurrection come? Some scholars have suggested that the author's non-speaking women bring an end to oral tradition; telling and retelling stories about Jesus turns into writing or recording stories about him. Since Mark's Gospel is the first to be written, it is the author's way of ending the oral tradition that preceded his writing for forty years. The three women cannot comprehend the meaning of an empty tomb. A tomb is where death exists, not life. Yet the young man has announced that Jesus is alive. The two perspectives do not fit together, and so the women run away from the tomb trembling and astonished, and they say nothing to anyone, because no one would believe them.

Evening
Antiphon: "Hallelujah! / Praise God in his sanctuary. / Praise him in his mighty expanse." (Ps 150:1, CSB) Alleluia!
Psalm: "God, save me by your name, / and vindicate me by your might! / God, hear my prayer; / listen to the words from my mouth. / God is my helper; / the Lord is the sustainer of my life. I will praise your name, LORD, / because it is good. / For he has rescued me from every trouble, / and my eye has looked down on my enemies." (Ps 54:1–2, 4, 6b–7, CSB)
Repeat Antiphon (above):
Reading: "Early on the first day of the week, after he had risen, he appeared first to Mary Magdalene.... She went and reported to those who had been with him, as they were mourning and weeping. Yet, when they heard that he was alive and had been seen by her, they did not believe it. After this, he appeared in a different form to two of them walking on their way into the country. And they went and reported it to the rest, who did not believe them either. Later he appeared to the Eleven themselves as they were reclining at the table. He rebuked their unbelief and hardness of heart, because they did not believe those who saw him after he had risen." (Mark 16:9–14, CSB)
Reflection: When reading the end of Mark's Gospel, many people are surprised when they find three endings given in most Bibles. The first

one is the original at 16:8. A shorter ending was adding to that later in history. Then, a longer ending was added in the early second century. The stories found in the shorter and longer endings differ in style from the rest of the gospel; this means that they were not written by the same person who wrote the rest of Mark's Gospel. The longer ending derives from Luke's Gospel (8:3, 24:12–35) and Matthew's Gospel (28:16, 19). In other words, after reading Luke's Gospel and Matthew's Gospel, someone summarized their endings and wrote what he considered to be a better ending for Mark's Gospel. Thus, Mark's Gospel has three endings. Likewise, John's Gospel has two endings. When it comes to the Bible, truth is plural.

Day 11: Wednesday of the Second Week of Easter

Morning
Antiphon: "The voice of the LORD shakes the wilderness; / the LORD shakes the wilderness . . . ." (Ps 29:8, CSB) Alleluia!
Psalm: "God is our refuge and strength, / a helper who is always found / in times of trouble. / Therefore we will not be afraid, / though the earth trembles / and the mountains topple / into the depths of the seas, / though its water roars and foams / and the mountains quake with its turmoil. / The LORD of Armies is with us . . . . / 'Stop fighting and know that I am God, / exalted among the nations, exalted on the earth.'" (Ps 46:1–3, 7a, 10, CSB)
Repeat Antiphon (above):
Reading: "After the Sabbath, as the first day of the week was dawning, Mary Magdalene and the other Mary went to view the tomb. There was a violent earthquake, because an angel of the Lord descended from heaven and approached the tomb. He rolled back the stone and was sitting on it. His appearance was like lightning, and his clothing was as white as snow." (Matt 28:1–3, CSB)
Reflection: The author of Matthew's Gospel considers Jesus' resurrection to be a theophany, an event of earthquake importance. In the HB (OT) an earthquake is an element of the theophany on Mount Sinai (Horeb) (Exod 19:18). The author of Matthew's Gospel makes use of the earthquake immediately and uniquely after Jesus dies on the cross (Matt 27:51) and again as two women are on their way to see the tomb in which Jesus was placed; unlike the Markan women who go to anoint Jesus' body, the Matthean women go only to view the tomb. The earthquake

heralds the appearance of an angel of the Lord, a code phrase for God, who, described wearing lightning and white clothes, descends from the divine realm above the dome over the earth to the earth and rolls away the stone covering the entrance to the cave-like tomb. He does that to show that there is no body inside. The angel in Matthew's Gospel replaces the young man in Mark's Gospel; in other words, the author of Matthew's Gospel has rewritten the empty-tomb story he found in Mark's Gospel. For the author of Matthew's Gospel, resurrection is bodily; there is no body in the tomb! With the earthquake God demonstrates his power over death. In the presence of the LORD, there is only life. Earthquakes can be found throughout the HB (OT), especially in the Psalms (18:7; 77:18; 99:1b; 114:7)—such as Psalm 46 above—in the HB (OT) (2 Sam 22:8; Isa 29:6; Hab 3:6; 2 Esd 3:18) and in the CB (NT) (Acts 16:25–26; Rev 6:12; 8:5; 11:13, 19; 16:18). An earthquake reveals the glory of God and the glory of the risen Jesus.

Evening
Antiphon: "The angel of the LORD encamps / around those who fear him, and rescues them." (Ps 34:7, CSB) Alleluia!
Psalm: "[The LORD] will give his angels orders concerning you, / to protect you in all your ways. / They will protect you in all your ways. / Because he has his heart set on me, [says the Most High], / I will deliver him; / I will protect him because he knows my name. / When he calls out to me, I will answer him; / I will be with him in trouble. / I will rescue him and give him honor. / I will satisfy him with a long life / and show him my salvation." (Ps 91:11–12, 14–16, CSB)
Repeat Antiphon (above):
Reading: "The guards [at Jesus' tomb] were so shaken by fear of [the angel of the Lord] that they became like dead men. The angel told the women, 'Don't be afraid, because I know you are looking for Jesus who was crucified. He is not here. For he has risen, just as he said. Come and see the place where he lay. Then go quickly and tell his disciples. "He has risen from the dead and indeed he is going ahead of you to Galilee; you will see him there." Listen, I have told you.'" (Matt 28:4–7, CSB)
Points to Ponder: First, guards at Jesus' tomb are unique to Matthew's Gospel. They are there because, according to the author, the chief priests and Pharisees asked Pilate for them, because they remembered having heard Jesus predict his resurrection and they conjectured that his disciples would steal his body and announce that he had been raised (Matt

28:62–65). The guards set a seal on the stone; thus, if the stone were moved, the seal would be broken. Second, there is a bit of irony in the author's description of the guards of a tomb becoming like dead men when the angel of the Lord appears! Third, at most biblical theophanies, the first response of people is fear; that is why the angel tells the two women (not three as in Mark's Gospel) not to be afraid. Fourth, the angel invites the women to view the shelf upon which was placed the body of Jesus; the absent body for the author of Matthew's Gospel stands for proof of the resurrection. Fifth, while the women are not told to go to Galilee, they are told by the angel that the risen Jesus is headed there. Sixth, then just to be sure the women have heard him, the angel tells them to listen carefully to what he said. Seventh, if you compare the words of Psalm 91 above to the narrative from Matthew's Gospel, what do you discover?

Day 12: Thursday of the Second Week of Easter

Morning

Antiphon: "You, LORD, will guard [me]; / you will protect [me] from this generation forever." (Ps 12:7, CSB) Alleluia!

Psalm: "The LORD reigns! Let the earth rejoice; / let the many coasts and islands be glad. / Clouds and total darkness surround him; / righteousness and justice are the foundation of his throne. / For you, LORD, / are the Most High over the whole earth; / you are exalted above all the gods. / You who love the LORD, hate evil! / He protects the lives of his faithful ones; / he rescues them from the power of the wicked. / Light dawns for the righteous, / gladness for the upright in heart. / Be glad in the LORD, you righteous ones, / and give thanks to his holy name." (Ps 97:1–2, 9–12, CSB)

Repeat Antiphon (above):

Reading: "As [the women] were on their way [to the disciples], some of the guards came into the city and reported to the chief priests everything that had happened. After the priests had assembled with the elders and agreed on a plan, they gave the soldiers a large sum of money and told them, 'Say this, "His disciples came during the night and stole him while we were sleeping." If this reaches the governor's ears, we will deal with him and keep you out of trouble.' They took the money and did as they were instructed, and this story has been spread among Jewish people to this day." (Matt 28:11–15, CSB)

Meditation/Journal: After comparing the verses from Psalm 97 to Matthew 28:11–15, what do you conclude? Explain.

Evening
Antiphon: "LORD, God of my salvation, / I cry out before you day and night. / May my prayer reach your presence; listen to my cry." (Ps 88:1–2, CSB) Alleluia!
Psalm: "I am counted among those going down to the Pit. / I am like a man without strength, / abandoned among the dead. / I am like the slain lying in the grave, / whom you [, LORD,] no longer remember, / and who are cut off from your care. / You have put me in the lowest part of the Pit, / in the darkest places, in the depths. / My eyes are worn out from crying. / LORD, I cry out to you all day long; / I spread out my hands to you. / Do you work wonders for the dead? / Will your faithful love be declared in the grave . . . ? / Will your wonders be known in the darkness / or your righteousness in the land of oblivion?" (Ps 88:4–6, 9–10a, 11a, 12, CSB)
Repeat Antiphon (above):
Reading: "The eleven disciples traveled to Galilee to the mountain where Jesus had directed them. When they saw him, they worshiped, but some doubted. Jesus came near and said to them, '. . . [R]emember, I am with you always to the end of the age.'" (Matt 28:16–18a, 20b, CSB)
Meditation/Journal: Answer the last three questions the psalmist poses to God in Psalm 88:10a, 11a, 12. What do you discover in your answers? What do you find interesting with the ending of Matthew's Gospel (28:16–18a, 20b)?

Day 13: Friday of the Second Week of Easter

Morning
Antiphon: "God, be exalted above the heavens, / and let your glory be over the whole earth." (Ps 108:5, CSB) Alleluia!
Psalm: "My heart is confident, God; / I will sing; I will sing praises / with the whole of my being. / Wake up, harp and lyre! / I will wake up the dawn. / I will praise you, LORD, among the peoples; / I will sing praises to you among the nations. / For your faithful love is higher than the heavens, / and your faithfulness reaches to the clouds." (Ps 108:1–4, CSB)
Repeat Antiphon (above):
Reading: "On the first day of the week, very early in the morning, [the women who had come with Jesus from Galilee to Jerusalem] came to the tomb, bringing the spices they had prepared. They found the stone rolled away from the tomb. They went in but did not find the body of the Lord

Jesus. While they were perplexed about this, suddenly two men stood by them in dazzling clothes." (Luke 24:1–4, CSB)
Reflection: This is the fourth version of the empty-tomb story told and retold in the CB (NT). The version of the account written by the author of Luke's Gospel keeps the journey of the women to the tomb he found in Mark's Gospel. The women, the reader was told earlier, observed where Jesus was placed and went home to prepare spices and perfumes (Luke 23:56). Thus, once the sun peeked over the horizon and they had enough light to see, they went to the tomb, finding the stone blocking its entrance rolled away. Upon entering and expecting to find the body of Jesus, they found no body. Indeed, they were perplexed, because a tomb is where dead people are found. The women had watched those carrying the dead body of Jesus to the tomb and placing it on a shelf. Therefore, the dead body should be where it was placed without spices and perfumes. Instead of a dead body, they see two men (not one as in Mark's Gospel) in dazzling clothes. The two men in dazzling clothes will appear again in Luke's second volume: The Acts of the Apostles (Acts 1:10). In the words of Psalm 108 (above), the women wake up the dawn. The absence of Jesus' body indicates that the author of Luke-Acts thinks that resurrection is bodily, but more characteristics will be displayed in the post-resurrection stories that fill the last chapter of Luke's Gospel (24:1–49). The resurrection of Jesus is, again in the words of Psalm 108, a demonstration of God's faithful love and faithfulness that reaches from the heavens (top story of a three-level universe) to the earth (middle story of a three-level universe).

Evening
Antiphon: ". . . [Y]ou, LORD, rescued me from death, / my eyes from tears, / my feet from stumbling." (Ps 116:8, CSB) Alleluia!
Psalm: "I love the LORD because he has heard / my appeal for mercy. / Because he has turned his ear to me, / I will call out to him as long as I live. / The ropes of death were wrapped around me, / and the torments of Sheol overcame me; / I encountered trouble and sorrow. / Then I called on the name of the LORD: / 'LORD, save me!' / I will walk before the LORD / in the land of the living. / The death of his faithful ones / is valuable in the LORD's sight." (Ps 116:1–4, 9, 15, CSB)
Repeat Antiphon (above):
Reading: ". . . [T]he women [at Jesus' tomb] were terrified [by the presence of two men in dazzling clothes] and bowed down to the ground.

'Why are you looking for the living among the dead?' asked the men. 'He is not here, but he has risen! Remember how he spoke to you when he was still in Galilee, saying "It is necessary that the Son of Man be betrayed into the hands of sinful men, be crucified, and rise on the third day"?' And they remembered his words. Returning from the tomb, they reported all these things to the Eleven and to all the rest." (Luke 24:5-9, CSB)

Reflection: In this unique Lukan scene, the women recognize the two men as heavenly creatures, and so they bow in worship. The men pose the obvious question: Why seek the living among the dead? See the scene is set at the tomb, in which one finds dead people lying on shelves and decaying. One does not go to a tomb to find the living; one goes to a tomb to find the dead. Yet, according to the two men in the tomb, the women, unknowingly, are in the wrong place, because Jesus has risen and is among the living. To convince the women, the men rehearse a theme that runs through Luke's Gospel, namely, that Jesus (the Son of Man) had to be betrayed, crucified, and rise on the third day (Luke 9:22, 43–45; 18:31–33). After the men spark the women's memory, they leave the place of the dead and find the Eleven living disciples and others with them, and they report what they have experienced. In other words, the women reporters are sent by the two men in dazzling clothes, who are later identified as angels (Luke 24:23), to the disciples that the living Jesus dwells with the living and not with the dead!

Day 14: Saturday of the Second Week of Easter

Morning

Antiphon: "The ropes of death were wrapped around me; / the torrents of destruction terrified me. / The ropes of Sheol entangled me; / the snares of death confronted me." (Ps 18:4–5, CSB) Alleluia!

Psalm: "[The LORD] reached down from on high / and took hold of me; / he pulled me out of deep water. / He rescued me from my powerful enemy / and from those who hated me, / for they were too strong for me. / They confronted me in the day of my calamity, / but the LORD was my support. / He brought me out to a spacious place; / he rescued me because he delighted in me. / The LORD rewarded me / according to my righteousness; / he repaid me / according to the cleanness of my hands. / LORD, you light my lamp; / my God illuminates my darkness." (Ps 18:16–20, 28, CSB)

SEASON OF EASTER

Repeat Antiphon (above):
Reading: "Mary Magdalene, Joanna, Mary the mother of James, and the other women with them were telling the apostles these things [they experienced at Jesus' tomb]. But these words seemed like nonsense to them, and they did not believe the women. Peter, however, got up and ran to the tomb. When he stooped to look in, he saw only the linen cloths. So he went away, amazed at what had happened." (Luke 24:10–12, CSB)
Reflection: In the culture of Jesus' day, women had no authority and were unreliable witnesses. Of course, this is one among many ironies that exist in the CB (NT). Those who are the most powerless, those who can only receive shame—and never honor—are sent to the male apostles with the good news of the resurrection! Peter, a man, responds to the women's message by going to the tomb himself. If he can see the truth, then he can believe it. By the time Peter gets to the tomb, the two men in dazzling clothes are gone, and all that Peter sees are the linen cloths that had been wound around Jesus' body lying on the shelf where the dead body had been placed three days previously. Either the risen body of Jesus is moving without clothes, or his risen body does not need clothes! Peter's response to the cloths is amazement. In other words, like the women before him, he is seeking the living one among the dead!

Evening
Antiphon: "I will meditate on your precepts [, LORD,] / and think about your ways." (Ps 119:15, CSB) Alleluia!
Psalm: "Open my eyes so that I may contemplate / wondrous things from your instruction [, LORD]. / My eyes grow weary / looking for what you have promised. / I am awake through each watch of the night / to meditate on your promise." (Ps 119:18, 82, 148, CSB)
Repeat Antiphon (above):
Reading: "Now that same day [—the first day of the week—] two of [the disciples] were on their way to a village called Emmaus, which was about seven miles from Jerusalem. Together they were discussing everything that had taken place. And while they were discussing and arguing, Jesus himself came near and began to walk along with them. But they were prevented from recognizing him." (Luke 24:13–16, CSB)
Points to Ponder: First, two disciples need one more to make three, a sacred number indicating the divine presence. Second, the village to which they are headed is seven miles from Jerusalem; seven is another sacred number, the sum of three (indicating the divine realm) and four

(indicating the earthly realm). God prevents them from recognizing the risen Jesus; thus, whatever a risen body is, it does not need clothes, and it is not recognizable by those with whom one traveled before being raised. Third, the two disciples, plus Jesus, are on a sacred or divine journey or pilgrimage to awakening or becoming aware of the divine presence.

Day 15: Third Sunday of Easter

Morning
Antiphon: "[God, y]ou rescued me from death, / even my feet from stumbling, / to walk before God in the light of life." (Ps 56:13, CSB) Alleluia!
Psalm: "God, listen to my prayer, / and do not hide from my plea for help. / Pay attention to me and answer me. / My heart shudders within me; / terrors of death sweep over me. / But I call to God, / and the LORD will save me. / I complain and groan morning, noon, and night, / and he hears my voice." (Ps 55:1–2a, 4, 16–17, CSB)
Repeat Antiphon (above):
Reading: "[Jesus asked Cleopas and his companion,] 'What is this dispute that you're having with each other as you are walking [from Jerusalem to Emmaus]?' And they stopped walking and looked discouraged. The one named Cleopas answered him, 'Are you the only visitor in Jerusalem who doesn't know the things that happened there in these days?' 'What things?' he asked them. So they said to him, 'The things concerning Jesus of Nazareth, who was a prophet powerful in action and speech before God and all the people. [Some women] arrived early at the tomb, and when they didn't find his body, they . . . reported that they had seen a vision of angels, who said he was alive.' He said to them, 'Wasn't it necessary for the Messiah to suffer these things and enter into his glory?'" (Luke 24:17–19, 22b–23, 25a, 26, CSB)
Reflection: In a unique Lukan account, Jesus joins two disciples walking on the road from Jerusalem to Emmaus. Jesus plus two disciples equal three, a sacred number indicating the presence of the divine. After the unrecognizable Jesus asks them about what they are discussing, they tell him that the Jesus, who was considered a prophet powerful in action and speech, has been raised from the dead; he died on a cross three days before. Then, the Lukan Jesus teaches the two disciples a theme that permeates Luke's Gospel: suffering leads to glory (Luke (9:21, 43–45; 18:31–33). While at first people living today may be taken aback by that theme, upon

careful reflection they can see that they have lived it. Any kind of disease is suffering; finding a doctor who can cure or a drug that can alleviate some of the pain is glory. Stress is a type of suffering; some people wear their stress. Getting a project completed, an exam completed, or a job interview finished can result in glory. Those who engage in sports often talk about all the suffering they have endured to win the medal of glory. Because people of the past are like the people of today, Jesus teaches two disciples on the road that the suffering he endured with his death on the cross has resulted in the glory of the resurrection, in a body that appears suddenly but can be seen and talks.

Evening
Antiphon: "Hallelujah! / Sing to the LORD a new song, / his praise in the assembly of the faithful." (Ps 149:1, CSB) Alleluia!
Psalm: "[The LORD] gave a command to the clouds above / and opened the doors of heaven. / He rained manna for [the Israelites] to eat; / he gave them grain from heaven. / People ate the bread of angels. / He sent them an abundant supply of food." (Ps 78:23–25, CSB)
Repeat Antiphon (above):
Reading: "[The two disciples and Jesus] came near the village where they were going, and he gave the impression that he was going farther. But they urged him, 'Stay with us, because it's almost evening, and now the day is almost over.' So he went in to stay with them. It was as he reclined at the table with them that he took the bread, blessed, and broke it, and gave it to them. Then their eyes were opened, and they recognized him, but he disappeared from their sight." (Luke 24:28–31, CSB)
Reflection: Both the verses from Psalm 78 and the passage from Luke's Gospel are about divine presence. The verses of Psalm 78 recall the event in the HB (OT) book of Exodus (16:3–7, 13b–35). God manifested his presence with manna, a substance that forms on plants in the desert and can be gathered and baked into bread. The event in Exodus is recalled in HB (OT) books of Numbers (11:6–9), Deuteronomy (8:3), Nehemiah (9:20); in the OT (A) book of Wisdom (16:20); and in the CB (NT) books of John's Gospel (6:31–51), Hebrews (9:4), and Revelation (2:17). The passage above from Luke's Gospel recalls the event of God feeding the Israelites with manna in the wilderness. Earlier in Luke's Gospel, the narrative about Jesus feeding five thousand men (Luke 9:10), and the narrative about the last Passover supper (Luke 22:19) prepares the reader for the two disciples' recognition of Jesus when he takes bread, blesses it,

breaks it, and gives it to them. With that the narrator, who had previous stated that God had kept them from recognizing him, declares that they recognize him in the breaking of bread. As soon as they know who it is who is at table with them, the risen Jesus disappears from their sight, indicating that his risen body can appear and disappear at will. In the history of transmission, the natural occurrence of manna in the desert becomes manna and grain raining from heaven and, because angels were understood to live with God, who lived above the dome of the sky, it became the bread of angels. Also, in the history of transmission, the act of Jesus taking bread, blessing it, breaking it, and distributing it becomes the action of the real presence of Eucharist. Both manna and bread are manifestations of the divine presence.

Day 16: Monday of the Third Week of Easter

Morning
Antiphon: "Come, let's shout joyfully to the LORD, / shout triumphantly to the rock of our salvation!" (Ps 95:1, CSB) Alleluia!
Psalm: "When I am afraid, / I will trust you [, God]. / In God, whose word I praise, / in God I trust; I will not be afraid. / What can mere mortals do to me? / In God, whose word I praise, / in the LORD, whose word I praise, / in God I trust; I will not be afraid. / What can mere humans do to me? / For you rescued me from death, / even my feet from stumbling, / to walk before God in the light of life." (Ps 56:3–4, 10–11, 13, CSB)
Repeat Antiphon (above):
Reading: "That very hour [the two disciples in Emmaus] got up and returned to Jerusalem. They found the Eleven and those with them gathered together, who said, 'The Lord has truly been raised and has appeared to Simon!' Then they began to describe what had happened on the road and how he was made known to them in the breaking of the bread." (Luke 24:33–35, CSB)
Meditation/Journal: What word gets most of your attention in the verses from Psalm 56 or Luke 24:33–35? What does the word mean to you? How does it make you aware of God's presence?

Evening
Antiphon: "Let's enter [the LORD's] presence with thanksgiving; / let's shout triumphantly to him in song." (Ps 95:2, CSB) Alleluia!

Psalm: "I will bless the LORD at all times; / his praise will always be on my lips. / I will boast in the LORD; / the humble will hear and be glad. / Proclaim the LORD's greatness with me; / let us exalt his name together. / The eyes of the LORD are on the righteous, / and his ears are open to their cry for help. / The righteous cry out, and the LORD hears, / and rescues them from all their troubles. / One who is righteous has many adversities, / but the LORD rescues him from them all." (Ps 34:1–3, 15, 17, 19, CSB)

Repeat Antiphon (above):

Reading: "As [the two disciples] were saying these things, [Jesus] himself stood in their midst. He said to them, 'Peace to you!' But they were startled and terrified and thought they were seeing a ghost. 'Why are you troubled?' he asked them. 'And why do doubts arise in your hearts? Look and see, because a ghost does not have flesh and bones as you can see I have.' Having said this, he showed them his hands and feet." (Luke 24:36–40, CSB)

Activity: Based on all that has been presented above about Luke's understanding of what a risen body is or is like, what does Luke 24:36–40 add to the discussion? Describe what you think the author of Luke's Gospel thinks resurrection is. What do the verses of Psalm 34 have to do with it?

Day 17: Tuesday of the Third Week of Easter

Morning

Antiphon: ". . . [A]scribe to the LORD glory and strength." (Ps 96:7b, CSB) Alleluia!

Psalm: "Answer me quickly, LORD; / my spirit fails. / Don't hide your face from me, / or I will be like those / going down to the Pit. / Let me experience / your faithful love in the morning / for I trust in you. / Reveal to me the way I should go / because I appeal to you. / Teach me to do your will, / for you are my God. / May your gracious Spirit / lead me on level ground. / For your name's sake, LORD, / let me live." (Ps 143:7–8, 10–11a, CSB)

Repeat Antiphon (above):

Reading: ". . . [W]hile [the Eleven and those with them] were amazed and in disbelief because of their joy, [Jesus] asked them, 'Do you have anything here to eat?' So they gave him a piece of broiled fish, and he took it and ate in their presence." (Luke 24:41–42, CSB)

Activity: Based on all that has been presented above about Luke's understanding of what a risen body is or is like, what does Luke 24:41–42 add to the discussion? Describe what you think the author of Luke's Gospel thinks resurrection is; you may need to revise what you thought about or wrote yesterday. What do the verses of Psalm 143 have to do with it?

Evening
Antiphon: "I waited patiently for the LORD, / and he turned to me and heard my cry for help." (Ps 40:1, CSB) Alleluia!
Psalm: "LORD my God, you have done many things—/ your wondrous works and your plans for us; / none can compare with you. / If I were to report and speak of them, / they are more than can be told. / 'I delight to do your will, my God, / and your instruction is deep within me.' / I proclaim righteousness in the great assembly; / see, I do not keep my mouth closed—/ as you know, LORD. / I did not hide your righteousness in my heart; / I spoke about your faithfulness and salvation; / I did not conceal your constant love and truth / from the great assembly." (Ps 40:5, 8–10, CSB)
Repeat Antiphon (above):
Reading: "[Jesus] told [the Eleven and the others with them], 'These are my words that I spoke to you while I was still with you—that everything written about me in the Law of Moses, the Prophets, and the Psalms must be fulfilled.' Then he opened their minds to understand the Scriptures. He also said to them, 'This is what is written: The Messiah will suffer and rise from the dead the third day, and repentance for forgiveness of sins will be proclaimed in his name to all the nations, beginning at Jerusalem. You are witnesses of these things. And look, I am sending you what my Father promised. As for you, stay in the city until you are empowered from on high.'" (Luke 24:44–49, CSB)
Meditation/Journal: When have you waited patiently for the LORD, and he heard your cry? What wondrous works has God done for you? With whom have you shared what God has done in your life? What connection do you find between the verses of Psalm 40 and Luke 24:44–49? Explain.

Day 18: Wednesday of the Third Week of Easter

Morning
Antiphon: "... [A]ll the ends of the earth / have seen our God's victory." (Ps 98:3cd, CSB) Alleluia!

Psalm: "Sing a new song to the LORD, / for he has performed wonders; / his right hand and holy arm / have won him victory. / The LORD has made his victory known; / he has revealed his righteousness / in the sight of the nations. / He has remembered his love / and faithfulness. . . . / Let the whole earth shout to the LORD; / be jubilant, shout for joy, and sing." (Ps 98:1–3ab, 4, CSB)
Repeat Antiphon (above):
Reading: Peter said, "This Jesus of Nazareth was a man attested to you by God with miracles, wonders, and signs that God did among you through him, just as you yourselves know. Though he was delivered up according to God's determined plan and foreknowledge, [he was nailed to a cross and killed]. God raised him up, ending the pains of death, because it was not possible for him to be held by death." (Acts 2:22b–24, CSB)
Reflection: The author of the CB (NT) book of the Acts of the Apostles is the same author of Luke's Gospel. In the Acts, the author portrays Peter giving a long speech and declaring that Jesus of Nazareth got his credentials from God, who worked through him with miracles, wonders, and signs. In that regard, the words of Peter connect to the words of Psalm 98. The psalmist declares that God worked wonders with his powerful and holy right hand and arm, revealing his righteousness and remembering his love and faithfulness. The whole earth should shout to the LORD, because he raised Jesus from the dead; that is something to be jubilant about, to shout for joy, and to sing about. According to the Lukan Peter, not only did God raise Jesus, but he put an end to death. According to Psalm 16:10, God would "not allow [his] faithful one to see decay." (Ps 16:10, CSB). By referring to those words, Peter is attempting to convince his hearers that Jesus has been raised from the dead. In other words, Peter's declaration of Jesus' resurrection is a statement that God has worked another miracle, wonder, and sign.

Evening
Antiphon: "I will praise you forever for what you have done [, God] . / In the presence of your faithful people, / I will put my home in your name, for it is good." (Ps 52:9, CSB) Alleluia!
Psalm: "My mouth will tell about your righteousness / and your salvation all day long [, LORD], though I cannot sum them up. / I come because of the mighty acts of the Lord GOD; / I will proclaim your righteousness, yours alone. / God, you have taught me from my youth, / and I still proclaim your wondrous works. / Even while I am old and gray, / God, do

not abandon me, / while I proclaim your power / to another generation." (Ps 71:15–18, CSB)
Repeat Antiphon (above):
Reading: Peter said, "God has raised this Jesus; we are all witnesses of this. Therefore, since he has been exalted to the right hand of God and has received from the Father the promised Holy Spirit, he has poured out what you both see and hear." (Acts 2:32–33, CSB)
Meditation/Journal: In the verses of Psalm 71 above, about what mighty act of the Lord GOD is Peter speaking? What does the word *righteousness* in Psalm 71 mean to you? What does the word *salvation* in Psalm 71 mean to you?

Day 19: Thursday of the Third Week of Easter

Morning
Antiphon: "I will sing about the LORD's faithful love forever. / I will proclaim your faithfulness to all generations / with my mouth." (Ps 89:1, CSB) Alleluia!
Psalm: [LORD God, "r]ighteousness and justice are the foundation / of your throne; / faithful love and truth go before you. / Happy are the people who know the joyful shout; / LORD, they walk in the light from you face. / They rejoice in your name all day long, / and they are exalted by your righteousness. / For you are their magnificent strength; / by your favor our horn is exalted. / Surely our shield belongs to the LORD, / our king to the Holy One . . . ." (Ps 89:14–18, CSB)
Repeat Antiphon (above):
Reading: Peter said, "The God of Abraham, Isaac, and Jacob, the God of our ancestors, has glorified his servant Jesus, whom you handed over and denied before Pilate, though he decided to release him. You denied the Holy and Righteous One . . . . You killed the source of life, whom God raised from the dead; we are witnesses of this." (Acts 3:13–15, CSB)
Points to Ponder: First, in Peter's long speech in the Acts of the Apostles, he identifies God as Abraham's, Isaac's, and Jacob's God; he is the God of Peter's ancestors. Second. That God has glorified his servant Jesus. A servant is one who ministers to another; in this case, according to the Lukan Peter, Jesus serves God. Third, Peter reminds his listeners that they handed Jesus over to Pilate, who, after he had decided to release him, told the governor to crucify him. Fourth, Peter declares Jesus to be the holy and righteous one, the person who did the right thing because it was the

right thing to do! Fifth, the Lukan Peter slips into irony; Jesus, the source of life, who was put to death, has been raised from the dead by the God of Abraham, Isaac, and Jacob.

Evening
Antiphon: "Sing to the LORD, bless his name; / proclaim his salvation from day to day." (Ps 96:2, CSB) Alleluia!
Psalm: "One generation will declare your works to the next [, LORD,] / and will proclaim your mighty acts. / I will speak of your splendor and glorious majesty / and your wondrous works. / [I] will proclaim the power of your awe-inspiring acts, / and will declare your greatness. / [I] will give a testimony of your great goodness / and will joyfully sing of your righteousness." (Ps 145:4–7, CSB)
Repeat Antiphon (above):
Reading: "[The] rulers, elders, and scribes assembled in Jerusalem. After they had Peter and John stand before them, they began to question them: 'By what power or in what name have you [healed a lame man]?' Then Peter was filled with the Holy Spirit and said to them, 'Rulers of the people and elders: If we are being examined today about a good deed done to a disabled man, by what means he was healed, let it be known to all of you and to all the people . . . , that by the name of Jesus Christ of Nazareth, whom you crucified and whom God raised from the dead—by him this man is standing here before you healthy." (Acts 4:5, 7–10, CSB)
Intercessions: I bless God's name for all who proclaim his mighty acts. I bless God's name for all who receive his wondrous works. I bless God's name for his great generosity. I bless God's name for his extravagant goodness. I bless God's name for raising Jesus of Nazareth from the dead. I bless God's name for all who heal in the name of Jesus. I bless God's name for all the disabled who come to Jesus to be cured.

Day 20: Friday of the Third Week of Easter

Morning
Antiphon: "Declare [the LORD's] glory among the nations, / his wondrous works among all peoples." (Ps 96:3, CSB) Alleluia!
Psalm: "All you have made will thank you, LORD; / the faithful will bless you. / They will speak of the glory of your kingdom / and will declare your might, / informing all people of your mighty acts / and of the glorious

splendor of your kingdom. / Your kingdom is an everlasting kingdom; / your rule is for all generations." (Ps 145:10–13a, CSB)
Repeat Antiphon (above):
Reading: "Peter and the apostles [said to the Sanhedrin and the high priest], 'We must obey God rather than people. The God of our ancestors raised up Jesus, whom you had murdered by hanging him on a tree. God exalted this man to his right hand as ruler and Savior, to give repentance . . . and forgiveness of sins. We are witnesses of these things, and so is the Holy Spirit whom God has given to those who obey him.'" (Acts 5:29–32, CSB)
Reflection: In the Acts of the Apostles, the second volume of a two-book work by the author of Luke's Gospel, in speeches given by Peter, who is presented as a Jesus follower hero, there is a formula used. The elements of the formula do not always appear in the same order in the speech, but they are present nevertheless. First, there is a statement about God raising Jesus. In the passage above, he is the God of the Jewish ancestors. Second, there is a statement about the Sanhedrin and high priest being responsible for Jesus' death on the cross through crucifixion; in the passage above it is referred to as hanging on a tree. Third, there is a statement about God exalting Jesus, placing him at God's right hand (the place of power), making him ruler and Savior. In the words of Psalm 145, he is ruler of an everlasting kingdom, which is entered through repentance—a change of mind that results in a change of behavior—with the forgiveness of sins, transgressions of Torah (Law). Fourth, Peter and the apostles serve as witnesses of what God has done; the Holy Spirit, the gift of God's self to people, also bears witness to what God has done. Fifth, all this is possible because people obey God; this is not a blind obedience, but one discerned and followed willingly.

Evening
Antiphon: ". . . [A]ll the ends of the earth / have seen our God's victory." (Ps 98:3b, CSB) Alleluia!
Psalm: "The LORD is faithful in all his words / and gracious in all his actions. / The LORD helps all who fall; / he raises up all who are oppressed. / All eyes look to you, / and you give them their food at the proper time. / You open your hand / and satisfy the desire of every living thing. / The LORD is righteous in all his ways / and faithful in all his acts. / The LORD is near all who call out to him, / all who call out to him with integrity. / The LORD guards all those who love him . . . . / My mouth will declare

the LORD's praise; / let every living thing / bless his holy name forever and ever. (Ps 145:13b–18, 20a, 21, CSB)
Repeat Antiphon (above):
Reading: "Peter began to speak [to Cornelius and his household]: 'Now I truly understand that God doesn't show favoritism, but in every nation the person who fears him and does what is right is acceptable to him. You know the events that took place throughout all Judea, beginning from Galilee after the baptism that John preached; how God anointed Jesus of Nazareth with the Holy Spirit and with power, and how he went about doing good and healing all who were under the tyranny of the devil, because God was with him. We ourselves are witnesses of everything he did in both the Judean country and in Jerusalem, and yet they killed him by hanging him on a tree. God raised up this man on the third day and caused him to be seen . . . . He commanded us to preach to the people and to testify that he is the one appointed by God to be the judge of the living and the dead. All the prophets testify about him that through his name everyone who believe in him receives forgiveness of sins.'" (Acts 10:34–35, 37–43, CSB)
Activity: Using the five elements of Peter's speeches in the Acts of the Apostles presented in the Reflection for Morning Prayer above, identify each in the Reading above from Acts 10:34–35, 37–43.

Day 21: Saturday of the Third Week of Easter

Morning
Antiphon: "Let the whole earth shout to the LORD; / be jubilant, shout for joy, and sing." (Ps 98:4, CSB) Alleluia!
Psalm: "The LORD reigns! Let the earth rejoice; / let the many coasts and islands be glad. / The heavens proclaim his righteousness; / all the peoples see his glory, / For you, LORD, / are the Most High over the whole earth; / you are exalted above all the gods. / Light dawns for the righteous, / gladness for the upright in heart. / Be glad in the LORD, you righteous ones, / and give thanks to his holy name." (Ps 97:1, 6, 9 11–12, CSB)
Repeat Antiphon (above):
Reading: "Paul stood up [in the synagogue in Pisidian Antioch] and motioned with his hand and said, 'Brothers and sisters, children of Abraham's race, and those among you who fear God, it is to us that the word of . . . salvation has been sent. Since the residents of Jerusalem and their rulers did not recognize [Jesus] or the sayings of the prophets that are

read every Sabbath, they have fulfilled their words by condemning him. Though they found no grounds for the death sentence, they asked Pilate to have him killed. When they had carried out all that had been written about him, they took him down from the tree and put him in a tomb. But God raised him from the dead, and he appeared for many days to those who came up with him from Galilee to Jerusalem, who are now his witnesses to the people. And we ourselves proclaim to you the good news of the promise that was made to our ancestors. God has fulfilled this for us, their children, by raising up Jesus . . . . Therefore, let it be known to you, brothers and sisters, that through this man forgiveness of sins is being proclaimed to you.'" (Acts 13:16a, 26–33a, 38, CSB)

Reflection/Activity: In the Acts of the Apostles, the second volume of a two-book work by the author of Luke's Gospel, in speeches given by Paul, who is presented as a Jesus follower hero, the formula used for Peter's speeches is also used for Paul's speeches. The elements of the formula do not always appear in the same order in the speeches, but they are present nevertheless. (1) There is a statement about God raising Jesus. (2) There is a statement about the Sanhedrin and high priest being responsible for Jesus' death on the cross through crucifixion. (3) There is a statement about God exalting Jesus. (4) Paul, Peter, and the apostles serve as witnesses to what God has done. And (5) all this is possible because people believe. Apply the elements of the formula to Paul's speech in the Acts of the Apostles 13:16a, 26–33a, 38, and identify the five elements in the speech.

Evening
Antiphon: "Confirm what you said to your servant [, LORD], for it produces reverence for you." (Ps 119:38, CSB) Alleluia!
Psalm: "Let your faithful love come to me, LORD, / your salvation, as you promised. / This is my comfort in my affliction: / Your promise has given me life. / I have sought your favor with all my heart; / be gracious to me according to your promise. / May your faithful love comfort me / as you promised your servant." (Ps 119:41, 50, 76, CSB)
Repeat Antiphon (above):
Reading: Paul said to King Agrippa: ". . . I stand on trial because of the hope in what God promised to our ancestors, the promise our twelve tribes hope to reach as they earnestly serve him night and day. King Agrippa, I am being accused by the Jews because of this hope. Why do any of you consider it incredible that God raises the dead?" (Acts 26:6–8, CSB)

Activity: What word or phrase from the verses of Psalm 119 or Acts 26:6–8 gets your attention? What does the word or phrase mean? How does the word or phrase make you aware of God's presence. What word or phrase connects the verses of Psalm 119 and Acts 26:6–8? Explain.

Day 22: Fourth Sunday of Easter

Morning
Antiphon: "... [Y]ou, LORD, be gracious to me and raise me up ...." (Ps 41:10a, CSB) Alleluia!
Psalm: "... [O]ne can see that the wise die; / the foolish and stupid also pass away. / Then they leave their wealth to others. / Their graves are their permanent homes, / their dwellings from generation to generation, / though they have named estates after themselves. / Like sheep they are headed for Sheol; / Death will shepherd them. / The upright will rule over them in the morning, / and their form will waste away in Sheol, / far from their lofty abode. / But God will redeem me / from the power of Sheol, / for he will take me." (Ps 49:10–11, 14–15, CSB)
Repeat Antiphon (above):
Reading: "In Joppa there was a disciple named Tabitha (which is translated Dorcas). She was always doing good works and acts of charity. . . . [S]he became sick and died. When [Peter] arrived, [two men] led him to the room upstairs [where her body was]. And all the widows approached him, weeping and showing him the robes and clothes that Dorcas had made while she was with them. Peter sent them all out of the room. He knelt down, prayed, and turning toward the body said, 'Tabitha, get up.' She opened her eyes, saw Peter, and sat up." (Acts 9:36–37a, 39b–40, CSB)
Reflection: In Luke's Gospel, the hero is Jesus of Nazareth. In the second volume, the Acts of the Apostles, Peter and Paul are the heroes. Whatever Jesus did in the gospel, Peter and Paul do in the Acts. In Luke's Gospel, Jesus raises a seemingly dead little girl (Luke 8:49–56), saying, "Child, get up!" (Luke 8:54, CSB). The author presents Peter raising Tabitha, saying, "Tabitha, get up" (Acts 9:40b, CSB). Ancient people conceived of the world as a three-floored sky scraper. God lived on the top floor (heaven); people lived on the middle floor (earth); and the dead lived on the first floor (Sheol). As the psalmist reflects, every person dies and is placed on a shelf in a tomb, where he or she lives forever. In Sheol, every person's body decays, and when the process is complete, his or her bones are gathered off the shelf and put in a box—called an ossuary—so that the shelf

can be used by another dead body. Jesus, acting like God, redeems the little girl by raising her from the dead; Sheol has no power over her. Peter, likewise, raises Tabitha from the dead; Sheol has no power over her. In other words, Jesus and Peter snatch people from the edge of the first level of the world and bring them back to the middle level. Christian hope is that Jesus will snatch people from the middle level and take them to the top level!—unless one no longer thinks of the universe as a three-floored skyscraper. Then, one must apply the raising of the dead biblical stories to a solar-centered universe and tease new meaning from the biblical accounts.

Evening

Antiphon: "It is not the dead who praise the LORD, / nor any of those descending into the silence of death." (Ps 115:17, CSB) Alleluia!

Psalm: "Not to us, LORD, not to us, / but to your name give glory / because of your faithful love, because of your truth. / Our God is in heaven / and does whatever he pleases. / You who fear the LORD, trust in the LORD! / He is their help and shield. / The LORD remembers us and will bless us. / [H]e will bless those who fear the LORD—/ small and great alike. / But we will bless the LORD, / both now and forever. / Hallelujah! (Ps 115:1, 3, 11–12a, 13, 18, CSB)

Repeat Antiphon (above):

Reading: In Troas, Paul spoke to a group of people until midnight. "There were many lamps in the room upstairs where we were assembled, and a young man named Eutychus was sitting on a window sill and sank into a deep sleep as Paul kept on talking. When he was overcome by sleep, he fell down from the third story and was picked up dead. But Paul went down, bent over him, embraced him, and said, 'Don't be alarmed, because he's alive.' They brought the boy home alive and were greatly comforted." (Acts 20:8–10, 12, CSB)

Reflection: As noted above in the Reflection for Morning Prayer, in Luke's Gospel, the hero is Jesus of Nazareth. In the second volume, the Acts of the Apostles, Peter and Paul are the heroes. Whatever Jesus did in the gospel, Peter and Paul do in the Acts. In Luke's Gospel, Jesus raises a seemingly dead little girl (Luke 8:49–56), saying, "Child, get up!" (Luke 8:54, CSB). The author presents Paul raising Eutychus—whose name means *fortunate*—saying, "He's alive." (Acts 20:10b, CSB). The astute Bible reader could conclude that he was alive by noting that he fell from the third story; three is the number for the divine presence. Furthermore,

Eutychus falls asleep, a metaphor for death. As already noted above, ancient people conceived of the world as three levels. God lived on the top level (heaven); people lived on the middle level (earth); and the dead lived on the first level (Sheol). As the psalmist reflects, God is in heaven, but he is both help and shield for those who trust him. He remembers people, like Eutychus, and blesses them. People who are blessed by the LORD thank God today and forever for not forgetting those who die. Just like Jesus saves the little girl from death, Paul saves Eutychus from his third-floor tumble. In other words, God through Jesus and Paul shield people from the edge of the first level of the world and pull them back to the middle level. Christian hope is that Jesus will snatch people from the middle level and take them to the top level!—unless one no longer thinks of the universe as a three-leveled universe. Then, one must apply the raising of the dead biblical stories to a solar-centered universe and tease new meaning from the biblical accounts in the hope of being fortunate!

Day 23: Monday of the Fourth Week of Easter

Morning

Antiphon: "Sing to [the LORD], sing praise to him; / tell about all his wondrous works!" (Ps 105:2, CSB) Alleluia!

Psalm: "Let the whole earth fear the LORD; / let all the inhabitants of the world stand in awe of him / For he spoke, and it came into being; / he commanded, and it came into existence. / But look, the LORD keeps his eye on those who fear him—/ those who depend on his faithful love / to rescue them from death / and keep them alive in famine." (Ps 33:8–9, 18–19, CSB)

Repeat Antiphon (above):

Reading: ". . . [T[he word of the LORD came to [Elijah]: 'Get up, go to Zarephath that belongs to Sidon and stay there. Look, I have commanded a woman who is a widow to provide for you there.' After this, the son of the woman, who owned the house, became ill. His illness got worse until he stopped breathing. . . . Elijah said to her, 'Give me your son.' So he took him from her arms, brought him up to the upstairs room where he was staying, and laid him on his own bed. Then he stretched himself out over the boy three times. He cried out to the LORD and said, 'LORD my God, please let this boy's life come into him again!' So the LORD listened to Elijah, and the boy's life came into him again, and he lived." (1 Kgs 17:8–9, 17, 19, 21–22, CSB)

Points to Ponder: Jesus, Peter, and Paul are not the only biblical characters who raise the dead. In the HB (OT) book of First Kings, the prophet Elijah raises the dead son of the widow of Zarephath. First, Zarephath is in Sidon, enemy territory! Not only has the LORD sent his prophet out of Israel, but he has sent him to live in enemy country with a widow. Second, the LORD informs Elijah that he has set in place the widow to provide for his needs. It is important to note here that the widow, a non-Israelite, is under God's control, because all people belong to God. Third, the son of the widow dies; this means that she has no man—husband or son—to take care of her. Fourth, just as God provided for Elijah in enemy territory, Elijah will provide for the widow by raising her son to life. Fifth, the sign of life is breath; just as God breathed the breath of life into the first man (Gen 2:7), Elijah, after stretching himself over the boy's dead body, breathed the breath of life into the son three times. Sixth, the three breaths indicate the divine presence, as Elijah prays that God will bring the boy back to life. Seventh, The LORD listens to Elijah's prayer, and acts on it. The boy lives. And Elijah provides for the widow, just as she has provided for him. In the words of the verses from Psalm 33, God has done a wondrous work; his faithful love has rescued the widow's son from death.

Evening
Antiphon: "LORD, God of my salvation, / I cry out before you day and night. / May my prayer reach your presence; / listen to my cry." (Ps 88:1–2, CSB) Alleluia!
Psalm: ". . . I have had enough troubles, [LORD], / and my life is near Sheol. / I am counted among those going down to the Pit. / I am like a man without strength, / abandoned among the dead. / I am like the slain lying in the grave, / whom you no longer remember, / and who are cut off from your care. / LORD, I cry out to you all day long; / I spread out my hands to you. / Do you work wonders for the dead? / Do departed spirits rise up to praise you? / Will your faithful love be declared in the grave . . . ? / Will your wonders be known in the darkness . . . ?" (Ps 88:3–5, 9b–11a, 12a, CSB)
Repeat Antiphon (above):
Reading: "Elisha said [to the Shunamite woman], 'At this time next year you will have a son in your arms.' The woman conceived and gave birth to a son at the same time the following year, as Elisha had promised. The child grew and one day went out to his father and the harvesters.

Suddenly he complained to his father, 'My head! My head!' The child sat on [his mother's] lap until noon and then died. She went up and laid him on the bed of the man of God, shut him in, and left. When Elisha got to the house, he discovered the boy lying dead on his bed. So he went in, closed the door . . . , and prayed to the LORD. Then he went up and lay on the boy; he put mouth to mouth, eye to eye, hand to hand. While he bent down over him, the boy's flesh became warm. Then he . . . bent down over him again. The boy sneezed seven times and opened his eyes. . . . Elisha said [to the Shunamite woman], 'Pick up your son.' She came, fell at his feet, and bowed to the ground; she picked up her son and left." (2 Kgs 4:15, 17, 18–19a, 20b–21, 32–34, 35bc, 36c–37, CSB)

Meditation/Journal: How would Elisha answer the questions posed by the psalmist in Psalm 88: LORD, do you work wonders for the dead? Do departed spirits rise up to praise you? Will your faithful love be declared in the grave? Will your wonders be known in the darkness? How would the Shunamite woman answer the questions posed by the psalmist in Psalm 88: LORD, do you work wonders for the dead? Do departed spirits rise to praise you? Will your faithful love be declared in the grave? Will your wonders be known in the darkness?

Day 24: Tuesday of the Fourth Week of Easter

Morning
Antiphon: "God arises." (Ps 68:1a, CSB) Alleluia!
Psalm: "The LORD is compassionate and gracious, / slow to anger and abounding in faithful love. / For as high as the heavens are above the earth, / so great is his faithful love / toward those who fear him. / As a father has compassion on his children, / so the LORD has compassion on those who fear him." (Ps 103:8, 11, 13, CSB)
Repeat Antiphon (above):
Reading: "One of the synagogue leaders, named Jairus, came, and when he saw Jesus, he fell at his feet and begged him earnestly, 'My little daughter is dying. Come and lay your hands on her so that she can get well and live.' While [Jesus] was still speaking, people came from the synagogue leader's house and said, 'You daughter is dead. Why bother the teacher anymore?' When Jesus overheard what was said, he told the synagogue leader, 'Don't be afraid. Only believe.' He went in [to the synagogue leader's house and said . . . 'The child is not dead but asleep.' Then he took the child by the hand and said to her, 'Talitha koum' (which is translated,

'Little girl, I say to you, get up'). Immediately the girl got up and began to walk." (Mark 5:22–23, 35–36, 39c, 41–42a, CSB)
Meditation/Journal: How does the story about Jesus raising Jairus' daughter from the dead in Mark's Gospel illustrate the LORD's compassion, grace, and faithful love in the verses from Psalm 103?

Evening
Antiphon: "In this very way / the man who fears the LORD / will be blessed." (Ps 128:6, CSB) Alleluia!
Psalm: "As for man [and woman], his [their] days are like grass—/ he [she] blooms like a flower of the field; / when the wind passes over it, it vanishes, / and its place is no longer known. / But from eternity to eternity / the LORD's faithful love is toward those who fear him, / and his righteousness toward the grandchildren / of those who keep his covenant, / who remember to observe his precepts. / Bless the LORD, all his works / in all the places where he rules. / My soul, bless the LORD!" (Ps 103:15–18, 22, CSB)
Repeat Antiphon (above):
Reading: "As [Jesus] was [talking], suddenly one of the leaders came and knelt down before him, saying, 'My daughter just died, but come and lay your hand on her, and she will live.' So Jesus and his disciples got up and followed him. When Jesus came to the leader's house, . . . he said, '[T]he girl is not dead but asleep.' . . . [H]e went in and took her by the hand, and the girl got up." (Matt 9:18–19, 23–25, CSB)
Meditation/Journal: How does the story about Jesus raising the leader's daughter from the dead in Matthew's Gospel illustrate the LORD's faithful love and his righteousness toward grandchildren of those who keep his covenant in the verses from Psalm 103? After comparing the account of Jesus raising the little girls in Mark's Gospel (5:22–23, 35–43) to Matthew's Gospel (9:18–19, 23–26) what do you conclude?

Day 25: Wednesday of the Fourth Week of Easter

Morning
Antiphon: "May the LORD add to your numbers, / both yours and your children's." (Ps 115:14, CSB) Alleluia!
Psalm: ". . . [Y]ou, LORD, are enthroned forever; / your fame endures to all generations. / You will rise up and have compassion . . . . [The LORD] has broken my strength in midcourse; / he has shortened my days. / I say,

'My God, do not take me / in the middle of my life!' / Your servants' children will dwell securely, / and their offspring will be established before you." (Ps 102:12–13a, 23–24, 28, CSB)

Repeat Antiphon (above):

Reading: "Just as [Jesus] neared the gate of the town [of Nain], a dead man was being carried out. He was his mother's only son, and she was a widow. A large crowd from the town was also with her. When the Lord saw her, he had compassion on her and said, 'Don't weep.' Then he came up and touched the open coffin, and the pallbearers stopped. And he said, 'Young man, I tell you, get up!' The dead man sat up and began to speak, and Jesus gave him to his mother." (Luke 7:12–15, CSB)

Reflection/Activity: On the surface, the unique Lukan account of Jesus raising the dead son of the widow of Nain looks like other resurrection-of-the-dead stories. However, there is another level to this narrative. In Jesus' world, a woman had no power; all power belonged to men. Since this woman is a widow—having no living husband—she is powerless, except for her son. After her son dies, she is even more powerless, having no man to take care of her. Thus, it is the widow who is raised to life. When Jesus gives her son back to her, he assures her of her livelihood. What connection can you make between the verses of Psalm 102 and Luke 7:12–15?

Evening

Antiphon: "Give thanks to the LORD, for he is good; / his faithful love endures forever." (Ps 107:1, CSB) Alleluia!

Psalm: "Others sat in darkness and gloom—/ prisoners in cruel chains—/ Then they cried out to the LORD in their trouble; / he saved them from their distress. / He brought them out of darkness and gloom / and broke their chains apart. Let them give thanks to the LORD / for his faithful love / and his wondrous works for all humanity." (Ps 107:10, 13–15, CSB)

Repeat Antiphon (above):

Readings:

(a) Jesus said to his disciples, "It is necessary that the Son of Man suffer many things and be rejected by the elders, chief priests, and scribes, be killed, and be raised the third day." (Luke 9:22, CSB)

(b) Jesus said to his disciples, "Let these words sink in: The Son of Man is about to be betrayed into the hands of men." (Luke 9:44, CSB)

(c) The Lord said, ". . . I have a baptism to undergo, and how it consumes me until it is finished." (Luke 12:50, CSB)

(d) Jesus said to some Pharisees, ". . . [I]t is necessary that I travel today, tomorrow, and the next day, because it is not possible for a prophet to perish outside of Jerusalem." (Luke 13:33, CSB)
(e) Jesus said to the Twelve: "See, we are going up to Jerusalem Everything that is written through the prophets about the Son of Man will be accomplished. For he will be handed over to the Gentiles, and he will be mocked, insulted, spit on, and after they flog him, they will kill him, and he will rise on the third day." (Luke 18:31–33, CSB)
(f) The two men in Jesus' tomb remind the spice- and perfume-bearing women about what Jesus said, "It is necessary that the Son of Man be betrayed into the hands of sinful men, be crucified, and rise on the third day." (Luke 24:7, CSB)
(g) Jesus said to the Eleven and those with them, "This is what is written: The Messiah will suffer and rise from the dead the third day . . . ." (Luke 24:47, CSB)

Reflection: The Lukan Jesus' predictions about his betrayal, death, and resurrection represent an expanded version of those found in Mark's Gospel (8:31; 9:31; 10:33–34). The author of Matthew's Gospel also took those predictions from Mark's Gospel and expanded them (Matt 16:21; 17:9, 23; 20:19; 26:32; 27:64). The purpose of Jesus' predictions (keeping in mind that the authors know how the story they are writing will end) is to spur the reader to finish the gospel to see if the predictions come true. Such a plot is the literary technique of the oldest author of a gospel: Mark (whoever he was). In film, this technique is called a flash-forward; something in a movie or TV show is predicted to happen; the viewer continues to watch to see if, indeed, it does happen—and, of course, it always does! While a person predicting his or her own death is credible (because everyone will die sooner or later), especially considering all the disturbance Jesus caused among the powers of his day, predicting one's resurrection is outrageous; in human experience, the dead stay dead! The author of Luke's Gospel uses the prediction technique throughout his gospel so that he can reuse (echo) it when his Jesus character makes post-resurrection appearances and he reminds his disciples of what he told them; these function as "I told you so" moments. In the resurrection predictions, Jesus was to rise on the third day. People often get confused about that. If he died on Friday and rose on Sunday, that is only two days—not three. The problem exists in that modern people presume zero. Zero before Jesus' Friday death to Saturday is one day, and from Saturday to Sunday is another day; with zero that adds to two days. However, even though zero was invented in the third century BCE, Arabic numbers featuring 0 for zero wasn't used until the tenth century CE. Also, most languages used letters for numbers (such as Roman Numerals: I = 1; V = 5, etc.). Thus, ancient people did not presume zero; they always began counting with one. Applying this to the author of Luke's Gospel, Friday would be the first day, Saturday would be the second day, and Sunday would be the third day. Jesus rose on the third day, as he had predicted he would. This fact is a good demonstration of how modern culture can impose its understanding—unknowingly or knowingly—upon an ancient text (biblical book) whose author does not share the current understanding or presupposes a different one.

Day 26: Thursday of the Fourth Week of Easter

Morning
Antiphon: "God arises." (Ps 68:1a, CSB) Alleluia!
Psalm: "God in his holy dwelling is / a father of the fatherless / and a champion of widows. / Sing to God, you kingdoms of the earth; / sing praise to the Lord, / to him who rides in the ancient, highest heavens. / Look, he thunders with his powerful voice! / Ascribe power to God. / His majesty is over [all]; / his power is among the clouds. / God, you are awe-inspiring in your sanctuaries. / . . . God . . . gives power and strength to his people. / Blessed be God!" (Ps 68:5, 32–35, CSB)
Repeat Antiphon (above):
Reading: Jesus said, ". . . [J]ust as the Father raises the dead and gives them life, so the Son also gives life to whom he wants. Truly I tell you, anyone who hears my word and believes him who sent me has eternal life [and] has passed from death to life." (John 5:21, 24 CSB)
Meditation/Journal: In what specific ways has Jesus given life to you? What specific experiences have you had of passing from death to life? Explain.

Evening
Antiphon: "Seek the LORD and his strength; / seek his face always." (Ps 105:4, CSB) Alleluia!
Psalm: "Let the name of the LORD be blessed / both now and forever. / From the rising of the sun to its setting, / let the name of the LORD be praised. / He raises the poor from the dust / and lifts the needy from the trash heap . . . ." (Ps 113:2–3, CSB)
Repeat Antiphon (above):

Reading: Jesus said: ". . . I have come down from heaven, not to do my own will, but the will of him who sent me. This is the will of him who sent me: that I should lose none of those he has given me but should raise them up on the last day. For this is the will of my Father: that everyone who sees the Son and believes in him will have eternal life, and I will raise him [her] up on the last day. No one can come to me unless the Father who sent me draws him [her], and I will raise him [her] up on the last day. The one who eats my flesh and drinks my blood has eternal life, and I will raise him [her] up on the last day." (John 6:38–40, 44, 54, CSB)

Reflection: The verses from John's Gospel are part of a much longer discourse in chapter 6. The Johannine Jesus can come down from heaven to earth only in a three-storied universe! According to the Johannine Jesus, he did not come down to earth to do his own will, but to do the will of God, who sent him. The will of God, according to John's Gospel, is that Jesus lose none of those God gave him; indeed, he will accomplish this by raising them on the last day. However, the Father also wills that people see the Son and believe in him to have eternal life—this theme of seeing and believing accompanies the seven major signs done by the Johannine Jesus and many of the minor ones. Those who believe in the Johannine Jesus will be raised on the last day. Assurance of eternal life and resurrection on the last day can be had by eating Jesus' flesh and drinking his blood, the topic of chapter 6 of John's Gospel, called by biblical scholars the bread of life discourse. In other words, those who partake of the eucharist have a solid hope for resurrection. The encounter they have now through the signs of bread and wine prepare them for their encounter on the last day, when Jesus will raise them from the dead. In the words of Psalm 113 above, the LORD raises the poor from the dust and lifts the needy from the trash heap.

Day 27: Friday of the Fourth Week of Easter

Morning

Antiphon: "As a deer longs for flowing streams, / so I long for you, God." (Ps 42:1, CSB) Alleluia!

Psalm: "Happy is the one who is considerate of the poor; / the LORD will save him [or her] in a day of adversity. / The LORD will keep him [or her] and preserve him [or her] . . . . / The LORD will sustain him [or her] on his [or her] sickbed; / you will heal him [or her] on the bed where he [or she] lies. / 'Something awful has overwhelmed him [or her], / and he [or

SEASON OF EASTER

she] won't rise again from where he [or she] lies!' / But you, LORD, be gracious to me and raise me up . . . ." (Ps 41:1–2a, 8, 10a, CSB)
Repeat Antiphon (above):
Reading: "Now a man was sick—Lazarus from Bethany the village of Mary and her sister Martha. . . . [I]t was [Mary's] brother Lazarus who was sick. So the sisters sent a message to [Jesus]: 'Lord, the one you love is sick.' When Jesus heard it, he said, 'This sickness will not end in death but is for the glory of God, so that the Son of God may be glorified through it.' Now Jesus loved Martha, her sister, and Lazarus." (John 11:1, 2b–5, CSB)
Meditation/Journal: What light shines on John 11:1, 2b–5 knowing that Lazarus means *God has helped*? What light shines on John 11:1, 2b–5 from the verses of Psalm 41? What do you expect Jesus to do?

Evening
Antiphon: "LORD, you light my lamp; / my God illuminates my darkness." (Ps 18:28, CSB) Alleluia!
Psalm: "LORD, you have searched me and know me. / You know when I sit down and when I stand up; / you understand my thoughts from far away. / If I go up to heaven, you are there; / if I make my bed in Sheol, you are there. / If I say, 'Surely the darkness will hide me, / and the light around me will be night'—/ even the darkness is not dark to you. / The night shines like the day; / darkness and light are alike to you." (Ps 139:1–2, 8, 11–12, CSB)
Repeat Antiphon (above):
Reading: "'Aren't there twelve hours in a day?' Jesus [asked his disciples]. 'If anyone walks during the day he doesn't stumble, because he sees the light of this world. But if anyone walks during the night, he does stumble, because the light is not in him.' He said this and then he told them, 'Our friend Lazarus has fallen asleep, but I'm on my way to wake him up.'" (John 11:9–10, CSB)
Reflection: The author of John's Gospel uses a lot of double entendres in his narrative. A double entendre is a figure of speech or a particular way of wording that is devised to have a double meaning, one of which is typically obvious, and the other often conveys a message that could be religiously unacceptable or offensive to state directly. Often, a double entendre is a word or phrase used ambiguously; it is open to several interpretations, one of which can be risqué or even indecent. In John's Gospel, the reader must determine what the author means. After presenting his Jesus character's reflection on the duality of light and darkness—also

addressed by the verses from Psalm 139—the author introduces walking, a double entendre. Walking can refer to navigating roads, paths, and houses during the day or during the night. But walking can also refer to following Jesus, who identifies himself as the light of the world. In the latter meaning, one walks by the light of faith and not by the darkness of non-belief. According to the psalmist, there is no duality. One cannot hide from God in the darkness, because there is no darkness from God's perspective; what we call darkness is light to God. In other words, God is both darkness and light; there is no duality in God. It is difficult to keep both meanings together for those who have been raised on duality! Sometimes we can see better in the dark. Furthermore, at the end of the Johannine passage the author introduces another double entendre. The author also employs sleep. According to the Johannine Jesus, his friend Lazarus has fallen asleep—either he is slumbering in his bed or he is dead. Jesus is going to awaken him—stir him to get up or raise him from the dead! The latter interpretations of sleep as death and awakening as resurrection make no sense and can sound offensive to those whose daily experience is that the dead remain dead!

Day 28: Saturday of the Fourth Week of Easter

Morning
Antiphon: "In vain you get up early and stay up late, / working hard to have enough food—/ yes, [the LORD] gives sleep to the one he loves." (Ps 127:2, CSB) Alleluia!
Psalm: "Consider me and answer, LORD my God. / Restore brightness to my eyes; / otherwise, I will sleep in death. / ... I have trusted in your faithful love; / my heart will rejoice in your deliverance. / I will sing to the LORD / because he has treated me generously." (Ps 13:3, 5-6, CSB)
Repeat Antiphon (above):
Reading: Jesus told his disciples, "'Our friend Lazarus has fallen asleep, but I'm on my way to wake him up.' Then the disciples said to him, 'Lord, if he has fallen asleep, he will get well.' Jesus, however, was speaking about his death, but they thought he was speaking about natural sleep. So Jesus then told them plainly, 'Lazarus has died. I'm glad for you that I wasn't there so that you may believe. But let's go to him.'" (John 11:11-15, CSB)
Reflection: As noted in yesterday evening's reflection, the author of John's Gospel uses double entendres in his narrative. A double entendre is a figure of speech or a particular way of wording that is devised to have

a double meaning, one of which is typically obvious, and the other often conveys a message that could be religiously unacceptable or offensive to state directly. Often, a double entendre is a word or phrase used ambiguously; it is open to several interpretations, one of which can be risqué or even indecent. In John's Gospel, the reader must determine what the author means. In the Johannine passage above, the author introduces the double entendre of sleep. According to the Johannine Jesus, his friend Lazarus has fallen asleep, which his disciples interpret as slumbering in his bed. The Johannine Jesus tells them that he is going to awaken him! The narrator interrupts the flow of the dialogue to inform the reader of what he considers to be the correct interpretation; Lazarus has died. And before he can explain that he intends to raise him from the dead, Jesus tells his disciples that Lazarus' death is for their benefit. Once they see what he is intending to do, they will believe in him. The Johannine Jesus does not say that he intends to raise Lazarus from the dead, as that would make no sense to his disciples; it could even sound offensive to those who know that once a person is dead, he or she remains dead!

Evening
Antiphon: "I will both lie down and sleep in peace, / for you alone, LORD, make me live in safety." (Ps 4:8, CSB) Alleluia!
Psalm: "My God, I cry by day, but you do not answer, / by night, yet I have no rest. / But you are holy . . . . Rescue my life . . . , / my only life . . . . / All who prosper on earth will eat and bow down; / all those who go down to the dust / will kneel before him—/ even the one who cannot preserve his life." (Ps 22:2–3a, 20, 29, CSB)
Repeat Antiphon (above):
Reading: "When Jesus arrived [in Bethany], he found that Lazarus had already been in the tomb four days. Many of the Jews had come to Martha and Mary to comfort them about their brother." (John 11:17, 19, CSB)
Reflection/Meditation/Journal: Jewish entombment custom was to wrap the deceased in linen and place the body on a shelf in the family tomb on the same day as death. The death of a person was considered final after three days; thus the editor's note about Lazarus having been in the tomb for four days means that he was really dead! Rituals surrounding death included not leaving home for the first week, except to visit the tomb. Relatives and friends visited the survivors to comfort them during that week. Compare and contrast modern death customs with

the biblical death customs noted above. What do you discover? What connection is there between the verses of Psalm 22 and John 11:17, 19?

Day 29: Fifth Sunday of Easter

Morning
Antiphon: "Your compassions are many, LORD; / give me life according to your judgments." (Ps 119:56, CSB) Alleluia!
Psalm: "I love the LORD because he has heard / my appeal for mercy. / Because he has turned his ear to me. / I will call out to him as long as I live. / The ropes of death were wrapped around me, / and the torments of Sheol overcame me; / I encountered trouble and sorrow. / Then I called on the name of the LORD: / 'LORD, save me!' / For you, LORD, rescued me from death, / my eyes from tears, / my feet from stumbling. / I will walk before the LORD / in the land of the living. / The death of his faithful ones / is valuable in the LORD's sight." (Ps 116:1–4, 8–9, 15, CSB)
Repeat Antiphon (above):
Reading: "As soon as Martha heard that Jesus was coming, she went to meet him, but Mary remained seated in the house. Then Martha said to Jesus, 'Lord, if you had been here, my brother wouldn't have died. Yet even now I know that whatever you ask from God, God will give you.' 'Your brother will rise again,' Jesus told her. Martha said to him, 'I know that he will rise again in the resurrection at the last day.' Jesus said to her, 'I am the resurrection and the life. The one who believes in me, even if he [or she] dies, will live. Everyone who lives and believes in me will never die. Do you believe this?' 'Yes, Lord,' she told him, 'I believe you are the Messiah, the Son of God, who comes into the world.'" (John 11:20–27, CSB)
Activity: What are the possible interpretations of the double entendres found in John 11:20–27: death, rise, resurrection, life, belief, Messiah?

Evening
Antiphon: "[The LORD] renews my life; / he leads me along the right paths / for his name's sake." (Ps 23:3, CSB) Alleluia!
Psalm: "LORD, you are my portion / and my cup of blessing; / you hold my future. / The boundary lines have fallen for me / in pleasant places; / indeed, I have a beautiful inheritance. / I will bless the LORD who counsels me—/ even at night when my thoughts trouble me. / I always let the LORD guide me. / Because he is at my right hand, / I will not be shaken. /

SEASON OF EASTER

Therefore my heart is glad / and my whole being rejoices; / my body also rests securely. / For you will not abandon me to Sheol; / you will not allow your faithful one to see decay. / You reveal the path of life to me; / in your presence is abundant joy; / at your right hand are eternal pleasures." (Ps 16:5–11, CSB)

Repeat Antiphon (above):

Reading: "The Jews who were with [Mary] in the house consoling her saw that Mary got up quickly and went out. They followed her, supposing that she was going to the tomb to cry there. As soon as Mary came to where Jesus was and saw him, she fell at his feet and told him, 'Lord, if you had been here, my brother wouldn't have died!'" (John 11:31–32, CSB)

Reflection/Intercessions: The astute reader will notice that both Martha and Mary say the same thing to Jesus: "Lord, if you had been here, my brother wouldn't have died!" Both understand death as natural and final, and both presume that Jesus could have stopped it from claiming their brother Lazarus, if Jesus had been present during Lazarus' illness. Mary's words are a petition, accompanied by her bodily posture for petition: kneeling at Jesus' feet.

For all who mourn the death of a spouse, I pray to you, Lord. For all who mourn the death of a sibling, I pray to you, Lord. For all who mourn the death of a child, I pray to you, Lord. For all who mourn the death of a parent, I pray to you, Lord. For all who mourn the death of a friend, I pray to you, Lord. Reveal the path of life to them and give them abundant joy and eternal pleasures in your presence forever. Amen.

Day 30: Monday of the Fifth Week of Easter

Morning

Antiphon: ". . . [T]he LORD has appointed the blessing—/ life forevermore." (Ps 133:3b, CSB) Alleluia!

Psalm: "It was you [, LORD,] who brought me out of the womb, / making me secure at my mother's breast. / I was given over to you at birth; / you have been my God from my mother's womb. / [The LORD] has not despised or abhorred / the torment of the oppressed. / He did not hide his face from him [her] / but listened when he [she] cried to him for help. / I will give praise in the great assembly / because of you; / I will fulfill my vows / before those who fear you." (Ps 22:9–10, 24–25, CSB)

Repeat Antiphon (above):

Reading: "When Jesus saw [Mary] crying, and the Jews who had come with her crying, he was deeply moved in his spirit and troubled. 'Where have you put him?' he asked. 'Lord,' they told him, 'come and see.' Jesus wept. Then Jesus deeply moved again, came to the tomb. It was a cave, and a stone was lying against it. 'Remove the stone.' Jesus said. (John 11:33–35, 38–39, CSB)

Meditation/Journal: What connection do you find between the womb in Psalm 22 and the tomb in John 11:38? In what specific ways are wombs and tombs alike?

Evening

Antiphon: "[The LORD our God] raises the poor from the dust / and lifts the needy from the trash heap." (Ps 113:7, CSB) Alleluia!

Psalm: "Open the gates of righteousness for me; / I will enter through them / and give thanks to the LORD. / This is the LORD's gate; / the righteous will enter through it. / The stone that the builders rejected / has become the cornerstone. / This came from the LORD; / it is wondrous in our sight. / This is the day the LORD has made; / let's rejoice and be glad in it." (Ps 118:19–20, 22–24, CSB)

Repeat Antiphon (above):

Reading: "'Remove the stone [from the tomb],' Jesus said. Martha, the dead man's sister, told him, 'Lord, there is already a stench because he has been dead four days.'" (John 11:39, CSB)

Points to Ponder: First, as the author of John's Gospel describes it, Lazarus' tomb is a cave with shelves in it. After being wrapped in linen, the deceased was laid on a shelf until all that remained was bones, which were gathered and placed in an ossuary (bone box), which was placed below the shelf so it could be used again. Second, rolling the stone away from the entrance to the tomb required several men with levers to push it; it was not an easy task to roll a circular- or oval-shaped stone from the entrance to a tomb; its purpose was to keep out grave robbers and wild animals. Third, Martha, who had told Jesus that she believed he was the resurrection, the life, and the Messiah, now is not so full of faith when faced with the stench coming from Lazarus' tomb once the stone is removed; after all, he has been decaying for four days! Once the stone was moved, the air coming out of the cave would have been strong enough to bowl over the whole crowd. Martha represents people who affirm their faith until confronted otherwise; then, the reality of life, death, decay, and stench takes over.

SEASON OF EASTER

Day 31: Tuesday of the Fifth Week of Easter

Morning
Antiphon: "I lie down and sleep; / I wake again because the LORD sustains me." (Ps 3:5, CSB) Alleluia!
Psalm: "The LORD is my strength and my song; / he has become my salvation. / There are shouts of joy and victory / in the tents of the righteous: / 'The LORD's right hand performs valiantly! / The LORD's right hand is raised. / The LORD's right hand performs valiantly!' / I will not die, but I will live / and proclaim what the LORD has done." (Ps 118:14–17, CSB)
Repeat Antiphon (above):
Reading: "Jesus said to [Martha], 'Didn't I tell you that if you believed you would see the glory of God?' . . . [T[hey removed the stone. Then Jesus raised his eyes and said, 'Father, I thank you that you heard me. I know that you always hear me, but because of the crowd standing here I said this, so that they may believe you sent me.' After he said this, he shouted with a loud voice, 'Lazarus, come out!' The dead man came out bound hand and foot with linen strips and with his face wrapped in a cloth. Jesus said to them, 'Unwrap him and let him go'" (John 11:40–44, CSB)
Meditation/Journal: Using the verses from Psalm 118, what do you think is the glory of God (John 11:40)? Does the raising of Lazarus narrative in John's Gospel help you believe that the Father sent Jesus? Explain.

Evening
Antiphon: "Protect my life, for I am faithful. / You are my God; save your servant who trusts in you." (Ps 86:2, CSB) Alleluia!
Psalm: "You answer us in righteousness, / with awe-inspiring works, / God of our salvation, / the hope of all the ends of the earth / and of distant seas. / You establish the mountains by your power; / you are robed with strength. / You silence the roar of the seas, / the roar of their waves, / and the tumult of the nations. / Those who live far away are awed by your signs; / you make east and west shout for joy." (Ps 65:5–8, CSB)
Repeat Antiphon (above):
Reading: ". . . [M]any of the Jews who came to Mary and saw what [Jesus] did believed in him. But some of them went to the Pharisees and told them what Jesus had done. So the chief priests and the Pharisees convened the Sanhedrin and were saying, 'What are we going to do since this man is doing many signs? If we let him go on like this, everyone will believe in him . . . .'" (John 11:45–48a, CSB)

Reflection: The word that ties Psalm 65 to John 11:45–48a is signs. A sign is a thing or action that points to something else. In the words of Psalm 65, people are awed by God's signs. In John's Gospel, people are awed by Jesus' signs. The heart of John's Gospel is organized around seven major signs done by Jesus: water into wine (John 2:1–11), curing of an official's son (John 4:46–54), curing a paralytic (John 5:1–15), feeding a crowd in Galilee (John 6:1–15), walking on water (John 6:16–21), curing a man born blind (John 9:1–41), and the last one: the raising of Lazarus (John 11:1–44). After witnessing a sign, some people in John's Gospel believe in Jesus. That is why the chief priests and the Pharisees convene the Sanhedrin to determine what they ought to do about him. In other words, his signs are a threat to their authority to govern Judaism. The Johannine Jesus is coloring outside the lines of established religious Judaism, and he is encouraging others to do the same. The raising of Lazarus sparks their plot to kill Jesus. From the point of view of officials in John's Gospel, the enacting of signs, awe-inspiring works, must be stopped to stop the belief that results from them. Modern application of this understanding are not hard to find. A department head or dean in a university stops a student protest about a certain course to stop bad press about it. A plant manager stops an employee from reporting a mistake made in the manufacturing of a product in order not to curb sales with a recall. Even churches put a quick end to a member disciple who challenges the pastor's interpretation of Scripture. The status quo must be maintained. The Johannine Jesus, however, turned upside down that presupposition by working signs.

Day 32: Wednesday of the Fifth Week of Easter

Morning
Antiphon: "[God, y]ou rescued me from death; / even my feet from stumbling, / to walk before God in the light of life." (Ps 56:13, CSB) Alleluia!
Psalm: "When you hide your face [, LORD, / all] are terrified; / when you take away their breath, / they die and return to the dust. / When you send your breath, / they are created, / and you renew the surface of the ground. / May the glory of the LORD endure forever; / may the LORD rejoice in his works. / He looks at the earth, and it trembles; / he touches the mountains, / and they pour out smoke. / I will sing to the LORD all my life; / I will sing praise to my God while I live." (Ps 104:29–33, CSB)
Repeat Antiphon (above):

Reading: Jesus spoke to [the Sadducees, who say there is no resurrection], 'Isn't this the reason why you're mistaken [about the woman who had been married to seven husbands]; you don't know the Scriptures or the power of God. For when they rise from the dead, they neither marry nor are given in marriage, but are like angels in heaven. And as for the dead being raised—haven't you read in the book of Moses, in the passage about the burning bush, how God said to him: I am the God of Abraham and the God of Issac and the God of Jacob? He is not the God of the dead but of the living. You are badly mistaken.'" (Mark 12:24–27, CSB)

Reflection: During a controversy the Markan Jesus has with the Sadducees, one of the many Jewish sects at Jesus' time, Jesus responds to the levirate marriage law: if a man's brother dies without having produced offspring, the brother is obligated to take her and raise offspring for his dead brother. Any children born of the union are considered the dead brother's offspring. The Sadducees present a hypothetical situation in which seven brothers successively marry the same woman after none of them father children. After the woman died, the Sadducees want to know whose wife will she be in the resurrection. The Markan Jesus responds that in the resurrection there is no marriage; thus, their question is mute! Jesus confronts the non-believing-in-the-resurrection Sadducees by reminding them that when Moses encounters the LORD in the burning bush, God identifies himself as the God of Abraham, Isaac, and Jacob—not the God of the deceased Abraham, Isaac, and Jacob. The LORD is the God of the living Abraham, Isaac, and Jacob; all three have passed through death to new life on the other side. They have been raised from the dead.

Evening

Antiphon: "God is my helper; / the Lord is the sustainer of my life." (Ps 54:4, CSB) Alleluia!

Psalm: "As a deer longs for flowing streams, / so I long for you, God. / I thirst for God, the living God. / When can I come and appear before God? / The LORD will send his faithful love by day; / his song will be with me in the night—/ a prayer to the God of my life. / Put your hope in God, for I will still praise him, / my savior and my God." (Ps 42:1–2, 8, 11cd, CSB)

Repeat Antiphon (above):

Reading: "Jesus told [the Sadducees], 'The children of this age marry and are given in marriage. But those who are counted worthy to take

part in that age and in the resurrection from the dead neither marry nor are given in marriage. For they can no longer die, because they are like angels and are children of God, since they are children of the resurrection. Moses even indicated in the passage about the burning bush that the dead are raised, where he calls the Lord the God of Abraham and the God of Isaac and the God of Jacob. He is not the God of the dead but of the living, because all are living to him'" (Luke 20:34–38, CSB)
Reflection: The original version of the controversy between Jesus and Sadducees is found in Mark's Gospel (12:24–27). The version of the controversy between Jesus and the Sadducees in Luke's Gospel (20:34–38) is derived from the one in Mark's Gospel. The author of Luke's Gospel tends to explain further material that he found in Mark's Gospel. He presents his Jesus character further clarifying that there is no marriage in the resurrection after death. Those who have been raised are like angels—an angel is a code word for God—who never die. Being children of God, they are children of eternal life, children of the resurrection. Indeed, the dead are raised, as Moses records the LORD telling him that God is the God of the living Abraham, Isaac, and Jacob. The LORD is not the God of the dead; he is the God of the living. To him Abraham, Isaac, and Jacob are alive. A contemporary way to state this would be that Abraham, Isaac, and Jacob are alive in him.

Day 33: Thursday of the Fifth Week of Easter

Morning
Antiphon: "The nobles of the peoples have assembled / with the people of the God of Abraham. / For the leaders of the earth belong to God; / he is greatly exalted." (Ps 47:9, CSB) Alleluia!
Psalm: "Seek the LORD and his strength; / seek his face always. / Remember the wondrous works he has done, / his wonders, and the judgments he has pronounced, / you offspring of Abraham his servant, / Jacob's descendants—his chosen ones. He remembers his covenant forever . . . , the covenant he made with Abraham, / swore to Isaac, / and confirmed to Jacob as a decree / and to Israel as a permanent covenant . . . . For he remembered his holy promise to Abraham his servant." (Ps 105:4–6, 8a, 9–10, 42, CSB)
Repeat Antiphon (above):
Reading: "[T]he promise to Abraham or to his descendants . . . was not through the law, but through the righteousness that comes by faith. This

is why the promise is by faith, so that it may be according to grace, to guarantee it to all the descendants—not only to the one who is of the law but also to the one who is of Abraham's faith. He is the father of all. As it is written: I have made you the father of many nations—in the presence of the God in whom he believed, the one who gives life to the dead and calls things into existence that do not exist. He believed, hoping against hope, so that he became the father of many nations according to what had been spoken: So will your descendants be. He did not weaken in faith when he considered his own body to be already dead (since he was about a hundred years old) and also the deadness of Sarah's womb. He did not waver in unbelief at God's promise but was strengthened in his faith and gave glory to God, because he was fully convinced that what God had promised, he was also able to do. Therefore, it was credited to him for righteousness. Now it was credited to him was not written for Abraham alone, but also for us. It will be credited to us who believe in him who raised Jesus our Lord from the dead." (Rom 4:13, 16–24, CSB)

Reflection: The covenant mentioned in the verses from Psalm 105 and in chapter 4 of Paul's letter to the Romans is God's agreement to make Abraham the father of many nations. Paul wants his readers to understand that the covenant was not in terms of the Torah (Law), because the agreement had been made before Moses received the Torah on Mount Sinai (Horeb). Paul is focused on Abraham's faith, which was credited to him for righteousness (Rom 4:9). That means that Abraham's trust of God put him in a good relationship with God. Throughout the patriarch's life, he trusted God to make him the father of many nations. Even when he and Sarah had no children of their own, Abraham continued to trust God, to hope against hope, to believe that God would do what he promised. Likewise, according to Paul, those who believe that God raised Jesus from the dead will be credited with righteousness. This opens the door of belief to both Jews and Gentiles. Righteousness, a gift of God's grace, cannot be earned by keeping Torah; it can only be received as an offer from the God who makes and keeps his covenant.

Evening

Antiphon: "Worthy is the Lamb who was slaughtered / to receive power and riches / and wisdom and strength / and honor and glory and blessing!" (Rev 5:12, CSB) Alleluia!

Canticle: "Our Lord and God, / you are worthy to receive / glory and honor and power, / because you have created all things, / and by your will / they exist and were created. / You [, the Lamb,] are worthy to take the scroll / and to open its seals, / because you were slaughtered, / and you purchased people / for God by your blood / from every tribe and language / and people and nation. / You made them a kingdom / and priests to our God, / and they will reign on the earth. / Blessing and honor and glory and power / be to the one seated on the throne, / and to the Lamb, forever and ever!" (Rev 4:11; 5:9–10, 13, CSB)

Repeat Antiphon (above):

Reading: ". . . [A]re you unaware that all of us who were baptized into Christ Jesus were baptized into his death? Therefore we were buried with him by baptism into death, in order that, just as Christ was raised from the dead by the glory of the Father, so we too may walk in newness of life. For if we have been united with him in the likeness of his death, we will certainly also be in the likeness of his resurrection. For we know that our old self was crucified with him so that the body ruled by sin might be rendered powerless so that we may no longer be enslaved to sin, since a person who has died is freed from sin. Now if we have died with Christ, we believe that we will also live with him, because we know that Christ, having been raised from the dead, will not die again. Death no longer rules over him. For the death he died, he died to sin once for all time; but the life he lives, he lives to God. So, you too consider yourselves dead to sin and alive to God in Christ Jesus" (Rom 6:3–11, CSB)

Reflection: Contrary to what many people think, Paul conceives of baptism as an experience of death. Ancient baptismal pools looked like graves excavated in a cemetery; there were three steps down on one end and three steps up on the other end. And the whole space was filled with water. After removing his or her clothes, the candidate for baptism stepped down into the pool, while the baptizing minister buried the person under the water. After a few seconds of drowning, the minister raised the newly baptized from the dead to newness of life. Paul understands baptism to be an experience of death, just like Jesus was crucified, died, and was entombed. But Paul also understands baptism to be an experience of resurrection, just like God raised Jesus from the dead. In Pauline thought, the old adam (mankind) goes into and under the water in the baptismal font and dies. Then, he or she is raised as the new adam, Christ. Just as Jesus will not die again, so will those who have been baptized not die again; indeed, they are living resurrected life now! They are dead to sin and alive to God in Christ Jesus.

SEASON OF EASTER

Day 34: Friday of the Fifth Week of Easter

Morning

Antiphon: "May the LORD answer you in a day of trouble; / may . . . God protect you." (Ps 20:1, CSB) Alleluia!

Psalm: "May [God] give you what your heart desires / and fulfill your whole purpose. / Let us shout for joy at your victory / and lift the banner in the name of our God. / May the LORD fulfill all your requests. / Now I know that the LORD gives victory to his anointed; / he will answer him from his holy heaven / with mighty victories from his right hand. / Some take pride in chariots, and others in horses, / but we take pride in the name of the Lord our God. / They collapse and fall, / but we rise and stand firm." (Ps 20:4–8, CSB)

Repeat Antiphon (above):

Reading: "If God is for us, who is against us? He did not even spare his own Son but gave him up for us all. How will he not also with him grant us everything? Who can bring an accusation against God's elect? God is the one who justifies. Who is the one who condemns? Christ Jesus is the one who died, but even more, has been raised; he also is at the right hand of God and intercedes for us. Who can separate us from the love of Christ? Can affliction or distress or persecution or famine or nakedness or danger or sword? No, in all these things we are more than conquerors through him who loved us. For I am persuaded that neither death nor life, nor angels nor rulers, nor things present nor things to come, nor powers, nor height nor depth, nor any other created thing will be able to separate us from the love of God that is in Christ Jesus our Lord." (Rom 8:31b—35, 37–39, CSB)

Activity: What word or phrase in the verses from Psalm 20 or Romans 8:31b–35, 37–39 gets your attention? What does the word or phrase mean? How does the word of phrase make you aware of God's presence?

Evening

Antiphon: "Restore us, God; / make your face shine on us, / so that we may be saved." (Ps 80:3, CSB) Alleluia!

Psalm: "I heard an unfamiliar language: / 'I relieved [Joseph's] shoulder from the burden; / his hands were freed from carrying the basket. You called out in distress, and I rescued you; / I answered you from the thundercloud. / Listen, my people, and I will admonish you. . . . [If[you would only listen to me! / I am the LORD your God, / who brought you

up from the land of Egypt. / Open your mouth wide, and I will fill it.'" (Ps 81:5b–7a, 8, 10, CSB)
Repeat Antiphon (above):
Reading: "The message is near you, in your mouth and in your heart. This is the message of faith that we proclaim. If you confess with your mouth, 'Jesus is Lord,' and believe in your heart that God raised him from the dead, you will be saved. One believes with the heart, resulting in righteousness, and one confesses with the mouth, resulting in salvation. For everyone who calls on the name of the Lord will be saved." (Rom 10:8b–10, 13, CSB)
Meditation/Journal: To what do you need God to restore you? Of what does faith consist for Paul in his letter to the Romans? Explain.

Day 35: Saturday of the Fifth Week of Easter

Morning
Antiphon: ". . . Jesus Christ is Lord, / to the glory of God the Father." (Phil 1:11b, CSB) Alleluia!
Canticle: "Adopt the same attitude as that of Christ Jesus, / who, existing in the form of God, / did not consider equality with God / as something to be exploited. / Instead he emptied himself / by assuming the form of a servant, / taking on the likeness of humanity. / And when he had come as a man, / he humbled himself by becoming obedient / to the point of death—/ even to death on a cross. / For this reason God highly exalted him / and gave him the name / that is above every name, / so that at the name of Jesus / every knee will bow—/ in heaven and on earth / and under the earth—/ and every tongue will confess / that Jesus Christ is Lord, / to the glory of God the Father." (Phil 2:5–11, CSB)
Repeat Antiphon (above):
Reading: "God raised up the Lord and will also raise us up by his power. Don't you know that your bodies are a part of Christ's body? . . . Anyone joined to the Lord is one spirit with him." (1 Cor 6:14–15a, 17, CSB)
Reflection/Journal/Meditation: In his letter to the Philippians, Paul exhorts his readers to adopt the attitude of Christ Jesus. Based on the ancient hymn he quotes in Philippians 2:5–11, of what would that attitude consist? In his First letter to the Corinthians, Paul reminds his readers that their bodies are a part of Christ's body through baptism, and just as God raised Jesus from the dead, he will raise from the dead all who have been baptized, who are members of the body of Christ, because they are

one spirit with him. In what specific ways do you experience being one spirit with Christ?

Evening
Antiphon: "Hallelujah! / Praise God in his sanctuary. / Praise him in his mighty expanse." (Ps 150:1, CSB) Alleluia!
Psalm: "God, the nations have invaded your inheritance, / desecrated your holy temple, / and turned Jerusalem into ruins. / They gave the corpses of your servants / to the birds of the sky for food, / the flesh of your faithful ones / to the beasts of the earth. / They poured out their blood / like water all around Jerusalem, / and there was no one to bury them. / [P]reserve those condemned to die. / Then we, your people, the sheep of your pasture, / will thank you forever; / we will declare your praise / to generation after generation" (Ps 79:1–3, 11c, 13, CSB)
Repeat Antiphon (above):
Reading: ". . . I passed on to you [, Corinthians,] as most important what I also received: that Christ died for our sins according to the Scriptures, that he was buried, that he was raised on the third day according to the Scriptures, and that he appeared to Cephas, then to the Twelve. Then he appeared to over five hundred brothers and sisters at one time, most of them are still alive, but some have fallen asleep. Then he appeared to James, then to all the apostles. Last of all, . . . he also appeared to me." (1 Cor 15:3–8, CSB)
Reflection: When Paul writes his First Letter to the Corinthians, he tells them that he is passing on to them what he had received and what he considered most important. Paul is passing on oral tradition about Jesus, as there was no written tradition earlier than Paul. The tradition that Jesus died, was entombed, and raised will become the key moments embedded in Mark's Gospel written about twenty years after Paul's writing. When Paul states that the tradition is according to the Scriptures, he is referring to what today is called the HB (OT). He cannot be referring to gospel, because the oldest, Mark's Gospel, was not written until 70 CE and Paul is writing in the early 50s CE. According to the Scriptures means that God is at work in the dying, entombment, and resurrection of Christ Jesus. Furthermore, for Paul it is not an empty-tomb story that proclaims resurrection, but the post-resurrection appearances of Christ, first to Peter (Cephas), then to a group of disciples called the Twelve (not necessarily twelve apostles), five hundred others at one time (of which there is no biblical account), his brother James, all the apostles (those

sent), and, last of all, to Paul. For Paul the multiple post-resurrection appearances confirm the resurrection. It is a useful meditation to reflect on the key events in the reader's life in which he or she has discovered Jesus (God) at work. A list of those key events stored in a journal can help recognize divine appearances.

Day 36: Sixth Sunday of Easter

Morning

Antiphon: "The LORD is good to everyone; / his compassion rests on all he has made." (Ps 145:9, CSB) Alleluia!

Psalm: "The LORD is great and is highly praised; / his greatness is unsearchable. / One generation will declare your works to the next / and will proclaim your mighty acts. / I will speak of your splendor and glorious majesty / and your wondrous works. / They will proclaim the power of your awe-inspiring acts, / and I will declare your greatness. / They will give a testimony of your goodness / and will joyfully sing of your righteousness." (Ps 145:3–7, CSB)

Repeat Antiphon (above):

Reading: "Now if Christ is proclaimed as raised from the dead, how can some of you say, 'There is no resurrection of the dead'? If there is no resurrection of the dead, then not even Christ has been raised; and if Christ has not been raised, then our proclamation is in vain, and so is your faith. Moreover, we are found to be false witnesses about God, because we have testified wrongly about God that he raised up Christ—whom he did not raise up, if in fact the dead are not raised. For if the dead are not raised, not even Christ has been raised. And if Christ has not been raised, your faith is worthless; you are still in your sins. Those, then, who have fallen asleep in Christ have also perished. If we have put our hope in Christ for this life only, we should be pitied more than anyone." (1 Cor 15:12–19, CSB)

Reflection: In chapter 15 of his First Letter to the Corinthians, Paul begins by accepting the truth that God raised Christ (anointed) from the dead. The resurrection is kerygma, the proclamation, the basis of the Christian message. Some people may have doubts about Christ not having been raised. Why? Because human experience dictates that once a person has died, he or she remains dead. Thus, the proclamation that God raised Christ from the dead is preposterous, because it contradicts basic, human experience. If the resurrection is denied in general, it eliminates

Christ's resurrection in particular. Not only is Paul's credibility at stake, because he has been preaching resurrection, but the credibility of faith is at stake, too. Basic Pauline faith is that Jesus died, and God raised Christ from the dead! If that is not true, then there are three consequences: faith is worthless, those who have died have perished, and pity is all that is left for those who put their hope in Christ for eternal life. But, using the verses of Psalm 145, the LORD, whose greatness is unsearchable by humans, deserves great praise for raising Christ from the dead. One generation passes on the truth of God's mighty act of resurrection to the next generation, which will find it awe-inspiring and worthy of the testimony about God's goodness and righteousness.

Evening
Antiphon: "Our God is a God of salvation, / and escape from death belongs to the LORD my Lord." (Ps 68:20, CSB) Alleluia!
Psalm: "Remember how short my life is [, LORD]. / Have you created everyone for nothing? / What courageous person can live and never see death? / Who can save himself from the power of Sheol? / Blessed be the LORD forever. / Amen and amen." (Ps 89:47–48, 52, CSB)
Repeat Antiphon (above):
Reading: ". . . Christ has been raised from the dead, the firstfruits of those who have fallen asleep. For since death came through a man, the resurrection of the dead also comes through a man. For just as in Adam all die, so also in Christ all will be made alive." (1 Cor 15:20–22, CSB)
Reflection: In Pauline thought, the first man, Adam (man) brought death into the world through his disobedience to God, as narrated in Genesis (3:1–24). The second Adam (Christ) brought resurrection through his obedience to God. Since all people die because of Adam, all people live because of Christ. In other words, just like the first Adam (man) was the beginning of something new, so the new Adam (Christ) was the beginning of something new. The old-new Adam dichotomy is best seen in Paul's understanding of baptism. People remove their clothes, like Adam wore no clothes, and descend three steps into the baptism pool, in the shape of a grave, in whose water they are plunged under to represent death. Once someone raises them from the water, they walk up three steps, looking like the new Adam; they have died and have been raised. Now, they look like Christ and share in eternal life. The first man to be raised from the dead was Christ; he is like the first picking of apples. He

is the first man to be raised from the dead; he becomes a pattern not only for baptism, but for all who die as members of his body.

Day 37: Monday of the Sixth Week of Easter

Morning
Antiphon: "... [T]he faithful shall abide with [the LORD] in love: / Because grace and mercy are with his holy ones, / and his care is with his elect." (Wis 3:9bcd, NAB) Alleluia!
Canticle: "... [T]he souls of the just are in the hand of God, / and no torment shall touch them. / They seemed, in the view of the foolish, to be dead; / and their passing away was thought an affliction / and their going forth from us, utter destruction. / But they are in peace. / For if before men [and women], indeed, they be punished, / yet is their hope full of immortality. / In the time of their visitation they shall shine, / and shall dart about as sparks through stubble." (Wis 3:1–4, 7, NAB)
Repeat Antiphon (above):
Reading: "... [S]omeone will ask, 'How are the dead raised? What kind of body will they have when they come?' You fool! What you sow does not come to life unless it dies. And as for what you sow—you are not sowing the body that will be, but only a seed, perhaps of wheat or another grain. But God gives it a body as he wants, and to each of the seeds its own body." (1 Cor 15:35–38, CSB)
Meditation/Journal: What connection do you find between the verses from the (OT) A book of Wisdom and the CB (NT) First Letter of Paul to the Corinthians 15:35–38?

Evening
Antiphon: "My lips will shout for joy / when I sing praise to you [, LORD,] / because you have redeemed me." (Ps 71:23, CSB) Alleluia!
Psalm: "The LORD will send his faithful love by day; / his song will be with me in the night—/ a prayer to the God of my life. / But you, LORD, be gracious to me and raise me up . . . . By this I know that you delight in me . . . . (Ps 42:8, 10a, 11a, CSB)
Repeat Antiphon (above):
Reading: "So it is with the resurrection of the dead: Sown in corruption, raised in incorruption; sown in dishonor, raised in glory; sown in weakness, raised in power, sown a natural body, raised a spiritual body.

If there is a natural body, there is also a spiritual body." (1 Cor 15:42–44, CSB)
Reflection: In his First Letter to the Corinthians, Paul employs the metaphor of seeds to explain what cannot be explained: resurrection. Every seed has a body unique to its species; after a seed is sown in the soil, it sprouts. Leaves appear, it grows into whatever it is supposed to be. Into what it grows is determined by its origin. Thus, an apple seed grows into an apple tree. Paul applies that understanding to resurrection. The human body is like a seed that must die or perish before it can grow into what God wants it to be. Once the human body dies, it is entombed or buried, just like one buries a seed. In other words, it is sown in corruption, but it is raised incorruptible. There is nothing more dishonorable than a decaying body, but it is raised to glory—brightness, radiance. Weakness characterizes the physical body, but power will characterize the raised body. In other words, what is entombed or buried is a physical body; what will be raised is a spiritual body, a raised body. Paul cannot know what a spiritual body is because he had not died and been raised. Only one person ever died and was raised: Christ Jesus. Because people attested seeing him after his death and resurrection, Paul presumes that there must be a spiritual body. Like there are different forms of life for seeds before and after burial, there are forms of life for people before and after entombment or burial. For Paul, a spiritual body—whatever that is—describes what resurrection is like on the other side of death.

Day 38: Tuesday of the Sixth Week of Easter
Morning
Antiphon: "God looks down from heaven on the human race / to see if there is one who is wise, / one who seeks God" (Ps 53:2, CSB) Alleluia!
Canticle: "God of my fathers [and mothers], LORD of mercy, / you who have made all things by your word / And in your wisdom have established man [and woman] / to rule the creatures produced by you, / To govern the world in holiness and justice, . . . / Give me Wisdom, the attendant at your throne . . . ." (Wis 9:1–3a, 4a, NAB)
Repeat Antiphon (above):
Reading: "The first man Adam became a living being; the last Adam became a life-giving spirit. However, the spiritual is not first, but the natural, then the spiritual. The first man was from the earth, a man of dust; the second man is from heaven. Like the man of dust, so are those who

are of the dust; like the man of heaven, so are those who are of heaven. And just as we have borne the image of the man of dust, we will also bear the image of the man of heaven." (1 Cor 15:47–49, CSB)

Reflection: In Pauline thought, as found in Paul's First Letter to the Corinthians, the apostle draws parallels between the first man, named Adam, and what he calls the last or second man, Christ Jesus. The first Adam received life when God breathed the breath (spirit) of life into him; the last or second Adam became a life-giving spirit; Christ gives resurrection. All human beings (along with animals) share Adam's dust; what is left after entombment or burial is dust. The last or second man comes from heaven, above the dome of the sky, where God lives. Those who have been baptized into Christ will one day be brought to resurrected life in the kingdom of God by breathing Christ's life-giving Spirit. Paul concludes his parallel between Adam and Christ by telling the Corinthians that just as they have looked like the man of dust, Adam, so they will also one day look like the man of heaven, Christ. First, they are natural—dusty—and, second, they will be spiritual (of the spirit).

Evening

Antiphon: "Consider me and answer, LORD my God. / Restore brightness to my eyes; / otherwise, I will sleep in death." (Ps 13:3, CSB) Alleluia!

Canticle: "Court not death by your erring way of life, / nor draw to yourselves destruction by the works of your hands. / Because God did not make death, / nor does he rejoice in the destruction of the living. / For he fashioned all things that they might have being; / and the creatures of the world are wholesome, / And there is not a destructive drug among them / nor any domain of the nether world on earth . . . ." (Wis 1:12–14, NAB)

Repeat Antiphon (above):

Reading: "Listen, I am telling you a mystery. We will not all fall asleep, but we will all be changed, in a moment, in the twinkling of an eye, at the last trumpet. For the trumpet will sound, and the dead will be raised incorruptible, and we will be changed. For this corruptible body must be clothed with incorruptibility, and this mortal body must be clothed with immortality." (1 Cor 15:51–53, CSB)

Points to Ponder: First, according to the author of the OT (A) book of Wisdom, God did not make death; God breathed the breath of life into people. Second, God does not rejoice in the destruction of the living; Jesus declared that God "is not the God of the dead but of the living" (Mark 12:27; Luke 20:38, CSB) Third, God fashioned all things to have being, existence—to have a share in divine existence. Fourth, Paul does not think that all his readers will die before Jesus returns; Paul thinks that he will be alive when Jesus returns in glory. People don't like hearing this, but Paul was wrong; the last trumpet has not sounded and the dead have not been raised. Fifth, what Paul was correct about is being changed. Transformation is a way of life for those who follow Jesus. They are always in the process of dying and rising; that process began with dying in the baptismal pool and being raised to new life from it. During the Season of Easter, people focus on living their transformed way of life.

Day 39: Wednesday of the Sixth Week of Easter

Morning

Antiphon: "What gain is there in my death [, LORD]: / If I go down to the Pit? / Will the dust praise you? / Will it proclaim your truth? (Ps 30:9, CSB) Alleluia!

Canticle: "Now with you [, God,] is Wisdom, who knows your works / and was present when you made the world; / Who understands what is pleasing in your eyes / and what is conformable with your commands. / Send her forth from your holy heavens / and from your glorious throne dispatch her / That she may be with me and work with me, / that I may know what is your pleasure. / For she knows and understands all things, / and will guide me discreetly in my affairs / and safeguard me by her glory . . . ." (Wis 9:9–11, NAB)

Repeat Antiphon (above):

Reading: "When this corruptible body is clothed with incorruptibility, and this mortal body is clothed with immortality, then the saying that is written will take place: / Death has been swallowed up in victory. / Where, death, is your victory? / Where, death, is your sting? / The sting of death is sin, and the power of sin is the law. But thanks be to God, who gives us the victory through our Lord Jesus Christ!" (1 Cor 15:54–57, CSB)

Points to Ponder: Frist, the Pauline understanding of what the first Adam (man) did and what the second man did are summarized in First Corinthians (15:54–57). Second, the first Adam introduced death's sting (corruptibility, mortality), sin, and law; the second man, Christ Jesus, introduced victory (incorruptibility, immortality), forgiveness of sin, and brought the law to fulfillment or completion. Third, all that was accomplished by God, who raised Jesus Christ from the dead, giving him victory over death. Fourth, using the verses of the OT (A) book of Wisdom (9:9–11), one can say that God dispatched Wisdom from his throne to reveal his work and to make known his pleasure. Wisdom guides whoever calls upon her and safeguards them with her glory.

Evening

Antiphon: ". . . [God] stands at the right hand of the needy / to save him [her] from those who would condemn him [her]." (Ps 109:31, CSB) Alleluia!

Canticle: "[Wisdom] gave the holy ones the recompense of their labors, / Conducted them by a wondrous road, / and became a shelter for them by day / and a starry flame by night. / . . . [God,] you have mercy on all, because you can do all things . . . . / For you love all things that are / and loathe nothing that you have made; / for what you hated, you would not have fashioned. / And how could a thing remain, unless you willed it; / or be preserved, had it not been called forth by you? / But you spare all things, because they are yours, O LORD and lover of souls, / for your imperishable spirit is in all things!" (Wis 10:17; 11:23a, 24–26; 12:1, NAB)

Repeat Antiphon (above):

Reading: ". . . [S]ince we have the same spirit of faith in keeping with what is written, I believed, therefore I spoke, we also believe, and therefore speak. For we know that the one who raised the Lord Jesus will also raise us with Jesus and present us with you [, Corinthians]. Indeed, everything is for your benefit so that, as grace extends through more and more people, it may cause thanksgiving to increase to the glory of God." (2 Cor 4:13–15, CSB)

Points to Ponder: First, in his Second Letter to the Corinthians, Paul writes about the spirit of faith, the capacity to believe; those who believe had heard the message, and they speak it so others will believe. Paul includes himself among those who have heard, believed, and now speak the good news to the Corinthians. Second, Paul is confident that God, who raised Jesus from the dead, will do the same for Paul and the Corinthians; in other words, the hope and faith are strong for Paul and among the Corinthians. Third, the Corinthians benefit from the grace that Paul has shared with them. In Pauline thought, grace is not a thing; grace is the act of God sharing himself with people. As God shares grace, people speak (extend) what they have received with others. The sharing doesn't stop. As one person shares his or her God-given grace (spirit of faith) with others, thanksgiving arises in the recipients to God, and it keeps increasing.

Day 40a: Ascension of the Lord

In some places, the Ascension of the Lord is moved to the Seventh Sunday of Easter. If that is the case, then go to Day 40b: Thursday of the Sixth Week of Easter. If today is Ascension, use the following Morning Prayer and Evening Prayer.

Morning
Antiphon: "God arises." (Ps 68:1a, CSB) Alleluia!
Psalm: "God, when you went out before your people, / when you marched through the desert, / the earth trembled and the skies poured rain / before God.... / Mount Bashan is God's towering mountain; / Mount Bashan is a mountain of many peaks. / Why gaze with envy, you mountain peaks, / at the mountain God desired for his abode? / The LORD will dwell there forever! / You ascended to the heights, taking away captives; / you received gifts from people, / even from the rebellious, / so that the LORD God might dwell there." (Ps 68:7–8b, 15–16, 18, CSB)
Repeat Antiphon (above):
Reading: "[Jesus] led [the Eleven and those with them] to the vicinity of Bethany, and lifting up his hands he blessed them. And while he was blessing them, he left them and was carried up into heaven. After worshiping him, they returned to Jerusalem with great joy. And they were continually in the temple praising God." (Luke 24:50–53, CSB)
Reflection: The context of the passage from Luke's Gospel (24:50–53) is the first day of the week, what we would call Easter Sunday. The author of Luke's Gospel ends his narrative with the account of the ascension of Jesus, which works as long as a person thinks of the world as constructed of three levels. God on the top level became incarnate on the middle level as Jesus of Nazareth; after he died and was raised on the middle level, he returned to the top level from where he came. For the author of Luke's Gospel, resurrection differs little from ascension. Many images and icons depicting the ascension feature a group of disciples gathered around Jesus being lifted into the sky like a rocket. In some images, only his feet are in the picture, since the rest of him is up and away! As will be noted below for Evening Prayer, the author of Luke's Gospel wrote a second narrative of the ascension, the one with which many people are familiar, in the Acts of the Apostles. That version of the ascension takes place forty days after Easter. In the modern world, one way to grasp this narrative is to consider it as an enthronement statement. The risen Jesus in his non-bodily body is seated next to his God and Father.

Evening
Antiphon: "The LORD will fulfill his purpose for me. / LORD, your faithful love endures forever." (Ps 139:8ab, CSB) Alleluia!
Psalm: "Where can I go to escape your Spirit [, LORD]? / Where can I flee from your presence? / If I go up to heaven, you are there. / If I make my bed in Sheol, you are there. / If I fly on the wings of the dawn / and settle down on the western horizon, / even there your hand will lead me; / your right hand will hold on to me. / If I say, 'Surely the darkness will hide me, / and the light around me will be night'—/ even the darkness is not dark to you. / The night shines like the day; / darkness and light are alike to you." (Ps 139:7-12, CSB)
Repeat Antiphon (above):
Reading: "After [Jesus] had suffered, he ... presented himself alive to [the apostles] by many convincing proofs, appearing to them over a period of forty days and speaking about the kingdom of God. . . . [H]e was taken up as [the apostles] were watching, and a cloud took him out of their sight. While he was going, they were gazing into heaven, and suddenly two men in white clothes stood by them." (Acts 1:3, 9-10, CSB)
Points to Ponder: First, whoever the author of Luke's Gospel is, he is also the author of the Acts of the Apostles. He indicates this (Luke 1:1-4; Acts 1:1-3). Second, in his gospel, he states that the ascension occurred on Easter Sunday evening (Luke 24:50-53), but in his second volume, the Acts of the Apostles, he states that it occurred forty days after Easter (Acts 1:3). Thus, ascension is not an historical event, but a theological one based on a three-storied or three-level cosmology. The Jesus, who lived on the top story became incarnate by the power of the Holy Spirit on the middle story and returns to the top story (except in Matthew's Gospel, where he promises to be present until the end of time [Matt 28:20]). Third, the two men in dazzling clothes, who appear to the women at the tomb (Luke 24:4) reappear at the ascension (Acts 1:10) to connect the two narratives theologically; in other words, for this author both resurrection and ascension are transcendent experiences. Fourth, the latter point is confirmed by the presence of a cloud that takes Jesus out of the sight of the apostles (Acts 1:9). A biblical cloud is a sign of divine presence (Exod 19:9; 24:15-18; 34:5; 40:34; Luke 1:35; 9:34). Fifth, unique to Luke's Gospel is the topic of discussion between Jesus, Moses, and Elijah in the transfiguration narrative: "his departure, which he was about to accomplish in Jerusalem" (Luke 9:31). The word translated into English as *departure* is *exodus* in Hebrew. Thus, in the

Acts, Jesus accomplishes his departure from the middle level and is exalted by God to the top level (Acts 7:56).

Day 40b: Thursday of the Sixth Week of Easter

When Ascension is moved to the following Sunday, the following Morning Prayer and Evening Prayer are used on Day 40 of the Season of Easter.

Morning
Antiphon: "Clap your hands, all you peoples; / shout to God with a jubilant cry." (Ps 47:1, CSB) Alleluia!
Psalm: ". . . [T]he LORD, the Most High, is awe-inspiring / a great King over the whole earth. / God ascends among shouts of joy, / the LORD with the sound of a ram's horn. / Sing praise to God, sing praise; / sing praise to our King, sing praise! / Sing a song of wisdom, / for God is King of the whole earth." (Ps 47:2, 5–7, CSB)
Repeat Antiphon (above):
Reading: "Long ago God spoke to our ancestors by the prophets at different times and in different ways. In these last days, he has spoken to us by his Son. God has appointed him heir of all things and made the universe through him. The Son is the radiance of God's glory and the exact expression of his nature, sustaining all things by his powerful word. After making purification for sins, he sat down at the right hand of the Majesty on high. So he became superior to the angels, just as the name he inherited is more excellent than theirs." (Heb 1:1–4, CSB)
Reflection: While it is called the letter to the Hebrews, the CB (NT) book bearing that name is misnamed; it is a treatise, sermon, or homily on the high priesthood of Jesus. Most likely, in the history of collecting and transmission this document was placed to the back of a collection of Paul's letters. When a copyist began making another copy of Paul's letters, he found this document and considered it another letter of Paul. While it used to be known as Paul's Letter to the Hebrews, biblical scholarship has demonstrated that Paul didn't write it, and it is not a letter. Nevertheless, it is a CB (NT) document, beginning with God speaking through prophets in the past, but then speaking through a Son, Jesus, appointed by God to be heir of all things and through whom the worlds were or the universe was created. Drawing upon the words of the HB (OT) book of Genesis about God creating man as a living being (Gen 2:7), the author of Hebrews states that Jesus is the reflection of God's glory and the imprint

of his very being; this means that he sustains everything by his powerful word. In other words, if one wants to see God, he or she can do so by looking at Jesus, who is superior to angel messengers, often presented biblically as God in disguise.

Evening
Antiphon: "The earth and everything in it, / the world and its inhabitants, / belong to the LORD." (Ps 24:1, CSB) Alleluia!
Psalm: "Who may ascend the mountain of the LORD? / Who may stand in his holy place? / The one who has clean hands and a pure heart, / who has not appealed to what is false, / and who has not sworn deceitfully. / He [or she] will receive blessing from the LORD, / and righteousness from the God of his [or her] salvation. / Such is the generation of those who inquire of him, / who seek the face of . . . God. / Lift up your heads, you gates! / Rise up, ancient doors! / Who is this King of glory? / The LORD, strong and mighty . . . ." (Ps 24:3–8b, CSB)
Repeat Antiphon (above):
Reading: ". . . [T]he Lord Jesus, after speaking to [the Eleven], was taken up into heaven and sat down at the right hand of God. And they went out and preached everywhere, while the Lord worked with them and confirmed the word by the accompanying signs." (Mark 16:19–20, CSB)
Reflection: In the history of transmission of the text of Mark's Gospel, various scribes added endings to it, because they did not like the original ending about the women leaving Jesus' tomb and saying nothing to anyone (Mark 16:8). If they said nothing to anyone, from where comes the empty tomb story? Biblical scholars are convinced that the original gospel ended at 16:8 with the conundrum parabolically intact. Someone added several sentences to that verse, which, if printed in Bibles, bears the subhead of the shorter ending of Mark's Gospel. Another scribe added another ending, Mark 16:9–20, known as the longer ending of Mark's Gospel, which is composed from the endings of Matthew (28:19), Luke (24:50–53) and Acts (1:1–11). The scribe who added the longer ending, from which the above reading is taken, did not remember that the Markan Jesus explicitly stated that no sign would be given (Mark 8:12) because he writes about accompanying signs. The three endings of Mark's Gospel is a good example of what happens when scribes copy manuscripts, which was the standard procedure before the invention of the printing press and then the copy machine! Scribes often got carried away while copying a manuscript, sometimes adding words to clarify something, omitting

words that were confusing, or even adding sentences and paragraphs to conclude the document in a better way.

Day 41: Friday of the Sixth Week of Easter

Morning
Antiphon: "Blessed be the LORD, my rock...." (Ps 144:1a, CSB) Alleluia!
Psalm: "LORD, part your heavens and come down. / Touch the mountains, and they will smoke. / Flash your lightning . . . ; / shoot your arrows . . . . / Reach down from on high; / rescue me . . . , and set me free . . . . / God, I will sing a new song to you; / I will play on a ten-stringed harp for you . . . ." (Ps 144:5–7b, 9, CSB)
Repeat Antiphon (above):
Reading: "Paul, an apostle . . . by Jesus Christ and God the Father who raised him from the dead . . . [t]o the churches of Galatia. Grace to you and peace from God the Father and our Lord Jesus Christ, who gave himself for our sins to rescue us . . . , according to the will of our God and Father. To him be the glory forever and ever. Amen." (Gal 1:1–5, CSB)
Activity: From the verses of Psalm 144 and Galatians 1:1–5, choose a word that ties them together. What does the word mean? How does it make you aware of God's presence?

Evening
Antiphon: [God, "l]et your hand be with the man at your right hand, / with the son of man / you have made strong for yourself." (Ps 80:17, CSB) Alleluia!
Canticle: ". . . [T[he souls of the just are in the hand of God, / and no torment shall touch them. / They seemed, in the view of the foolish, to be dead; / and their passing away was thought an affliction / and their going forth from us, utter destruction. / But they are in peace. / Those who trust in [the LORD] shall understand truth, / and the faithful shall abide with him in love; / Because grace and mercy are with his holy ones, / and his care is with his elect." (Wis 3:1–3, 9, NAB)
Repeat Antiphon (above):
Reading: "[God] exercised [his] power in Christ by raising him from the dead and seating him at his right hand in the heavens . . . . And he subjected everything under his feet and appointed him as head over everything for the church, which is his body, the fullness of the one who fills all things in every way." (Eph 1:20, 22–23, CSB)

Reflection: In biblical understanding, the right hand is the place of power, and the left hand is the place of weakness. In Latin, the right hand is *dexter*, and the left hand is *sinister*. *Dexter* contributes to the English language with *dexterity* (strength) and *ambidextrous* (two right hands). *Sinister* contributes to the English language with *sinister*, evil in some way, powerless. That is why the psalmist asks God to use his hand to strengthen the man at his right hand (Ps 80:17). That is also why the author of the OT (A) book of Wisdom states that the spirits of the just are in the hand of God. It is also why the author of the CB (NT) letter to the Ephesians writes about God exercising his power in Christ by raising him from the dead and seating him at his right hand, the place of power. With its lofty language, the author of Ephesians displays the meaning of God's right hand; the risen Christ is not only seated on a throne to the right of God's throne in the heavens, but God has subjected everything to him—biblically placing everything under his feet—and made him head of the church, which is also his body. Like God, the risen Christ possesses the fullness of the divinity of God, who fills all things in every way. The basic idea of being baptized into the body of Christ is genuinely from Paul, but the headship of the church is the addition of the author of Ephesians for the next generation of Pauline readers.

Day 42: Saturday of the Sixth Week of Easter

Morning

Antiphon: "... [T]he age that is honorable comes not with the passing of time, / nor can it be measured in terms of years. / Rather, understanding is the hoary crown for men [and women], / and an unsullied life, the attainment of old age." (Wis 4:8–9, NAB) Alleluia!

Canticle: "... [T]he just live forever, / and in the LORD is their recompense, / and the thought of them is with the Most High. / Therefore shall they receive the splendid crown, / the beauteous diadem, from the hand of the LORD—/ For he shall shelter them with his right hand, / and protect them with his arm. / He shall take his zeal for armor .... / He shall don justice for a breastplate / and shall wear sure judgment for a helmet; / He shall take invincible rectitude as a shield.... / Well-aimed shafts of lightings shall go forth / and from the clouds as from a well-drawn bow shall leap to the mark...." (Wis 5:15–16, 17a, 18–19a, 21, NAB)

Repeat Antiphon (above):

SEASON OF EASTER

Reading: "... [T]he entire fullness of God's nature dwells bodily in Christ, and you have been filled by him, who is the head over every ruler and authority. You were also circumcised in him with a circumcision not done with hands, but putting off the body of flesh, in the circumcision of Christ, when you were buried with him in baptism, in which you were also raised with him from the dead." (Col 2:9–12, CSB)
Activity: In the Antiphon, the author of the OT (A) book of Wisdom redefines old age as understanding and an unsullied life. In the Canticle, the author of the OT (A) book of Wisdom presents the LORD as a great warrior defending the just, who live forever. In the Reading from the CB (NT) book of Colossians, the author defines baptism as circumcision. Which of those three images get most of your attention? How does the image make your aware of God's presence?

Evening
Antiphon: "... [T]he just man [or woman], though he [or she] die early, shall be at rest." (Wis 4:7, NAB) Alleluia!
Canticle: "He [She] who pleased God was loved .... / Having become perfect in a short while, / he [she] reached the fullness of a long career; / for his [her] soul was pleasing to the LORD .... / But the people saw and did not understand .... / For they see the death of the wise man [woman] / and do not understand what the LORD intended for him [her], / or why he made him [her] secure." (Wis 4:10, 13–14ac, 17, NAB)
Repeat Antiphon (above):
Reading: "... [I]f you have been raised with Christ, seek the things above, where Christ is seated at the right hand of God. Set your minds on things above, not on earthly things. For you died, and your life is hidden with Christ in God. When Christ, who is your life, appears, then you also will appear with him in glory." (Col 3:1–4, CSB)
Activity: Choose an idea you like from the verses of the OT (A) book of Wisdom or from the verses from chapter 3 of the letter to the Colossians and reflect or meditate on it. For example, the author of Wisdom reflects on the one who pleased God and was loved by God. How have you pleased God? How have you experience God's love?

Day 43a: Ascension of the Lord

If today is the Ascension of the Lord, use 40a. If today is the Seventh Sunday of Easter, use 43b.

Day 43b: Seventh Sunday of Easter

Morning

Antiphon: "Blessed are you, and praiseworthy, O Lord, the God of our fathers [and mothers], and glorious forever is your name." (Dan 3:26 [Sg Three 1:3], NAB) Alleluia!

Canticle: O Lord, "[d]o not take away your mercy from us, / for the sake of Abraham, your beloved, / Isaac your servant, and Israel your holy one, / To whom you promised to multiply their offspring / like the stars of heaven, / or the sand on the shore of the sea. / Do not let us be put to shame, / but deal with us in your kindness and great mercy. / Deliver us by your wonders, / and bring glory to your name, O Lord." (Dan 3:35, 42–43 [Sg Three 1:12–13, 19–20], NAB)

Repeat Antiphon (above):

Reading: "By faith Abraham, when he was tested, offered up Isaac. He received the promises and yet he was offering his one and only son, the one to whom it had been said, Your offspring will be traced through Isaac. He considered God to be able even to raise someone from the dead; therefore, he received him back, figuratively speaking." (Heb 11:17–19, CSB)

Reflection: The passage from the CB (NT) Letter to the Hebrews illustrates the verses from the Canticle from the prophet Daniel, commonly called the Prayer or Song of Azariah and the Song of the Three Jews. The author of Hebrews reflects on the faith of the ancients. He attributes faith—"the reality of what is hoped for, the proof of what is not seen" (Heb 11:1)—to Abraham, to whom God had promised numerous descendants. After a long wait without a son, Sarah and Abraham became pregnant in their older years; in other words, God showed mercy to them. However, God also called Abraham to take his only son, slaughter him, and offer him as a sacrifice to God. Abraham was ready with the knife to kill his son, when God grabbed his hand and stopped him. Abraham's willingness to kill the son through whom God would fulfill his promise to provide Abraham with many descendants is, according to the author of Hebrews, faith that God could raise Isaac from the dead. After God stopped the patriarch from slaughtering Isaac, the author of Hebrews states that Abraham received back Isaac, as if he had been raised from the dead. In other words, Isaac was as good as dead, but God raised him to life by giving him back to his father, Abraham. God showed mercy both to Abraham and to Isaac.

SEASON OF EASTER

Evening
Antiphon: "Blessed are you, O Lord, the God of our fathers [and mothers], / praiseworthy and exalted above all forever; / And blessed is your holy and glorious name, / praiseworthy and exalted above all for all ages." (Dan 3:52 [Sg Three 1:29–30], NAB) Alleluia!
Canticle: "Blessed are you who look into the depths / from your throne upon the cherubim, / praiseworthy and exalted above all forever. / Blessed are you in the firmament of heaven, / praiseworthy and glorious forever." (Dan 3:55–56 [Sg Three 1:32, 34], NAB)
Repeat Antiphon (above):
Reading: "If you appeal to the Father who judges impartially according to each one's work, you are to conduct yourselves in reverence during your time living as strangers. For you know that you were redeemed from your empty way of life inherited from your ancestors, not with perishable things like silver or gold, but with the precious blood of Christ, like that of an unblemished and spotless lamb. He was foreknown before the foundation of the world but was revealed in these last times for you. Through him you believe in God, who raised him from the dead and gave him glory, so that your faith and hope are in God." (1 Pet 1:17–21, CSB)
Points to Ponder: First, the Canticle reflects two places where God was located in the ancient world. He could be found in the Jerusalem Temple sitting on his throne, cherubim with wings stretched over the ark of the covenant. He could also be located on the first level of the three-level universe, referred to as the firmament of heaven. No matter where God was located, he could see into the depths. Second, the author of the First Letter of Peter in the CB (NT) urges his readers to be reverent during their time of sojourn on earth. The reverence should spring from their awareness that they were redeemed by the blood of Christ shed on the cross. Third, Jesus' death was a Passover sacrifice. Like the Passover lamb, he was unblemished and spotless. Even though he existed since before God created the world, he was not known until now. Fourth, through Christ, people have come to faith in God, who raised Christ from the dead and shared his glory with him. Fifth, because Peter's readers believe that God raised Jesus from the dead, their faith and hope are centered in God. People have access to God, who is not located in any place, but whose presence fills the universe.

Day 44: Monday of the Seventh Week of Easter

Morning
Antiphon: "Give thanks to the Lord, for he is good, / for his mercy endures forever." (Dan 3:89 [Sg Three 1:67], NAB) Alleluia!
Canticle: "You sons [and daughters] of men [and women] bless the Lord; / praise and exalt him above all forever. / Servants of the Lord, bless the Lord; / praise and exalt him above all forever. / Spirits and souls of the just, bless the Lord; / praise and exalt him above all forever." (Dan 3:82, 85–86 [Sg Three 1:60, 63–65], NAB)
Repeat Antiphon (above):
Reading: Jesus said to the Sadducees: ". . . [A]s for the dead being raised—haven't you read in the book of Moses, in the passage about the burning bush how God said to him: I am the God of Abraham and the God of Isaac and the God of Jacob? He is not the God of the dead but of the living." (Mark 12:26–27a, CSB)
Reflection: According to the Markan Jesus, the resurrection of the dead can be found in the HB (OT) book of Exodus in the passage where Moses meets God in the burning bush (Exod 3:1–6). God tells Moses that he is the God of the patriarchs, who have been dead for years, but who are alive in God, who is not the God of the dead but of the living. The full impact of that Markan Jesus' statement cannot be felt until one is aware that the Sadducees, one of many Jewish groups at the time of Jesus, do not believe in the resurrection. In other words, with his words, the Markan Jesus slams their belief structure. The dead do not pass out of existence; they remain alive in God, who raises them to new life. Nothing that God made ever goes out of existence; like energy, they are changed. The consequences apply not only to people, but they apply to every created thing. God cannot let any kind of life bow and exit; it came from him and it returns to him, and he keeps it alive. Pet dogs, cats, fish, etc. once alive remain alive in some form. That is why the author of the song sung by the three Jews in the fiery furnace exhorts all spirits and souls of the just to bless the Lord, that is, to praise and exalt him above all forever.

Evening
Antiphon: O Lord, ", . . blessed is your holy and glorious name, / praiseworthy and exalted above all for all ages." (Dan 3:52cd [Sg Three 1:30], NAB) Alleluia!
Canticle: ". . . [B]less the Lord; / praise and exalt him above all forever. / For he has delivered us from the nether world, / and saved us from the

power of death; / He has freed us from the raging flame / and delivered us from the fire. / Give thanks to the Lord, for he is good, / for his mercy endures forever. / Bless the God of gods, all you who fear the Lord; / praise him and give him thanks, / because his mercy endures forever." (Dan 3:88–90 [Sg Three 1:66–68], NAB)
Repeat Antiphon (above):
Reading: Jesus said to the Pharisees: "You are mistaken, because you don't know the Scriptures or the power of God. Now concerning the resurrection of the dead, haven't you read what was spoken to you by God: I am the God of Abraham and the God of Isaac and the God of Jacob. He is not the God of the dead, but of the living." (Matt 22:29, 31–32, CSB)
Reflection: Jesus' encounter with the Sadducees in the CB (NT) Gospel of Matthew has been taken from Mark (12:26–27a) and slightly adapted by the author for his audience. The message remains that God is the God of the living. The patriarchs are alive in him. In the words of the Canticle from the HB (OT) book of Daniel—known as the Song of Azariah and the three Jews in the OT (A)—God delivers from the nether world, another name for Sheol, the lowest level of a three-level universe. God saves people from the power of death; people on the middle level of the universe (earth) call it resurrection. Therefore, it behooves the living to give thanks to the good God, whose mercy extends throughout the universe and endures forever. In other words, every human deserves eternal death, but God rescues all for eternal life. And there is nothing any person can do to earn or achieve it; all people can do is accept such a gift with grace and praise.

Day 45: Tuesday of the Seventh Week of Easter

Morning
Antiphon: "LORD, I have heard the report about you; / LORD, I stand in awe of your deeds. / Revive your work in these years; / make it known in these years. / . . . [R[emember mercy! (Hab 3:2, CSB) Alleluia!
Canticle: "[God's] splendor covers the heavens, / and the earth is full of his praise. / His brilliance is like light; / rays are flashing from his hand. / This is where his power is hidden. / You come out to save your people, / to save your anointed. / Though the fig tree does not bud / and there is no fruit on the vines, / though the olive crop fails / and the fields produce no food, / though the flocks disappear from the pen / and there are no herds in the stalls, / yet I will celebrate in the LORD; / I will rejoice in the God of my salvation!" (Hab 3:3b–4, 13a, 17–18, CSB)

Repeat Antiphon (above):
Reading: Jesus said to the Sadducees, "who say there is no resurrection: . . . '[T]hose who are counted worthy to take part in that age and in the resurrection from the dead . . . can no longer die, because they are children of the resurrection. Moses even indicated in the passage about the burning bush that the dead are raised, where he calls the Lord the God of Abraham and the God of Isaac and the God of Jacob. He is not the God of the dead but of the living, because all are living to him.'" (Luke 20:27, 35–38, CSB)
Reflection: The author of Luke's Gospel took the passage he found in Mark (12:12:24–27) and adapted it for his audience. God is one who saves, as the writer of the HB (OT) book of Daniel makes clear. God saves by delivering from the nether world, otherwise known as Sheol. He saves from the power of death. He saves out of his abundant mercy, which endures forever. The LORD is the God of the living, and all who live exist to/for/in him. Using images from ancient culture, the psalmist puts his trust in the LORD to save him, even if there are no figs, no grapes, no olives, no crops, no flocks, and no herds. Nothing can shake one's trust in the LORD.

Evening
Antiphon: "Hallelujah!" (Ps 149:9c, CSB)
Psalm: "Answer me quickly LORD; / my spirit fails. / Let me experience / your faithful love in the morning, / for I trust in you. / Reveal to me the way I should go / because I appeal to you. / Teach me to do your will, / for you are my God. / May your gracious Spirit / lead me on level ground." (Ps 143:7ab, 8, 10 CSB)
Repeat Antiphon (above):
Reading: ". . . [Jesus] rejoiced in the Holy Spirit and said, 'I praise you, Father, Lord of heaven and earth, because you have hidden these things from the wise and intelligent and revealed them to infants. Yes, Father, because this was your good pleasure. All things have been entrusted to me by my Father. No one knows who the Son is except the Father, and who the Father is except the Son, and anyone to whom the Son desires to reveal him.'" (Luke 10:21–22, CSB)
Reflection: The Lukan Jesus is a Spirit-child. His mother experiences the Holy Spirit coming upon her and the power of the Most High overshadowing her for her to conceive Jesus (Luke 1:35). Jesus himself experiences the Holy Spirit descend upon him (Luke 3:22), making him full of the

Holy Spirit (Luke 4:1). In the synagogue in Nazareth he quotes Isaiah's words about the Spirit of the Lord being on him (Luke 4:18a). This is why he rejoices in the Holy Spirit in Luke's Gospel. In a Johannine manner, he reveals the Father, who entrusts all things to him, and declares that the only way to know the Father is through the Son. Throughout Luke's Gospel, the Holy Spirit is present—anticipating his fiery presence in the Acts of the Apostles. The Holy Spirit is the mark of the Father's reign, as demonstrated in the role the Spirit plays in both the Gospel and its second volume, the Acts of the Apostles.

Day 46: Wednesday of the Seventh Week of Easter

Morning
Antiphon: "Return to us, God of our salvation . . . ." (Ps 85:4a, CSB) Alleluia!
Psalm: "Show us your faithful love, LORD, and give us your salvation. / I will listen to what God will say; / surely the LORD will declare peace / to his people, his faithful ones, / and not let them go back to foolish ways. / His salvation is very near those who fear him, / so that glory may dwell in our land. / Faithful love and truth will join together, / righteousness and peace will embrace. / Truth will spring up from the earth, / and righteousness will look down from heaven. / Also, the LORD will provide what is good. . . . / Righteousness will go before him / to prepare the way for his steps." (Ps 85:7–12a, 13, CSB)
Repeat Antiphon (above):
Reading: Jesus said to his disciples: ". . . [W]hen they arrest you and hand you over don't worry beforehand what you will say, but say whatever is given to you at that time, for it isn't you speaking but the Holy Spirit." (Mark 13:11, CSB)
Reflection: The Markan Jesus explains to his followers that they will share his fate. Like Jesus, his disciples will be arrested and handed over to Jewish and Gentile authorities—what was happening at the time this gospel was written, 70 CE. It is safe for the author to present his Jesus character predicting arrest and being handed over, because it had been occurring! When the disciples are handed over to authorities because they are proclaiming the good news, the Markan Jesus tells them not to be concerned about what they will say. They receive a promise that the Holy Spirit will speak through them. In other words, they will be saved. In the words of the verses of Psalm 85, the LORD will give them salvation; near salvation

brings with it righteousness, peace, and truth, marks of the Spirit's presence. While the Markan Jesus' disciples experience persecution, they are promised that they will experience a healthy relationship with God and inner peace as the Spirit of truth speaks through them.

Evening
Antiphon: "LORD, I appeal to you." (Ps 25:1, CSB) Alleluia!
Psalm: "Make your ways known to me, LORD; / teach me your paths. / Guide me in your truth and teach me / for you are the God of my salvation; / I wait for you all day long. / The LORD is good and upright; / therefore he shows sinners the way. / He leads the humble in what is right / and teaches them his way. / All the LORD's ways show faithful love and truth / to those who keep his covenant and decrees." (Ps 25:4-5, 8-10, CSB)
Repeat Antiphon (above):
Readings:
(a) Jesus said to the Twelve: ". . . [W]hen they hand you over, don't worry about how or what you are to speak. For you will be given what to say at that hour, because it isn't you speaking but the Spirit of your Father is speaking through you." (Matt 10:19-20, CSB)
(b) Jesus said to his disciples: "Whenever they bring you before synagogues and rulers and authorities, don't worry about how you should defend yourselves or what you should say. For the Holy Spirit will teach you at the very hour what must be said." (Luke 12:11-12, CSB)
Activity: The source for the Reading from Matthew's Gospel and Luke's Gospel is Mark's Gospel (11:13, the Reading for Morning Prayer above). Compare the passage from Matthew's Gospel to the one in Mark's Gospel. What do you discover? In what specific ways do your discoveries help you know the intended audience of Matthew's Gospel? Compare the passage from Luke's Gospel to the one in Mark's Gospel. What do you discover? In what specific ways do your discoveries help you know the intended audience of Luke's Gospel?

Day 47: Thursday of the Seventh Week of Easter

Morning
Antiphon: "God, create a clean heart for me / and renew a steadfast spirit within me." (Ps 51:10, CSB) Alleluia!

SEASON OF EASTER

Psalm: "Do not banish me from your presence [, God,] / or take your Holy Spirit from me. / Restore the joy of your salvation to me, / and sustain me by giving me a willing spirit. / Save me . . . , God—/ God of my salvation—/ and my tongue will sing of your righteousness." (Ps 51:11–12, CSB)
Repeat Antiphon (above):
Reading: "On the last and most important day of the festival, Jesus stood up and cried out, 'If anyone is thirsty, let him come to me and rink. The one who believes in me, as the Scripture has said, will have streams of living water flow from deep within him.' He said this about the Spirit. Those who believed in Jesus were going to receive the Spirit, for the Spirit had not yet been given because Jesus had not yet been glorified." (John 7:37–39, CSB)
Reflection: The festival mentioned in the passage from John's Gospel is Tabernacles (Booths), an autumn rain celebration. Jesus has been in attendance. The festival recalls the water from the rock in the HB (OT) book of Numbers (20:2–11) along with Isaiah (12:3). The eight-day celebration began every morning with a priest going to the pool of Siloam and filling a golden vessel with water from the pool. Then, he would bring it to the Temple, where it was mixed with a jug of wine, poured into silver bowls, and brought to the altar, where it was poured into the ground by way of tubes; this is a type of fertility ritual meant to petition God to send the autumn rains to grow the crops. The words of the Johannine Jesus—the words of the author of the gospel—invites the thirsty to come to him and drink. Anyone who believes in him will become like a flowing river. The narrator of the gospel specifies that Jesus is speaking about the Spirit, which had not yet been given in this gospel, because Jesus had not yet been glorified—crucified, died, and resurrected. In John's Gospel, the Spirit, sent by the Father, replaces Jesus after his resurrection. Also, the author of John's Gospel consistently presents Jesus replacing Jewish celebrations. Here, Jesus replaces Tabernacles; he gives drink (Spirit) to the thirsty, just like the priests gave drink to the altar. Jesus brings forth new life with the Spirit, just like the autumn rains gave new life to the crops, which gave new life to the people. The verses from Psalm 51 petition God not to remove his Spirit, but to restore the joy of salvation while sustaining a willingness in the petitioner. Physical life is dependent upon water, and spiritual life is dependent upon Spirit.

Evening
Antiphon: "Let your faithful love come to me, LORD, / your salvation, as you promised." (Ps 119:41, CSB) Alleluia!
Psalm: "This is my comfort in my affliction: / Your promise [, LORD,] has given me life. / LORD, I remember your judgments from long ago / and find comfort. / May your faithful love comfort me / as you promised your servant. / My eyes grow weary / looking for what you have promised; / I ask, 'When will you comfort me?'" (Ps 119:50, 52, 76, 82, CSB)
Repeat Antiphon (above):
Reading: Jesus said: "When the Counselor comes, the one I will send to you from the Father—the Spirit of truth who proceeds from the Father—he will testify about me." (John 15:26, CSB)
Reflection: The Greek word *Paraclete* is translated into English as *Counselor, Comforter*, and *Advocate;* sometimes it is merely transliterated as *Paraclete*. Only the author of John's Gospel uses the word, which is why it is difficult to find an English word that captures the full intent of the Greek word. This is known as the promise of the Father in Luke's Gospel. In Johannine understanding, Jesus, who has been seen physically, sends the invisible Spirit that comes from the invisible Father. He is called the Spirit of truth because he bears witness about Jesus. In the words of the verses of Psalm 119, the Spirit will offer comfort, give life, and fulfill God's promise. Like the psalmist looking forward to what God promised, the author of John's Gospel looks forward to the Spirit coming from God. The fulfillment of God's promise is celebrated in three days, Pentecost.

Day 48: Friday of the Seventh Week of Easter

Morning
Antiphon: "Lord, who can dwell in your tent? / Who can live on your holy mountain?" (Ps 15:1–2, CSB) Alleluia!
Psalm: "I have been young and now I am old / yet I have not seen the righteous abandoned / . . . . / . . . [T]he LORD . . . will not abandon his faithful ones. / They are kept safe forever. / The righteous will inherit the land / and dwell in it permanently. / The mouth of the righteous utters wisdom; / his [her] tongue speaks what is just. / The instruction of his [her] God is in his [her] heart; / his [her] steps do not falter." (Ps 37:25ab, 28abc, 29–31, CSB)
Repeat Antiphon (above):

SEASON OF EASTER

Reading: Jesus said to his disciples: ". . . I will ask the Father, and he will give you another Counselor to be with you forever. He is the Spirit of truth. The world is unable to receive him because it doesn't see him or know him. But you do know him, because he remains with you and will be in you." (John 13:16–17, CSB)
Meditation/Journal: What connections do you make between the verses of Psalm 37 and John 13:16–17? Explain.

Evening
Antiphon: "[The LORD] will judge the world with righteousness / and the peoples with his faithfulness." (Ps 96:13cd, CSB) Alleluia!
Psalm: "Send your light and your truth; let them lead me [, God]. / Let them bring me to your holy mountain, to your dwelling place. Put your hope in God, for I will still praise him, / my Savior and my God." (Ps 43:3, 5bcd, CSB)
Repeat Antiphon (above):
Reading: Jesus said to his disciples: "When the Spirit of truth comes, he will guide you into all the truth. For he will not speak on his own, but he will speak whatever he hears. He will also declare to you what is to come. He will glorify me, because he will take from what is mine and declare it to you. Everything the Father has is mine. This is why I told you that he takes from what is mine and will declare it to you." (John 16:13–15, CSB)
Meditation/Journal: What connections do you make between the verses of Psalm 43 and John 16:13–15? Explain.

Day 49: Saturday of the Seventh Week of Easter

Morning
Antiphon: "The words of the LORD are pure words, / like silver refined in an earthen furnace, / purified seven times." (Ps 12:6, CSB) Alleluia!
Psalm: "You are my shelter and my shield [, LORD]; / I put my hope in your word. / Sustain me as you promised, and I will live. / My eyes grow weary looking for your salvation / and for your righteous promise. / Make my steps steady through your promise . . . ." (Ps 119:114, 116a, 123, 133a, CSB)
Repeat Antiphon (above):
Reading: "While Jesus was with [the apostles], he commanded them not to leave Jerusalem, but to wait for the Father's promise. 'Which,' he said,

'you have heard me speak about; for John baptized with water, but you will be baptized with the Holy Spirit in a few days." (Acts 1:4–5, CSB)
Reflection: In Luke-Acts, two CB (NT) books written by the same author, the Father's promise uniquely refers to the gift of the Holy Spirit. By the time that Luke's Gospel and the Acts of the Apostles were written (90–110 CE), a controversy had arisen as to who was greater: Jesus or John the Baptist. It is not a question of today, but it was for anyone who had read Mark's Gospel (70 CE). If John the Baptist baptized Jesus, as he clearly does in Mark's Gospel (1:9–11), the logical conclusion is that the greater (John the Baptized) baptized the lesser (Jesus). The way the author of Luke's Gospel and the Acts of the Apostles chose to solve the controversy was to change Jesus' baptismal scene in his gospel. John the Baptist is in prison (Luke 3:20), when Jesus is baptized (Luke 3:21–22). John the Baptist's baptism is diminished so that Jesus can be enhanced and shown to be greater than John. The Acts of the Apostles continues to diminish John and his Baptism. After Pentecost, Peter tells his listeners that Jesus received the promised Holy Spirit and poured it upon the apostles (Acts 2:33). Those who had only received John's baptism needed to be rebaptized (Acts 18:24; 19:1–3). Thus, as the importance of John the Baptist's baptism was narrated as decreasing, the importance of Jesus' baptism with the Holy Spirit continued to increase. The author of Luke-Acts carefully points this out when his risen Jesus tells the apostles to stay in Jerusalem until they received the promise of the Father, because John the Baptist baptized only with water, but they will be baptized with the Holy Spirit. After reading Luke's Gospel and the Acts of the Apostles, there is no doubt in the reader's mind as to who is greater!

Evening
Antiphon: "God has spoken once; / I have heard this twice: / strength belongs to God, / and faithful love belongs to you, Lord." (Ps 62:11–12a, CSB) Alleluia!
Psalm: "I wait for the LORD; I wait / and put my hope in his word. / I wait for the Lord / more than watchmen for the morning—/ more than watchmen for the morning. / . . . [P]ut your hope in the LORD. / For there is faithful love with the LORD, / and with him is redemption in abundance." (Ps 130:5–7, CSB)
Repeat Antiphon (above):

Reading: Jesus said to the apostles, "... [Y]ou will receive power when the Holy Spirit has come on you, and you will be my witnesses in Jerusalem, in all Judea and Samaria, and to the ends of the earth." (Acts 1:8, CSB)
Points to Ponder: First, the words in the reading are the last spoken by the Lukan Jesus in the Acts of the Apostles before he ascends into the heavens. Second, in biblical understanding, the spoken word is believable. God speaks to people through the word recorded in Bibles and elsewhere. The psalmist reflects on what he has heard about God's strength (Ps 62:11). Another psalmist waits—like watchmen patrolling the city walls during the night until daybreak—to hear God speak, while putting his hope in his word. Third, the power the apostles are to receive when the Holy Spirit comes upon them is like the power announced by Gabriel to Mary: "The Holy Spirit will come upon you, and the power of the Most High will overshadow you" (Luke 1:35a). The result of such power will be a pregnancy not achieved by intercourse. In other words, power is a sign of divine authority. Fourth, the author gives the reader the geographic outline for the CB (NT) Acts of the Apostles: Jerusalem, Judea, Samaria, and the ends of the earth—Rome. As the travel narrative moves along, the apostles witness to Jesus, his words, and they baptize.

Day 50: Pentecost

Morning
Antiphon: "My soul, bless the LORD! / LORD my God, you are very great; / you [make] the winds [your] messengers, / flames of fire [your] servants." (Ps 104:1ab, 4, CSB) Alleluia!
Psalm: "From his temple [God] heard my voice, / and my cry to him reached his ears. / Then the earth shook and quaked; / the foundations of the mountains trembled .... / Smoke rose from his nostrils, / and consuming fire came from his mouth; / coals were set ablaze by it. / From the radiance of his presence / his clouds swept onward with hail and blazing coals. / The LORD thundered from heaven; / the Most High made his voice heard." (Ps 18:6cd–7ab, 8, 12–13, CSB)
Repeat Antiphon (above):
Readings:
(a) Jesus said to the Eleven and those with them, "... I am sending you what my Father promised. As for you, stay in the city until you are empowered from on high." (Luke 24:49, CSB)

(b) The angel said to Mary: "The Holy Spirit will come upon you, and the power of the Most High will overshadow you. Therefore, the holy one to be born will be called the Son of God." (Luke 1:35, CSB)
(c) "When the day of Pentecost had arrived, [the apostles and others] were all together in one place. Suddenly a sound like that of a violent rushing wind came from heaven, and it filled the whole house where they were staying. They saw tongues like flames of fire that separated and rested on each one of them. Then they were all filled with the Holy Spirit and began to speak in different tongues, as the Spirit enabled them." (Acts 2:1-4, CSB)
Reflection: The author of the Acts of the Apostles prepares for the fireworks of Pentecost in Luke's Gospel. Mary is told by an angel—a manifestation of God—that she will conceive a child by the Holy Spirit. Before he disappears, the Lukan Jesus tells his apostles to stay in Jerusalem to receive from him the Father's promise—the Holy Spirit. The Acts of the Apostles opens with the fulfillment of the Father's promise. The author presents a theophany, a manifestation of the presence of God. The violent rushing wind sends the reader to the HB (OT) book of Genesis, where the Spirit of God was hovering over the surface of the waters (Gen 1:2). In other words, a new creation is taking place. The tongues like flames of fire sends the reader to the HB (OT) book of Exodus, where Moses encountered God in a bush that was on fire but was not consumed (Exod 3:1). In other words, God is making his presence available. Being filled with the presence of God, enabled the apostles to speak different languages. The reader is sent back to the HB (OT) book of Genesis, where the whole earth had the same language and vocabulary until God confused their language so they could not understand each other (Gen 11:1-9). In other words, Pentecost undoes what God did at the tower of Babel; instead of scattering people, he has brought them together. The Lukan John the Baptist had told his audience that the one coming after him would baptize with the Holy Spirit and fire (Luke 3:16). The Lukan Jesus declares that he came to bring fire on the earth (Luke 12:49). The Lukan description of Pentecost, a Jewish celebration occurring fifty days after Passover, brings to fulfillment wind, tongues—languages, and fire in the Lukan plot structure.

Evening
Antiphon: "When you hide your face [, LORD], / [your creatures] are terrified; / when you take away their breath, / they die and return to the

dust. / When you send your breath, / they are created, / and you renew the surface of the ground." (Ps 104:29–30, CSB) Alleluia!
Psalm: "LORD, make me aware of my end / and the number of my days / so that I will know how short-lived I am. / In fact, you have made my days just inches long, / and my life span is as nothing to you. / Yes, every human being stands as only a vapor. / Yes, a person goes about like a mere shadow. / Indeed, they rush around in vain, / gathering possessions / without knowing who will get them. / . . . [Y]es, every human being is only a vapor. / Hear my prayer, LORD, / and listen to my cry for help; / do not be silent at my tears. / For I am here with you as an alien, / a temporary resident like all my ancestors." (Ps 39:4–6, 11c–12, CSB)
Repeat Antiphon (above):
Reading: ". . . [Jesus] breathed on [the disciples] and said, 'Receive the Holy Spirit.'" (John 20:22, CSB)
Reflection: While Pentecost is presented by the author of Luke-Acts with wind, fire, and tongues fifty days after the resurrection of Christ, the author of John's Gospel presents it on the evening of the resurrection (Easter Sunday) with an appearance of the risen Christ, who breathes on his disciples and gives them the Holy Spirit. In other words, the Johannine Jesus imitates God in the HB (OT) book of Genesis; he breathes the breath of life into people's nostrils so that they become eternal, living beings (Gen 2:7). In the words of the verses from Psalm 39, people are finite. They have only so many days on the third planet from the sun. A human finite lifespan cannot begin to compare to the divine infinite lifespan. The psalmist uses three images worthy of reflection. He compares human beings to vapor, a substance that disappears quickly, like fog in the sunshine. He compares human beings to mere shadows, who disappear once the sunlight grows bright. And he compares human beings to resident aliens, who, after being on the earth for a short time, die and disappear. In other words, the psalmist thinks that breath is very short. The Johannine Jesus breathed divine breath (Holy Spirit) into his disciples, so that they and all who believe in him will live forever.

The Most Holy Trinity

First Sunday after Pentecost
Morning
Antiphon: ". . . [T]he word of the LORD is right; / And all his work is done in faithfulness." (Ps 33:4, AMP)

Psalm: "Let all the earth fear and worship the LORD; / Let all the inhabitants of the world stand in awe of Him. / For He spoke, and it was done; / He commanded, and it stood fast. / The counsel of the LORD stands forever; / The thoughts and plans of His heart through all generations. / Blessed [fortunate, prosperous, and favored by God] is the nation whose God is the LORD, / The people whom He has chosen as His own inheritance. / The LORD looks [down] from heaven; / He sees all the sons [and daughters] of man [and woman]; / From His dwelling place He looks closely / Upon all the inhabitants of the earth—/ He who fashions the hearts of them all, / Who considers and understands all that they do." (Ps 33:8–9, 11–15, AMP)

Repeat Antiphon (above):

Reading: "We firmly believe and confess without reservation that there is only one true God, eternal, infinite and unchangeable, incomprehensible, almighty, and ineffable, the Father and the Son and the Holy Spirit; three persons indeed, but one essence, substance, or nature entirely simple. The mystery of the Most Holy Trinity is the central mystery of Christian faith and life. It is the mystery of God in himself. It is therefore the source of all the other mysteries of faith, the light that enlightens them. . . . The whole history of salvation is identical with the history of the way and the means by which the one true God, Father, Son, and Holy Spirit, reveals himself to men [and women] . . . ." (CCC, pars 202, 234)

Reflection: Contrary to what many people think, the doctrine of the Trinity is not found in the Bible. Yes, there are mentioned the Father, the Son, and the Holy Spirit, but the doctrine of one God and three persons is not formulated until 325 CE during the First Council of Nicaea, long after the books of the Bible had been collected. Thus, the feast of the Most Holy Trinity on the Sunday after Pentecost is a doctrinal celebration. The verses of Psalm 33, while they are about the LORD (Yahweh), help to focus on the Trinitarian dogma. Of particular importance is the exhortation of the psalmist to stand in awe of the Trinitarian God, who is creator, redeemer, and sanctifier of the people he has chosen. Of course, the psalmist expresses the cosmology of his time and place. His God lives on the top level of the three-storied universe, and from there he can look down on the second story—the earth—where he can observe his creations and understand what they do. He sent his Son to redeem people, and he made them holy, like himself, by sending his Holy Spirit.

Evening
Antiphon: "O LORD, our Lord, / How majestic and glorious and excellent is Your name in all the earth!" (Ps 8:1ab, AMP)
Psalm: "You [, LORD,] have displayed Your splendor above the heavens. / When I see and consider Your heavens, the work of Your fingers, / The moon and the stars, which You have established, / What is man [or woman] that You are mindful of him [or her], / And the son [daughter] of (earthborn) man [and woman] that You care for him [or her]? / Yet You have made him [and her] a little lower than God. / And You have crowned him [and her] with glory and honor. / You made him [and her] to have dominion over the works of Your hands; / You have put all things under his [and her] feet.... / O LORD, our LORD, / How majestic and glorious and excellent is Your name in all the earth!" (Ps 8:1b, 3–6, 9, AMP)
Repeat Antiphon (above):
Reading: "We worship one God in the Trinity and the Trinity in unity, without either confusing the persons or dividing the substance; for the person of the Father is one, the Son's is another, the Holy Spirit's another but the Godhead of the Father, Son, and Holy Spirit is one, their glory equal, their majesty coeternal." (CCC, par 266)
Intercessions: Father, creator of heaven and earth, have mercy upon me. Son, redeemer of the world, have mercy upon me. Holy Spirit, sanctifier of all people, have mercy upon me. Holy, blessed, and glorious Trinity, one God, have mercy upon me and all people. Eternal LORD, bless all your people, whom you have redeemed through your Son, Jesus Christ, and whom you have made sacred with your Holy Spirit; have mercy today, tomorrow, and forever.

The Most Holy Body and Blood of Christ (Corpus Christi)

Sunday after the Most Holy Trinity or Second Sunday after Pentecost
Morning
Antiphon: "Praise the LORD! / For it is good to sing praises to our [gracious and majestic] God; / Praise is becoming and appropriate." (Ps 147:1, AMP)
Psalm: "Sing to the LORD with thanksgiving; / Sing praises to our God with the lyre, / Who covers the heavens with clouds, / Who provides rain for the earth, / Who makes grass grow on the mountains. / Praise the LORD...! / Praise your God...! / He has blessed your children.... /

He satisfies you with the finest of the wheat. / His word runs very swiftly." (Ps 147:7–8, 12, 13b, 14b, 15b, AMP)
Repeat Antiphon (above):
Reading: "... I [, Paul,] received from the Lord Himself that [instruction] which I passed on to you, that the Lord Jesus on the night in which He was betrayed took bread; and when He had given thanks, He broke it and said, 'This is (represents) My body, which is [offered as a sacrifice] for you. Do this in [affectionate] remembrance of Me.' In the same way, after supper He took the cup, saying, 'This cup is the new covenant [ratified and established] in My blood; do this, as often as you drink it, in [affectionate] remembrance of Me.' For every time you eat this bread and drink this cup, you are [symbolically] proclaiming [the fact of] the Lord's death until He comes [again]." (1 Cor 11:23–26, AMP)
Reflection: Leaving behind the multiple interpretations of Jesus' actions during the last meal he shared with his disciples—even though the Amplified Holy Bible passage above adds its editor's own interpretation—the day honoring the body and blood of Christ, otherwise known as the Eucharist or the Lord's Supper, is a celebration of his absence, according to Paul in his First Letter to the Corinthians. While Paul considers himself to be a link in the chain of passing on the tradition of the supper, he interprets what he has received from the Lord after he has presented the tradition! Bread represents life; the cup (of wine) represents the blood of sacrifice. Thus, the supper signifies the end of life of the Lord—his death. One must bear in mind that Paul thought that he would see the day of Jesus' return; Paul was wrong. Because he was waiting for Jesus to return in glory, his understanding of remembering Jesus with bread and cup is a remembrance of his absence. Thus, the supper, according to Paul, is celebrated to remember his absence from the day of his resurrection to his coming again (Parousia).

Evening
Antiphon: "Praise the LORD! (Hallelujah)" (Ps 116:19c, AMP)
Psalm: "What will I give to the LORD [in return] / For all His benefits toward me? / [How can I repay Him for His precious blessings?] / I will lift up the cup of salvation / And call on the name of the LORD. / I will offer to You the sacrifice of thanksgiving, / And will call on the name of the LORD." (Ps 116:12–13, 17, AMP)
Repeat Antiphon (above):

Reading: "Moses wrote down all the words of the LORD. Then he got up early in the morning, and built an altar [for worship] at the foot of the mountain [Sinai, Horeb] with twelve pillars (memorial stones) representing the twelve tribes of Israel. Then he sent young Israelite men, and they offered burnt offerings and sacrificed young bulls as peace offerings to the LORD. Moses took half of the blood and put it in large basins, and [the other] half of the blood he sprinkled on the altar. Then he took the Book of the Covenant and read it aloud to the people, and they said, 'Everything that the LORD has said we will do, and we will be obedient.' So Moses took the blood [which had been placed in the large basins] and sprinkled it on the people, and said, 'Behold the blood of the covenant, which the LORD has made with you in accordance with all these words.'" (Exod 24:4-8, AMP)

Reflection: In the Israelite world, blood represents life. In our world, blood represents life. When one cuts a finger or scrapes a knee, a little blood flows out, and without speaking most people see life flowing out of a person. Blood drives urge us to give the gift of life. After leading the Israelites out of Egypt and to Mount Sinai (Horeb), where Moses first encountered the LORD, he inscribes God's words in a book. Then, Moses builds an altar with twelve pillars; the altar represents God, and the twelve pillars represent his people. After reading the words inscribed in the Book of the Covenant, Moses takes blood and sprinkles it on the altar and on the people, In essence, God and the people become blood brothers and sisters; they are united in the sign of life: blood. In the CB (NT) Jesus' shed blood on the cross is declared to be the blood of the covenant (Mark 14:24; Matthew 26:28) and the blood of the new covenant (Luke 22:20; 1 Cor 11:25). That the author of CB (NT) books differ on the meaning of the cup should not surprise the reader. The tradition has kept two basic strands about the meaning of the blood of the covenant: (1) Mark's Gospel and the derivative gospels of Matthew and Luke, and (2) Paul. Drinking from the cup of wine (blood) gives life and unites all who share the cup as blood brothers and sisters.

The Most Sacred Heart of Jesus

Friday after the Second Sunday after Pentecost or Friday after the Most Holy Body and Blood of Christ (Corpus Christi)

Morning

Antiphon: "The LORD is merciful and gracious, / . . . abounding in compassion and lovingkindness." (Ps 103:8, AMP)

Psalm: "Bless and affectionately praise the LORD, O my soul, / and all that is [deep] within me, bless His holy name. / Bless and affectionately praise the LORD, O my soul, / And do not forget any of His benefits; . . . / Who redeems your life from the pit, / Who crowns you [lavishly] with lovingkindness and tender mercy; / Who satisfies your years with good things, / So that your youth is renewed like the [soaring] eagle. / For as the heavens are high above the earth, / So great is His lovingkindness toward those who / fear and worship Him [with awe-filled respect and deepest reverence]. / As far as the east is from the west, / So far has He removed our transgressions from us. / Just as a father [and mother] loves his [her] children, / So the LORD loves those who fear and worship Him [with awe-filled respect and deepest reverence]. / For He knows our [mortal] frame; / He remembers that we are [merely] dust." (Ps 103:1–2, 4–5, 11–14, AMP)

Repeat Antiphon (above):

Reading: Moses said to the Israelites: ". . . [Y]ou are a holy people [set apart] to the LORD your God; the LORD your God has chosen you out of all the peoples on the face of the earth to be a people for His own possession [that is, His very special treasure]. The LORD did not love you and choose you because you were greater in number than any of the other people, for you were the fewest of all peoples. But because the LORD loves you and is keeping the oath which He swore to your fathers [and mothers], the LORD has brought you out [of Egypt] with a mighty hand and redeemed (bought) you from the house of slavery, from the hand of Pharaoh king of Egypt. Therefore know [without any doubt] and understand that the LORD your God, He is God, the faithful God, who is keeping His covenant and His [steadfast] lovingkindness to a thousand generations with those who love Him . . . ." (Deut 7:6–9, AMP)

Reflection: The feast of the Most Sacred Heart of Jesus is like Valentine's Day in June or July. In the biblical world, the heart is the chief bodily focus of emotional activity; also, it is the seat of intelligence. The verses from Psalm 103 and the HB (OT) book of Deuteronomy express God's love for people using the word *lovingkindness*. The English lovingkindness is a translation of the Hebrew *hesed*, often translated into English as *mercy*. Because *hesed* has no singular English equivalent, the idea behind it is faithful love in action; instead of getting what people deserve—because they are dust—God goes beyond love and takes care of his people. Using a modern idiom, his heart goes out to people; he is moved with pity to show them his mercy, his lovingkindness.

Evening
Antiphon: ". . . [W]ith joy you will draw water / From the springs of salvation." (Isa 12:3, AMP)
Canticle: "I will give thanks to You, O LORD . . . . / Behold, God, my salvation! / I will trust and not be afraid, / For the LORD GOD is my strength and song; / Yes, He has become my salvation. / Give thanks to the LORD, call on His name [in prayer]. / Make His deeds known among the people [of the earth]; / Proclaim [to them] that His name is exalted! / Sing praises to the LORD, for He has done excellent and glorious things; / Let this be known throughout the earth. / Rejoice and shout for joy. . . . / For great in your midst is the Holy One . . . ." (Isa 12:1b, 2, 4–6, AMP)
Repeat Antiphon (above):
Reading: ". . . [H]ope [in God's promises] never disappoints us, because God's love has been abundantly poured out within our hearts through the Holy Spirit, who was given to us. While we were still helpless [powerless to provide for our salvation], at the right time Christ died [as a substitute] for the ungodly. . . . God clearly shows and proves His own love for us, by the fact that while we were still sinners, Christ died for us. Therefore, since we have now been justified [declared free of the guilt of sin] by His blood, [how much more certain is it that] we will be saved . . . . Not only that, but we also rejoice in God [rejoicing in His love and perfection] through our Lord Jesus Christ, through whom we have now received and enjoy our reconciliation [with God]." (Rom 5:5–6, 8–9, 11, AMP)
Meditation/Journal: Has hope in God's promises ever disappointed you? Explain. In what specific ways have you experienced God's love abundantly poured within your heart? Today, for what do you rejoice in God through the Lord Jesus Christ?

9

Major Special Days

Major Special Days Introduction

Throughout the liturgical year, there are major special days, as can be found below; in general, Major Special Days are celebrated unless they fall on a Sunday, when they are omitted that year. These days are classified as solemnity (top rank) or feast (second from the top rank). When a special day falls during Advent, it can be celebrated, but not on Sunday; all the Major Special Days of Christmas fall during the Season of Christmas; Major Special Days that fall during Lent are observed according to the directions found in the Season of Lent Introduction. During the Season of Easter, except for the first week, Major Special Days are celebrated as indicated. And during Ordinary Time, Major Special Days are celebrated as indicated, unless they fall on Sunday. However, during Ordinary Time the following Major Special Days are marked on Sunday: The Presentation of the Lord (February 2), The Nativity of St John the Baptist (June 24), Sts. Peter and Paul, Apostles (June 29), The Transfiguration of the Lord (August 6), The Assumption of the Blessed Virgin Mary (August 15), The Exaltation of the Holy Cross (September 14), All Saints (November 1), The Commemoration of All the Faithful Departed (November 2), and The Dedication of the Lateran Basilica (November 9).

While The Most Holy Trinity, The Most Holy Body and Blood of Christ (Corpus Christi), and The Most Sacred Heart of Jesus are Major Special Days that occur during Ordinary Time, they are listed at the end of the Season of Easter. In the Season of Easter Introduction, the dates are given for these celebrations. In general, The Most Holy Trinity is the first Sunday after Pentecost; the Most Holy Body and Blood of Christ (Corpus Christi) is on the Sunday after the Most Holy Trinity or the Second Sunday after Pentecost. And The Most Sacred Heart of Jesus is on the Friday after the Second Sunday after Pentecost or the Friday after the Most Holy Body and Blood of Christ (Corpus Christi). The last Sunday in Ordinary Time is the Major Special Day called Our Lord Jesus Christ, King of the Universe; it is found at the end of the Season of Ordinary Time, chapter 3, and the dates for its celebration are found in Season of Ordinary Time Introduction.

Other books by Mark G. Boyer that follow the same structure of Morning Prayer and Evening Prayer that can be used—in substitution for what is provided here—Major Special Days—include: *Weekday Saints: Reflections on Their Scriptures* (Eugene, OR: Wipf & Stock, 2014); *Very Short Reflections—for Advent and Christmas, Lent and Easter, Ordinary Time, and Saints—through the Liturgical Year* (Eugene, OR: Wipf & Stock, 2020).

In general, Antiphons, Psalms, and Readings for the Major Special Days are taken from the *English Standard Version* (ESV) (Wheaton, IL: Crossway, 2001); some come from *The New American Bible* (NAB) (New York: Catholic Book Publishing Co., 1970, 1986), *The Catechism of the Catholic Church* (CCC) (Washington, DC: United States Catholic Conference, 1994), and "The Proto-Gospel of James" in *The Apocryphal Gospels* by Bart Ehrman and Zlatko Plese (New York: Oxford University Press, 2011). Antiphons, Psalms, and Readings from October 18 through December 9 are taken from the *Amplified Holy Bible* (AMP) (Grand Rapids, MI: Zondervan, 2018).

Days in Major Special Days

The Conversion of St. Paul the Apostle

January 25
Morning
Antiphon: "Go into all the world and proclaim the gospel to the whole creation." (Mark 16:15, ESV)

Psalm: "Praise the LORD, all nations! / Extol him, all peoples! / For great is his steadfast love toward us, / and the faithfulness of the LORD endures forever. / Praise the LORD!" (Ps 117:1–2, ESV)
Repeat Antiphon (above):
Reading: "... [T]he gospel that was preached by me [, Paul,] is not man's gospel. For I did not receive it from any man, nor was I taught it, but I received it through a revelation of Jesus Christ. For you have heard of my former life in Judaism, how I persecuted the church of God violently and tried to destroy it. And I was advancing in Judaism beyond many of my own age among my people, so extremely zealous was I for the traditions of my fathers. But when he who had set me apart before I was born, and who called me by his grace, was pleased to reveal his Son to me, in order that I might preach him among the Gentiles, I did not immediately consult with anyone . . . ." (Gal 1:11–16, ESV)
Meditation/Journal: What do you understand the word *conversion* to mean? How is your definition illustrated in Galatians 1:11–16?

Evening
Antiphon: "Go . . . and make disciples of all nations . . . ." (Matt 28:19, ESV)
Psalm: "You [, LORD,] delivered me from strife with the people; / you made me the head of the nations, / people whom I had not known served me. / As soon as they heard of me they obeyed me; / foreigners came cringing to me. / The LORD lives, and blessed be my rock, / and exalted be the God of my salvation . . . . / For this I will praise you, O LORD, among the nations, / and sing to your name." (Ps 18:43–44, 46, 49, ESV)
Repeat Antiphon (above):
Reading: ". . . I [, Paul,] delivered to you [, Corinthians,] as of first importance what I also received: that Christ died for our sins in accordance with the Scriptures, that he was buried, that he was raised on the third day in accordance with the Scriptures, and that he appeared to Cephas, then to the twelve. Then he appeared to more than five hundred brothers at one time, most of whom are still alive, though some have fallen asleep. Then he appeared to James, then to all the apostles. Last of all, as to one untimely born, he appeared also to me. For I am the least of the apostles unworthy to be called an apostle, because I persecuted the church of God. But by the grace of God I am what I am, and his grace toward me was not in vain." (1 Cor 15:3–10a, ESV)

Reflection: In common understanding, *conversion* usually refers to changing religions or changing beliefs. In Pauline understanding, *conversion* is a response to God's call; it is usually accompanied by a change in lifestyle. Paul was convinced that he was called to go to the Gentiles to bring them to faith in Jesus, who was proclaimed to be the Messiah (Anointed One). For Paul, raised and educated as a Pharisee, his conversion was a life experience which changed him. Besides the two narratives of his conversion noted above, there are four more in the CB (NT): Acts 9:1–19; 22:6–21; 26:12–18; 2 Cor 12:1–7. Biblical scholars distinguish the conversion of Paul in the genuine Pauline letters (Galatians and First and Second Corinthians) from the three Lukan (or Acts) narratives of Paul's conversion. In the telling and retelling of the life-changing experience, the focus keeps changing and the interpretation of the experience with it. No matter how Saul's experience of Paul's conversion is narrated, the man called the apostle in biblical literature understood that the Jewish perspective had changed in light of Christ Jesus. Righteousness could not be earned by keeping Torah; righteousness was a divine gift offered to Jews and Gentiles alike; if the gift was accepted, a person's lifestyle indicated it.

The Presentation of the Lord

February 2
Morning
Antiphon: "Who is this King of glory? / The LORD, strong and mighty . . . ." (Ps 24:8ab, ESV)
Psalm: "The earth is the LORD's and the fullness thereof, / the world and those who dwell therein, / for he founded it upon the seas / and established it upon the rivers. / Who shall ascend the hill of the LORD? / And who shall stand in his holy place? / He who has clean hands and a pure heart, / who does not lift up his soul to what is false / and does not swear deceitfully. / He will receive blessing from the LORD / and righteousness from the God of his salvation. / Such is the generation of those who seek him, / who seek the face of . . . God . . . . / Lift up your heads, O gates! / And lift them up, O ancient doors, / that the King of glory may come in." (Ps 24:1–6, 9, ESV)
Repeat Antiphon (above):
Reading: ". . . [A]t the end of eight days, when [the child] was circumcised, he was called Jesus, the name given by the angel before he was

conceived in [Mary's] womb. And when the time came for their purification according to the Law of Moses, they brought him up to Jerusalem to present him to the Lord (as it is written in the Law of the Lord, 'Every male who first opens the womb shall be called holy to the Lord') and to offer a sacrifice according to what is said in the Law of the Lord, 'a pair of turtledoves, or two young pigeons.'" (Luke 2:21-24, ESV)

Reflection: Following Torah, the baby Jesus is circumcised—incorporated into the Abrahamic covenant—on the eighth day after his birth (Lev 12:3). Then, again following Torah, the woman who gives birth to a male child is ceremonially unclean for thirty-three days; it is a time of blood purification (Lev 12:4). The flow of blood with childbirth with the dangerous mixture of life (the birth of a child) and death (the blood flow) renders the mother ritually unclean for thirty-three days. The divine period (thirty-three) is capped with a sacrifice. For those who are unable to afford a sheep, two turtledoves or two pigeons can be substituted (Lev 12:7b). The priest makes atonement on the woman's behalf—needed because she is unclean from her contact with blood—and she becomes clean. This is the reason Mary and Joseph go to the Jerusalem Temple. The author of Luke's Gospel has combined the dedication of the firstborn (Exod 13:2) with the purification of the mother. The child's presence was not necessary for the mother's purification, and the redemption of the firstborn was not connected to the Temple. There is an inherent irony present in this narrative, as the Son of God is presented to God in God's house. There is also a devaluation of the Temple taking place in the narrative; God's presence shifts from the building (Temple) to the person (Jesus), as will be seen in the Reading for Evening Prayer.

Evening

Antiphon: "Glory to God in the highest, / and on earth peace among those with whom he is pleased!" (Luke 2:14, ESV)

Canticle: "Lord, now you are letting your servant depart in peace, according to your word; / for my eyes have seen your salvation that you have prepared in the presence of all people, / a light for revelation to the Gentiles, and for glory to your people Israel." (Luke 2:29-32, ESV)

Repeat Antiphon (above):

Reading: ". . . [T]her was a man in Jerusalem, whose name was Simeon, and this man was righteous and devout, waiting for the consolation of Israel, and the Holy Spirit was upon him. And it had been revealed to him by the Holy Spirit that he would not see death before he had seen the Lord's Christ. And he came in the Spirit into the temple, and when the parents brough in the child Jesus, to do for him according to the custom of the Law, he took him up in his arms and blessed God.... And Simeon blessed them and said to Mary his mother, 'Behold, this child is appointed for the fall and rising of many in Israel, and for a sign that is opposed (and a sword will pierce through your own soul also) so that the thoughts from many hearts may be revealed.'" (Luke 2:25–28, 34–35, ESV)

Points to Ponder: First, this unique Lukan narrative is about an encounter between a man named Simeon (meaning *God has heard*) and Jesus. Simeon is described by the author as righteous—in good standing with God—and devout—faithful. Second, he is waiting for God to console, redeem, do something for the Jews, who returned to Jerusalem and are under domination by a foreign power (Rome). Third, he is full of the Holy Spirit (before Pentecost), another unique Lukan theme. Fourth, he is the recipient of divine revelation: he would not die until he had seen the Lord's Messiah (Anointed One). Fifth, in his canticle, Simeon thanks God for letting him see and touch salvation that God is offering to all peoples: Gentiles and Jews. Sixth, in Luke's first volume, the gospel, Jesus brings divine light to the Jews, who will not accept him; in his second volume, the Acts of the Apostles, his followers bring divine light to the Gentiles, who accept Jesus.

The Chair of St. Peter the Apostle

February 22
Morning
Antiphon: "... I tell you, you are Peter, and on this rock I will build my church...." (Matt 16:18, ESV)
Psalm: "The LORD is my shepherd; I shall not want. / He makes me lie down in green pastures. / He leads me beside still waters. He restores my soul. / He leads me in paths of righteousness for his name's sake. / Even though I walk through the valley of the shadow of death, I will fear no evil, / for you are with me; your rod and your staff, they comfort me. / You prepare a table before me ...; you anoint my head with oil; my cup overflows. / Surely goodness and mercy shall follow me all the days of my life, / and I shall dwell in the house of the LORD forever." (Ps 23:1–6, ESV)
Repeat Antiphon (above):

Reading: "... When Jesus came into the district of Caesarea Phillipi, he asked his disciples, 'Who do people say that the Son of Man is?' Simon Peter relied, 'You are the Christ, the Son of the living God.' And Jesus answered him, 'Blessed are you, Simon Bar-Jonah! For flesh and blood has not revealed this to you, but my Father who is in heaven. And I tell you, you are Peter, and on this rock I will build my church, and the gates of hell shall not prevail against it. I will give you the keys of the kingdom of heaven, and whatever you bind on earth shall be bound in heaven, and whatever you loose on earth shall be loosed in heaven.' (Matt 16:13, 15-19, ESV)

Reflection: The source for the narrative above between the Matthean Jesus and Peter is Mark's Gospel (8:27-30). A quick comparison between the two accounts reveals that the author of Matthew's Gospel has added a lot to his source. Biblical scholars refer to this as Special M or Special Matthew, since it is material found only in Matthew's Gospel. And in this case, it is special Petrine material. The author of Matthew's Gospel builds the character of Peter from the stupid disciple the author of Mark's Gospel presents into a knowledgeable rock. This doctrinal celebration is named the chair of St. Peter, but it has nothing to do with a physical chair; the chair is a sign of the authority the Matthean Jesus gives to Peter, indicated in Matthew's Gospel by the words *rock* and *keys*, and to the authority enjoyed by the successors of Peter, commonly known as popes.

Evening

Antiphon: "I will give you the keys of the kingdom of heaven, and whatever you bind on earth shall be bound in heaven, and whatever you loose on earth shall be loosed in heaven." (Matt 16:19, ESV)

Psalm: "Give ear, O Shepherd . . . , / you who lead . . . like a flock. You who are enthroned upon the cherubim, shine forth . . . , / stir up your might and come to save us! Restore us, O God; / let your face shine, that we may be saved!" (Ps 80:1-3, ESV)

Repeat Antiphon (above):

Reading: "The Lord made Simon alone, whom he named Peter, the 'rock' of his Church. He gave him the keys of his Church and instituted him shepherd of the whole flock. 'The office of binding and loosing which was given to Peter was also assigned to the college of apostles united to its head.' This pastoral office of Peter and the other apostles belongs to the Church's very foundation and is continued by the bishops under the primacy of the Pope. The *Pope*, Bishop of Rome and Peter's successor, 'is

the perpetual and visible source and foundation of the unity both of the bishops and of the whole company of the faithful.' 'For the Roman Pontiff, by reason of his office as Vicar of Christ, and as pastor of the entire Church has full, supreme, and universal power over the whole Church, a power which he can always exercise unhindered.'" (CCC, pars 881–82)
Intercessions: For the pope, may he be a source of unity among the members of the church, I pray to you, Lord. For the bishops, may they be worthy pastors of the members of the church, I pray to you, Lord. For priests and deacons who share in the authority of the pope and bishops, may they exercise their offices with care, I pray to you, Lord. For all members of the church, may they be one in heart and mind with their leaders and with Christ, I pray to you, Lord.

St. Joseph, Spouse of the Blessed Virgin Mary

March 19
Morning
Antiphon: "My faithfulness and my steadfast love shall be with [my servant], and in my name shall his horn be exalted." (Ps 89:24, ESV)
Psalm: "The heavens are yours [, O LORD God]; the earth also is yours; / the world and all that is in it, you have founded them. / The north and the south, you have created them . . . . You have a mighty arm; / strong is your hand, high your right hand. / Righteousness and justice are the foundation of your throne; / steadfast love and faithfulness go before you. / Blessed are the people who know the festal shout, / who walk, O LORD, in the light of your face, / who exult in your name all the day / and in your righteousness are exalted. / For you are the glory of their strength; / by your favor our horn is exalted. / For our shield belongs to the LORD, / our king to the Holy One . . . ." (Ps 89:11–12a, 13–18, ESV)
Repeat Antiphon (above):
Reading: "Jacob [was] the father of Joseph the husband of Mary, of whom Jesus was born, who is called Christ. Now the birth of Jesus Christ took place in this way. When his mother Mary had been betrothed to Joseph, before they came together she was found to be with child from the Holy Spirit. And her husband Joseph, being a just man and unwilling to put her to shame, resolved to divorce her quietly. But as he considered these things, behold, an angel of the Lord appeared to him in a dream, saying, 'Joseph, son of David, do not fear to take Mary as your wife, for that which is conceived in her is from the Holy Spirit.' When Joseph woke

from sleep, he did as the angel of the Lord commanded him; he took his wife.... (Matt 1:16, 18–20, 24, ESV)

Points to Ponder: First, the account of Joseph, Mary, and the birth of Jesus above is unique to Matthew's Gospel; this means that it is Special M or Special Matthew. Second, the Joseph in Matthew's Gospel is modeled on the Joseph in the HB (OT) book of Genesis. He is the son of Jacob, and he is a dreamer. Third, Joseph is uniquely identified as a son of David, because David is mentioned in his genealogy (Matt 1:6). Fourth, in a dream NT (CB) Joseph is visited by an angel of the Lord, a code phrase for God. Fifth, Matthew creates the Joseph story to introduce his theme of higher righteousness; do the right thing because it is the right thing to do. According to Torah (Law), discovering his engaged pregnant should have resulted in public divorce and stoning to death; Joseph, an example of the higher righteousness, takes Mary as his wife. In other words, he breaks Torah in order to be righteous! Sixth, the reader is left puzzled about how a woman conceives by the Holy Spirit. Seventh, the antiphon and verses from Psalm 89 mention horn: In HB (OT) understanding, a horn (from a ram, goat, or ox) is a metaphor for strength and dignity.

Evening
Antiphon: "Let your fountain be blessed, / and rejoice in the wife of your youth, a lovely deer, a graceful doe." (Prov 5:18, ESV)
Psalm: "Blessed is everyone who fears the LORD, / who walks in his ways! / You shall eat the fruit of the labor of your hands; / you shall be blessed, and it shall be well with you. / Your wife will be like a fruitful vine within your house; / your children will be like olive shoots around your table. / Behold, thus shall the man be blessed / who fears the Lord. / May you see your children's children! (Ps 128:1–4, 6a, ESV)
Repeat Antiphon (above):
Reading: "... [Jesus'] parents went to Jerusalem every year at the Feast of the Passover. And when he was twelve years old, they went up according to custom. And when the feast was ended, as they were returning, the boy Jesus stayed behind in Jerusalem. His parents did not know it. After three days they found him in the temple, studying among the teachers, listening to them, and asking them questions. And when his parents saw him, they were astonished. And his mother said to him, 'Son, why have you treated us so? Behold, your father and I have been searching for you in great distress.' And he said to them, 'Why were you looking for me?

Did you not know that I must be in my Father's house?'" (Luke 2:41–43, 46, 48–49, ESV)
Reflection: While there is more focus on Joseph in Matthew's Gospel, there is more focus on Mary in Luke's Gospel. In Luke's Gospel, Joseph is mentioned by name five times (Luke 1:27; 2:4, 16; 3:23; 4:22). His presence is presumed in other places, such as in the unique childhood account of Jesus staying in Jerusalem after his parents have headed home after Passover. The author of Luke's Gospel considers Joseph, spouse of Mary, Jesus' earthly father, while also insisting that he is the Son of God conceived by the Holy Spirit in Mary's womb (Luke 1:35). The trip to the Jerusalem Temple when Jesus was twelve years old is the only mention of Jesus going to Jerusalem in Luke's account until he goes there for his last Passover (Luke 19:28). Also, Jesus' engagement with the Temple teachers prepares the reader for their opposition to him later in the gospel (Luke 20:1–47). While there are other childhood stories in apocryphal gospels, this is the only one in the CB (NT).

Annunciation of the Lord

March 25
Morning
Antiphon: "... [T]hose who know your name [, O LORD,] put their trust in you, / for you, O LORD, have not forsaken those who seek you." (Ps 9:10, ESV)
Psalm: "I will give thanks to the LORD with my whole heart; / I will recount all of your wonderful deeds. / I will be glad and exult in you; / I will sing praise to your name, O Most High. / ... [T]he LORD sits enthroned forever; / he has established his throne for justice, / and he judges the world with righteousness; / he judges the peoples with uprightness. (Ps 9:1–2, 7–8, ESV)
Repeat Antiphon (above):
Reading: "... [T]he angel Gabriel was sent from God to a city of Galilee named Nazareth, to a virgin betrothed to a man whose name was Joseph, of the house of David. And the virgin's name was Mary. And the angel said to her, 'Do not be afraid, Mary, for you have found favor with God. And behold, you will conceive in your womb and bear a son, and you shall call his name Jesus. He will be great and will be called the Son of the Most High. The Holy Spirit will come upon you, and the power of the

Most High will overshadow you; therefore the child to be born will be called holy—the Son of God.'" (Luke 1:26–27, 30–32a, 35, ESV)
Reflection: The angel Gabriel announces to Mary of Nazareth that she has been chosen to be the mother of the Most High's son. In this unique Lukan account, Gabriel, whose name means *God is strong*, announces that God is strong enough to conceive a child in the virgin's womb using the power of the Holy Spirit. As the angel, a code name for God, explains, the child will be called the holy Son of God. Mary accepts the announcement as a servant of the Lord. Announcements from God are not rare in biblical literature, nor are they rare in human experience. Announcements concerning a baby shower, the birth of a baby, a graduation, and a wedding are common occurrences, but there are divine announcements pronounced daily in the words of a loved one, in the sunrise or sunset, in the ocean pawing the shore, and, of course, in the words of scripture of all kinds. It is a sign of wisdom to sit quietly and listen to the announcements that are being made.

Evening
Antiphon: "... [Y]our steadfast love [, O LORD,] is before my eyes, / and I walk in your faithfulness." (Ps 26:3, ESV)
Psalm: "I wash my hands in innocence / and go around your altar, O LORD, / proclaiming thanksgiving aloud, / and telling all your wondrous deeds. / O LORD, I love the habitation of your house / and the place where your glory dwells. / My foot stands on level ground; / in the great assembly I will bless the LORD." (Ps 26:6–8, 12, ESV)
Repeat Antiphon (above):
Reading: "... [T]he LORD spoke to Ahaz: 'Ask a sign of the LORD your God....' But Ahaz said, 'I will not ask, and I will not put the LORD to the test.' Therefore the Lord himself will give you a sign. Behold, the virgin shall conceive and bear a son, and shall call his name Immanuel." (Isa 7:10–12, 14, ESV)
Reflection: Ahaz is king of Judah, whose capital was Jerusalem. His kingdom is about to be attacked by the kings of Aram and Israel, who have entered an alliance (Isa 7:1). Judah is a small kingdom, and the kings of Aram and Israel intend to capture it and depose King Ahaz. However, Ahaz enters an alliance with the powerful Assyrians. Using the names of children, the prophet Isaiah conveys a message (sign) to King Ahaz. Only the name of the middle child concerns us here. The middle child is named Immanuel, a name that means *God is with us*. Because Isaiah is

not clear about whose child this was (the first and third are the prophet's children; therefore, it is reasonable to conclude that the middle child is also the prophet's child, conceived by the prophet's wife, a young woman (says the Hebrew; not a virgin, a story that has been heavily influenced by translation errors and the narrative about the announcement of the conception of Jesus in Luke's Gospel). The second child could also be a royal heir to the throne, who would assure the future of the royal, Davidic dynasty. Like the other two children, the child becomes the unasked-for sign to King Ahaz; it may be a child from one of his wives. The point of the story in Isaiah is that even though Judah is under attack, God is with his people. God will protect them; that is the message or announcement that the name of the second child brings to King Ahaz.

St. Mark, Evangelist

April 25
Morning
Antiphon: ". . . [T]he foolishness of God is wiser than men, and the weakness of God is stronger than men." (1 Cor 1:25, ESV)
Psalm: "Righteousness and justice are the foundation of your throne [, LORD]; / steadfast love and faithfulness go before you. / Blessed are the people who know the festal shout, / who walk, O LORD, in the light of your face, / who exult in your name all the day / and in your righteousness are exalted. / For you are the glory of their strength, / by your favor our horn is exalted. / For our shield belongs to the LORD, / our king to the Holy One . . . .' (Ps 89:14–18, ESV)
Repeat Antiphon (above):
Reading: "The beginning of the gospel of Jesus Christ, the Son of God. As it is written in Isaiah the prophet, 'Behold, I send my messenger before your face, / who will prepare your way, / the voice of one crying in the wilderness: / "Prepare the way of the Lord, / make his paths straight."' John appeared, baptizing in the wilderness and proclaiming a baptism of repentance for the forgiveness of sins. In those days Jesus came from Nazareth of Galilee and was baptized by John in the Jordan." (Mark 1:1–4, 9, ESV)
Points to Ponder: First, the first verse of Mark's Gospel is the author's title of the work: The Gospel of Jesus Anointed. Second, the word *gospel* is the English translation of the Greek *euanggelion*, which means *good news*. Third, the author of this work declares it to be the good news of

Jesus Anointed, the meaning of the Greek word usually transliterated *Christ*. Fourth, in many manuscripts, the phrase *the Son of God* does not appear. This means that it was added by a scribe later, when making a copy of the original manuscript. Fifth, using two verses from the prophet Isaiah totally out of context, the author of the oldest gospel (called Mark for the sake of convenience) interprets the prophet as referring to John the Baptist. The original context of Isaiah 40:3 is a call to the reader to bring a message of comfort to the Jewish exiles in Babylon; their period of captivity is over. The message of hope employs the image of a highway stretching across the desert from Babylon to Jerusalem. In its original context, Isaiah's words have nothing to do with John the Baptist. Sixth, the author of Mark's Gospel gives no background information; John the Baptist appears (Mark 1:4); Jesus appears (Mark 1:9). Seventh, in Mark's Gospel there is no birth of Jesus account, no infancy stories, no account of Jesus' sinlessness.

Evening

Antiphon: I proclaim "thanksgiving aloud, and [tell] of your wondrous deeds [, O LORD]." (Ps 26:7, ESV)

Psalm: "I will tell of your name to my brothers [and sisters], / in the midst of the congregation I will praise you [, O LORD]. / You who fear the LORD, praise him! / . . . [G]lorify him, / and stand in awe of him . . . . / For he has not despised or abhorred / the affliction of the afflicted, / and he has not hidden his face from him, / but has heard, when he cried to him. / The afflicted shall eat and be satisfied; / those who seek him shall praise the LORD! / May your hearts live forever! / All the ends of the earth shall remember / and turn to the LORD, / and all the families of the nations / shall worship before you. / For kingship belongs to the LORD, / and he rules over the nations." (Ps 22:22–24, 26–28, ESV)

Repeat Antiphon (above):

Reading: "In those days Jesus came from Nazareth of Galilee and was baptized by John in the Jordan. And when he game up out of the water, immediately he saw the heavens being torn open and the Spirit descending on him like a dove. And a voice came from heaven, 'You are my beloved Son; with you I am well pleased.'" (Mark 1:9–11, ESV)

Reflection: Mark's Gospel is short and to the point. This means that events occur quickly in the narrative. John the Baptist appears (Mark 1:4) and Jesus appears and is baptized by John in the Jordan River (Mark 1:9). There is no doubt that John baptized Jesus, as the fact is mitigated by the derivative gospels attributed to Matthew (3:13–17) and Luke (3:21–22). If John baptized Jesus, then, the reasoning concluded, he must be greater. Thus, the author of Matthew tones down the Markan narrative by inserting dialogue between John, who defers to baptize Jesus, and Jesus, who insists that he do it (Matt 3:13–17). The author of Luke's Gospel conveniently places John in prison before Jesus is baptized (Luke 3:20); thus, while Jesus is baptized, John didn't do it! The other important point needing attention is Mark's note about the heavens being torn open. In a three-leveled universe, where God lives above the dome of the sky stretched over the second level of the flat, plate-like surface of the earth, if the heavens were torn open, God would fall to the earth. Again, the authors of Matthew's and Luke's gospels mitigate that bit of information (Matt 3:16; Luke 3:21) because it displaces God. According to the author of Mark's Gospel, God falls to the earth as Spirit, descending on Jesus, like a dove flies out of the sky to the earth. Yet, at the same time, God remains in his heavenly abode, for the voice echoes from heaven, claiming Jesus as the Son with whom God is pleased. Later in the Markan narrative, the curtain in the Jerusalem Temple will be torn from top to bottom (Mark 15:38) to indicate that God escaped from the place where many people located him. By paying attention to story details rich in theological nuances, it is easy to see why both the authors of Matthew's Gospel and Luke's Gospel decided to rewrite what they found in Mark's Gospel.

Sts. Philip and James, Apostles

May 3
Morning
Antiphon: "Let the words of my mouth and the meditation of my heart / be acceptable in your sight, / O LORD, my rock and my redeemer" (Ps 19:14, ESV)
Psalm: "The heavens declares the glory of God, / and the sky above proclaims his handiwork. / Day to day pours out speech, / and night to night reveals knowledge. / There is no speech, nor are there words, / whose voice is not heard. / Their voice goes out through all the earth, / and their words to the end of the world. / In them he has set a tent for the sun, / which comes out like a bridegroom leaving his chamber, / and, like a strong man, runs its course with joy. / Its rising is from the end of the heavens, / and its circuit to the end of the them, / and there is nothing hidden from its heat." (Ps 19:1–6, ESV)

Repeat Antiphon (above):
Reading: "Philip said to [Jesus], 'Lord, show us the Father, and it is enough for us.' Jesus said to him, 'Have I been with you so long, and you still do not know me, Philip? Whoever has seen me has seen the Father. How can you say, "Show us the Father"? Do you not believe that I am in the Father and the Father is in me? The words that I say to you I do not speak on my own authority, but the Father who dwells in me does his works. Believe me that I am in the Father and the Father is in me, or else believe on account of the works themselves.'" (John 14:8-11, ESV)
Meditation/Journal: This morning what are the words of your mouth and the meditation of your heart? What word gets most of your attention in the verses from Psalm 19 above? What does it mean? How does it make you aware of God's presence? In whom do you see the Father? Explain.

Evening
Antiphon: "Be exalted, O LORD, in your strength! / We will sing and praise your power." (Ps 21:13, ESV)
Psalm: "The law of the LORD is perfect, / reviving the soul; / the testimony of the LORD is sure, / making wise the simple; / the precepts of the LORD are right, / rejoicing the heart; / the commandment of the LORD is pure, / enlightening the eyes; / the fear of the LORD is clean, / enduring forever; / the rules of the LORD are true, / and righteous altogether. / More to be desired are they than gold, / even much, fine gold, / sweeter also than honey / and drippings of the honeycomb." (Ps 19:7-10, ESV)
Repeat Antiphon (above):
Reading: ". . . [Jesus] called to him his twelve disciples and gave them authority over unclean spirits, to cast them out, and to heal every disease and every affliction. The names of the twelve apostles are these: first, Simon, who is called Peter, and Andrew his brother; James the son of Zebedee, and John his brother; Philip and Bartholomew; Thomas and Matthew the tax collector; James the son of Alphaeus, and Thaddaeus; Simon the Zealot, and Judas Iscariot, who betrayed him." (Matt 10:1-4, ESV)
Reflection: The feast of the apostles Philip, whose name means *lover of horses*, and James, the Anglicized form of Jacob, the son of Alphaeus, appear in all the CB (NT) lists (Mark 3:18; Matt 10:3; Luke 6:14-15; Acts 1:13). While Philip appears more in John's Gospel (John 1:43, 45-46; 6:5-7; 12:21-22; 14:8-10), James, son of Alphaeus, also known as James the Less or the brother of the Lord (Mark 6:3, Matt 13:55, Gal 1:19), was prominent in the church in Jerusalem (Acts 12:17; 15:13-23; 21:18; 1

Cor 15:7; Gal 2:9, 12). James was martyred around 62 CE. It is important to note in the Matthean list above that they are called disciples before Jesus chooses them and apostles after they are chosen.

St. Matthias, Apostle

May 14
Morning
Antiphon: "Praise the LORD!" (Ps 113:9c, ESV)
Psalm: "Praise the LORD! / Praise, O servants of the LORD, / praise the name of the LORD! / Blessed be the name of the LORD / from this time forth and forevermore! / From the rising of the sun to its setting, / the name of the LORD is to be praised! / The LORD is high above all nations, / and his glory above the heavens! / Who is like the LORD our God, / who is seated on high, / who looks far down / on the heavens and the earth?" (Ps 113:1–6, ESV)
Repeat Antiphon (above):
Reading: "[The eleven apostles] returned to Jerusalem . . . . And when they had entered, they went up to the upper room, where they were staying, Peter and John and James and Andrew, Philip and Thomas, Bartholomew and Matthew, James the son of Alphaeus and Simon the Zealot and Judas the son of James. All these with one accord were devoting themselves to prayer, together with the women and Mary the mother of Jesus, and his brothers [and sisters]." (Acts 1:12–14, ESV)
Reflection: According to the author of the Acts of the Apostles—the same author of Luke's Gospel—after the death of Judas (Iscariot) (Acts 1:15–19), there were eleven apostles. After Jesus' ascension (Acts 1:6–11), the eleven apostles and some women return to the upper room in Jerusalem to pray and to await the coming of the Holy Spirit. The reader will notice that the name Matthias is not on the list, because he has not yet been elected to fill the vacant seat of Judas (Iscariot). In Matthew's Gospel, the vacant seat is not filled (Matt 28:16) nor is there any reference to filling it in Mark's Gospel or in Luke's Gospel. In John's Gospel, there is no list of apostles.

Evening
Antiphon: "You are my God, and I will give thanks to you; / you are my God; I will extol you." (Ps 118:28, ESV)
Psalm: "Open to me the gates of righteousness, / that I may enter through them / and give thanks to the LORD. / This is the gate of the LORD; / the

righteous shall enter through it. / I thank you that you have answered me / and have become my salvation. / The stone that the builders rejected / has become the cornerstone. / This is the LORD's doing; / it is marvelous in our eyes. / This is the day that the LORD has made; / let us rejoice and be glad in it. / Save us, we pray, O LORD! / O LORD, we pray, give us success!" (Ps 118:19–25, ESV)
Repeat Antiphon (above):
Reading: ". . . Peter stood up among the brothers . . . and said, '. . . [O]ne of the men who ha[s] accompanied us during all the time that the Lord Jesus went in and out among us . . . —one of these men must become with us a witness to his resurrection.' And they put forward two, Joseph called Barsabbas, who was also called Justus, and Matthias. And they prayed and said, 'You, Lord, who know the hearts of all, show which one of these two you have chosen.' And they cast lots for them, and the lot fell on Matthias, and he was numbered with the eleven apostles." (Acts 1:15, 21, 22b–24, 26, ESV)
Points to Ponder: First, Matthias' sole purpose is to reconstitute the twelve apostles in preparation for Luke-Acts Pentecost (Acts 2:1–13). Second, Matthias never appears again in the Acts of the Apostles nor in any other CB (NT) book! Third, the way Matthias is chosen is by lot, an oracular device employed to select one from several choices. In other words, a lot is a form of divination, to ascertain God's will. Fourth, the usual way to cast lots was to mark two stones or pottery fragments to represent Joseph and Matthias and place them in a jar or bag. The container was shaken until a stone or pottery piece fell out, determining upon whom the lot fell. Fifth, Because the stone or pottery piece representing Matthias fell out first, he was declared to be God's choice for apostle number twelve.

The Visitation of the Blessed Virgin Mary

May 31
Morning
Antiphon: "How awesome are your deeds!" [O God]. (Ps 66:3a, ESV)
Psalm: "'Because the poor are plundered, because the needy groan, / 'I will now arise,' says the LORD; / 'I will place him [or her] in the safety for which he [or she] longs.' / The words of the LORD are pure words, / like silver refined in a furnace on the ground, / purified seven times. / You, O LORD, will keep them; / you will guard us from this generation forever." (Ps 12:5–7, ESV)

Repeat Antiphon (above):
Reading: ". . . Mary arose and went with haste into the hill country, to a town in Judah, and she entered the house of Zechariah and greeted Elizabeth. And when Elizabeth heard the greeting of Mary, the baby leaped in her womb. And Elizabeth was filled with the Holy Spirit, and she exclaimed with a loud cry, 'Blessed are you among women, and blessed is the fruit of your womb! . . . [W]hen the sound of your greeting came to my ears, the baby in my womb leaped for joy.'" (Luke 1:39–42, 44, ESV)
Reflection: The scene of Mary of Nazareth visiting Elizabeth of the hill country is unique to Luke's Gospel. It serves as a bridge between the announcement of the birth of John the Baptist to Zechariah and the announcement of the birth of Jesus to Mary. Furthermore, it illustrates one of the author's favorite techniques: pairing a story about a man with one about a woman. Because Elizabeth's pregnancy is in its sixth month (Luke 1:26), the baby kicks, as the author of Luke's Gospel narrates the story; he interprets the kicking as the forerunner (John the Baptist) being excited about the appearance of the Son of God (Jesus). As the author has prepared his opening plot structure, John the Baptist will appear (Luke 3:1–20) to prepare the way for Jesus and his baptism. Thus, both will be brought together again. One pregnant woman visits another and, in doing so, brings awareness of the divine presence to her. It is useful to reflect upon all the people in life who bring the awareness of the divine presence to us. Among such people are repair men and women, mail carriers, cab drivers, shuttle operators, etc. Even dogs can be bearers of the divine presence.

Evening
Antiphon: "Praise is due to you, O God, . . . / and to you shall vows be performed." (Ps 65:1, ESV)
Psalm: "By awesome deeds you answer us with righteousness, / O God of our salvation, / the hope of all the ends of the earth / and of the farthest seas . . . . / You visit the earth and water it; / you greatly enrich it; / the river of God is full of water; / you provide their grain, / for so you have prepared it. / You water its furrows abundantly, / settling its ridges, / softening it with showers, / and blessing its growth. / You crown the year with your bounty, / your wagon tracks overflow with abundance. / The pastures of the wilderness overflow, / the hills gird themselves with joy, / the meadows clothe themselves with flocks, / the valleys deck themselves with grain, / they shout and sing together for joy." (Ps 65:5, 9–13, ESV)
Repeat Antiphon (above):

Reading: "Sing aloud, O daughter of Zion; / shout, O Israel! / Rejoice and exult with all your heart, / O daughter of Jerusalem! / The LORD your God is in your midst, / a mighty one who will save; / he will rejoice over you with gladness; / he will quiet you by is love; / he will exult over you with loud singing." (Zeph 3:14, 17, ESV)
Intercessions: For all who upon recognizing the visitation of the LORD rejoice and exult with all their heart, I pray to you, O God. For all who experience the saving power of the LORD, I pray to you, O God. For all who rejoice with gladness over the members of their families, I pray to you, O God. For all who are quieted by the LORD's love in times of upheaval, I pray to you, O God. For all who listen in silence for the LORD's exultation and loud singing, I pray to You, O God.

St. Barnabas, Apostle

June 11
Morning
Antiphon: ". . . [L]et the hills sing for joy together / before the LORD, for he comes . . . ." (Ps 98:8b–9a, ESV)
Psalm: "Oh sing to the LORD a new song, / for he has done marvelous things! / His right hand and his holy arm / have worked salvation for him. / The LORD has made known his salvation; / he has revealed his righteousness in the sight of the nations. / He has remembered his steadfast love and faithfulness . . . . / All the ends of the earth have seen / the salvation of our God. / Make a joyful noise to the LORD, all the earth; / break forth into joyous song and sing praises! / Sing praises to the LORD with the lyre, / with the lyre and the sound of melody! / With trumpets and the sound of the horn / make a joyful noise before the King, the LORD!" (Ps 98:1–6, ESV)
Repeat Antiphon (above):
Reading: ". . . [T]here were in the church at Antioch prophets and teachers, Barnabas . . . and Saul [Paul]. While they were worshiping the Lord and fasting, the Holy Spirit said, 'Set apart for me Barnabas and Saul for the work to which I have called them.' Then after fasting and praying they laid their hands on them and sent them off." (Acts 13:1–3, ESV)
Reflection: One cannot find the name Barnabas in any list of apostles in any CB (NT) gospel. He is called an apostle only in the Acts of the Apostles (14:14), although his name appears over twenty times in the Acts. His name means *son of encouragement* (Acts 4:36), and that is what he does

MAJOR SPECIAL DAYS

as Paul's (Saul's) companion as narrated by the same author who wrote Luke's Gospel. Barnabas brings Paul to the apostles (Acts 9:27). Later in the account, Barnabas travels to Antioch (Acts 11:22), from which he travels to Tarsus to find Saul (Acts 11:25). Barnabas and Paul began their mission going to Jewish synagogues, but later began to preach to the Gentiles (Acts 13:46). The acceptance of their preaching to and the belief of the Gentiles raised a question about circumcision; because Christianity emerged out of Judaism, some Jews were saying that the Gentiles needed to be circumcised before becoming Christian. As will be seen below in the reading for Evening Prayer, Barnabas and Paul traveled to meet with the apostles and elders there to determine an answer to that question. After returning to Antioch (Acts 15:35), Barnabas and Paul have a sharp disagreement and part company (Acts 15:39). Because Paul, too, is called an apostle (Acts 14:14), the number of apostles has reached fifteen—counting Matthias—by the end of the Acts of the Apostles!

Evening
Antiphon: "Exalt the LORD our God; / worship at his footstool! / Holy is he!" (Ps 99:5, ESV)
Psalm: "Make a joyful noise to the LORD, all the earth! / Serve the LORD with gladness! / Come into his presence with singing! / Know that the LORD, he is God! / It is he who made us, and we are his, / we are his people, and the sheep of his pasture. / Enter his gates with thanksgiving, / and his courts with praise! / Give thanks to him; bless his name! / For the LORD is good; / his steadfast love endures forever; / and his faithfulness to all generations." (Ps 100:1–5, ESV)
Repeat Antiphon (above):
Reading: ". . . [S]ome men came . . . from Judea [to Antioch] and were teaching the brothers, 'Unless you are circumcised according to the custom of Moses, you cannot be saved.' And after Paul and Barnabas had no small dissension and debate with them, Paul and Barnabas and some of the others were appointed to go . . . to Jerusalem to the apostles and the elders about this question. . . . [A]ll the assembly fell silent, and they listened to Barnabas and Paul as they related what signs and wonders God had done through them among the Gentiles. After they finished speaking, James replied, . . . '[M]y judgment is that we should not trouble those of the Gentiles who turn to God . . . .' Then it seemed good to the apostles and the elders, with the whole church, to choose men from among them and send them to Antioch [with a letter] with Paul and

Barnabas: '[I]t has seemed good to the Holy Spirit and to us to lay on you no greater burden . . . .' Paul and Barnabas remained in Antioch, teaching and preaching the word of the Lord, with many others also." (Acts 15:1–2, 12–13a, 19, 22a, 28, 35, ESV)

Reflection: Once Paul's and Barnabas' mission to the Jews comes to an end and they begin to teach and preach to the Gentiles, they make many converts among the Gentiles. It must be kept in mind that in the ancient world, from a Jewish male perspective, one was either a Jew or a Gentile. A male Jew was circumcised on the eighth day after his birth; Gentiles considered circumcision to be mutilation, and, thus, did not practice it. For Jews, the removal of the male's foreskin was a sign of incorporation into the covenant God had entered with Abraham. Thus, when Paul and Barnabas begin to have convert success among the Gentiles in Antioch, they are confronted by Jews from Jerusalem who insist that male Gentiles need to be circumcised; needless to say, the male Gentile converts are not excited by the proposition. Such talk precipitates a trip to Jerusalem to meet with apostles and elders to discuss the question: Do Gentiles have to become Jews (circumcised) before being counted among the followers of Jesus of Nazareth? In Jerusalem, Barnabas and Paul report on God's success through them among the Gentiles. An earth-shaking decision is reached: Male Gentile believers do not have to undergo circumcision to follow Jesus. Upon hearing that news, Gentile men jump up and down for joy! It is very difficult to appreciate the radicalness of this decision in a culture that circumcises all—or almost all—male babies! Determining that Gentiles do not need to be circumcised to follow Jesus is a decision that helps to split off Christianity from its Jewish mother. And right there in the thick of it is Barnabas, a son of encouragement.

The Nativity of St. John the Baptist

June 24
Morning
Antiphon: ". . . [Y]ou, child, will be called the prophet of the Most High; / for you will go before the Lord to prepare his ways . . . ." (Luke 1:76, ESV)
Psalm: O LORD, ". . . you formed my inward parts, / you knitted me together in my mother's womb. / I praise you, for I am fearfully and wonderfully made. / Wonderful are your works; / my soul knows it very well. / My frame was not hidden from you, / when I was being made in secret, / intricately woven in the depths of the earth. / Your eyes saw my

unformed substance; / in your book were written, every one of them, / the days that were formed for me, / when as yet there was none of them. / How precious to me are your thoughts, O God! / How vast is the sum of them! / If I would count them, they are more than the sand, / I awake, and I am still with you." (Ps 139:13–18, ESV)

Repeat Antiphon (above):

Reading: ". . . [T]here was a priest named Zechariah, . . . [a]nd he had a wife . . . and her name was Elizabeth. And they were both righteous before God, walking blamelessly in all the commandments and statutes of the Lord. But they had no child, because Elizabeth was barren, and both were advanced in years. Now while he was serving as priest before God . . . [Zechariah] was chosen by lot to enter the temple of the Lord and burn incense. And there appeared to him an angel of the Lord . . . . [T]he angel said to him, 'Do not be afraid Zechariah, for your prayer has been heard, and your wife Elizabeth will bear you a son, and you shall call his name John. And you will have joy and gladness, and many will rejoice at his birth. And he will turn many of the children of Israel to the Lord their God, and he will go before him in the spirit and power of Elijah . . . . to make ready for the Lord a people prepared.'" (Luke 1:5–9, 11, 13–14, 16–17, ESV)

Reflection: The only biblical account of the birth of John the Baptist is found in Luke's Gospel. The carefully crafted story is a retelling of the Abraham and Sarah account before the birth of Isaac. It also contains some elements of the Samson birth narrative. The author of the narrative has created it to balance the announcement of Jesus' birth later in the gospel. This author likes to balance a story about a man (Zechariah) with one about a woman (Mary). The outline followed by both is (1) prediction of birth, (2) birth (nativity), (3) appearance, and (4) arrest, imprisonment, and death. The material about John the Baptist is much shorter than the material about Jesus. In other words, John fulfills his mission of preparing people for the coming of the Lord, and then he disappears from the narrative. Once his function, as the author of Luke's Gospel understands it, is completed, he is no longer needed in the story.

Evening

Antiphon: The Lord God has shown "the mercy promised to our fathers [and mothers]" and has remembered "his holy covenant." (Luke 1:79, ESV)

Psalm: "O God, from my youth you have taught me, / and I still proclaim your wondrous deeds. / So even to old age and gray hairs, / O God, do not

forsake me, / until I proclaim your might to another generation, / your power to all those to come. / Your righteousness, O God, / reaches the high heavens. / You who have done great things, / O God, who is like you? / You who have made me see many troubles and calamities / will revive me again; / from the depths of the earth / you will bring me up again. / You will increase my greatness / and comfort me again." (Ps 71:17–21, ESV)
Repeat Antiphon (above):
Reading: "... [T]he time came for Elizabeth to give birth, and she bore a son. And on the eighth day they came to circumcise the child.... [T]hey made signs to his father, inquiring what he wanted him to be called. And he asked for a writing tablet and wrote, 'His name is John.'" (Luke 1:57, 59a, 62–63, ESV)
Activity/Meditation/Journal: Just like there is a Markan Jesus, a Matthean Jesus, a Lukan Jesus, and a Johannine Jesus, there is a Markan John the Baptist, a Matthean John the Baptist, a Lukan John the Baptist, and a Johannine John the Baptist. Before exploring each John the Baptist character, it is important for the meditator to become aware of his or her presupposed John the Baptist character. Thus, who is John the Baptist for you? For the author of Mark's Gospel, John the Baptist is a preacher announcing the end of time; he baptizes Jesus. For the author of Matthew's Gospel, John the Baptist assists Jesus in fulfilling all righteousness; he baptizes Jesus reluctantly. For the author of Luke's Gospel, John submits to Jesus; Jesus is superior, even in birth. John's mission is to preach repentance. John does not baptize Jesus, as John is imprisoned before Jesus is baptized. And for the author of John's Gospel, John the Baptist is a witness to Jesus; John steers some of his disciples to Jesus. There is no scene of John baptizing Jesus in John's Gospel.

Sts. Peter and Paul, Apostles

June 29
Morning
Antiphon: "... Peter said [to a lame man], 'I have no silver and gold, but what I do have I give to you. In the name of Jesus Christ of Nazareth, rise up and walk.'" (Acts 3:6, ESV)
Psalm: "The heavens declare the glory of God, / and the sky above proclaims his handiwork. / Day to day pours out speech, / and night to night reveals knowledge. / There is no speech, nor are there words, / whose voice is not heard. / Their voice goes out through all the earth, / and their

words to the end of the world. / In them he has set a tent for the sun, / which comes out like a bridegroom leaving his chamber, / and, like a strong man, runs its course with joy. / Its rising is from the end of the heavens, / and its circuit to the end of them, / and there is nothing hidden from its heat." (Ps 19:1–6, ESV)

Repeat Antiphon (above):

Reading: ". . . Peter and John were going up to the temple at the hour of prayer . . . . And a man lame from birth was being carried, whom they laid daily at the gate of the temple that is called the Beautiful Gate to ask alms of those entering the temple. . . . Peter said [to the lame man], 'I have no silver and gold, but what I do have I give to you. In the name of Jesus Christ of Nazareth, rise up and walk.' And he took him by the right hand and raised him up, and immediately his feet and ankles were made strong. And leaping up, he stood and began to walk, and entered the temple with them, walking and leaping and praising God." (Acts 3:1–2, 6–8, ESV)

Meditation/Journal: What connection(s) do you find between the verses of Psalm 19 and Acts 3:1–2, 6–8? Explain.

Evening

Antiphon: "Paul, an apostle—not from men nor through men, but through Jesus Christ and God the Father, who raised him from the dead." (Gal 1:1, ESV)

Psalm: "I will bless the LORD at all times; / his praise shall continually be in my mouth. / My soul makes its boast in the LORD; / let the humble hear and be glad. / Oh, magnify the LORD with me, / and let us exalt his name together. / The eyes of the LORD are toward the righteous / and his ears toward their cry. / When the righteous cry for help, the LORD hears / and delivers them out of their troubles. / The LORD is near to the brokenhearted / and saves the crushed in spirit. / The LORD redeems the life of his servants; / none of those who take refuge in him will be condemned." (Ps 34:1–3, 15, 17–18, 22, ESV)

Repeat Antiphon (above):

Reading: ". . . [A]fter three years [in Arabia and Damascus] I [, Paul,] went up to Jerusalem to visit Cephas and remained with him fifteen days. But I saw none of the other apostles except James the Lord's brother. . . . I was still unknown in person to the churches of Judea that are in Christ. They only were hearing it said, 'He who used to persecute us is now preaching the faith he once tied to destroy.' And they glorified God because of me." (Gal 1:18–19, 22–24, ESV)

A BIBLICAL MORNING & EVENING PRAYER MANUAL

Meditation/Journal: What connection(s) do you find between the verses of Psalm 34 and Galatians 1:18–19, 22–24? Explain.

St. Thomas, Apostle

July 3
Morning
Antiphon: "Thomas answered [Jesus], 'My Lord and my God!'" (John 20:28, ESV)
Psalm: "Praise the LORD, all nations! / Extol him, all peoples! / For great is his steadfast love toward us, / and the faithfulness of the Lord endures forever. / Praise the LORD!" (Ps 117:1–2, ESV)
Repeat Antiphon (above):
Reading: ". . . Thomas, one of the twelve, called the Twin, was not with [the disciples] when Jesus came [after his resurrection]. So the other disciples told him, 'We have seen the Lord.' But he said to them, 'Unless I see in his hands the mark of the nails, and place my finger into the mark of the nails, and place my hand into his side, I will not believe.' Eight days later, his disciples were inside again, and Thomas was with them. Although the doors were locked, Jesus came and stood among them and said, 'Peace be with you.' Then he said to Thomas, 'Put your finger here and see my hands, and put out your hand, and place it in my side. Do not disbelieve, but believe.' Thomas answered him, 'My Lord and my God!' Jesus said to him, 'Have you believed because you have seen Me? Blessed are those who have not seen and yet have believed.'" (John 20:24–29, ESV)
Points to Ponder: First, Thomas, whose name means *twin*, makes three appearances in John's Gospel (11:16; 14:5; 20:24), like other major characters do. Second, Thomas is mentioned in chapter 21:2, but that chapter was added later to the gospel; that fact is easy to determine from the original ending (John 20:30–31). Third, throughout John's Gospel, various people—especially disciples—see signs and believe. For example, the author states that Jesus' disciples saw the sign of water become wine at the wedding in Cana and believed in Jesus (John 2:11). Fourth, for the generation following the disciples, there are no signs to see and believe. Thus, the process of seeing and believing must conclude in the gospel. And that is what the author of John's Gospel does with the narrative about Thomas wanting to see and believe and Jesus telling him that those who have not seen are blessed because they believe. With that unique

Johannine dialogue, the process of seeing and believing is finished; new believers no longer need to see signs to believe. Fifth, while Thomas is known as Twin, no CB (NT) literature identifies his twin.

Evening
Antiphon: "Praise the LORD! Praise the LORD, O my soul!" (Ps 146:1, ESV)
Psalm: "I will praise the LORD as long as I live; / I will sing praise to my God while I have my being. / Blessed is he [she] whose help is . . . God . . . , / who made heaven and earth, / the sea, and all that is in them, / who keeps faith forever. / [T]he LORD opens the eyes of the blind. / The LORD lifts up those who are bowed down; / the LORD loves the righteous. / The LORD watches over the sojourners . . . ." (Ps 146:2, 5–6, 8–9a, ESV)
Repeat Antiphon (above):
Reading: Jesus said to his disciples: "Let not your hearts be troubled. Believe in God; believe also in me. In my Father's house are many rooms. If it were not so, would I have told you that I go to prepare a place for you? And if I go and prepare a place for you, I will come again and will take you to myself, that where I am you may be also. And you know the way to where I am going.' Thomas said to him, 'Lord, we do not know where you are going. How can we know the way?' Jesus said to him, 'I am the way, and the truth, and the life. No one comes to the Father except through me.'" (John 14:1–6, ESV)
Meditation/Journal: When have you most recently experienced a troubled heart? Explain. What do you think the Johannine Jesus means by belief in God and belief in him? What do you think the Johannine Jesus means by many rooms in his Father's house? What do you think the Johannine Jesus means by being the way, the truth, and the life?

St. Mary Magdalene

July 22
Morning
Antiphon: "Mary Magdalene went and announced to the disciples, 'I have seen the Lord . . . .'" (John 20:18, ESV)
Psalm: "O God, you are my God; earnestly I seek you; / my soul thirsts for you, / my flesh faints for you, / as in a dry and weary land where there is no water. / So I have looked upon you in the sanctuary, / beholding your power and glory. / Because your steadfast love is better than life,

/ my lips will praise you. / So I will bless you as long as I live; / in your name I will lift up my hands." (Ps 63:1–4, ESV)
Repeat Antiphon (above):
Reading: ". . . [O]n the first day of the week Mary Magdalene came to [Jesus'] tomb early, while it was still dark, and saw that the stone had been taken away from the tomb. So she ran and went to Simon Peter and the other disciple, the one whom Jesus loved, and said to them, 'They have taken the Lord out of the tomb, and we don't know where they have laid him.' Mary stood weeping outside the tomb, and as she wept she stooped to look into the tomb. And she saw two angels in white, sitting where the body of Jesus had lain, one at the head and one at the feet. . . . [S]he turned around and saw Jesus standing, but she did not know that it was Jesus. Supposing him to be the gardener, she said to him, 'Sir, if you have carried him away, tell me where you have laid him, and I will take him away.' Jesus said to her, 'Mary.' She turned and said to him in Aramaic, 'Rabboni' (which means Teacher)." (John 20:1–2, 11–12, 14, 15c–16, ESV)
Points to Ponder: First, throughout John's Gospel, there is a dichotomy between darkness (disbelief) and light (belief). This is why Mary Magdalene, apostle to the apostles, goes to Jesus' tomb in early morning darkness; she does not believe that he has been raised. She goes to the tomb expecting to find the stone rolled over the entrance to the cave-like tomb. Second, she runs to where Simon Peter and the unnamed disciple Jesus loved are housed; her message is that she found the stone rolled away from the tomb and the body not lying on the shelf where it should have been. Third, after completing her mission as apostle to the apostles, she went back to the tomb, and looking inside saw two angels dressed in divine white sitting on the shelf where Jesus' body should have been. Angel is a code name for God! Fourth, she sees the risen Jesus, but, thinking he was the gardener, she does not recognize him; she is still looking for a dead body. Fifth, the risen Jesus says her name, and that is the trigger that makes her aware that the gardener is not the gardener, but the Jesus she had known raised from the dead. She responds by calling him her teacher. Sixth, she becomes the apostle to the apostles in truth, when she goes to them and announces that she has seen the Lord. The woman who began her day in the dark has emerged into the light!

Evening
Antiphon: "For God alone my soul waits in silence; / from him comes my salvation." (Ps 62:1, ESV)
Psalm: "My soul will be satisfied as with fat and rich food, / and my mouth will praise you [, God,] with joyful lips, / when I remember you upon my bed, / and meditate on you in the watches of the night; / for you have been my help, / and in the shadow of your wings I will sing for joy. / My soul clings to you; / your right hand upholds me." (Ps 63:5–8, ESV)
Repeat Antiphon (above):
Reading: "There were . . . women looking on [Jesus' crucifixion] from a distance, among whom were Mary Magdalene. . . . When he was in Galilee, they followed him and ministered to him, and there were also many other women who came up with him to Jerusalem. Mary Magdalene . . . saw where he was laid [, entombed, after he was taken down from the cross]. When the sabbath was past, Mary Magdalene . . . bought spices, so that [she] might go and anoint him." (Mark 15:40–41, 47; 16:1, ESV)
Activity: Choose a word or phrase from either the verses of Psalm 63 or Mark 15:40–41, 46; 16:1. What does the word or phrase mean? How does the word or phrase make you aware of God's presence?

St. James, Apostle

July 25
Morning
Antiphon: "Do good, O LORD, to those who are good, / and to those who are upright in their hearts!" (Ps 125:4, ESV)
Psalm: ". . . [O]ur mouth was filled with laughter [, LORD,] / and our tongue with shouts of joy; / when [others] said among the nations, / 'The LORD has done great things . . .' / The LORD has done great things for us; / we are glad. / Those who sow in tears / shall reap with shouts of joy! / He [She] who goes out weeping, / bearing the seed for sowing, / shall come home with shouts of joy, / bringing his [her] sheaves with him [her]." (Ps 126:2–3, 5–6, ESV)
Repeat Antiphon (above):
Reading: ". . . [T[he mother of the sons of Zebedee came up to [Jesus] with her sons, and kneeling before him she asked him for something. And he said to her, 'What do you want?' She said to him, 'Say that these two sons of mine are to sit, one at your right hand and one at your left, in your kingdom.' Jesus answered, 'You do not know what you are asking.

Are you able to drink the cup that I am to drink?' They said to him, 'We are able.'" (Matt 20:20–22, ESV)
Reflection: On this feast of St. James, traditionally described as *the Greater* (to distinguish him from James, son of Alphaeus, the Less), a lesson in biblical editing is presented. Throughout Mark's Gospel, Jesus' disciples are characterized as dumb. After teaching them about self-loss and humility, they don't comprehend. Instead, "James and John, the sons of Zebedee, came up to [Jesus] and said to him, 'Teacher, we want you to do for us whatever we ask of you.' And he said to them, 'What do you want me to do for you?' And they said to him, 'Grant us to sit, one at your right hand and one at your left, in your glory.' Jesus said to them, 'You do not know what you are asking. Are you able to drink the cup that I drink, or to be baptized with the baptism with which I am baptized?' And they said to him, 'We are able' (Mark 10:35–39a). To present Jesus' disciples in a favorable light, the author of Matthew's Gospel presents the mother of James and John asking for the power position on the right of Jesus and the next power position on the left of Jesus in his kingdom. Because James and John do not ask Jesus, they are not presented as not comprehending his teaching, as they are in Mark's Gospel. The author of Luke's Gospel doesn't bother with the story. Nevertheless, this narrative is a good example of what one gospel writer (Matthew) did with an earlier gospel writer's (Mark's) work. A slight alteration in the account changes the characterization of James and John. Finally, it is important to note that in Matthew's story, it is a powerless woman who seeks power for her apostolic sons!

Evening
Antiphon: "Praise the LORD!" (P 149:9c, ESV)
Psalm: "Praise the LORD! / Sing to the LORD a new song, / his praise in the assembly of the godly! / Let them praise his name with dancing, / making melody to him with tambourine and lyre! / For the LORD takes pleasure in his people, / he adorns the humble with salvation. / Let the godly exult in glory; / let them sing for joy on their beds. / Let the high praises of God be in their throats . . . . / This is honor for all his godly ones. (Ps 149:1, 3–6a, 9b, ESV)
Repeat Antiphon (above):
Reading: ". . . [Jesus] appointed twelve (whom he also named apostles) so that they might be with him and he might send them out to preach . . . . He appointed the twelve: Simon (to whom he gave the name Peter); James the son of Zebedee and John the brother of James (to whom he gave the

name Boanerges, that is, Sons of Thunder); Andrew and Philip, and Bartholomew, and Matthew, and Thomas, and James the son of Alphaeus, and Thaddaeus, and Simon the Zealot, and Judas Iscariot, who betrayed him." (Mark 3:14, 16–19, ESV)

Reflection: James and John, the sons of Zebedee, appear in all biblical lists of apostles (Mark 3:17; Matt 10:2), but without their father's name (Luke 6:14; Acts 1:13) and as unnamed sons of Zebedee (John 21:2). Simon Peter is always the first name on the list (Mark 3:16; Matt 10:2; Luke 6:14; John 21:2; Acts 1:13); sometimes Peter is listed with his brother Andrew (Matt 10:2; Luke 6:14); at other times Andrew is listed with no identification with Peter (Mark 3:18; Acts 1:13). Philip appears on the list (Mark 3:18; Matt 10:3; Luke 6:14; Acts 1:13). Bartholomew appears on all the synoptic lists (Mark 3:18; Matt 10:3; Luke 6:14; Acts 1:13), as does Matthew (Mark 3:18; Matt 10:3; Luke 6:15; Acts 1:13); only in Matthew's Gospel is he identified as the tax collector (Matt 10:3). Thomas appears on all the synoptic lists (Mark 3:18; Matt 10:3; Luke 6:15; Acts 1:13). James son of Alphaeus also appears on all the synoptic lists (Mark 3:15; Matt 10:3; Luke 6:15; Acts 1:13). Thaddaeus appears only on the list in Mark (3:18) and Matthew (10:3). Simon the Cananaean is on the list in Mark (3:18) and in Matthew (10:4); in Luke (6:15) and Acts (1:13) he is identified as a Zealot. Likewise, there is a Judas son of James on Luke's list in his gospel and on his list in the Acts (Luke 6:16; Acts 1:13). At the end of all synoptic lists is Judas Iscariot, who betrayed Jesus (Mark 3:19; Matt 19:4; Luke 6:16; Acts 1:16) and Matthias, who is chosen to replace him (Acts 1:26). In addition to all these apostles, in John's Gospel there is one named Nathaniel of Cana in Galilee (John 21:2), two unnamed disciples (21:2) and the disciple Jesus loved (John 13:23; 19:26; 20:2), who originally made three appearances in John's Gospel, like Nicodemus and Thomas, but with the addition of chapter 21, made two more appearances (John 21:7, 20). Not to be forgotten on the list of apostles is Barnabas and Saul (Paul) (Acts 14:14). Thus, when comparing CB (NT) lists, there are as few as twelve apostles or as many as twenty or twenty-one!

The Transfiguration of the Lord

August 6
Morning
Antiphon: "Oh sing to the LORD a new song, for he has done marvelous things!" (Ps 98:1a, ESV)

Psalm: "The LORD reigns, let the earth rejoice; / let the many coastlands be glad! / Clouds and thick darkness are all around him; / righteousness and justice are the foundation of his throne. / Fire goes before him .... / His lightnings light up the world; / the earth sees and trembles. / The mountains melt like wax before the LORD, / before the Lord of all the earth. / The heavens proclaim his righteousness, / and all the peoples see his glory." (Ps 97:1-6, ESV)
Repeat Antiphon (above):
Readings:
(a) "... [A]fter six days [after teaching disciples and the crowd] Jesus took with him Peter and James and John, and led them up a high mountain by themselves. And he was transfigured before them, and his clothes became radiant, intensely white, as no one on earth could bleach them. And there appeared to them Elijah with Moses, and they were talking with Jesus. And Peter said to Jesus, 'Rabbi, it is good that we are here. Let us make three tents, one for you and one for Moses and one for Elijah.' For he did not know what to say, for they were terrified. And a cloud overshadowed them, and a voice came out of the cloud, 'This is my beloved Son; listen to him.' And suddenly, looking around, they no longer saw anyone with them but Jesus only." (Mark 9:2-8, ESV)

(b) "... [A]fter six days [after teaching his disciples] Jesus took with him Peter and James, and John his brother, and led them up a high mountain by themselves. And he was transfigured before them, and his face shone like the sun, and his clothes became white as light. And behold, there appeared to them Moses and Elijah, talking with him. And Peter said to Jesus, 'Lord, it is good that we are here. If you wish, I will make three tents here, one for you and one for Moses and one for Elijah.' He was still speaking when, behold, a bright cloud overshadowed them, and a voice from the cloud said, 'This is my beloved Son, with whom I am well pleased; listen to him.' When the disciples heard this, they fell on their faces and were terrified. But Jesus came and touched them, saying, 'Rise, and have no fear.' And when they lifted up their eyes, they saw no one but Jesus only." (Matt 17:1-8, ESV)

(c) "... [A]bout eight days after [pronouncing some] sayings [Jesus] took with him Peter and John and James and went up on the mountain to pray. And as he was praying, the appearance of his face was altered, and his clothing became dazzling white. And behold, two men were talking with him, Moses and Elijah, who appeared in glory and spoke of his departure, which he was about to accomplish at Jerusalem. Now Peter and those who were with him were heavy with sleep, but when they became fully awake, they saw his glory and the two men who stood with him. And as the men were parting from him, Peter said to Jesus, 'Master, it is good that we are here. Let us make three tents, one for you and one for Moses and one for Elijah'—not knowing what he said. As he was saying these things, a cloud came and overshadowed them, and they were afraid as they entered the cloud. And a voice came out of the cloud saying, 'This is my Son, my Chosen One; listen to him!' And when the voice had spoken, Jesus was found alone. And they kept silent and told no one in those days anything of what they had seen." (Luke 9:28–36, ESV)

Reflection: One element that all three accounts of Jesus' transfiguration have in common is a cloud. In Mark's Gospel, the cloud overshadows Jesus, Peter, John, and James. In Matthew's Gospel, a bright cloud overshadows them. And in Luke's Gospel, the cloud overshadows them, and they enter it. The cloud is a sign of divine presence, as can be seen in the verses from Psalm 97. In the HB (OT), the LORD often makes his appearance as a storm cloud, thick and dark. His fire flashes across the skies. His thunder rattles the earth. Dark clouds, lightning, and thunder not only herald God's presence, but they are considered manifestations of his glory. It is important to know this when reading the original account of Jesus' transfiguration in Mark's Gospel. The mention of the cloud indicates who the author of Mark's Gospel thought Jesus was: God. The author of Matthew's Gospel copied the account he found in Mark's Gospel and further enhanced the divine presence in it. And the author of Luke's Gospel not only copied the account he found in Mark's Gospel, but he used it to illustrate some of his themes: praying, exodus, and journey to Jerusalem. The cloud sparks fear in the three disciples with Jesus, because, biblically, one cannot see the divine presence and live. Today, most people do not immediately think of the divine presence when a thunder storm approaches; however, when approaching both the HB (OT) and the CB (NT), a reader should pay close attention to the divine presence manifested in a cloud!

Evening

Antiphon: "The LORD has made known his salvation; / he has revealed his righteousness in the sight of the nations." (Ps 98:2, ESV)

Psalm: ". . . [Y]ou, O LORD, are most high over all the earth; / you are exalted far above all gods. / Light is sown for the righteous, / and joy for the upright in heart. / Rejoice in the LORD, O you righteous, / and give thanks to his holy name!" (Ps 97: 9, 11–12, ESV)

Repeat Antiphon (above):
Reading: "... [W]e were eyewitnesses of [our Lord Jesus Christ's] majesty. For when he received honor and glory from God the Father, and the voice was borne to him by the Majestic Glory, 'This is my beloved Son, with whom I am well please,' we ourselves heard this very voice borne from heaven, for we were with him on the holy mountain. And we have the prophetic word more fully confirmed, to which you will do well to pay attention as to a lamp shining in a dark place, until the day dawns and the morning star rises in your hearts." (2 Pet 1:16–19, ESV)
Reflection: Whoever the author of the Second Letter of Peter is, he knows the synoptic tradition concerning the transfiguration. This letter, written in the late second century CE, uses the transfiguration account to give "eyewitness" authority to the writer. In other words, someone other than Simon Peter wrote this letter in the apostle's name, and he uses an edited form of the transfiguration account found in Matthew's Gospel to assure his readers of his authenticity. The author of Second Peter interprets the transfiguration narrative he was reading as God the Father's honor and glory bestowed upon Jesus Christ. However, in Mark's Gospel the transfiguration account is a misplaced resurrection story, which is transformed by both the author of Matthew's Gospel and the author of Luke's Gospel to conform to each's specific gospel themes. Worthy of reflection is First Peter's urging that his readers pay attention to the word, as they would on a lamp shining in a dark place; in other words, the author is urging the recipients of the letter to be focused until the day of Christ's return occurs. The author also has access to the CB (NT) book of Revelation, which refers to Christ as the morning star (Rev 22:16).

St. Lawrence, Deacon and Martyr

August 10
Morning
Antiphon: "Praise the LORD!" (Ps 112:1a, ESV)
Psalm: "Blessed is the man [or woman] who fears the LORD, / who greatly delights in his commandments! / Wealth and riches are in his [or her] house, / and his [or her] righteousness endures forever. / Light dawns in the darkness for the upright; / he [or she] is gracious, merciful, and righteous. / For the righteous will never be moved; / he [or she] will be remembered forever. / His [or her] heart is ready; he [or she] will not be afraid. . . . / He [or she] has distributed freely; he [or she] has given to

the poor, / his [or her] righteousness endures forever; / his [or her] horn is exalted in honor." (Ps 112:1bc, 3-4, 6, 8a, 9, ESV)
Repeat Antiphon (above):
Reading: Jesus said: "Truly, truly, I say to you, unless a grain of wheat falls into the earth and dies, it remains alone; but if it dies, it bears much fruit. Whoever loves his life loses it, and whoever hates his life in this world will keep it for eternal life. If anyone serves me, he [she] must follow me; and where I am, there will my servant be also. If anyone serves me, the Father will honor him [her]." (John 12:24-26, ESV)
Reflection: The verses of Psalm 112 and John 12:24-26 are a help to understand Lawrence as a third-century CE martyr. As a young man, Lawrence traveled from Spain to Rome with another man, who became Pope Sixtus II in 257 and ordained Lawrence a deacon and appointed him archdeacon of Rome, first among seven deacons. As archdeacon, Lawrence was placed in charge of the treasury and other riches of the church; he distributed alms to the poor. In the words of Psalm 112, he feared the LORD, and the wealth and riches in his house he distributed freely to the poor. After the Roman Emperor Valerian ordered a persecution of Christians in 258, the prefect of Rome reminded and demanded that Lawrence turn over the riches of the church, as the property of executed Christians was confiscated by the state. Lawrence gave away everything, becoming a light to the destitute. He emptied the treasury with graciousness, mercifulness, and righteousness; the poor received everything as alms. When Lawrence presented the crippled, blind, and suffering to the prefect as the treasure of the church, the prefect was so angered that he ordered a gridiron with hot coals prepared and placed Lawrence on it; later, he was decapitated. And, thus, he is remembered for his steady heart and trust of God. Like a grain of wheat planted in the earth, he died, but what sprouted from his martyrdom produced many grains. He followed Jesus as a servant; by despising his life in this world, he kept it for the next.

Evening
Antiphon: "The LORD has done great things for us; / we are glad." (Ps 126:3, ESV)
Psalm: ". . . [O]ur mouth was filled with laughter, / and our tongue with shouts of joy . . . . / Those who sow in tears / shall reap with shouts of joy! / He [She] who goes out weeping, / bearing the seed for sowing, / shall come home with shouts of joy, / brining his [her] sheaves with him [her]." (Ps 126:2ab, 5-6, ESV)

Repeat Antiphon (above):
Reading: ". . . [W]hoever sows sparingly will also reap sparingly, and whoever sows bountifully will also reap bountifully. Each one must give as he [she] has decided in his [her] heart, not reluctantly or under compulsion, for God loves a cheerful giver. And God is able to make all grace abound to you, so that having all sufficiency in all things at all times, you may abound in every good work. He who supplies seed to the sower and bread for food will supply and multiply your seed for sowing and increase the harvest of your righteousness." (2 Cor 9:6–8, 10, ESV)
Reflection/Meditation/Journal: While Paul is reflecting on the collection he hopes to take to Jerusalem in his Second Letter to the Corinthians, he uses an agricultural metaphor. Everyone knows that sowing a few seeds results in a small harvest, while sowing many seeds results in an abundant harvest. When it comes to people offering funds for a collection, each person must decide freely what to give; one cannot be forced to contribute. Whatever is given is done so because one chooses to give. Paul's mention of grace is a gift that God gives. People imitate God by giving what the Holy One has given to him or her. The more one gives away what he or she has received from God, the more God will give to him or her. In other words, there is a reciprocity to giving. Giving begets giving. What application can you make of Second Corinthians 9:6–8, 10 to St. Lawrence? In what specific ways has your giving to worthy causes resulted in more giving? Whom have you influenced to contribute to a cause by your own contribution?

The Assumption of the Blessed Virgin Mary

August 15
Morning
Antiphon: "Death is swallowed up in victory." (1 Cor 15:54b, ESV)
Psalm: "Remember, O LORD, in David's favor, / all the hardships he endured, / how he swore to the LORD / and vowed to the Mighty One . . . , 'I will not enter my house / or get into my bed. / I will not give sleep to my eyes / or slumber to my eyelids, / until I find a place for the LORD, / a dwelling place for the Mighty One . . . .' / Arise, O LORD, and go to your resting place, / you and the ark of your might." (Ps 132:1–5, 8, ESV)
Repeat Antiphon (above):
Reading: ". . . Christ has been raised from the dead, the first-fruits of those who have fallen asleep. For as by a man came death, by a man has

MAJOR SPECIAL DAYS

come also the resurrection of the dead. For as in Adam all die, so also in Christ shall all be made alive. When the perishable puts on the imperishable, and the mortal puts on immortality, then shall come to pass the saying that is written: 'Death is swallowed up in victory. / O death, where is your victory? / O death, where is your sting?' The sting of death is sin, and the power of sin is the law. But thanks be to God, who gives us the victory through our Lord Jesus Christ." (1 Cor 15:20–22, 54–57, ESV)
Reflection: This doctrinal feast of the Assumption of the Blessed Virgin Mary is also known as the Dormition of the Blessed Virgin Mary. The doctrine is based on her son's resurrection. God raised sinless Jesus from the dead. In Paul's thought, the first Adam (man) brought death into the world, but the second Adam (Jesus Christ) brought the resurrection into the world. Just as all die in Adam, including Mary of Nazareth, so all are made alive in Christ, including Mary of Nazareth; that is why this feast is known as the dormition, the falling asleep of Mary. Just as her son, Jesus, was raised from the dead and ascended into heaven, his sinless mother shared in his resurrection and was assumed into heaven. Their perishable nature became imperishable; and their mortality became immortality. In other words, their deaths were swallowed in God's victory, accomplished through Jesus Christ.

Evening
Antiphon: "Hear my prayer, O LORD, / let my cry come to you!" (Ps 102:1, ESV)
Psalm: ". . . "[Y]ou, O LORD, are enthroned forever; / you are remembered throughout all generations. / Let this be recorded for a generation to come, / so that a people yet to be created may praise the LORD: / that he looked down from his holy height; / from heaven the LORD looked at the earth, . . . that [people] may declare . . . the name of the LORD, and . . . his praise, / when peoples gather together / . . . to worship the LORD." (Ps 102:12, 18–19, 21–22, ESV)
Repeat Antiphon (above):
Reading: "'. . . [T]he Immaculate Virgin, preserved free from all stain of original sin, when the course of her earthly life was finished, was taken up body and soul into heavenly glory, and exalted by the Lord as Queen over all things. So that she might be the more fully conformed to her Son, the Lord of lords and conqueror of sin and death.' The Assumption of the Blessed Virgin is a singular participation in her Son's Resurrection and in anticipation of the resurrection of other Christians . . . ." (CCC, par 966)

Meditation/Journal: What role does the biblical presumption of a three-storied universe (level 1 is Sheol, where the dead live; level 2 is the flat plate-like place where the living live; and level 3 above the dome in the sky is where God lives) have in understanding the assumption of the Blessed Virgin Mary? How does a solar-centered universe affect the doctrinal understanding of the assumption of the Blessed Virgin Mary?

St. Bartholomew (Nathanael), Apostle

August 24

Morning

Antiphon: "The LORD is gracious and merciful . . . ." (Ps 145:8a, ESV)

Psalm: "I will extol you, my God and King, / and bless your name forever and ever. / Every day I will bless you / and praise your name forever and ever. / Great is the LORD, and greatly to be praised, / and his greatness is unsearchable. / One generation shall commend your works to another, / and shall declare your mighty acts. / On the glorious splendor of your majesty, / and on your wondrous works I will meditate. / They shall speak of the might of your awesome deeds, / and I will declare your greatness. / They shall pour forth the fame of your abundant goodness / and shall sing aloud of your righteousness." (Ps 145:1–7, ESV)

Repeat Antiphon (above):

Reading: "Philip found Nathanael and said to him, 'We have found him of whom Moses in the Law and also the prophets wrote, Jesus of Nazareth, the son of Joseph.' Nathanael said to him, 'Can anything good come out of Nazareth?' Philip said to him, 'Come and see.' Jesus saw Nathanael coming toward him . . . . Nathanael said to him, 'How do you know me?' Jesus answered hm, 'Before Philip called you, when you were under the fig tree, I saw you.' Nathanael answered him, 'Rabbi, you are the Son of God! You are the King of Israel!'" (John 1:45–49, ESV)

Points to Ponder: First, the name Bartholomew, which means *son of Tolmai*, is found in the synoptic lists as one of the twelve (Mark 3:18; Matt 10:3; Luke 6:14; Acts 1:13). Nathanael, which means *God has given*, is found only in John's Gospel (1:45–49; 21:2), and in tradition has been identified with Bartholomew. Second, the account of the call of Nathanael of Cana in Galilee illustrates a peculiarity of John's Gospel: One disciple calls another one. For example, Andrew is called by Jesus, and then Andrew calls his brother Peter (John 1:40–42). Jesus calls Philip, who, in turn, calls Nathanael (John 1:43–49). Third, when calling Nathanael, Philip refers to the Law and Prophets, indicating Scripture. Fourth, Nathanael is at first doubtful about anyone from Galilean Nazareth. Fifth, nevertheless, Philip invites him to come and see. Seeing is believing—that's a theme of John's Gospel. The theme occurs throughout the narrative, until the Johannine Jesus pronounces blessed those who believe without seeing (John 20:29). Six, the Johannine Jesus possesses supernatural knowledge; he saw Nathanael under a fig tree. Seventh, Nathanael, becomes a follower by declaring Jesus a rabbi (teacher), as did Andrew (John 1:38), and Son of God and King of Israel, his supernatural rank.

Evening
Antiphon: "The LORD is righteous in all his ways / and kind in all his works." (Ps 145:17, ESV)
Psalm: "All your works shall give thanks to you, O LORD, / and all your saints shall bless you! / They shall speak of the glory of your kingdom / and tell of your power, / to make known to the children of man [and woman] your mighty deeds, / and the glorious splendor of your kingdom. / Your kingdom is an everlasting kingdom, / and your dominion endures throughout all generations." (Ps 145:10–13, ESV)
Repeat Antiphon (above):
Reading: "... [O]ne of the seven angels ... spoke to me [, John of Patmos], saying, 'Come, I will show you the Bride, the wife of the Lamb.' And he carried me away in the Spirit to a great, high mountain, and showed me the holy city Jerusalem coming down out of heaven from God. It had a great high wall.... And the wall of the city had twelve foundations, and on them were the twelve names of the twelve apostles of the Lamb." (Rev 21:9–10, 12a, 14, ESV)
Meditation/Journal: What connection do you find between the verses of Psalm 145 and Revelation 21:9–10, 12a, 14? For what work do you thank the LORD today? Why do you think the twelve names of the twelve apostles of the Lamb form the twelve foundations of the wall for the holy city Jerusalem coming down out of heaven?

The Nativity of the Blessed Virgin Mary

September 8
Morning
Antiphon: "Posterity shall serve [the LORD]; / it shall be told of the Lord to the coming generation ...." (Ps 22:30, ESV)

Psalm: ". . . [Y]ou [, God,] are he who took me from the womb; / you made me trust you at my mother's breast. / On you was I cast from my birth, / and from my mother's womb you have been my God. / All the ends of the earth shall remember / and turn to the LORD, / and all the families of the nations / shall worship before you. / For kingship belongs to the LORD, / and he rules over the nations." (Ps 22:9–10, 27–28, ESV)
Repeat Antiphon (above):
Reading: ". . . [B]ehold, an angel of the Lord appeared and said to [Anna], 'Anna, Anna, the Lord has heard your prayer. You will conceive a child and give birth, and your offspring will be spoken of throughout the entire world.' Anna replied, 'As the Lord God lives, whether my child is a boy or a girl, I will offer it as a gift to the Lord my God, and it will minister to him its entire life.' For an angel of the Lord had descended to Joachim and said, 'Joachim, Joachim, the Lord God has heard your prayer. Go down from here; see, your wife Anna has conceived a child.'" (Proto-Gospel of James 4:1–2)
Reflection: Otherwise known as the *Protoevangelium Jacobi*, the Proto-Gospel of James, a gospel prior to the gospel, is one of many other gospels that were written but for one reason or another were never accepted as Scripture. The Proto-Gospel of James, written in the late second century CE, is an account of the events leading up to and immediately following the birth of Jesus. The gospel's focus is on Jesus' mother, Mary. It gives rise to many Marian feast days, such as the Nativity of the Blessed Virgin Mary. Her birth is preceded by her miraculous conception. As are Abraham and Sarah, Joachim and Anna, Mary's parents, have no children, but an angel appears to each of them to notify them that Anna will conceive a child. It is easy to see how HB (OT) accounts of conceptions and births of famous people have influenced the narratives in the Proto-Gospel of James.

Evening
Antiphon: "O God, be not far from me; / O my God, make haste to help me!" (Ps 71:12, ESV)
Psalm: ". . . [Y]ou, O Lord, are my hope, / my trust, O LORD, from my youth. / Upon you I have leaned from before my birth; / you are he who took me from my mother's womb. / My praise is continually of you. / My mouth is filled with your praise, / and with your glory all the day. / . . . I will hope continually / and will praise you [, my God,] yet more and more. / My mouth will tell of your righteous acts, / of your deeds of salvation all the day, / for their number is past my knowledge. / With the

mighty deeds of the Lord GOD I will come; / I will remind them of your righteousness, yours alone. / O God, from my youth you have taught me, / and I still proclaim your wondrous deeds." (Ps 71:5–6, 8, 14–17, ESV)
Repeat Antiphon (above):
Reading: "Some six months came to completion for Anna; and in the seventh month she gave birth. She asked the midwife, 'What is it?' The midwife replied, 'A girl.' Anna said, 'My soul is exalted today.' And she laid the child down. When the days came to completion, Anna washed off the blood of her impurity, gave her breast to the child, and named her Mary." (Proto-Gospel of James 5:2)
Reflection: In the account of the nativity of Mary, the writer does not think that the child was only in Anna's womb for seven months. The use of the number six indicates incompletion, while the number seven indicates completion or fullness. Another account of the nativity of Mary, based on the Proto-Gospel of James, is found in the Gospel of Pseudo-Matthew, and it presents the usual nine-month gestation period: ". . . [W]hen her nine months were completed, Anna brought forth a daughter and named her Mary" (Gospel of Pseudo-Matthew 4:1). Like many of the other gospels that exist, both the Proto-Gospel of James and the Gospel of Pseudo-Matthew were written to fill in what someone observed as a missing piece. In the canonical gospels (Mark, Matthew, Luke, and John), no background concerning the nativity of Mary is given. In the oldest canonical gospel—Mark—Jesus is identified as the son of Mary (Mark 6:3). Mary's first appearance in Matthew's Gospel is as the wife of Joseph (Matt 1:16), in Luke's Gospel as a virgin engaged to Joseph (Luke 1:27), and in John's Gospel as the unnamed mother of Jesus (John 2:1). Thus, all a writer (or anyone else) had to do was ask: Who was Mary? Answering that question led back to presenting parents, modeled on HB (OT) characters, and events of the birth of a young woman and more until the canonical gospels picked up the story. As any writer will admit, it is much easier to fill in the past than it is to predict the future (unless one already knows what the future brought).

The Exaltation of the Holy Cross

September 14
Morning
Antiphon: "[The people] remembered that God was their rock, / the Most High God their redeemer." (Ps 78:35, ESV)

Psalm: "Give ear, O my people, to my teaching; / incline your ears to the words of my mouth! / I will open my mouth in a parable; / I will utter dark sayings from of old, / things that we have heard and known, / that our fathers [and mothers] have told us. / We will not hide them from their children, / but tell to the coming generation / the glorious deeds of the LORD, and his might, / and the wonders that he has done. / He established a testimony . . . , which he commanded our fathers [and mothers] / to teach to their children, / that the next generation might know them, / the children yet unborn, / and arise and tell them to their children, / so that they should set their hope in God / and not forget the works of God . . . ." (Ps 78:1–7ab, ESV)
Repeat Antiphon (above):
Reading: "Have this mind among yourselves, which is yours in Christ Jesus, who though he was in the form of God, did not count equality with God a thing to be grasped, but emptied himself, by taking the form of a servant, being born in the likeness of men. And being found in human form, he humbled himself by becoming obedient to the point of death, even death on a cross. Therefore God has highly exalted him and bestowed on him the name that is above every name, so that at the name of Jesus every knee should bow, in heaven and on earth and under the earth, and every tongue confess that Jesus Christ is Lord, to the glory of God the Father." (Phil 2:5–11, ESV)
Reflection: The feast of the Exaltation of the Holy Cross is like Good Friday in September! Its focus is clearly on the cross, the instrument of Jesus' death, a form of Roman capital punishment. Originally, the feast commemorated the finding of what was called the true cross by St. Helena in the fourth century CE and the dedication of churches built by her son, Constantine, on the site of the Holy Sepulcher and the return of the true cross to Jerusalem by Heraclius in 629 CE after it had been taken by the Persian Emperor Chosroes II in 614 CE. In his letter to the Philippians, Paul presents Jesus crucified as a model of humility, quoting a hymn he knew. Even though Jesus was in the form of God, according to Paul, he put others ahead of himself; he didn't even consider his equality with God. In other words, he emptied himself, first, by becoming human and, second, by dying on the cross. God exalted him by, first, raising him from the dead, and, second, by giving him a name that is above every name. Thus, when hearing the name of Jesus, every knee in the presumed three-storied universe must bend—above the heavens, on the earth, and below the earth (Sheol), while every tongue declares that Jesus Christ is

Lord. The cross planted into the earth reaches above to the heavens and below to Sheol. Thus, it is exalted because it unites the three stories of the universe in one. In the words of Psalm 78, it is a parable concerning the exaltation of death and life that is narrated to others so as not to forget the works of God.

Evening
Antiphon: "Sing to the LORD, for he has triumphed gloriously . . . ." (Exod 15:21a, ESV)
Canticle: "I will sing to the LORD, for he has triumphed gloriously . . . . / The LORD is my strength and my song, / and he has become my salvation; / this is my God, and I will praise him, / my father's [and mother's] God, and I will exalt him. / Who is like you, O LORD, among the gods? / Who is like you, majestic in holiness, / awesome in glorious deeds, doing wonders? / The LORD will reign forever and ever." (Exod 15:1a, 2, 11, 18, ESV)
Repeat Antiphon (above):
Reading: Jesus said to Nicodemus, ". . . [A]s Moses lifted up the serpent in the wilderness, so must the Son of Man be lifted up, that whoever believes in him may have eternal life." (John 3:14–15, ESV)
Points to Ponder: First, the Johannine Jesus' reference to Moses lifting the serpent in the wilderness sends the reader to the HB (OT) book of Numbers. After the Israelites have complained against God, he "sent fiery serpents among the people, and they bit the people, so that many people . . . died." (Num 21:6). The people go to Moses and repent. The LORD tells Moses, "Make a fiery serpent and set it on a pole, and everyone who is bitten, when he [or she] sees it, shall live" (Num 21:8). Moses did as he was told; he made a bronze serpent, mounted it on a pole, and anyone who had been bitten by a serpent would look at it and live (Num 21:9). Second, just as the bronze serpent brought healing to those people bitten by snakes, so Jesus—referring to himself as the Son of Man—brings healing to anyone who believes in him. Third, the serpent on a pole is called a caduceus; it is a winged staff entwined with two serpents, originally representing Hermes, Mercury, and Asclepius, the Greek god of healing. It is found frequently on ambulances, hospitals, and doctors' offices. Fourth, those who looked upon the serpent on a pole in the wilderness were saved; those who look upon Jesus exalted on the cross and believe in him will be saved for eternal life, according to Johannine thought.

St. Matthew, Apostle and Evangelist

September 21

Morning

Antiphon: The rules of the LORD are "sweeter . . . than honey / and drippings of the honeycomb." (Ps 19:10cd, ESV)

Psalm: "The heavens declare the glory of God, / and the sky above proclaims his handiwork. / Day to day pours out speech, / and night to night reveals knowledge. / There is no speech, nor are there words / whose voice is not heard. / Their voice goes out through all the earth, / and their words to the end of the world. / Let the words of my mouth and the meditation of my heart / be acceptable in your sight, / O LORD, my rock and my redeemer." (Ps 19:1-4ab, 14, ESV)

Repeat Antiphon (above):

Reading: "[Jesus] went out . . . beside the sea, and all the crowd was coming to him, and he was teaching them. And as he passed by, he saw Levi, the son of Alphaeus sitting at the tax booth, and he said to him, 'Follow me.' And he rose and followed him." (Mark 2:13-14, ESV)

Points to Ponder: First, if the reader has never heard of the apostle Levi, that is because the author of Mark's Gospel, after narrating his call by Jesus and identifying him as the son of Alphaeus (Mark 2:14), changes his name to Matthew (Mark 3:18) in his list of the twelve! Following his Markan source, the author of Luke's Gospel does the same; in the call narrative, he refers to him merely as Levi (Luke 5:27)—having removed Mark's "son of Alphaeus"—but names him Matthew in his list of the twelve (Luke 6:15)! The author of Luke's Gospel keeps the "son of Alphaeus" descriptive in his list of disciples for James, hoping that he has removed any confusion between Levi and "James the son of Alphaeus" (Mark 3:18; Luke 6:15). Because the name Levi does not appear in the list of the twelve in Mark and Luke, and because the author of Matthew's Gospel changes the call of Levi to the call of Matthew—as will be seen in the Evening Prayer Reading below—the feast day honors Matthew, apostle and evangelist (gospel writer). Second, Levi is a tax collector in both Mark's Gospel and Luke's Gospel. At the time of Jesus, a tax collector was an employee of Herod Antipas, who represented the Roman occupation forces. Levi collected land taxes, taxes on the transport of goods, tolls, and custom duties at a public building. Jews despised the Jewish tax collectors, because they worked for the occupation forces and made their living by raising the stated amount of the tax and pocketing the difference! The Markan and Lukan Jesus called one of these men to be numbered among his twelve apostles. Furthermore, he goes to eat with Levi, who invites other tax collectors to dine with them; such a scene upset the scribes (Mark 2:15-17; Luke 5:29-32).

Evening
Antiphon: "O God, save me by your name, / and vindicate me by your might." (Ps 54:2, ESV)
Psalm: "Give ear O my people to my teaching; / incline your ears to the words of my mouth! / I will open my mouth in a parable; / I will utter dark sayings from of old, / things that we have heard and known, / that our fathers [and mothers] have told us. / We will not hide them from their children, / but tell to the coming generation / the glorious deeds of the LORD, and his might, / and the wonders that he has done." (Ps 78:1-4, ESV)
Repeat Antiphon (above):
Reading: "As Jesus passed on . . . , he saw a man called Matthew sitting at the tax booth, and he said to him, 'Follow me.' And he rose and followed him. And as Jesus reclined at table in the house, behold, many tax collectors . . . came and were reclining with Jesus and his disciples. And when the Pharisees saw this, they said to his disciples, 'Why does your teacher eat with tax collectors . . . ? But when he heard it, he said, 'Those who are well have no need of a physician, but those who are sick. Go and learn what this means: "I desire mercy, and not sacrifice." For I came not to call the righteous, but sinners.'" (Matt 9:9-13, ESV)
Reflection: In the author of Matthew's Gospel rewrite of the call of Levi in Mark's Gospel, the author of Matthew's Gospel changes Levi to Matthew—probably to reflect the name of the gospel—and makes sure in the list of twelve apostles to identify him as "Matthew, the tax collector" (Matt 10:3). Instead of the Markan scribes of the Pharisees (Mark 2:16), the author of Matthew's Gospel presents Pharisees, Jesus' great, Jewish opponent in Matthew's Gospel. A characteristic of the author of Matthew's Gospel is the use of HB (OT) quotations. "I desire mercy, and not sacrifice" is not a direct quotation from the HB (OT) prophet Hosea 6:6a, where the LORD states, ". . . I desire steadfast love and not sacrifice . . . ." Either the author altered the quotation (as he does elsewhere [Matt 1:23]) or he is recalling the passage from memory. The Matthean Jesus makes it very clear that he did not come to call the righteous—those who have a healthy relationship with God, and an important Matthean theme—but

sinners, and included in that category are tax collectors, of whom Matthew, apostle and evangelist, is one.

Sts. Michael, Gabriel, and Raphael, Archangels
September 29
Morning
Antiphon: "Bless the LORD, O you his angels, / you mighty ones who do his word, / obeying the voice of his word!" (Ps 103:20, ESV)
Psalm: "Praise the LORD! / Praise the LORD from the heavens, / praise him in the heights! / Praise him, all his angels, / praise him, all his hosts! / Praise him, sun and moon, / praise him, all you shining stars! / Praise him, you highest heavens, / and you waters above the heavens! / Let them praise the name of the LORD! / For he commanded and they were created. / Let them praise the name of the LORD, / for his name alone is exalted; / his majesty is above earth and heaven." (Ps 148:1–5, 13, ESV)
Repeat Antiphon (above):
Reading: ". . . [A] word was revealed to Daniel . . . . And the word was true . . . . And he understood the word and had understanding of the vision. In those days I, Daniel . . . lifted up my eyes and looked, and behold, a man clothed in linen, with a belt of fine gold . . . around his waist. His body was like beryl, his face like the appearance of lightning, his eyes like flaming torches, his arms and legs like the gleam of burnished bronze, and the sound of his words like the sound of a multitude. Then I heard the sound of his words, and as I heard the sound of his words, I fell on my face in deep sleep with my face to the ground. And behold, a hand touched me and set me trembling on my hands and knees. And he said to me, 'O Daniel, man greatly loved, understand the words that I speak to you, and stand upright, for now I have been sent to you. . . . Michael, one of the chief princes, . . . came to make you understand what is to happen to your people in the latter days. For the vision is for days to come. . . . I will tell you what is inscribed in the book of truth; there is none who contends by my side . . . except Michael, your prince. . . . Michael, the great prince who has charge of your people [shall arise]. . . . At that time your people shall be delivered, everyone whose name shall be found written in the book. And many of those who sleep in the dust of the earth shall awake, some to everlasting life . . . .'" (Dan 10:1–2a, 5–6, 9–11a, 13b, 14, 21; 12:1–2, ESV)

MAJOR SPECIAL DAYS

Reflection: The name Michael, meaning *who is like God*, is presented in biblical literature, especially by the prophet Daniel, as a heavenly spirit who watches over the Jews—the name Michael is another way to say that God watches over his people! The name is used for individuals eight times in the HB (OT) First Book of Chronicles and Second Book of Chronicles; it also appears one time in Numbers, Ezra, 1 Esdras in the OT (A), three times in the prophet Daniel (as noted above), and two times in the CB (NT). The author of the Letter of Jude calls Michael an archangel (Jude 1:9), from which comes the title for this feast. Gabriel, whose name means *God is strong*—who is not called an archangel in biblical literature—appears in the HB (OT) book of Daniel as an interpreter of a vision and in the CB (NT) as the announcer of the birth of John the Baptist and the birth of Jesus. Raphael, the third archangel is discussed below. Some people add to the archangel list one named Uriel, meaning *God is my light* or *flame of God*, who makes several appearances in the OT (A) book of Second Esdras. An archangel is a chief or named angel among many unnamed angelic spirits. An angel or archangel is not a human with wings, as is often depicted, nor is it a head with wings! An angel or archangel is bodiless, because it is another way to speak about God, who is spirit. A good way to think about angels and archangels is to presume that they are God in disguise. Archangels have specific divine functions, as their names imply.

Evening
Antiphon: "The LORD is merciful and gracious, / slow to anger and abounding in steadfast love." (Ps 103:8, ESV)
Psalm: "Because you have made the LORD your dwelling place—/ the Most High, who is my refuge—/ no evil shall be allowed to befall you, / no plague come near your tent. / For he will command his angels concerning you / to guard you in all your ways. / On their hands they will bear you up, / lest you strike your foot against a stone. / 'Because he [she] holds fast to me in love, I will deliver him [her]; / I will protect him [her], because he [she] knows my name. / When he [she] calls at me, I will answer him [her]; / I will be with him [her] in trouble; / I will rescue him [her] and honor him [her]. / With long life I will satisfy him [her] / and show him [her] my salvation.'" (Ps 91:9–12, 14–16, ESV)
Repeat Antiphon (above):
Reading: "Tobiah went to look for someone acquainted with the roads who would travel with him to Media. As soon as he went out, he found

the angel Raphael standing before him, though he did not know that this was an angel of God. Tobiah said, 'Do you know the way to Media?' The other replied: 'Yes, I have been there many times. I know the place well and I know all the routes.' Tobiah said to him, 'Wait for me, young man, till I go back and tell my father; for I need you to make the journey with me. I will, of course, pay you.' Raphael replied, 'Very well, I will wait for you; but do not be long.' When Raphael entered the house, Tobit greeted him first. Raphael said, 'Hearty greetings to you!' Tobit replied: 'What joy is left for me any more? Here I am, a blind man who cannot see God's sunlight, but must remain in darkness, like the dead who no longer see the light! Though alive, I am among the dead. I can hear a man's voice, but I cannot see him.' Raphael said, 'Take courage! God has healing in store for you; so take courage!'" (Tob 5:4, 5d, 6ab, 7-8, 10a-h, NAB)

Reflection: Raphael, whose name means *God heals*, has a primary role in the OT (A) book of Tobit. As he leads Tobit's son, Tobiah, to Media to claim some money Tobit left there, Raphael guards the journey. However, he also functions as God healing. First to be healed of a demon is Sarah, daughter of Raguel and Edna; Sarah has had seven husbands, but a demon has killed every one of them on their wedding night. The next man entitled to marry Sarah is Tobiah, whom Raphael instructs about what to do on his wedding night. After retrieving the money, Raphael, Tobiah, and Sarah head home. Once they get there, Raphael again instructs Tobiah how to heal his father's blindness. Thus, the function of Raphael, who is not called an archangel in biblical literature, is to be the healing presence of God.

St. Luke, Evangelist

October 18

Morning

Antiphon: "The LORD is gracious and full of compassion, / . . . and abounding in lovingkindness." PS 145: 8, AMP)

Psalm: "I will exalt You, my God, O King, / and [with gratitude and submissive wonder] I will bless / Your name forever and ever. / Every day I will bless You and lovingly praise You; / Yes, [with awe-inspired reverence] I will praise Your / name forever and ever. / Great is the LORD, and highly to be praised. / And His greatness is [so vast and profound as to be] / unsearchable [incomprehensible to man {or woman}]. One generation shall praise Your works to another, / And shall declare Your mighty and remarkable acts. / On the glorious splendor of Your majesty / And on Your wonderful works, I will meditate. / People will speak of the power of Your awesome acts, / And [with gratitude and submissive wonder] I will tell of Your greatness. / They will overflow [like a fountain] when they speak of / Your great and abundant goodness / and will sing joyfully of Your righteousness." (Ps 145:1-7, AMP)

Repeat Antiphon (above):

Reading: "Since [as is well known] many have undertaken to compile an orderly account of the things which have been fulfilled among us [by God], exactly as they were handed down to us by those [with personal experience] who from the beginning [of Christ's ministry] were eyewitnesses and ministers of the word [that is, of the teaching concerning salvation through faith in Christ], it seemed fitting for me as well, [and so I have decided] after having carefully searched out and investigated all the events accurately, from the very beginning, to write an orderly account for you, most excellent Theophilus, so that you may know the exact truth about the things you have been taught [this is, the history and doctrine of the faith]. (Luke 1:1-4, AMP)

Reflection: Among the four canonical gospels, the author of Luke's Gospel is unique insofar as he writes an introduction in the first person. He makes clear that others—Mark, Q, Special L—have preceded him in preparing orderly accounts about Jesus. However, he does not think that they have done the best of jobs, because he has decided to present what he considers to be a more accurate orderly account. The author tells the reader that he has done his research and investigated events. He is writing his gospel for Theophilus, whose name means *God-lover*, and who could be either his patron (paying him to write the book) or anyone who loves God. His goal is to present the truth as he has come to understand it. Whoever the author of Luke's Gospel was, the feast of St. Luke, evangelist (gospel writer), honors his work.

Evening

Antiphon: "My mouth will speak the praise of the LORD, / And all flesh will bless and gratefully praise His holy name forever and ever." (Ps 145:21, AMP)

Psalm: "All Your works shall give thanks to You and praise You, O LORD, / And Your godly ones will bless You. / They shall speak of the glory of Your kingdom / And talk of Your power, / To make known to the sons [and daughters] of men [and women] Your mighty acts / And the glorious majesty of Your kingdom. / Your kingdom is an everlasting kingdom, / And Your dominion endures throughout all generations. / The LORD upholds all those [of His own] who fall / And raises up all those who are bowed down. / The eyes of all look to You [in hopeful expectation], / And You give them their food in due time. / You open Your hand / And satisfy the desire of every living thing. / The LORD is [unwaveringly] righteous in all His ways / And gracious and kind in all His works. / The LORD is near to all who call on Him, / To all who call on Him in truth [without guile]." (Ps 145:10–18, AMP)

Repeat Antiphon (above):

Reading: "The first account I made, Theophilus, was [a continuous report] about all the things that Jesus began to do and to teach until the day when He ascended to heaven, after He had by the Holy Spirit given instruction to the apostles (special messengers) whom He had chosen. To these [men] He also showed Himself alive after His suffering [in Gethsemane and on the cross] by [a series of] many infallible proofs and unquestionable demonstrations, appearing to them over a period of forty days and talking to them about the things concerning the kingdom of God. While being together and eating with them, He commanded them not to leave Jerusalem, but to wait for what the Father had promised, 'Of which,' He said, 'you have heard Me speak.'" (Acts 1:1–4, AMP)

Reflection: The introduction to the CB (NT) Acts of the Apostles is like the introduction to Luke's Gospel. Thus, whoever wrote Luke's Gospel also wrote the Acts of the Apostles. Biblical scholars consider them to be two books by the same author. Theophilus, anyone who loves God, is addressed in both books. One event that confuses scholars is the fact that the gospel ends with the ascension of Jesus on Easter Sunday (Luke 24:50–53), while the Acts of the Apostles opens with Jesus' ascension forty days later (Acts 1:9–11). Most likely, the author did not consider the ascension to be an historical event. It is theological event, created to remove Jesus from the scene so that the apostles can receive the Holy Spirit and launch the mission to the Jews and the Gentiles. In other words, the apostles cannot do what Jesus did until Jesus disappears. That is why Luke's narrative of the ascension looks very similar to his narrative of the resurrection; he considers them to be one and the same. Luke-Acts, written by the same person, is the longest continuous narrative about Jesus and his apostles in the CB (NT).

Sts. Simon and Jude, Apostles

October 28

Morning

Antiphon: "Let the words of my mouth and the meditation of my heart / Be acceptable and pleasing in Your sight, / O LORD, my [firm, immovable] rock and my Redeemer." (Ps 19:14, AMP)

Psalm: "The law of the LORD is perfect (flawless), restoring, and refreshing the soul; / The statutes of the LORD are reliable and trustworthy, making wise the simple. / The precepts of the LORD are right, bringing joy to the heart; / The commandment of the LORD is pure, enlightening the eyes. / The fear of the LORD is clean, enduring forever; / The judgments of the LORD are true, they are righteous altogether. / They are more desirable than gold, yes, than much fine gold; / Sweeter also than honey and the drippings of the honeycomb. / Moreover, by them Your servant is warned [reminded, illuminated, and instructed], / In keeping them there is great reward. / Who can understand his [her] errors or omissions? Acquit me of hidden (unconscious, unintended) faults. (Ps 19:7–12, AMP)

Repeat Antiphon (above):

Reading: "... [A]nd [Jesus] also appointed] ... Thaddaeus (Judas the son of James), and Simon the Zealot . . . ." (Mark 3:18, AMP)

Reflection: The *Amplified Holy Bible* attempts to make sense of the various lists of apostles that occur in the synoptic gospels (Mark, Matthew, and Luke) to maintain a list of only twelve apostles. Mark's list includes a Thaddaeus and a Simon the Cananaean—which *The Amplified Holy Bible* identifies as Simon the Zealot (as he is found in Luke 6:15). The author of Matthew's Gospel copied what he found in Mark's Gospel. Luke's list contains "Simon, who was called the Zealot, and Judas son of James." As can be seen from the passage from Mark's Gospel, the *Amplified Holy Bible* equates Thaddaeus with Judas (Jude) the son of James and keeps Simon the Zealot. The Acts of the Apostles presents "Simon the Zealot and Judas son of James" (Acts 1:13), but there is no Thaddaeus! The discrepancy has been solved by identifying Thaddaeus with Judas the son of James to keep the list of apostles at twelve. Because there was no master list of twelve apostles, it is impossible to guess what names would have been on it. While most people think in terms of twelve apostles to parallel the twelve tribes of Israel and indicate that a new people of God was coming into existence, there were probably more than twelve apostles, just like there were never twelve tribes of Israel (Joseph was never a tribe). In other words, both are fictions preserving the number twelve, which indicates all God's people. There is also the apostle named Judas Iscariot, who appears in Mark's list with the moniker "who betrayed him" (Mark 3:19), the "one who betrayed Him" (Matt 10:4), "who became a traitor [to the Lord]" (Luke 6:16). In Mark's Gospel and Luke's Gospel, Judas merely disappears from the narrative after betraying Jesus; in Matthew's Gospel Judas hangs himself after betraying Jesus (Matt 27:5), and in the Acts of the Apostles (Luke's second volume), he buys a field and falls headfirst bursting open and his bowels gushing out (Acts 1:18). In John's Gospel, the author identifies Judas as the son of Simon Iscariot (John 6:71); he was about to betray Jesus (John 12:4; 13:2, 26). The author of the Fourth Gospel—who does not have a list of apostles—adds to the confusion by presenting another "Judas (not Iscariot)" (John 14:22), who makes but one appearance in the narrative. Thus, harmonizing all the lists of apostles in the CB (NT), there emerges the following apostles: Simon (Peter), James and John (sons of Zebedee), Andrew, Philip, Bartholomew, Matthew, Thomas, James son of Alphaeus, Thaddaeus, Simon the Cananaean, Simon the Zealot, Judas son of James, Nathaniel of Cana in Galilee, Judas Iscariot, the disciple whom Jesus loved, Levi, Matthias, Barnabas, and Saul (Paul). That makes twenty apostles! Biblical scholars think that there were two groups of disciples following Jesus; one group, called the Twelve, and another group called Apostles. Over time, the two groups got melded into twelve apostles. That explains why there are different names on lists of apostles.

Evening
Antiphon: "Go into all the world and preach the gospel to all creation." (Mark 16:15, AMP)
Psalm: "I waited patiently and expectantly for the LORD; / And He inclined to me and heard my cry. / He brought me up out of a horrible pit [of tumult and of / destruction], out of the miry clay, / And He set my feet upon a rock, steadying my footsteps / and establishing my path. / He put a new song in my mouth, a song of praise to our God; / Many will see and fear [with great reverence] / And will trust confidently in the LORD. / Blessed [fortunate, prosperous, and favored by God] is / the man [or woman] who makes the LORD his [or her] trust, / And does not regard the proud nor those who lapse into lies. / Many, O LORD my God, are the wonderful works which / You have done, / And Your thoughts toward

us; / There is none to compare with You. / If I would declare and speak of your wonders, / They would be too many to count." (Ps 40:1-5, AMP)
Repeat Antiphon (above):
Reading: "Now at this time Jesus went off to the mountain to pray, and He spent the whole night in prayer to God. When day came, He called His disciples and selected twelve of them, whom He also named apostles (special messengers, personally chosen representatives): Simon, whom He also named Peter, and his brother Andrew; and [the brothers] James and John; and Philip, and Bartholomew [also called Nathanael]; and Matthew (Levi, the tax collector) and Thomas, and James the son of Alphaeus, and Simon who was called the Zealot; Judas [also called Thaddaeus], the son of James, and Judas Iscariot, who became a traitor [to the Lord]." (Luke 6:12-16, AMP)
Points to Ponder: First, the Lukan Jesus, unlike the Markan and Matthean Jesus, prays before every major decision. Second, the list of apostles presented by the author of Luke's Gospel in *The Amplified Holy Bible* demonstrates the melding of names to maintain a list of twelve apostles. Nowhere in the CB (NT) is Bartholomew also called Nathanael; nowhere in the CB (NT) is Matthew also called Levi; nowhere in the CB (NT) is Judas called Thaddaeus. Furthermore, in Christian tradition, Judas called Thaddaeus is known as Jude. Third, Luke's identifying Simon as being called the Zealot may be a mistranslation of zealous (zeal). Simon could not have belonged to the political party known as the Zealots, because that party did not come into existence until the winter of 67-68 CE. Some biblical scholars propose that Judas Iscariot is a type of Judah the patriarch, because he sold his brother Joseph into slavery, like Judas Iscariot sold Jesus.

All Saints

November 1
Morning
Antiphon: "To You, O LORD, I lift up my soul." (Ps 25:1, AMP)
Psalm: "The earth is the LORD's, and the fullness of it, / The world, and those who dwell in it. / For He has founded it upon the seas / And established it upon the streams and the rivers. / Who may ascend onto the mountain of the LORD? / And who may stand in His holy place? / He [She] who has clean hands and a pure heart, / Who has not lifted up his [her] soul to what is false, / Nor has sworn [oaths] deceitfully. / He [She]

shall receive a blessing from the LORD, / And righteousness from the God of his [her] salvation. / This is the generation (description) of those who / diligently seek Him and require Him as their greatest need, / Who seek Your face . . . ." (Ps 24:1–6, AMP)
Repeat Antiphon (above):
Reading: "I [, John of Patmos,] heard how many were sealed, a hundred and forty-four thousand . . . . I looked, and this is what I saw: a vast multitude which no one could count, [gathered] from every nation and from all the tribes and peoples and languages [of the earth], standing before the throne and before the Lamb (Christ), dressed in white robes, with palm branches in their hands; and in a loud voice they cried out, saying, 'Salvation [belongs] to our God who is seated on the throne, and to the Lamb [our salvation is the Trinity's to give, and to God the Trinity we owe our deliverance].' And all the angels were standing around the throne and . . . saying, 'Amen! Blessing and glory and majesty and wisdom and thanksgiving and honor and power and might belong to our God forever and ever. Amen.'" (Rev 7:4, 9–12, AMP)
Reflection: All Saints Day is a doctrinal feast celebrating those men and women who have been examples of holiness. According to the *Catechism*, the Christian "discovers [holiness] in the spiritual tradition and long history of the saints who have gone before" (CCC, par 2030). Because the saints—those acknowledged officially and unofficially—are "more closely united to Christ, those who dwell in heaven fix the whole Church more firmly in holiness. . . . [B]y their fraternal concern [human] weakness [is] greatly helped" (CCC, par 956). According to the *Catechism*, "a saint . . . is a disciple who has lived a life of exemplary fidelity to the Lord" (CCC, par 2156). Saints are "[t]he witnesses who have preceded us into the kingdom" and "share in the living tradition of prayer by the example of their lives, the transmission of their writing, and their prayer today" (CCC, par 2683). A single day during the year honors all saints. "In the communion of saints, many and varied spiritualities have been developed throughout . . . history . . . ." (CCC, par 2684); the saints bear witness to the variety of ways to experience the divine presence, like that narrated in the CB (NT) book of Revelation.

Evening
Antiphon: "Praise the LORD (Hallelujah!)" (Ps 150:6b, AMP)
Psalm: "Praise the LORD! / Praise God in His sanctuary, / Praise Him in His mighty heavens. / Praise Him for His mighty acts; / Praise Him

according to [the abundance of] His greatness. / Praise Him with trumpet sound; / Praise Him with harp and lyre. / Praise Him with tambourine and dancing; / Praise Him with stringed instruments and flute. / Praise Him with resounding cymbals; / Praise Him with loud cymbals. / Let everything that has breath and every breath of life praise the LORD!" (Ps 150:1–6a, AMP)
Repeat Antiphon (above):
Reading: "See what an incredible quality of love the Father has shown to us, that we would [be permitted to] be named and called and counted the children of God! Beloved, we are [even here and] now children of God, and it is not yet made clear what we will be [after {Jesus' second} coming]. We know that when He comes and is revealed, we will [as His children] be like Him, because we will see Him just as He is [in all His glory]. And everyone who has this hope [confidently placed] in Him purifies himself, just as He is pure (holy, undefiled, guiltless). (1 John 3:1a, 2–3, AMP)
Meditation/Journal: What does it mean for you to consider yourself to be a child of God? Is it the same as being (becoming) a saint? Explain. Do you think Jesus will come again, as the author of First John presupposes? If you think Jesus will come again, how do you think he will look?

The Commemoration of All the Faithful Departed

November 2
Morning
Antiphon: "To You, O LORD, I lift up my soul." (Ps 25:1, AMP)
Psalm: "O my God, in You I [have unwavering] trust [and I rely / on You with steadfast confidence], / Do not let me be ashamed or my hope in You be disappointed.... / Indeed, none of those who [expectantly] wait for You will be ashamed.... / Let me know Your ways, O LORD; / Teach me Your paths. / Guide me in Your truth and teach me, / For You are the God of my salvation; / For You [and only You] I wait [expectantly] all the day long. / Remember, O LORD, Your [tender] compassion and Your lovingkindnesses, / For they have been from of old. / According to Your lovingkindness remember me, / For Your goodness' sake, O LORD." (Ps 25:2ab, 3a, 4–6, 7b, AMP)
Repeat Antiphon (above):
Reading: "... [H]ope [in God's promises] never disappoints us, because God's love has been abundantly poured out within our hearts through the Holy Spirit who was given to us. While we were still helpless [powerless

to provide for our salvation], at the right time Christ died [as a substitute] for the ungodly.... God clearly shows and proves His own love for us, by the fact that while we were still sinners, Christ died for us. Therefore, since we have now been justified [declared free of the guilt of sin] by His blood, [how much more certain is it that] we will be saved.... Not only that, but we also rejoice in God [rejoicing in His love and perfection] through our Lord Jesus Christ through whom we have now received and enjoy our reconciliation [with God]." (Rom 5:5–6, 8–9, 11, AMP)

Reflection: The Commemoration of the Faithful Departed, what at one time was called All Souls Day, is a doctrinal feast of the remembrance of all who have died in the hope that God would save them. Death brings an end to human life. Doctrinally, soul "refers to human life or the entire human person." However, it "also refers to the innermost aspect of [people], that which is of greatest value..., that by which [one] is most especially in God's image: soul signifies the spiritual principle..." (CCC, par 363). "... [E]very spiritual soul is created immediately by God ... and it is immortal: it does not perish when it separates from the body at death" (CCC, par 366). While the *Catechism* distinguishes between soul and spirit—"signifying that from creation [the person] is ordered to a supernatural end and that his [or her] soul can gratuitously be raised beyond all it deserves to communion with God" (CCC, par 367)—this author prefers to use the word *spirit* to designate the spiritual principle. Soul, the non-material, immortal essence of a person, represents a philosophy borrowed from Aristotle and Plato. According to the first story of creation in the HB (OT) book of Genesis, "... God said, 'Let Us (Father, Son, Holy Spirit) make man in Our image, according to Our likeness [not physical, but a spiritual personality and moral likeness] ....' So God created man in His own image, in the image and likeness of God He created him, male and female He created them" (Gen 1:26–27, AMP). In the second story of creation,..."[T]he LORD God formed [that is, created the body of] man from the dust of the ground, and breathed into his nostrils the breath of life, and the man became a living being [an individual complete in body and spirit] (Gen 2:7). The Hebrew word translated into English as spirit is *ruah*, which can also be translated into English as *breath* or *wind*. Thus, "the breath of life" can also be translated as "the spirit of life." The spiritual principle of people, therefore, is best referred to as spirit—not soul. Spirituality, then, is the connection between Spirit and spirit. The Commemoration of All the Faithful Departed is the day to remember all those whose spirits connected to our spirit and who are now connected forever to Spirit.

Evening
Antiphon: "I would have despaired had I not believed that I would see the goodness of the LORD, / In the land of the living." (Ps 27:13, AMP)
Psalm: "The LORD is my light and my salvation . . . . / The LORD is the refuge and fortress of my life . . . . / One thing I have asked of the LORD, and that I will seek: / That I may dwell in the house of the LORD [in His / presence] all the days of my life, / To gaze upon the beauty [the delightful loveliness and / majestic grandeur] of the LORD / And meditate in His temple. / Hear, O LORD, when I cry aloud; / Be gracious and compassionate to me and answer me. / When You said, 'Seek My face [in prayer, require My / presence as your greatest need],' my heart said to You, 'Your face, O LORD, I will seek [on the authority of Your word].'" (Ps 27:1ac, 4, 7-8, AMP)
Repeat Antiphon (above):
Reading: "If God is for us, who can be [successful] against us? He who did not spare [even] His own Son, but gave Him up for us all, how will He not also, along with Him, graciously give us all things? Who will bring any charge against God's elect (His chosen ones)? It is God who justifies us [declaring us blameless and putting us in a right relationship with Himself]. Who is the one who condemns us? Christ Jesus is the One who died [to pay our penalty], and more than that, who was raised [from the dead], and who is at the right hand of God interceding [with the Father] for us. Who shall ever separate us from the love of Christ? Will tribulation, or distress, or persecution, or famine, or nakedness, or danger, or sword? Yet in all these things we are more than conquerors and gain an overwhelming victory through Him who loved us [so much that He died for us]. For I am convinced [and continue to be convinced—beyond any doubt] that neither death, nor life, nor angels, nor principalities, nor things present and threatening, nor things to come, nor powers, nor height, nor depth, nor any other created thing will be able to separate us from the [unlimited] love of God, which is in Christ Jesus our Lord." (Rom 31b-35, 37-39, AMP)
Meditation/Journal: Write a detailed answer to the following Pauline questions: (1) "If God is for us, who can be [successful] against us?" (2) "Who shall ever separate us from the love of Christ?" Of what are you convinced concerning the spirits of the dead?

The Dedication of the Lateran Basilica

November 9
Morning
Antiphon: "The LORD of hosts is with us; / . . . God . . . is our stronghold [our refuge, our high tower]." (Ps 46:11, AMP)
Psalm: "God is our refuge and strength [mighty and impenetrable], / A very present and well-proved help in trouble. / There is a river whose steams make glad the city of God, / The holy dwelling places of the Most High. / God is in the midst of her [His city], she will not be moved; / God will help her when the morning dawns. / The LORD of hosts is with us; / . . . God . . . is our stronghold [our refuge, our high tower]; / 'Be still and know (recognize, understand) that I am God. / I will be exalted among the nations! I will be exalted in the earth'" (Ps 46:1, 4-5, 7, 10, AMP)
Repeat Antiphon (above):
Reading: ". . . [H]e [, my guide,] brought me [, Ezekiel,] . . . to the door of the house [the temple of the LORD]; and behold, water was flowing from under the threshold of the house [temple] toward the east, for the front of the temple was facing east. And the water was flowing down from under, from the right side of the house, from south of the altar. Then he brought me out by way of the north gate and led me around on the outside to the outer gate by the way of the gate that faces east. And behold, water was spurting out from the south side [of the gate]. Then he said to me, 'These waters go out toward the eastern region and go down into the Arabah (the Jordan Valley); then they go toward the sea, being made to flow into the sea, and the waters of the Dead Sea shall be healed and become fresh. It will come about that every living creature which swarms in every place where the river goes, will live. And there will be a very great number of fish because these waters go there so that the waters of the sea are healed and become fresh; so everything will live wherever the river goes. By the river on its bank, on one side and on the other, will grow all kinds of trees for food. Their leaves will not wither and their fruit will not fail. They shall bear every month because their water flows from the sanctuary, and their fruit will be for food and their leaves for healing.'" (Ezek 47:1-2, 8-9, 12, AMP)
Points to Ponder: First, the prophet Ezekiel, who went into Babylonian captivity with the Israelites, is led in a vision to the Jerusalem Temple, from which he sees water flowing. The temple faces east, the direction of the rising sun, representing the fecundity of God. This story is a creation

story; the temple represents God creating the Israelite world again. Second, the water indicates the fluidity of the divine presence along with its creating power. Wherever the water runs and whatever it touches—even the Dead Sea—is made fresh or healed. All swarming creatures and all fish in the stream of God's presence live. The trees along the river bank are so abundant that they produce fruit every month, and their leaves never wither and fall. Third, in the creative presence of God, strength and healing flow everywhere. Fourth, today's feast is a celebration of the dedication of a major church in Rome in the fourth century: St. John Lateran; the church is dedicated to St. John the Evangelist and St. John the Baptist. Lateran in the title refers to the name of the palace that stands beside it; the Lateran Palace was the main papal residence at one time. Fifth, it is the cathedral of the bishop of Rome; a cathedral is a church in which is located the bishop's chair, a sign of his authority to teach, govern, and sanctify. The word *cathedral* comes from a Latin word for chair, *cathedra*. A cathedral, like St. John Lateran, is the church in which the bishop's chair is located. Six, St. John Lateran is named a basilica, more specifically an archbasilica. A basilica indicates that the building is titled; it is a privileged place. The Lateran Basilica is the mother of all churches; it signifies the universality of the church and the unity of the churches in communion with her under the leadership of the bishop of Rome (the pope). Sixth, a church is a house of God, the dwelling place of God, a holy temple, and a building of God; a church is an edifice in which God's people dwell. In other words, the building is a visible sign representing the pilgrim people who live and worship in it.

Evening

Antiphon: "The stone which the builders rejected / Has become the chief corner stone." (Ps 118:22, AMP)

Psalm: "O give thanks to the LORD, for He is good; / for His lovingkindness endures forever. / The stone which the builders rejected / Has become the chief corner stone. / This is from the LORD and is His doing; / it is marvelous in our eyes. / This [day in which God has saved me] is the day which the LORD has made; / Let us rejoice and be glad in it. / O LORD, save now, we beseech You; / O LORD, we beseech You, send now prosperity and give us success! / Blessed is the one who comes in the name of the LORD; / We have blessed you from the house of the LORD [you who come into His sanctuary under His guardianship]. / The LORD is God, and He has given us light [illuminating us with His grace and freedom and joy]. / You are my God, and I give thanks to You; / [You are] my God, I extol You." (Ps 118:1, 22–27a, 28, AMP)

Repeat Antiphon (above):

Reading: ". . . [W]e are God's fellow workers [His servants working together]; you [, Corinthians,] are God's cultivated field [His garden, His vineyard], God's building. According to the [remarkable] grace of God which was given to me [, Paul,] [to prepare me for my task], like a skillful master builder I laid a foundation, and now another is building on it. But each one must be careful how he builds on it, for no one can lay a foundation other than the one which is [already] laid, which is Jesus Christ. Do you not know and understand that you [the church] are the temple of God, and that the Spirit of God dwells [permanently] in you [collectively and individually]? If anyone destroys the temple of God [corrupting it with false doctrine], God will destroy the destroyer; for the temple of God is holy (sacred), and that is what you are." (1 Cor 3: 9–11, 16–17, AMP)

Intercessions: For all the church buildings throughout the world that they be worthy dwelling places for God, I pray to you, O Lord. For all members of churches that they never cease to pray for unity among themselves, I pray to you, O Lord. For all ministers that they be good cultivators of God's church, field, garden, and vineyard, I pray to you, O Lord. For an abundance of grace given to all people that they build upon the foundation who is Jesus Christ, I pray to you, O Lord. For a deeper awareness among people that God's Spirit dwells collectively and individually in each one of them, I pray to you, O Lord. For all people in need of healing that God's love flowing from his temple will bring them healing and strength, I pray to you, O Lord.

St. Andrew, Apostle

November 30

Morning

Antiphon: "Praise the LORD! (Halleluiah!)" (Ps 111:1a, AMP)

Psalm: "I will give thanks to the LORD with all my heart, / In the company of the upright and in the congregation. / Great are the works of the LORD, / Studied by all those who delight in them. / Splendid and majestic is His work, / And His righteousness endures forever. / He has made His wonderful acts to be remembered; / The LORD is gracious and merciful and full of loving compassion. / He has declared and made known to His people the power of His works, / In giving them the

heritage of the nations. / The works of His hands are truth and [absolute] justice; / All His precepts are sure (established, reliable, trustworthy), / They are upheld forever and ever; / They are done in [absolute] truth and uprightness. / He has sent redemption to His people; / He has ordained His covenant forever; / Holy and awesome is His name—[inspiring reverence and godly fear]." (Ps 111:1b-4, 6-9, AMP)
Repeat Antiphon (above):
Reading: "As Jesus was walking by the shore of the Sea of Galilee, He saw Simon [Peter] and Simon's brother, Andrew, casting a net in the sea; for they were fishermen. And Jesus said to them, 'Follow Me [as My disciples, accepting Me as your Master and Teacher and walking the same path of life that I walk], and I will make you fishers of men.'" (Mark 1:16-17, AMP)
Reflection: Unlike other apostles who may have had multiple names or were more than twelve in number, Andrew, whose name means *manly*, in the oldest gospel, Mark, is identified as Simon Peter's brother, but he does not use the moniker in his list of apostles (Mark 3:18). The author of Matthew's Gospel alters the text he found in Mark very little, making sure to follow his Markan source in identifying Andrew as Simon Peter's brother (Matt 4:18-19; 10:2). However, the author of Luke's Gospel ignores his Markan source and focuses only on Peter and a miraculous catch of fish (Luke 5:1-11), which is also found in chapter 21 of the Fourth Gospel, added to John's Gospel (John 21:3-11). When the author of Luke's Gospel presents his list of apostles, he identifies Andrew as Peter's brother (Luke 6:14). While Andrew appears elsewhere in Mark's Gospel (1:29; 13:3), his name is found nowhere else in Matthew or Luke; however, Luke does include him in the list of apostles in the Acts of the Apostles (1:13). Andrew has a starring role in John's Gospel, as will be seen below.

Evening
Antiphon: "I will walk [in submissive wonder] before the LORD / In the land of the living." (Ps 116:9, AMP)
Psalm: "I love the LORD, because He hears [and continues to hear] / My voice and my supplications (my pleas, my cries, my specific needs). / Because He has inclined His ear to me, / Therefore I will call on Him as long as I live. / . . . I called on the name of the LORD: 'O LORD, please save my life.' / Gracious is the LORD, and [consistently] righteous; / Yes, our God is compassionate. / The LORD protects the simple (childlike); / I was brought low [humbled and discouraged], and He saved me. / Return to your rest, O my soul, / For the LORD has dealt bountifully with you.

/ O LORD, truly I am Your servant; / I am Your servant, the son of Your handmaid; / You have unfastened my chains." (Ps 116:1–2, 4–7, 16, AMP)
Repeat Antiphon (above):
Reading: ". . . John [the Baptist] was standing with two of his disciples, and he looked at Jesus as He walked along, and said, 'Look! The Lamb of God!' The two disciples heard him say this, and they followed Jesus. One of the two who heard what John said and [as a result] followed Jesus was Andrew, Simon Peter's brother. He first looked for and found his own brother Simon and told him, 'We have found the Messiah' (which translated means the Christ). Andrew brought Simon to Jesus. Jesus looked at him and said, 'You are Simon the son of John. You shall be called Cephas (which is translated Peter)'" (John 1:35–37, 40–42, AMP)
Points to Ponder: First, in John's Gospel, John the Baptist has disciples, one of whom is Andrew. Second, John the Baptist identifies Jesus as the Lamb of God (also in John 1:29) indicating that Jesus will die at the same time as the Passover lambs are being slaughtered in the temple (John 19:16–22, 31). Second, after hearing John the Baptist identify Jesus as the Lamb of God, Andrew follows him. Third, following a unique device of one disciple calling another one, Andrew finds his brother Simon; here it is important to note that Simon is not called first—Andrew is called first, and he is called by John the Baptist before Jesus calls him. Fourth, when Andrew calls Simon, he identifies Jesus as the Messiah; the Greek word for Messiah is *Christ*; the English translation of both words is *Anointed*. Messiah, Christ, and Anointed indicate a person called by God to a specific task. Fifth, once Andrew brings Simon to Jesus, Jesus changes his name to Cephas, which can be translated into English as Peter or Rock. The name Peter is derived from the Greek word *petros*, meaning rock. Sixth, in John's Gospel, Andrew is identified as coming from Bethsaida, the same city as Philip and Peter (John 1:44). Andrew reports to Jesus that he has found a boy with five barley loaves of bread and two fish (John 6:8). When some Greeks want to see Jesus, Andrew receives the message from Philip and goes with him to tell Jesus (John 12:22).

The Immaculate Conception of the Blessed Virgin Mary

December 8
Morning
Antiphon: "Let the mountains sing together for joy and delight / Before the LORD, for He is coming . . . ." (Ps 98:8b–9a, AMP)

Psalm: "O sing to the LORD a new song / For He has done marvelous and wonderful things; / His right hand and His holy arm have gained the victory for Him. / He has [graciously] remembered His lovingkindness and his faithfulness; / All the ends of the earth have witnessed the salvation of our God. / Shout joyfully to the LORD, all the earth; / Shout [in jubilation] and sing for joy and sing praises. / Sing praises to the LORD with the lyre, / With the lyre and the sound of melody, / With trumpets and the sound of the horn / Shout with joy before the King, the LORD." (Ps 98:1, 3–6, AMP)

Repeat Antiphon (above):

Reading: "Through the centuries the Church has become ever more aware that Mary, 'full of grace' through God, was redeemed from the moment of her conception. That is what the dogma of the Immaculate Conception confesses, as Pope Pius IX proclaimed in 1854: The most Blessed Virgin Mary was, from the first moment of her conception, by a singular grace and privilege of almighty God and by virtue of the merits of Jesus Christ, Savior of the human race, preserved immune from all stain of original sin." (CCC par 491)

Reflection: This is a doctrinal feast. It begins with the redemption brought by Jesus Christ and looks backward from him to his mother, Mary. For her to bear the Son of God, she, the doctrine states, would have to be free from original sin; the mother of God could not be tainted by original sin. Thus, from the first moment of her conception in the womb of her mother Anna, wife of Joachim (according to the Proto-Gospel of James), she was redeemed by God's singular grace. Original sin, transferred to every other human being, was not transferred to her. Thus, she is a unique person, immaculately conceived.

Evening

Antiphon: "O sing to the LORD a new song; / Sing to the LORD, all the earth!" (Ps 96:1, AMP)

Psalm: "Shout joyfully to the LORD, all the earth. / Serve the LORD with gladness and delight; / Come before His presence with joyful singing. / Know and fully recognize with gratitude that the LORD Himself is God; / It is He who has made us, not we ourselves [and we are His]. / We are His people and the sheep of His pasture. / Enter his gates with a song of thanksgiving / And His courts with praise. / Be thankful to Him, bless and praise His name. / For the LORD is good; / His mercy and

lovingkindness are everlasting. / His faithfulness [endures] to all generations" (Ps 100:1-5, AMP)
Repeat Antiphon (above):
Reading: "The 'splendor of an entirely unique holiness' by which Mary is 'enriched from the first instant of her conception' comes wholly from Christ: she is 'redeemed, in a more exalted fashion, by reason of the merits of her Son.' The Father blessed Mary more than any other created person 'in Christ with every spiritual blessing in the heavenly places' and chose her 'in Christ before the foundation of the world, to be holy and blameless before him in love.'" [Eph 1:3-4] (CCC, par 492)
Activity: Choose a word or phrase from the verses of Psalm 100 or the Reading from paragraph 492 of the *Catechism of the Catholic Church*. What does the word or phrase mean? How does it help you understand the Immaculate Conception of the Blessed Virgin Mary? How does it help make you more aware of God's presence?

Our Lady of Guadalupe

December 12
Morning
Antiphon: "Let your every creature serve you [, LORD,]; / for you spoke, and they were made. / You sent forth your spirit, and they were created; / no one can resist your word." (Jdt 16:14, NAB)
Canticle: "Blessed are you, daughter, by the Most High God, above all the women on earth; and blessed be the LORD God, the creator of heaven and earth . . . . Your deed of hope will never be forgotten by those who tell of the might of God. May God make this redound to your everlasting honor, rewarding you with blessings . . . ." (Jdt 13:18-20a, NAB)
Repeat Antiphon (above):
Reading: ". . . [T]he temple of God which is in heaven was opened; and the ark of His covenant appeared in His temple, and there were flashes of lightning, loud rumblings and peals of thunder and an earthquake and a great hailstorm. And a great sign [warning of an ominous and frightening future event] appeared in heaven: a woman clothed with the sun, with the moon beneath her feet, and on her head a crown of twelve stars. She was with child (the Messiah) and she cried out, being in labor and pain to give birth. And she gave birth to a Son, a male Child, who is destined to rule (shepherd) all the nations with a rod of iron; and her Child was caught up to God and to His throne." (Rev 11:19—12:2, 5, AMP)

MAJOR SPECIAL DAYS

Reflection: Mary, the mother of Jesus, is known by many titles. For example, she is called Our Lady of Grace, Our Lady of Fatima, Our Lady of Lourdes, etc. In Mexico, she is called Our Lady of Guadalupe. On December 9, 1521, she appeared to Juan Diego and instructed him to gather roses blooming on a hill in the winter. When he opened his tilma, her figure was impressed on the inside of the cloak. The tilma is enshrined in the basilica (church) build in her honor. The image on Diego's tilma features a life-sized, dark-haired, olive-skinned young woman standing with her head inclined to her right. She holds her hands in prayer, and she wears a pink dress with a floral design, a dark ribbon tied above her waist indicates that she is pregnant, and a blue-green mantle over all. As indicated in the CB (NT) book of Revelation, she stands on a crescent moon; the moon is supported by an angel; and she is surrounded by a golden sunburst. She is described as a representation of the Immaculate Conception. Her image on the tilma calls to mind the vision seen by John of Patmos in the book of Revelation. She is surrounded by the sun with the moon under her feet, and she is pregnant with the Messiah.

Evening
Antiphon: "A new hymn I will sing to my God. / O LORD, great are you and glorious, / wonderful in power and unsurpassable." (Jdt 16:13, NAB)
Canticle: "Strike up the instruments, / a song to my God with timbrels, / chant to the LORD with cymbals; / Sing to him a new song, / exalt and acclaim his name. / . . . [T]he LORD Almighty thwarted [the enemy], / by a woman's hand he confounded them. / Not by youths was their mighty [Holofernes] struck down, / nor did titans bring him low, / nor huge giants attack him; / But Judith, the daughter of Merari, / by the beauty of her countenance disabled him." (Jdt 16:1, 5–6, NAB)
Repeat Antiphon (above):
Reading: "'Sing for joy and rejoice . . . ; for behold, I am coming, and I will dwell in your midst,' declares the LORD. 'I will dwell in your midst, and you shall know (recognize, understand fully) that the LORD of hosts has sent Me to you. Be still before the LORD, all mankind [and womankind]; for He is roused (raised up) from his holy habitation [in response to His . . . people].'" (Zech 2:10, 11b, 13, AMP)
Reflection: The HB (OT) prophet Zechariah is addressing the exiles, who have returned from Babylon to Jerusalem, to give them hope. The prophet exhorts them to sing and rejoice, because the LORD, who had been considered to have left Jerusalem, promised to return, just like the

exiles were returning. Basically, God tells the returnees that he is sending himself to them. Their response should be silence before the divine presence. He has been awakened from his living quarters above the dome of the sky, and he is coming to Jerusalem to comfort and live with his people. The same idea is found in the Canticle from the OT (A) book of Judith. The widow Judith defeated the enemy of her people; it was not young warriors or titans who brought down the leader of her enemy's people; it was a woman, a widow, who used her beauty to defeat the powerful and mighty Holofernes. The LORD reveals his divine presence through exiles, a woman, and Our Lady of Guadalupe. In a three-storied universe, the Holy One leaves his habitation on the top level to live with those on the middle level.

Bibliography

The Amplified Outreach Bible. Grand Rapids, MI: Zondervan, 2018.
Catechism of the Catholic Church. Washington, DC: United States Catholic Conference—Libreria Editrice Vaticana, 1994.
The Contemporary English Version. Nashville, TN: Thomas Nelson, 1995.
Ehrman, Bart D., and Zlatko Plese. "Gospel of Pseudo-Matthew." In the Apocryphal Gospels, 73–113. New York: Oxford University Press, 2011.
———"The Proto Gospel of James." In *The Apocryphal Gospels*, 40–71. New York: Oxford University Press, 2011.
The Holy Bible: Christian Standard Bible. Nashville, TN: Holman Bible, 2018.
The Holy Bible: English Standard Version. Wheaton, IL: Crossway, 2001.
Holy Bible: New International Version. Grand Rapids, MI: Zondervan, 2023.
The New American Bible. New York: Catholic Book, 1970.
New American Standard Bible. La Habra, CA: The Lockman Foundation, 2020.
O'Day, Gail R, and David Peterson. *The Access Bible: New Revised Standard Version with the Apocryphal/Deuterocanonical Books.* New York: Oxford University Press, 1999.
Peterson, Eugene, and William Griffin. *The Message: Catholic/Ecumenical Edition, The Bible in Contemporary Language.* Chicago: ACTA, 2013.
Sandmel, Samuel, ed. *The New English Bible with Apocrypha.* New York: Oxford University Press, 1976.

Recent Books by Mark G. Boyer

Nature Spirituality: Praying with Wind, Water, Earth, Fire

A Spirituality of Ageing

Weekday Saints: Reflections on Their Scriptures

Human Wholeness: A Spirituality of Relationship

A Simple Systematic Mariology

Praying Your Way through Luke's Gospel and the Acts of the Apostles

An Abecedarian of Animal Spirit Guides: Spiritual Growth through Reflections on Creatures

Overcome with Paschal Joy: Chanting through Lent and Easter—Daily Reflections with Familiar Hymns

Taking Leave of Your Home: Moving in the Peace of Christ

An Abecedarian of Sacred Trees: Spiritual Growth through Reflections on Woody Plants

Divine Presence: Elements of Biblical Theophanies

Fruit of the Vine: A Biblical Spirituality of Wine

Names for Jesus: Reflections for Advent and Christmas

Talk to God and Listen to the Casual Reply: Experiencing the Spirituality of John Denver

RECENT BOOKS BY MARK G. BOYER

Christ Our Passover Has Been Sacrificed: A Guide through Paschal Mystery Spirituality—Mystical Theology in The *Roman Missal*

Rosary Primer: The Prayers, The Mysteries, and the New Testament

From Contemplation to Action: The Spiritual Process of Divine Discernment Using Elijah and Elisha as Models

Love Addict

All Things Mary: Honoring the Mother of God—An Anthology of Marian Reflections

Shhh! The Sound of Sheer Silence: A Biblical Spirituality that Transforms

What is Born of the Spirit is Spirit: A Biblical Spirituality of Spirit

Very Short Reflections—for Advent and Christmas, Lent and Easter, Ordinary Time, and Saints—through the Liturgical Year

Living Parables: Today's Versions

My Life of Ministry, Writing, Teaching, and Traveling: The Autobiography of an Old Mines Missionary

300 Years of the French in Old Mines: A Narrative History of the Oldest Village in Missouri

Journey into God: Spiritual Reflections for Travelers

Monthly Entries for the Spiritual but not Religious through the Year: Texts, Reflections, Journal/Meditations, and Prayers for the Spiritual but not Religious

The Shelbydog Chronicles by Shelby Cole as Recorded by Mark G. Boyer: A Novel

Four Catholic Pioneers in Missouri: Lamarque, Kenrick, Fox, and Hogan: Irish Missionaries and Their Supporter

Smothered with Inexhaustible Mercy: An Anthology of Poems

Spirituality for the Solitary: A Handbook for Those Who Live Alone

Seasons of Biblical Spirituality: Spring, Summer, Autumn, Winter

RECENT BOOKS BY MARK G. BOYER

Biblical Names for God: An Abecedarian Anthology of Spiritual Reflections for Anytime

More Shelbydog Chronicles: Reflections on a Dog's Life by Her Friend, Knowing Your Pet

His Mercy Endures Forever: Biblical Reflections on Divine Mercy for Anytime

The Roman Catholic Lectionary and the Bible: Analysis, Conclusions, Suggested Alternatives

The Spirit of the Lord God: Biblical Names and Images for the Holy Spirit; An Abecedarian Anthology of Spiritual Reflections for Anytime

www.ingramcontent.com/pod-product-compliance
Lightning Source LLC
Chambersburg PA
CBHW071141300426
44113CB00009B/1039